Monitoring the EU Accession Process:

Equal Opportunities for Women and Men

COUNTRY REPORTS

BULGARIA
CZECH REPUBLIC
ESTONIA
HUNGARY
LITHUANIA
POLAND
ROMANIA

2002

Published by

OPEN SOCIETY INSTITUTE

Október 6. u. 12.
H-1051 Budapest
Hungary

400 West 59th Street
New York, NY 10019
USA

© OSI/EU Accession Monitoring Program, 2002
All rights reserved.

◎ TM and Copyright © Open Society Institute 2002

JOINT PROGRAM OF THE NETWORK WOMEN'S PROGRAM
AND THE OPEN SOCIETY FOUNDATION ROMANIA

Október 6. u. 12.
H-1051 Budapest
Hungary

Website
<www.eonet.ro>

ISBN: 1-891385-21-6

Library of Congress Cataloging-in-Publication Data.
A CIP catalog record for this book is available upon request.

Copies of the book can be ordered from the EU Accession Monitoring Program
<euaccession@osi.hu>

Printed in Gyoma, Hungary, September 2002
Design & Layout by Q.E.D. Publishing

Table of contents

Introduction 5
Overview 9
Country reports 57
    Bulgaria 57
    Czech Republic 123
    Estonia 179
    Hungary 233
    Lithuania 297
    Poland 355
    Romania 421

Introduction

The Program on *Equal Opportunities for Women and Men in the European Accession Process* (EOWM) is a joint initiative of the Open Society Foundation Romania and the Network Women's Program of the Open Society Institute. Its conception stems from the Open Society Institute project to monitor the progress of candidate countries as they prepare themselves for integration into the European Union and ensure that they meet the Copenhagen political criteria, particularly in relation to the independence of the judiciary, minorities' rights, and anti-corruption. Given the *acquis communautaire* in the field of equal opportunities for women and men, which the countries in accession are required to adopt and comply with, an independent programme to evaluate the status of accession countries from this perspective was developed.

An assessment of the status of equal opportunities, *de jure* and *de facto,* was carried out in seven of the candidate countries: Bulgaria, the Czech Republic, Estonia, Hungary, Lithuania, Poland and Romania, and the EU Directives on equal opportunities provided the framework for monitoring and analysing the corresponding legislation, institutions and practices. The Directives related to the principle of equal pay for work of equal value; equal treatment as regards employment, protection of pregnant, breastfeeding women and women who recently gave birth, the burden of proof in cases of sex-based discrimination and non-discrimination against part-time workers were analysed in 2001; while the remaining Directives on self-employed workers, parental leave, and social security schemes were assessed in 2002.

The Programme Director, with the assistance of an expert working group comprised of experts from Western and Eastern Europe, devised the methodology based on the content of the EU Directives and EU case law. The experts were also charged with supervising the completion of the Monitoring Reports by the national experts. Questions related to each specific Directive were issued, addressing key aspects from a legal, conceptual and factual point of view. The research was carried out in each candidate country by teams of local experts from various backgrounds: lawyers, sociologists, scholars, women's rights advocates from local NGOs or international agencies or from trade unions. Throughout the project, debates were organised within each country to enable a discussion and critique of the draft reports, sections of which were discussed with different constituencies and presented to the European Commission.

Each country report provides concrete recommendations on how to ensure full compliance with all of the Directives and outlines specific areas of concern. The country reports contain the latest information available as of 15 July 2002. On-going legislative updates will be available on the EOWM website (www.eonet.ro).

The findings of the reports illustrate how women's human rights and equal opportunities for women and men are perceived in the candidate countries, all of whom have undertaken several steps in order to comply with EU standards, adopting a host of new laws and in most cases amending their Labour Codes. The overall assessment is that the EU accession is a positive process for raising social standards, and standards on gender equality in particular. The process has primarily influenced legislation in the field of employment, specifically equal pay and access to employment, the establishment of gender equality institutions and special legislation. The shift in the burden of proof and the adoption of provisions on parental leave provisions can be seen in some countries, as can the removal of certain measures that claim to be protective towards women, but which are in fact discriminatory.

The Opinion of the European Parliament from April 2002 commends countries in accession, including the Czech Republic and Hungary, and to some extent Poland, Lithuania and Estonia, for the progress they have made. Bulgaria and Romania still lag behind the standards in many respects, although the recent adoption of the Law on Equal Opportunities in Romania will certainly bring the country into the above group that has been commended, at least from the formal point of view of legal harmonisation.

This critical assessment is valid despite the fact that as of June 2002 all of the countries under review had already closed Chapter 13 "Employment and social policy" of the negotiation process. The Chapter was closed with certain conditions dictated by the Commission for these countries, including in the field of gender equality. The fulfilment of these conditions must be thoroughly monitored by the European Commission, the European Parliament, and the NGOs in the countries in accession.

In order to promote further progress, EU bodies and, in particular, the European Commission, which is responsible for the enlargement process, should monitor the implementation of the Directives under review around the critical issues presented in the national reports and in this overview. Pressure should be put on governments that do not demonstrate enough flexibility, and more specifically, pressure should be exerted to ensure the following:

- the explicit introduction of the principle of equal treatment;
- the introduction of a legal definition of indirect discrimination;
- the introduction of a provision for the shift in the burden of proof;
- the adoption of the possibility for introducing positive action;

- the establishment and strengthening, through financial and personal resources, of institutional mechanisms for gender equality.

In addition, the reports all collectively underline the following points:

- The adoption of special gender equality legislation should be strongly encouraged.
- There should be a special focus on supporting the elimination of gender stereotypes through broad educational campaigns, and new educational programmes.
- There should be explicit mention throughout the entire negotiation process, and beyond it, of the integration of a gender approach into other aspects of the negotiation process with the EU. Gender equality standards should accordingly be emphasised through and beyond the accession process.
- The implementation of the commitments made during the negotiation process should be thoroughly observed and monitored, with a special focus on the gender issues raised through these national reports.
- Special attention should be paid and resources should be allocated for the establishment and strengthening of institutional gender equality structures, and for the development of respective policies by the governments.
- The increased role of civil society, namely of NGOs, in the process of accession should be taken into consideration and a permanent dialogue with EU bodies should be established.
- Dialogue between the governments of the candidate countries and civil society should be strongly encouraged.
- Financial resources should be allocated towards raising gender awareness and the implementation of the EU gender equality standards at the local level in the accession countries.
- Financial resources should be allocated for programmes and projects of NGOs, as well as government programmes with NGO assistance, in the field of research, awareness raising of EU standards, training of professionals and the judiciary, and for respective pilot initiatives, contributing to the fulfilment in letter and in practice of the *acquis communautaire*.

The Open Society Institute, through its Network Women Program and national foundations and in cooperation with local and European NGOs, will continue to closely monitor the developments in these countries and to advocate for a gender inclusive approach to EU accession.

We would like to thank all the individuals who were involved in this programme and whose work and support made the publications of these reports possible. In particular, we would like to acknowledge the invaluable contributions of:

Roxana Tesiu	*(Director of EOWMP)*
Anastasia Posadskaya-Vanderbeck	*(Director of the Network Women Program of OSI)*
Éva Földvári	*(NWP-OSI)*
Florentina Bocioc	*(EOWMP)*
Rachel Guglielmo	*(EUMAP-OSI)*
Emma Basker	*(OSI Brussels)*
Megan Ireland	*(OSI Brussels)*
Ana Maria Draganica	*(EOWMP)*

Expert working group:

Nathalie Wuiame	Krisztina Morvai
Genoveva Tisheva	Enikő Pap
Nicole Watson	Renate Weber

The local research teams:

Bulgaria	Plamenka Markova, Lilia Abadjieva, Raina Karcheva, Jivka Marinova, Genoveva Tisheva;
Czech Republic	Darina Lisuchova, Radka Machackova, Marketa Hunkova, Jolana Novakova;
Estonia	Carita Rammus, Marika Linntam, Milvi Jänes;
Hungary	Krisztina Morvai, Tamás Gyulavári, Judit Czuglerné Iványi, Istvánné Szabó, Enikő Pap;
Lithuania	Indre Mackeviciute, Saule Vidrinskaite, Laima Vaiciuniene;
Poland	Eleonora Zielińska;
Romania	Doina Dimitriu, Valentina Contescu, Florentina Negrutiu, Georgiana Macavei, Livia Aninosanu, Daniela Martis.

Special thanks to the coordinators of the Network Women's Programs within each national foundation.

The editorial team: Nicole Watson, Ursula Lindenberg, Miklós Vörös.

Overview

This overview is based on the findings of the "Equal Opportunities for Women and Men (EOWM) in the European Accession Program" (2000–2002), a joint initiative of the Open Society Foundation Romania and the Network Women's Program of the Open Society Institute. The aim of the OSI EOWM reports is to determine to what extent seven candidate countries (Bulgaria, the Czech Republic, Estonia, Hungary, Lithuania, Poland, and Romania) comply with EU standards in the field of gender equality, and to assess the level of commitment to equal opportunities in these countries, in terms of political will, legal reform and social policy, as well as a commitment to raising social standards prior to joining the European Union. The reports further aim to outline specific areas of concern related to each EU Directive, and issue concrete recommendations to ensure their full implementation.

1. THE CHALLENGES OF EU ACCESSION

1.1 The EU standards on gender equality

The standards of the European Union regarding the equal treatment of men and women are part of both the primary and secondary law of the EU, provided for by several Articles of the 1997 Amsterdam Treaty[1] and contained in the Directives under review, which have all been transposed into the legislation of the Member States. The Treaty of the European Union obliges Member States to promote equality between women and men and to ensure that the principle of equal pay for male and female workers for equal work or work of equal value is applied. In addition, the Amsterdam Treaty contains a new Article 13 that empowers the Council of Ministers, acting unanimously, to take 'appropriate action' to combat discrimination based on sex, racial or ethnic origin, religion or belief, disability, age, or sexual orientation, although so far

---

[1] Article 2 declares equality between men and women as one of the main tasks of the Community, Article 3(2) states that "In all the activities referred to in this Article, the Community shall aim to eliminate inequalities, and to promote equality between men and women;" Article 137 empowers the Council of Ministers to adopt Directives by a qualified majority aimed at reinforcing Community action namely in the area of equality between men and women with regard to labour market opportunities and treatment at work.

only a framework and directive on racial discrimination have been adopted based on general anti-discrimination provisions.

The main tenets of EU policy on gender equality are contained in the secondary law, specifically in *Council Directive 75/117/EEC* of 10 February 1975 on equal pay, *Council Directive 76/207/EEC* of 9 February 1976 on equal treatment at the work place, *Council Directive 92/85/EEC* of 19 October 1992 on safety and health at work of pregnant workers and workers who have recently given birth or are breastfeeding, *Council Directive 97/80/EC* of 15 December 1997 on the burden of proof, *Council Directive 97/81/EC* of 15 December 1997 on part-time work, *Council Directive 86/613/EEC* of 11 December 1986 on equal treatment for self-employed and their assisting spouses, *Council Directive 96/34/EC* of 3 June 1996 on parental leave, and *Council Directive 96/97/EC* of 20 December 1996 on equal treatment for men and women in occupational social security schemes.

In addition to primary and secondary legislation, there exists a body of EU case law,[2] which, together with five programs and a variety of 'soft law', indicates that gender equality is high on the political agenda of the EU.

1.2 The acquis communautaire

The anticipated enlargement of the European Union towards Central and Eastern Europe ought to see its first results in 2003, at which time several of the countries currently seeking accession will become full members. As the EU is a union with legal dimensions, candidate countries must accordingly transpose existing EU law, the so-called 'legal *acquis*', into their national legislation. The adoption of this law is the result of a long process of negotiation between the European Commission, representing the EU, and the candidate countries, during which different negotiation positions are discussed and agreed upon. Gender equality is among the fields to which the *acquis* applies; however, the reports issued within this program measure not only the level of implementation of concrete obligations undertaken by the governments of the candidate countries during the negotiation process, but also the candidate countries' ability to adhere to their commitments as well as the level of understanding of the broader need for and benefits of equal opportunities for women and men.

---

[2] Over 100 cases have been decided by the European Court of Justice (ECJ), including *Kalanke v City of Bremen* – Case C-450/93; *Marschall v Northrhine-Westphalia* – Case C-409/95; *Defrenne v Belgian State, Defrenne I and II* – Cases 80/70 and 43/75; *The Queen v Secretary of State for Employment, ex parte Seymour-Smith and Perez* – Case C-167/97. See also *Equality Quarterly News* (http://europe.eu.int/comm/dg05/equ_opp/index_en.htm).

Historically, the *acquis communautaire* in the field of equal treatment has concentrated mainly on the field of employment and social security because the Union, which was established in 1957 as an economic community, had an interest in the direct economic impact of the principle of equal pay from the very beginning.[3] Nowadays, the policy on gender equality is part and parcel of EU policies and programs. It is significant that in its report based on the national reports on the European Employment Strategy for the period 1999–2000,[4] the European Commission clearly stressed the fact that equal opportunities for men and women are an economic necessity and that approximately one-fifth of the annual increase of the GNP in EU countries (2.3 percent) was due to the increased participation of women in the labour force. This explains why the principle of equality does not exclude positive action, which allows for the provision of specific advantages in order to make it easier for the underrepresented sex to pursue a vocational activity, or to prevent or be compensated for disadvantages in professional life.

At the same time, the Community has always been explicitly committed to social policy, and accordingly has impressed upon accession countries the need to improve their social standards, including those on gender equality. It is therefore critical for the accession countries to appreciate that the policy on gender equality and gender mainstreaming, as enshrined in the Amsterdam Treaty, secondary EU law and soft law, is a priority for the EU *beyond* the principle of equal treatment and the prohibition of discrimination based on sex. It is a requirement for a comprehensive gender equality policy that would cut across all the policies and programs of the Union.

Policy developments regarding sexual harassment, violence against women, and more recently on issues such as political participation and reproductive rights, reflect some of the more contemporary trends in the field of women's rights. These are all areas that generate concern in terms of gender equality in accession countries as well in Member States. Civil society has already been working on these issues in depth, and the accession process provides a valuable opportunity for EU-based NGOs, together with NGOs from the accession countries, to a major role in shaping and lobbying for greater and broader requirements. In addition, NGOs from the candidate countries can mobilise and lobby

---

[3] Accordingly, it regulated economic matters. Article 119 of the Treaty of Rome of 1957 obliged Member States to respect the principle of equal pay for men and women. This provision lay dormant until 1971, when the ECJ held that Article 119 could be directly referred to by individuals claiming discrimination in pay.

[4] Following the adoption of the Amsterdam Treaty it was agreed at the Luxembourg Jobs Summit in November 97 that the European Employment Strategy (EES) should be built on thematic priorities: four Pillars described in the Employment Guidelines. Each year these Guidelines must be translated into NAP for employment in each country (NAPs), which are analysed by the Commission. The report and its the conclusions are used to reshape the Guidelines and to make country-specific recommendations to the Member States.

their respective governments on new, emerging issues, and can be of support to the EU institutions in terms of any prospective changes they seek to adopt.

2. CANDIDATE COUNTRIES AND THEIR BACKGROUND ON GENDER EQUALITY

2.1 The communist legacy

One major obstacle towards achieving real equality between women and men is rooted in the belief that gender equality had already been achieved during communism. An actual examination of women's participation in the labour force prior to democratisation, however, reveals that this in fact was not the case.[5] Against a backdrop of formal equality between the sexes, in the initial period of the planned socialist economy, the model of 'emancipated women' was imposed through a variety of economic, legal, and social mechanisms. Women were strongly encouraged to participate in all forms of labour on a par with men, although one major factor in the high employment rate of women was the low salary rates that led families to seek to increase their income. As the legal underpinnings of equality between men and women developed though, at the same time and by virtue of past traditions, women were taking on the double burden of childrearing and housework.

Accordingly, there were three major aspects of women's participation in the socialist economy: work, the socio-political life of the nation, and the family. In order to facilitate women's balanced fulfilment of these different responsibilities, the state created favourable legal and economic conditions: well-paid maternity leave was introduced, women's right to abortion was recognised in most countries, childcare facilities were set up, etc.[6] However, the encouragement for women to participate in

---

[5] Based on the English version of the report of the Bulgarian Gender Research Foundation "Impact of Privatisation on Women's Social and Economic Rights in the Period of Economic Restructuring in Bulgaria" (Sofia, 1999).

[6] As a result of the above-mentioned social policies, women in Eastern Europe enjoyed a much higher rate of labour force participation than women in other European countries. International statistics on the comparative representation of women in the labour force from 1950–2000 confirm this. For example, while the average coefficient of women's labour representation in developed countries was 31.8, in Eastern European countries it was approximately 40. The figures for 1985 were as follows: 36.1 in developed countries; 38.4 in North America; 43.8 in Eastern Europe and 49.5 in Bulgaria. This coefficient decreased after 1990. *Women in Economic Activity. A Global Statistical Survey 1950–2000*, ILO, ISTRAW, UN (New York, 1985).

national economies during socialism did not automatically guarantee women *de facto* equal status with men. One basic source of discrimination, for example, was the fact that women were defined and understood by society in terms of their role as both mothers and workers. Bearing the burden of the double workday and the accompanying responsibilities was a constant source of stress for many women and the formal benefits of the legislation often had the reverse effect of actually reinforcing stereotypical roles and unequally distributing men and women's family responsibilities. As a result, many women regarded their right to work more as a duty than an inalienable human right. A notable accomplishment, however, was women's high level of education, an asset that has unfortunately not been effectively utilised in the period of economic transformation due to the inability of the state to sustain full employment.

2.2 The challenges for newly emerged democracies

The general perception that gender equality had already been achieved under communism continued to hold sway during the period of economic, social and political transition. In fact, despite the incontestably positive elements that were introduced, real gender equality was never achieved, and discrimination did occur under the old regimes, although it was largely ignored, and never documented, admitted, or punished. At the same time, the communist policy implied various types of representation, particularly on gender and national belonging, in some central and local leading bodies. Of course, this representation was based rather on party affiliation and support than on people's competence and skills, and in most cases those representatives were perceived as bringing no value to the structures to which they were assigned. It was merely a matter of reports and statistics. It was thus not particularly surprising that after 1990 the idea of quota representation for women, of 'positive discrimination' or 'special measures' aimed at better representation for women, was rejected by the political elite of these countries and the public as well. These difficult lessons of the past have been constantly invoked in discussions on positive action, although the previous practice had nothing in common with the human rights approach of affirmative action. It has taken a decade to overcome, at least partially, these old prejudices.

The issue of gender equality in transition received the attention of governments for the first time in the mid-1990s, in the process of preparation, participation and follow-up to the 4th World Conference on Women in Beijing. The fact that most accession countries had no explicit legal provisions and mechanisms on equal pay and equal treatment until very recently illustrates the degree to which this topic was underestimated at the time.

In the period of transition, new problems added to these past preconceptions:

a) *Economic constraints*

The relatively high proportion of female participation in the workforce was grounded in the principles of the planned economy, a state monopoly on industrial property, and artificially sustained employment that could be maintained only by paying extremely low salaries. The collapse of the socialist economy and the introduction of supply and demand market principles brought to a head the disintegration of outdated practices, and precipitated a decrease in the rate of women's participation in the national workforce. A pattern of the violation of women's labour rights also set in, which further discouraged them from actively participating in the national economies.

It became clear that standards for the social and special protection of women are difficult to implement, and can even be weakened and eroded, by the process of market liberalisation.[7] Certain of these standards, which are also regulated by ILO conventions, must therefore be reviewed in the context of EU accession.

b) *Low legal culture and weak institutional infrastructures*

A common weakness in all of the countries seeking accession is the low level of implementation of laws, even those that formally comply with the *acquis* of the EU. This concern also holds true for new legislation that was adopted during the process of accession negotiations, and is largely due to weak and under-resourced institutions, a limited awareness of social rights and standards and gender equality, and to the absence of case law on gender issues.

The lack of sufficient financial resources in the accession countries during the period of economic restructuring is also a serious issue that ought to be addressed by the European Commission in order to strengthen the implementation of EU standards and to establish and develop institutional mechanisms for gender equality. Investing more in education and in career development with a view to supporting the development of effective administration and expertise in the field of EU integration is a major challenge, but improvement in this area would positively influence the accession process.

---

[7] For example, the general provision for equal pay for work of equal value was abolished from the Bulgarian Labour Code in 1992 and reintroduced only recently in 2001 as equal pay for women and men.

3. Adopting the Acquis Communautaire

3.1 Priorities for change

Within the context of the accession process, candidate countries established different priorities that influenced their respective negotiations with the EU. Countries such as Hungary and Bulgaria, for example, considered it a priority to ensure gender equality through the reform of their labour legislation, while Lithuania undertook the adoption of a Gender Equality Act and the establishment of the office of the Ombudsperson on Equal Opportunities. Romania and Bulgaria gave priority to the adoption of general anti-discrimination legislation.

Following the initiation of the negotiation process, most candidate countries began adjusting their legislation in the field of equal treatment in employment, leaving the adoption of the standards in social security for the second phase.

The principle of equal treatment is being gradually introduced into the legislation of the candidate countries, with most of them first introducing the principle of equal pay, and afterwards the principle of equal treatment in the access to employment, promotion and working conditions. A few candidate countries have also introduced new legal provisions banning discriminatory advertisements and practices.[8]

One way to comprehensively regulate the issue of equal treatment is through the adoption of a Gender Equality Act, which has so far been adopted only in Lithuania (1999) and Romania (2002). Such an approach is important because the lack of gender equality legislation and specific mechanisms are among the main reasons for the absence of cases and litigation on gender equality in the accession countries.

The notion of indirect discrimination based on sex is a relatively new issue, both legally and conceptually, that has not yet been introduced in most of the accession countries and which has met with certain resistance. Changes in the Bulgarian Labour Code in 2001 introduced a ban on both direct and indirect discrimination on grounds of, *inter alia*, sex. Indirect discrimination is explicitly prohibited in Romania and Hungary, and similar changes are expected also in Estonia. However, greater effort is required to ensure that this concept is effectively understood and implemented.

The notion of sexual harassment is another new concept for Eastern European countries and has so far only been regulated in the Czech Republic, Lithuania, and recently in Romania, though new legislative provisions are expected in Bulgaria and Estonia as well.

---

[8] That is, in Bulgaria, Hungary, Lithuania, and Romania.

Nearly all of the countries examined lag behind in harmonising the fields of occupational social security schemes, part-time work, and recognising the work of contributing family members.

3.2 Anti-discrimination or gender equality policy and legislation?

These are two components of the *acquis* that are negotiated under Chapter 13 "Employment and social policy:" anti-discrimination legislation and gender equality policy, both of which are essential and complementary, and must be integrated into law and policy by the time of accession.

The Amsterdam Treaty clearly differentiates between the two issues, while at the same time recognising the inevitable links. On the one hand, the promotion and mainstreaming of gender equality features among the tasks of the EU and is one of its transversal objectives. At the same time, Article 13 introduces a general legislative power to tackle a broad range of forms of discrimination, which includes but is not limited to discrimination based on sex. The difference also exists in the secondary law of the EU, and it is important to note that the European Court of Justice in its ample practice on gender equality has also recognised that in order to achieve equal opportunities for women and men it is necessary on occasion to go beyond the eradication of discrimination, and that positive action may be appropriate.[9]

The limited understanding of the differences and interrelation of the two concepts by candidate countries has led sometimes to the assumption that gender equality policy is covered by adopting anti-discrimination, and sometimes to the assertion that 'positive rights' for women contradicts the principle of non-discrimination. In countries such as Bulgaria and Romania, governments proceeded directly to considerations to adopt general anti-discrimination legislation, trying to satisfy both EU standards for the equal treatment of women and men and anti-discrimination more generally at the same time. The principle of equal treatment of men and women has often been lost in the context of these much broader considerations. (Because this is not an easy task and requires more in-depth knowledge and consideration, the results have not always had a positive impact on the principle of equal treatment of men and women, which has been largely ignored). One negative outcome of this approach that has been observed, and which may follow for other countries, is the difficulty associated with promoting special gender equality legislation whenever there has been a decision to adopt broader anti-

---

[9] For this purpose, the Court is in favour of giving Member States the discretion to take positive action to redress the societal discrimination faced by women, in particular.

discrimination legislation. This is the case in Bulgaria;[10] and was the case in Romania prior to the adoption of the Law on Equal Opportunities.[11] Similar problems may also arise in the Czech Republic.

3.3 The shortage of gender policies and the need to strengthen gender equality institutions

Legislative endeavours will remain limited in value unless effective means for the implementation exist, and this underlies the critical need for institutions and mechanisms on gender equality and appropriate policies to be set up and operate so as to ensure an approach of 'mainstreaming.' Although explicit reference to 'gender mainstreaming' has been made by the EU more recently and the Council Directives concerning gender equality represent concrete tools to give effect to the EU's commitment to gender equality, the negotiation process has focused mainly on legal harmonisation and the extent to which the *acquis communautaire* is transposed into the national legislations of the candidate countries. It was only last year that clear progress was made on this issue in negotiations, and due to the latest amendments to Directive 76/207/EEC that the mainstreaming approach and establishment of institutional mechanisms for gender equality have become a legal obligation and integral part of the *acquis*.

As a result of the pressure of the negotiation process, new gender equality bodies were established in a number of accession countries, mainly as departments at the level of the ministries of labour, for example in Hungary, Czech Republic, Estonia, and Lithuania. In Romania, the Ministry of Labour and Social Solidarity heads the hierarchy of the institutional mechanism for equal opportunities of women and men. The establishment in November 2001 of the Office of the Governmental Plenipotentiary on Equal Opportunities for Women and Men in Poland is a good example of a higher-level institution, directly subordinated to and established with an Ordinance of the Council of Ministers. So far, Bulgaria is the only country examined that does not have any gender equality machinery. Nevertheless, the effectiveness of these bodies remains to be seen and should be subject to continued monitoring beyond accession.

The Office of the Gender Equality Ombudsperson in Lithuania is a unique and particularly successful institution that deserves special attention. Established by the *Seimas* (Parliament) of the Republic of Lithuania according to the Law on Equal

---

[10] The elaboration of an Anti-Discrimination Act is under way. The Draft Act on Equal Opportunities of Women and Men, elaborated in the beginning of 2001, was rejected with the justification that a comprehensive act should be adopted.

[11] Statutory Order No.137 of 2000 for the Prevention and Punishment of All Forms of Discrimination was adopted in 2000, while the draft Act on Equal Opportunities was pending.

Opportunities, which entered into force on 1 March 1999, the Office of the Equal Opportunities Ombudsperson was given the status of an independent public institution on 25 May 1999 and has since played a key role in the national machinery on equal opportunities. Parliamentary commissions or sub-commissions dealing with equal opportunities, such as those that exist in the Czech Republic and Lithuania, also have an important role to play.

Although special governmental programs on gender equality have been launched by the governments in the Czech Republic and Hungary, the lack of gender policies and means for their implementation constitutes one of the major weaknesses of these institutional mechanisms. Other problems these institutions face include a lack of adequately trained staff and a shortage of financial resources. Support from the EU in this regard, particularly in terms of providing appropriate training, would go a long way in helping to overcome these obstacles.

3.4 Gender equality litigation and a shift in the burden of proof: The necessary metamorphosis

The OSI EOWM country reports all show that very few cases on gender equality, if any, have been brought to the national courts in recent years and that the question of shifting the burden of proof has been rejected – either vigorously or gently – even in those countries where it is legally permitted.

In general, the adoption of new legislation is certainly a crucial first step in raising legal awareness and facilitating litigation on gender issues. However, it is not enough: the lack of information on EU standards and case law, the general lack of citizens' awareness of their rights, and the absence of appropriate training for judges and lawyers are all underlying factors in the shortage of impact litigation. Moreover, in most countries employees are not offered protection from retaliatory measures taken by employers if the employee seeks to legally protect his/her rights.[12]

Another disincentive to bringing cases concerning sex discrimination to court is the fact that the burden of proof has not, in all countries, been shifted in favour of the plaintiff. At present, only the Czech Republic has introduced this principle in a consistent way.[13] Due to the climate of conservatism in which dominates among candidate state judiciaries, it is important that harmonisation and accompanying legal reforms in the candidate countries are introduced step by step, together with judicial training, because the transformation from having very few standards in this area to the

---

[12] Such protection has been introduced in the Czech Republic, Lithuania, and Romania.

[13] In Bulgaria and Lithuania, harmonisation with the burden of proof Directive is underway.

very high EU standards and requirements could find both society and the courts unprepared.[14] The new legal concepts and provisions should also be accompanied by concrete mechanisms to encourage their implementation and, most importantly, by awareness-raising campaigns.

One important means of bringing more gender equality cases to court and creating impact legislation would be to provide NGOs with *locus standi,* which would allow them to represent victims of discrimination before courts. So far, Romania is the only country examined where NGOs have been given the power to bring such cases to court and even to represent victims, which is a significant breakthrough.[15]

3.5 An awareness that is missing everywhere

As all the OSI EOWM reports reveal, awareness of gender issues is generally low for a number of reasons. Firstly, the ways in which the issue was approached during communism, and the belief that gender equality was secured, led to its later trivialisation. In addition, during the process of democratisation and transition, due to many other political and economic problems, gender equality was not identified as a priority either by society at large or by the decision-makers. At the same time, the lack of gender research and specific statistics means that there was no background against which this information could be placed. In fact, the legislative changes that have occurred in this field in some countries have only seldom been presented to the public or discussed by experts or specialised NGOs, and there has been little media coverage of gender issues. As a result, the importance of issues such as sexual harassment, indirect discrimination, parental leave, and the shift of the burden of proof, has been minimised and dismissed due to ignorance.

---

[14] Like in the case of the adoption of general anti-discrimination acts encompassing the requirements of the Article 13 Directives and the gender equality Directives.

[15] Statutory Order No.137 of 2000.

4. A comparison of the implementation of the directives under review in the accession countries: regional and national trends and recurrent issues

4.1 Equal treatment in employment

A. *The principle of equal pay for work of equal value and compliance with Council Directive 75/117/EEC of 10 February 1975*

General considerations

Article 141 of the Amsterdam Treaty, stipulating the guarantees for equal pay for work of equal value, and Council Directive 75/117/EEC represent the *acquis communautaire* in the field of equal pay for men and women, which is further reinforced by Council Directive 97/80/EC on the burden of proof in cases of discrimination based on sex. Accession countries must measure their progress through the implementation of the following elements of the principle of equal pay:

- The elimination of all discrimination on grounds of sex for the same work or work of equal value with regard to all aspects and conditions of remuneration;

- The establishment of job classifications systems applying the same criteria for men and women in order to prevent discrimination on grounds of sex;

- The introduction of protective measures in cases of the violation of the principle of equal pay by judicial process after possible recourse to out of court procedures;

- The abolishment of all discriminatory laws, regulations or administrative provisions contrary to the principle of equal pay;

- The establishment of mechanisms to declare null and void or amend provisions of collective agreements, wage scales, and agreements and individual contracts that are contrary to the principle of equal pay;

- The provision of the necessary measures to protect employees against dismissal in reaction to a complaint or any legal proceedings aimed at enforcing the principle of equal pay;

- The establishment of effective guarantees for the application of the principle of equal pay;

- Ensuring that employees are informed by all appropriate means of the provisions on the principle of equal pay.

The principle of equal pay is a core EU standard in the field of equal treatment between men and women and as such is one of the first requirements that accession countries must meet in the process of harmonisation. Although this principle is enshrined in UN human rights documents and is part of the core ILO standards, for most of the countries under review the declaration of this principle in their domestic legislation came only after the beginning of the negotiation process. Surprisingly enough, the former communist countries did not have this principle explicitly declared in their legislation previously, which is further evidence of the more formal approach of the state towards equality between the sexes adopted by those regimes.

In addition, for most of the countries under consideration, the accession process began several years after the beginning of transition and in the interim there were no social safeguards or legal provisions in the field of equal treatment, including on equal pay. Meanwhile, the movement towards a market economy and trade liberalisation created additional risks for vulnerable groups and for gender equality in the labour market, and the acceleration and promotion of privatisation and private business were not accompanied by social guarantees and adequate control mechanisms. The issue of the gender pay gap is closely related to the large income discrepancies in societies in transition and with the problem of the minimum wage, which in many countries can barely cover the minimum subsistence.

Another common feature in this area is the lack of effective mechanisms for the implementation of existing and recently adopted legislation in the field of equal treatment, which is further exacerbated by the general infra-structural weakness of existing institutions, labour inspections, trade unions, etc.

Notwithstanding the progressive adoption of the new EU standards, deep-rooted gender stereotypes persist in all of the countries surveyed, and will require concerted broader educational efforts that ought to be carried out in conjunction with the education and information specific to the equal treatment standards of the EU. The weak legal culture and legal awareness about how to protect human rights during the previous regime remain obstacles to legal protection and remedy for persons whose rights to equal treatment and equal pay are infringed.

The general level of compliance with the principle of equal pay can be assessed as satisfactory in terms of the formal adoption of the standard, but the principle is far from being realised in practice in any of the countries under review. The reports do demonstrate that the process of adopting the *acquis* is a highly dynamic one,[16] which is more advanced in countries such as Lithuania and the Czech Republic, and is being actively transposed in countries such as Estonia, Hungary, and Bulgaria.

Legal framework and institutional structures

The basis for the principle of equal pay is set forth in the constitutions of the countries under review as a guarantee for non-discrimination, *inter alia* based on sex, and for the protection of social rights. In Poland it is enshrined explicitly as a principle in the 1997 Constitution, and a general principle of equal pay and non-discrimination in the field of equal compensation for equal work, including on grounds of sex, is established in the Hungarian Constitution.

All of the countries under review have ratified the basic human rights instruments related to equal pay, including the International Covenant on Economic, Social and Cultural Rights, CEDAW, the ILO Conventions 100 and 111, and most countries have ratified the Revised European Social Charter. The transposition of laws and regulations comprises the essential part of the harmonisation with regard to this principle, and the countries present a rich variety of solutions to doing this. Labour Codes are most often amended in order to accommodate these standards. In Poland, for example, the Labour Code guarantees equal rights for the fulfilment of the same obligations and prohibition of discrimination in employment; in Romania the principle of equal pay for equal work has been a part of the Labour Code since 1972; in Bulgaria the accession process provoked the adoption in March 2001 of a special provision on equal pay (Section 243 of the Labour Code guarantees the right to equal pay for the same work or work of equal value). The principle is also regulated by other laws, such as the Wages Act in Lithuania and the Act on Wages in the Czech Republic.

The guarantees for equal pay in specialised gender equality and anti-discrimination acts deserve special attention. The acts in Lithuania and Romania both confirm the principle of equal pay for equal work and constitute a model for establishing mechanisms for the implementation of the principle of equal treatment. In Bulgaria, in addition to the provision in the Labour Code, a new comprehensive Act for the Prevention of Discrimination will contain a general provision on equal pay. Despite this progress in the formal adoption of the principle of equal pay, serious concerns about its implementation in practice have been reported. Difficulties with the full transposition of the principle for 'work of equal value' persist in certain countries like

---

[16] In Estonia, many pieces of new legislation have entered into force since the beginning of 2002, including the Employment Contract Act, the Holidays Act, the Working and Rest Time Act, the amendments of the Wages Act, the Unemployment Insurance Act; and a new Draft Employment Act is awaiting a second reading. In Hungary, the recent amendments to the Labour Code introduced equal pay not only for equal work, but also for work of equal value.

Lithuania, where only equal pay for 'equal work' formally exists. Furthermore, not 'all the aspects and conditions of remuneration' are encompassed in the notion of equal pay. The development of legislation and legal practice in this area though will hopefully ensure the full transposition of EU standards.[17]

There are no legal provisions contrary to the principle of equal pay in the countries under review and that the guarantees are valid both for the public and private sectors. However, with the exception of the Czech Republic there are no unified job classification systems for the two sectors, ensuring the factual implementation of the principle of equal pay. Strict criteria for remuneration in the public sector are observed in all of the countries, especially for civil servants, and usually depend on the rank, job position and evaluation, and practically exclude discrimination if applied correctly. This is provided for by the Public Service Act of Estonia, and the Act on Civil Servants and the Public Administration Act and respective regulations in Bulgaria.

This statutory regulation of the public sector is typical for accession countries, where prior to the democratic changes the labour market was comprised almost exclusively by the public sector. Attempts to regulate pay in the private sector in countries such as Romania and the Czech Republic are relatively new, and were first observed in the Collective Work Agreements for the private sector in Romania and in the special unified job classification adopted in the Czech Republic in 2001. In order to ensure equal pay and, more specifically, non-discrimination in the private sphere, the Czech Ministry of Social Affairs issued regulations for the application of a special analytical method of assessing the value of the different jobs.

Monitoring to ensure application of the principle of equal pay is carried out by different state institutions in accession countries, although the role of the labour inspections as departments of the respective ministries of labour is a common characteristic. In general, the competence, power and performance of the traditional labour inspection have proven insufficient for the effective implementation of the principle of equal treatment, and more specifically, of equal pay. This issue does not always fall under the explicit competence of the inspection; in Poland, Bulgaria, or Hungary, for example, it cannot act *ex officio* in cases of discrimination. A lack of awareness on behalf of the respective state officials and the limited power of the inspection have been noted, with some exceptions, as further concerns.[18] The Labour Inspectorate of Lithuania, which has an agreement with the Ombudsperson on Equal Opportunities in the field of equal treatment, is in a more advantageous position.

---

[17] For example, the notion of 'work of equal value' was adopted in Hungary at the beginning of 2002.

[18] The Inspectorate in Romania has the power to ask for the removal of the enterprise from the Commercial Register.

Other institutions that were noted include the Council for Women's issues (with the participation of women's organisations) and the National ILO Council for the implementation of the principle of equal pay according to the ILO Convention 100 at the Ministry of Labour in Hungary.

In addition to the specialised Ombudsperson in Lithuania, the development of the general institution of the ombudsman in countries such as Hungary, Romania, and the Czech Republic can offer additional guarantees for the effective implementation of the principle of equal pay.

Because the principle of equal pay is in the initial stages of implementation in the candidate countries, it is difficult at this stage to assess the impact of harmonisation with the Directive, and it would be unrealistic to expect positive results within such a short timeframe. For this reason, the situation that has been reported *de facto* remains valid. Specifically, equal pay remains an area where women face discrimination related to gender stereotypes and the existing job segregation, whereby women prevail in low paid sectors such as the public sector (health, education, public services) or in low paid industries such as the textile and clothing industries. However, newly feminised sectors such as banking, insurance, and also entrepreneurship, clearly improve this negative balance.

The gender pay gap is notable in all of the countries examined: 79 percent in Poland in 1999, where 75 percent of people earning less than the average were women; 72 percent in Estonia in 1997; 79 percent in Hungary in 1999; 73 percent in the Czech Republic in 1999; and 88 percent in Lithuania in 2001. In all these countries official statistical institutes monitor the pay gap. Official statistics on equal opportunities are provided regularly in Lithuania, and also by certain specialised institutes like the National Institute of Research in the field of labour and social protection, and the National Research and Methodological Centre for labour relations and monitoring the level of wages. A special governmental program for action and priorities in promoting equal opportunities for women and men in the Czech Republic gives a mandate to the Minister of Labour and Social Affairs and the President of the national statistics to regularly conduct research in the field of equal treatment. There is no consistent system of state statistics in Bulgaria concerning equal pay.[19]

Procedures available for the implementation of the principle of equal pay

In order to ensure full compliance with Articles 2 and 6 of the Directive, the governments in countries in accession must adopt or adjust existing procedures to enable persons whose right to equal treatment was violated to have recourse to the

---

[19] Private research data for the public sector pay gap of 69% in 1997 is not sufficiently reliable and has not been updated.

competent authorities and seek redress, including by judicial process. However, several weaknesses of the existing systems for protection can be identified. In particular:

- No consistent case law can be observed, despite the existence of some precedents.
- There is a lack of awareness among representatives of the legal profession.
- The existing mechanisms are not applied in a satisfactory manner.

The lack of alternatives to judicial protection in most of the countries is obvious; the main 'missing link' for effective protection being the shift in the burden of proof in cases of sex-based discrimination. With a few exceptions, such as the Czech Republic, this principle has not yet been adopted in accession countries.

Among the positive trends concerning protection in court, it is possible to note the exemption of the applicant from all the judicial costs related to the procedure for protecting labour rights, including the right to equal pay. In many countries the employee is considered the weaker party in proceedings, and in Poland this party is entitled to assistance from the court and social organisations. Legal assistance from the state is available if income criteria are met in Estonia, Romania, Hungary, and Lithuania. A serious improvement and an important breakthrough concerning the opportunities for legal protection is Statutory Order No.137 of 2000 of Romania regarding the Prevention and Punishment of All Forms of Discrimination, which entrusts human rights NGOs with *locus standi* in cases in their field of activity and which prejudice a community or a group of persons and also at the request of an individual whose rights are violated. Among the procedures available for the violation of the principle of equal pay, the vast powers of the Ombudsperson on Equal Opportunities of Lithuania bear repeating.[20]

In relation to the legal means available to persons in cases of the violation of the principle of equal treatment, the following trends can be observed: unsatisfactory conciliation opportunities, no substantive role and control through the trade unions or collective agreements, and no clear information procedures. The possibility for conciliation by a Conciliation Committee is envisaged in the Labour Code of Poland, although it does not yet apply to cases of the violation of the principle of equal pay. A similar procedure exists in Hungary, too, but these institutions need further development.

Trade unions in the candidate countries can play a more effective role in the practical implementation of the principle of equal pay, since the laws there confer a broad competence upon them with respect to the protection of the rights of employees.[21] In

---

[20] The request of the Equal Opportunities Ombudsperson is binding since all legal and natural persons are obliged to immediately submit the material and necessary explanations upon the request of the Ombudsperson. The latter can act both in the public and private sectors.

[21] For example, in Bulgaria.

particular, trade unions participate in consultations and the drafting of labour and social security legislation, defend the rights of workers before the government and the employers, and actively participate in tripartite consultations and collective bargaining, etc. The trade unions in most countries have an especially important right, which is to provide legal representation in court at the request of the worker or employee.

Although the establishment of women's committees or associations in the trade unions of Estonia, Romania, and Hungary, is a positive trend, the reality is that the unions in the candidate countries are not yet conscious of their critical role in this field, and require greater awareness raising and training on the EU standards.

Although very formal at first glance, the requirements of Article 5 (protection against dismissal in reaction to a complaint) and Article 7 of the Directive (the right of employees to be informed about the principle of equal pay) are among those elements that have not yet been transposed. Employees' right to protection exists to some extent in the Act on Equal Opportunities of Lithuania, which states that "An employer must [...] take appropriate means to prevent the persecution of an employee who has lodged a complaint on grounds of discrimination." A similar provision exists in the Romanian Act on Equal Opportunities. The obligation to inform employees of the equal pay standards has not been implemented in the countries under review, although the draft Wages Act of Estonia does contain such a legal obligation.

B. Equal treatment for women and men as regards access to employment, vocational training and promotion, and working conditions and compliance with Council Directive 76/207/EEC of 9 February 1976

General considerations

In this field, the *acquis* is composed primarily of the provisions of EU primary law; specifically, Articles 13, 137, and 141 of the Amsterdam Treaty, stipulating the adoption of measures for fighting discrimination, including on grounds of sex, EU support for the measures of the member states in the field of equal opportunities for men and women in the labour market, and the adoption of affirmative action for the underrepresented sex in the field of employment. Furthermore, the *acquis* includes Council Directive 76/207/EEC and Council Directive 97/80/EC on the burden of proof in cases of discrimination based on sex. The burden of proof and the notion of indirect discrimination are key elements when dealing with equal treatment in the labour market.

The main standards in this field include:

- The elimination of discrimination on grounds of sex either directly or indirectly, in particular by reference to marital and family status;

- The exclusion from the field of application of the Directive those occupational activities that by reason of their nature or the context in which they are carried out, consider that the sex of the worker constitutes a determining factor;
- The application of the Directive without prejudice to provisions concerning the protection of women, particularly as regards pregnancy and maternity;
- The application of the Directive without prejudice to measures to promote equal opportunities for men and women, and the elimination of discrimination on grounds of sex in the selection criteria, for access to all jobs or posts, sectors or branches of activity, and at all levels of the occupational hierarchy;
- The abolishment of all discriminatory provisions in laws, regulations, administrative procedures, collective agreements, individual contracts, etc.;
- The revision of all protective provisions that are no longer justified;
- The application of the principle of equal treatment with regard to vocational training, and with regard to working conditions;
- The provision of measures ensuring the possibility for protection against the violation of the principle of equal treatment by judicial process after recourse to other competent authorities; and protection against dismissal in reaction to lodging a complaint;
- Informing employees about the principle of equal treatment.

The Directive has undergone further development with the addition of clear standards on the adoption of affirmative action, where necessary, and with regard to measures for the elimination of sexual harassment as a form of sex discrimination. Accordingly, this Directive is a strong example of the progressive development of EU standards in the field of equal treatment.

The requirements for equal treatment contained in this Directive are fundamental to an understanding of this principle in the accession countries. For this reason, the process of implementation here is indicative of the level of awareness of gender equality, and of the attitudes of decision-makers, which touch upon the most firm gender stereotypes in the respective countries. In order for the standards to be successfully harmonised, it is essential also to understand the gender equality standards inherited in each country from the socialist regime, since these form the basis for adopting new legislation. For example, in societies where gender equality was expressly declared and where women benefited to a large extent from social protection, it is remarkably difficult now to pass gender equality laws and gender sensitive legislation. The myth that everything was already achieved in the field of gender equality, combined with the paternalistic approach and gender stereotypes that remained intact, go a long way in explaining the reluctance of the political elite to align with European standards. What renders compliance with this Directive particularly sensitive, and at the same time most crucial, is its specific purpose of bridging the gap between *de jure* and *de facto* equality.

Another sensitive point is the differentiation in the Directive between special protective measures for women and affirmative action, which may seem obvious to the EU, but which is less obvious for the governments in accession countries. Special measures are often presented as measures for promoting women or positive discrimination. Protective legislation, however, where not reviewed, brought inequality for women and men in the labour market. The special protection of women and the fact that they assume, in most cases, the exclusive burden of raising the children, make employers reluctant to hire and invest in them as part of the labour force. They also estimate that the costs of having women in the labour force are higher than those sustained for men. All of these factors made women more vulnerable to the fluctuations of the labour market. Under these conditions, from the entire period of transition prior to the beginning of the accession process, there was no protection, for example, in the field of access to employment in all its elements or against sexual harassment, and there were no guarantees (which is still the case in most countries) against dismissals in retaliation to lodging a complaint, etc. At the same time, the excessive focus on the reproductive role of women and on women as mothers serves as an obstacle towards the enforcement of parental leave rights and to sharing parental and family responsibilities.

The new economic conditions render the traditional protection by the Labour Codes less effective, and the social guarantees in terms of social security benefits for maternity and childcare leave are not sufficient and do not constitute a real guarantee for women. Thus, where stronger protection exists, it is much more 'on paper' than in reality.

The impact of economic transition and the restructuring on the labour force is most visible on the working conditions and women's factual situation. In most countries women prevail among the unemployed, especially the long-term unemployed, and in many cases they are forced to accept any job, under any conditions. This leads to the worsening of labour conditions and has clear gender connotations.[22]

The lack of provisions on the shift of the burden of proof in most national legal system constitutes a serious obstacle to the judicial protection of the rights guaranteed by the Directive, and hence to its full implementation. The traditional general rule on the burden of proof still prevailing in most countries in accession puts workers at an additional disadvantage, since workers claiming their rights and plaintiffs are in a

---

[22] In Poland, a country from the first wave of accession countries, the gender gap in unemployment in 1999 was 18.4% for women and 14.4% for men, with a tendency to broaden. In Bulgaria, women prevail among long-term unemployed and comprise 53% of the registered unemployed.

weaker position than the employer. The absence of case law in countries that have harmonised substantive provisions but not yet introduced the shift in the burden of proof confirms the dissuasive effect of the existing procedure.

The implementation of the Directive, which is highly comprehensive, requires the establishment of institutional mechanisms for gender equality, and while this has been done in some countries, they are not sufficiently strong or effective. Such specialised institutions and their respective mechanisms, however, are the only way to ensure the implementation of the principle of equal treatment.

National legal frameworks on equal treatment

The review of the implementation of the principle of equal treatment in the accession countries clearly illustrates the influence the negotiation process has had on their legislation. While the principle is being slowly but progressively implemented, at least *de jure,* the *de facto* effects have yet to be seen and evaluated. In general, the progress can be assessed as satisfactory, although some countries such as Lithuania and the Czech Republic are more advanced.

No directly discriminatory provisions contrary to the Directive were reported in any of the countries under review. Certain elements of discrimination, though, can be observed in connection with the protective measures for women, which can also constitute discrimination against men and will be discussed further.

The principle of equal treatment is enshrined in the constitutions of the countries in accession, and both Poland and Hungary contain special provisions on equality between women and men in their constitutions. The labour codes and labour legislation further develop the principle, both as a general provision on non-discrimination and equal treatment, as in the Bulgarian Labour Code, or as specific provisions on equal treatment on grounds of sex.[23] The principle is set forth in special gender equality legislation also, for example in the Act on Equal Opportunities of Lithuania and in the Act on Equal Opportunities of Women and Men of Romania.[24]

Notwithstanding the constitutional provisions noted above, the principle of equal treatment is not established *expressis verbis* in most of the countries, and this is viewed as a shortcoming according to the national reports. A key issue for compliance with and implementation of the principle of equal treatment as required by the Directive, is the difference between the concept of equal treatment and the concept of non-discrimination. The implementation of the principle of equal treatment, as defined in

---

[23] In the Czech Republic, Poland, and in the Act on Employment Contracts of Lithuania.

[24] Romania is an interesting example where the principle of equal treatment for all citizens is declared in the Act on the Prevention of Discrimination, Statutory Order No.137 of 2000.

EU primary and secondary law, implies the adoption of effective policy on gender mainstreaming, going beyond the mere adoption of gender equality legislation. It also requires the establishment of institutional mechanisms for gender equality. In many countries influenced by the accession process this policy began with the establishment of new institutions. In Lithuania, as described earlier, this entailed an Equal Opportunities Ombudsperson and the Act on Equal Opportunities. The policy of gender mainstreaming in the Czech Republic began in 1997 when the government assigned special functions to the Minister of Labour and Social Affairs to coordinate the gender equality policy. There is an Office on women's issues at the Ministry of Labour in Hungary, and a recent example of such an institution is the office of the governmental Plenipotentiary on Equal Opportunities in Poland (2001).

The best regulation of the principle of equal treatment among countries in accession so far can be found in the Act on Equal Opportunities of Lithuania. Areas such as access to employment (job advertisements and selection procedure), vocational training and promotion, which are usually problematic because they are not expressly included in the labour legislation, are covered by this law. The new Act on Equal Opportunities in Romania appears even more comprehensive. In Bulgaria, some issue of equal treatment (in the process of job hunting, prohibition of discriminatory advertisements, including on grounds of sex) are regulated by the new Act on Employment Promotion, which entered into force in January 2002.

A trend of favouring more general anti-discrimination over gender equality legislation can be observed, and it will soon be possible to evaluate how effective anti-discrimination acts can be in the field of gender equality in employment if they are not combined with the gender equality mechanisms.

The concept of discrimination on grounds of sex

The lack of a clear concept and definition of discrimination based on sex is a major concern in most of the countries, as is the absence of family and marital status among the possible grounds for discrimination.[25] Examples of good practice in this field though include Estonia, where the new Employment Contracts Act prohibits discrimination on grounds of sex by reference to marital and family status, and Bulgaria, where the amended Labour Code (2001) explicitly prohibits direct and indirect discrimination and provides a definition of indirect discrimination.[26]

---

[25] This ground for non-discrimination was introduced with latest amendments to the Labour Code of Hungary.

[26] In most countries a definition of direct and indirect discrimination was lacking as of 2001, but latest developments show that the notion of indirect discrimination was introduced in Hungary and Romania, too.

It is important to note that in the countries under review the provision of Article 1 of CEDAW is in force and is part of their domestic legislation, and the concepts of both direct and indirect discrimination can be derived from this definition of discrimination against women. The same consideration holds true for the ILO Convention 111 Concerning Discrimination (Employment and Occupation), where both discrimination and affirmative action are defined.

With regard to the procedures for protection, most of the considerations made in the review of the principle of equal pay are valid for all of the countries: the administrative control and mechanisms of punishment of the labour inspections are not effective enough, the legal grounds for filing a complaint are not explicitly specified in most cases, there are scarce and ineffective out-of-court possibilities for settling disputes on equal treatment, and the right of a victim of discrimination to compensation is not clearly specified or ensured.

The following examples illustrate these assessments: In Poland, there has not been any case law on equal treatment in the practice of the Supreme Court or the Constitutional Court. No specific practice of the Ombudsperson has been observed either. The practice is developed only in the field of equal treatment in social security, where there are clear means for protection and a clear procedure. No cases on the violation of the principle of equal treatment under the Constitution of Estonia are pending before the Legal Chancellor of Estonia and the new Labour Dispute Committee in Estonia, as an extra-judicial independent institution for cases under individual contracts, does not deal with cases of access to employment. In Romania, the recently established National Council for the Prevention of Discrimination can be addressed in cases of discrimination also on grounds of sex, but it is questionable whether a body that is part of the central public administration and which falls under the authority of the government can take independent decisions.

Affirmative action is not explicitly recognised or defined in law in any of the countries examined, although the provisions of CEDAW (Article 4) and of the ILO Convention 111 contain clear definitions of these positive measures aimed at the establishing equality *de facto*. Positive measures are perceived as a means of eliminating discrimination in the new Statutory Order No.137 of 2000 of Romania, and in this respect the new Act on Equal Opportunities in Romania providing for affirmative action in the field of gender equality is a real milestone. Positive discrimination is defined in Lithuania following amendments to the Law on Equal Opportunities of 18 June 2002. Although not clearly defined, importance is given to these developments and changes can be expected in Hungary, Estonia, and Bulgaria.

Protective measures regarding women's participation in the labour market and the prohibition of dismissal

As a matter of principle, women in all of the accession countries under review benefit from protection against harmful and hazardous types of work because of their biological and reproductive functions and such measures are not considered discriminatory. Sometimes this general protection is afforded to them as women, in addition to any protection they are granted while pregnant, breastfeeding or caring for children. Working conditions such as night work, overtime, business trips, and protection against dismissal also form part of the protective measures.

At the heart of compliance with the Directive in this field is the need to strike a balance between ensuring both equal treatment for men and women and a fair division of tasks in the family, while at the same time removing any obstacles that women face in the labour market as a result of this protection. Under the pressure of transition and accession to the EU, many accession countries are revising these protective measures. This exercise requires thorough consideration as it is related to social safeguards and, occasionally, contradicts certain strong ILO standards. A few examples illustrate the nature of the debate and the direction of the changes envisaged: In Hungary and Poland it is declared that excessive protective measures, especially for women who are not pregnant or breastfeeding, are unjustified and solutions are sought in the direction of affirming the right of individual choice. Some radical feminist views have been expressed in Poland in reaction to the excessive protection, but the measures have not yet been removed. Certain protective measures, such as the absolute ban on business trips for mothers of children up to three years of age in Bulgaria, and the ban on night work in Slovakia, have been removed.

Protection against dismissal for a person who claims to be a victim of the violation of the principle of equal treatment is not yet regulated in all the candidate countries in a consistent manner. Countries that introduced such protection into their Labour Codes include the Czech Republic and Hungary, where the provision is against retaliation for bringing legal action. Lithuania introduced such protection into the Act on Equal Opportunities, and Romania recently did the same. Such a measure is expected to be introduced in Estonia with the adoption of the Gender Equality Act.

Informing employees about their rights under the Directive is again very weakly regulated and even when this principle exists on paper; it is not implemented in practice. In Romania the obligation and the respective right to information are provided for by the Act on Equal Opportunities. NGOs, alone or together with trade unions, can play a crucial role in this respect: organising awareness campaigns, providing institutions with legal and gender expertise, ensuring literacy among workers and employees, and providing employers with awareness training. In addition, they can actively participate in national consultative bodies established through the institutional mechanisms for gender equality, and conduct impact litigation on gender issues.

The legal status of sexual harassment

Protection against sexual harassment is another field where the challenges are many, particularly since full compliance with EU standards requires measures to be adopted in the fields of labour law, criminal law, general civil law and administrative law.

Due to persisting stereotypes, there has been a strong resistance to recognise sexual harassment as a typical phenomenon also in Eastern European countries,[27] and reluctance on behalf of the states to ensure the respective legal protection. Clearly though, the first step to combating the phenomenon is to recognise its existence and provide for its definition in the national law of the candidate countries.

Protection against sexual harassment in the workplace is regulated in the Czech Republic, which is in compliance with the EU standards. It is also regulated by the Law on Equal Opportunities in Lithuania and Romania,[28] although one could hardly observe any improvements in daily practice. Changes ought to be forthcoming in Bulgaria with the new Act on the Prevention of Discrimination, and in Estonia once the draft Gender Equality Act is adopted. In Bulgaria and Poland, the matter is treated in the labour law as an obligation to ensure dignity at work, but it does not touch upon the essence of the problem and requires further and specific development in the legislation.

---

[27] Firstly, sexual harassment also existed during socialist times, but was part of the culture of 'tolerance' and hypocrisy typical of the former regime. Although formal gender equality was declared and was also part of the official ideology and policy, feminist movements and issues were not accepted. Secondly, during the period of transition general anti-feminist attitudes persisted, as did the lack of sensitivity towards how women, who comprise the most part of victims of sexual harassment, feel. Thirdly, the fact that most feminist movements, ideas and issues were brought into Eastern European countries by American women's organisations created the impression that these problems, including sexual harassment, were imported by these organisations. And finally, in most of the countries the problem was under-researched and only women's NGOs presented data to the governments.

[28] This country adopted a comprehensive approach for eliminating the phenomenon, including changes in the Criminal Code punishing the worst forms of sexual harassment.

4.2 From special protection to affirmative action

A. *Council Directive 92/85/EC on Maternity Protection: General Considerations and Level of Compliance*

General considerations

The main standards in the protection of maternity relate to:

- An assessment by the employer of the specific safety risks at work for pregnant women, and women who have recently given birth or are breastfeeding, and taking measures to avoid these risks;

- Information about the potential risks;

- Avoiding exposure by moving the woman to another job if necessary or, if that is not possible, by granting leave;

- To respect defined minimum standards to avoid risks and hazards;

- Banning night work during pregnancy and for some period after giving birth;

- Transfer to daytime work or granting of leave if necessary; entitlement to at least 14 weeks of maternity leave before and after birth with a period of two weeks compulsory maternity leave;

- Granting of time off with pay for antenatal examinations; and apart from exceptional cases and with the consent of the respective authorities, prohibition of dismissal from the beginning of pregnancy until the end of the maternity leave;

- The requirement for duly substantiated grounds in case of dismissal and protection from the consequences of unlawful dismissal;

- Ensuring employment rights plus pay and respective allowances during maternity leave;

- The possibility for women to defend their rights in court;

- An additional standard shifting the burden of proof.

As a matter of fact, all of the countries examined have more favourable core provisions on maternity protection, leaving only some elements that are not in compliance with the Directive. However, an analysis of the legislation shows that the length of the leave in itself, the most favourable element, does not guarantee effective protection.

The legislation in Romania still leaves much to be desired concerning the procedure for risk assessment and the explicit prohibition of certain minimum risky and hazardous types of work. Again in Romania, but also in Poland and Lithuania, for example, there is no procedure for transferring a pregnant woman to daytime work, or for granting leave. In relation to night work, the provisions range from an absolute ban, which has been criticised, to a lack of protection during the first five months of pregnancy, as is the case in Romania. Estonia has the most democratic solution, whereby night work cannot be imposed on women under maternity protection. Polish case law also veers in the direction of supporting a woman's individual choice.

Another general concern is the lack of sufficient guarantees for returning back to the same conditions of work. This is reported as a serious problem in Hungary, but is a common concern in all of the countries, where new economic realities make the implementation of this protection difficult in practice.

This inadequate implementation of laws is also characteristic of protection against unlawful dismissal, where it is suggested that further protection be sought through special laws on equal opportunities, despite changes that have already been brought to the labour laws. Lithuania is an example of good practice in this regard, because in addition to the special law, the Criminal Code foresees criminal responsibility for the dismissal or refusal to employ a pregnant or breastfeeding woman. Bulgaria is very close to compliance with this Directive, but needs further steps to be taken because the provisions concerning the dismissal of pregnant women and mothers still allow for subjective decision-making, and do not cover the entire pregnancy period.

No effective judicial protection of women is possible without ensuring a shift in the burden of proof from the plaintiff to the defendant. This radical legislative change has taken place in the Czech Republic, and is under way in Lithuania and Bulgaria.

B. Compliance with Council Directive 96/34/EC on the Framework Agreement on Parental Leave

General considerations

The main standards for equal treatment in granting parental leave relate to:

- Granting male and female workers the individual right to parental leave;
- Enabling them to take care of the child for at least three months until a given age up to eight years;
- Granting the right to leave on a non-transferable basis;
- Protecting workers against dismissal on the grounds of applying for or taking parental leave;
- Ensuring the right to return to the same job under the same conditions and to maintain the rights acquired during the period of the leave;

- Ensuring the right to time off for work in case of emergencies for family reasons.

Research carried out on the sharing of family responsibilities and the reconciliation of family/parental and professional obligations shows that women's and men's traditional roles prevail in all of the accession countries, although some positive trends can be noted.

A significant obstacle to the implementation of this principle is the hardship caused by economic transition, which, in most of countries, requires the work and income of both parents. The gender pay gap, which can be noted both in accession countries and EU member states, reinforces this trend. Thus, in many cases the standards outlined in the Directive are unaffordable for both women and men. The lack of opportunities for flexible work schedules in most of the countries examined render these obstacles even more acute, and the absence of consistent research and gender statistics, not to mention public discussions on the role both parents should play in the family and in relation to their children, makes it even more difficult to adopt the appropriate legislation and policies.

Legal framework and policy

Despite the difficulties and challenges outlined above, the Directive is gradually being transposed in most of the countries under review, and the main elements, such as the granting of the right to parental leave in principle to fathers and the respective social security coverage, already existed in most of the countries.[29] All of the countries have provisions on childcare allowances for both parents according to the respective economic standards, and the length of the leave is in many instances above the minimum requirements of the Directive.

Legislation on this issue in countries such as Estonia and Romania has been clearly influenced by the accession process. According to the new Holiday Act of Estonia in force since the beginning of 2002, for example, there is a special provision on 'father's leave' and the father has the right to 14 calendar days of paid leave during the mother's pregnancy and maternity leave, or during the two months following the birth of the child. This is in addition to the parental leave granted upon request to the mother or the father to raise a child up to three years of age. In Romania, the Act on Parental Leave, the National Collective Agreement and the National Plan for Occupancy are aimed at further implementing the Directive and at reconciling professional and family life. Even in the absence of full compliance, this trend is positive. The recent provision in Polish law, giving the opportunity for simultaneous parental leave of three months, although paid only for one of the parents, is indicative of the variety of solutions that might be adopted.

---

[29] For example, this principle was already introduced in the 1980s and 1990s in countries such as Bulgaria, Poland, and Hungary.

The non-transferable nature of the leave is a critical point that has not been resolved in many of the countries. In Bulgaria, for example, the childcare leave following maternity leave is granted to both parents, but the mother must consent to this. In these circumstances it is not considered 'real' parental leave. Similarly, the father can take the childcare leave instead of the mother upon the family's decision.

Other common weaknesses include the lack of clear provisions for protection against dismissal,[30] a lack of guarantees for returning to the same job and working conditions and maintaining the rights acquired, and a lack of flexible schemes for taking advantage of the parental leave.[31] No specific affirmative action encouraging fathers to take childcare leave was observed, and the new provision on father's leave in Estonia, once adopted, will be a good test in this regard.

4.3 The missing links: Burden of proof and part-time work

A. *The burden of proof in cases of discrimination based on sex and compliance with Council Directive 97/80/EC of 15 December 1997*

General considerations

The main standards on the burden of proof in cases of discrimination based on sex relate to:

- A definition of equal treatment as non-discrimination based on sex, either directly or indirectly;

- A definition of indirect discrimination;

- Application of the Directive to situations of discrimination based on sex covered by Directives 75/117/EEC, 76/207/EEC, 92/85/EEC, and 96/34/EC;

- Application of the Directive to all civil and administrative procedures concerning the public or private sector with the exception of out-of-court procedures of a voluntary nature or provided for in national law;

- Introduction of a rule of evidence, as a minimum standard, in favour of the person wronged by the act of discrimination;

- Informing all persons concerned about the measures taken pursuant to the Directive and already in force in this field.

---

[30] It is explicitly regulated in Romania.
[31] Although Poland offers a good example.

The Directive is a relatively new standard in itself, not only for accession countries, but also for EU member states, and it entails a major shift in the legal theory and practice. Adoption of this standard is therefore particularly difficult in countries in accession, where the legal systems are based on classical rule of evidence.

The major challenges of the Directive are twofold: firstly, to define indirect discrimination and secondly to shift the burden of proof in cases of discrimination based on sex. The new rules of evidence are indispensable to the real exercise of the right to equal treatment and for ensuring the 'equality of arms' in the procedures for its enforcement. It is also the only way for the weaker party to successfully bring and defend her/his cause in court. Although very slow, the progressive implementation of these standards in the countries in accession shows that, gradually, this concept is gaining ground.

Legal framework on indirect discrimination

The notion of indirect discrimination has been extensively regulated in Bulgarian legislation since changes were brought to the Labour Code in April 2001. Clearly precipitated by the accession process, this breakthrough is expressed in various ways: the concept is mentioned in the general prohibition of discrimination in labour relations, it is explicitly defined in the Labour Code, and it is mentioned and defined in the Act on Employment Promotion of 2002. Indirect discrimination on different grounds, including sex, will be prohibited in the new Act on the Prevention of Discrimination, which is currently being elaborated. There is no separate definition of such discrimination based on sex.

As mentioned above, the provisions recognising and banning indirect discrimination have also been in effect in Hungary since the beginning of 2002 and in Romania since 2000. Because these provisions are very recent, it is not yet possible to measure their impact. The practice of the Ombudsperson in Poland proposes interesting solutions that involve an elaboration and interpretation of the concept.[32]

---

[32] For example in the taxation of revenues of single parents, who are predominantly women. Furthermore, the Ombudsperson has submitted a document to the Minister of Labour and Remuneration expressing his concern that the unequal treatment of men and women in access to employment is visible, *inter alia,* in attempts to dismiss women in the first place within so-called group lay-offs and in the fact that women take leave from work relatively more often due to their care duties for children and family. The Ombudsperson has also proposed that preferences for women within work employment should be facultative, because otherwise, in the present conditions, they act against women.

The burden of proof in litigation concerning the violation of the principle of equal treatment for women and men

A general observation that can be made is that there are no specific procedures in the countries under consideration concerning the enforcement of the principle of equal treatment. Besides administrative responsibility, which can be initiated by the labour inspections, there are no clear rules of procedure and compensation for cases of discrimination based on sex. In Lithuania, the Act on Equal Opportunities treats direct discrimination as a prohibited act and provides for administrative sanctions for this violation of between €28 and €1,130, imposed by the Ombudsperson on Equal Opportunities. As mentioned earlier, the procedures of individual complaints before the Constitutional courts can be used in Poland and the Czech Republic. Despite the existing court procedures, both civil and special labour procedures, no case law has been observed in the field of equal treatment. Individual cases have only been reported in Hungary, where the courts considered cases related to a discriminatory job description and to the extension of protection in termination of contracts to fathers.

One reason for the absence of case law, in addition to the lack of awareness and a reluctance to bring such cases to court, is the fact that the burden of proof lies with the plaintiff. In this respect the candidate countries can be divided into three groups: those that have adopted the new rule of evidence, those who are in the process of adopting it, and those who are still reluctant to do so. Hungary and the Czech Republic fall into the first group. In Hungary the Labour Code provides that in the event of any dispute related to a violation of the prohibition of discrimination, the employer shall be required to prove that his actions did not violate this prohibition. No court decisions are reported with respect to the 'objective justifiability' of the employer's action. The amended Civil Procedure Code of the Czech Republic provides for the shift in the burden of proof in cases of discrimination in employment matters. In countries such as Estonia and Bulgaria, the shift in the burden of proof will be provided for once the new legislation, the Gender Equality Act of Estonia and the Act on the Prevention of Discrimination in Bulgaria, is adopted. In Romania, the draft Act on Equal Opportunities provided for the shift in the burden of proof, but Parliament rejected the shift once the act was adopted, stating that judges must play an active role and can therefore oblige the defendant to provide all the necessary evidence. However, it must be stressed that this is not an obligation, and a lack of evidence on behalf of the defendant will not be considered in favour of the plaintiff.

For the remaining countries under review, the principle *actori incumbit probatio* is valid and no inference of discrimination is possible if the respondent fails to produce evidence. According to the civil procedure in Bulgaria, if the respondent creates obstacles to collecting evidence admitted by the court, the discrimination may be considered as proved. This alternative to the classical rule of evidence can also be used in cases of discrimination based on sex. Under the Lithuanian civil court practice related to the application of labour laws, the burden of proof in disputes related to violations of labour laws falls on the defendant. An interesting example of the non-application of the shift of the burden of proof according to Article 4(3) of the Directive is the investigation procedure of the Lithuanian Ombudsperson on Equal Opportunities.[33]

B. Non-discrimination against part-time workers and compliance with Council Directive 97/81/EC of 15 December 1997

General considerations

The main standards relating to part-time workers include:

- The protection of part-time workers with an employment contract or in an employment relationship;

- A definition of 'part-time worker' with reference to 'comparable full-time worker';

- Non-discrimination of part-time workers with respect to employment conditions;

- Protection against the termination of employment for workers who refuse to be transferred from full-time to part-time work or vice versa;

- The consideration of requests for a transfer from full-time to part-time or vice-versa should the opportunity arise;

- Information about the availability of full-time and part-time positions in order to facilitate transfers;

- The facilitation of access to part-time work at all levels of the enterprise, including skilled and managerial positions and easier access to vocational training.

---

[33] She/he is the main subject who must collect evidence, examine the individual who committed the violation and submit a justified explanation to the Ombudsperson within a fixed term. Such an investigation procedure for complaints involving the application of the principle of equal treatment for men and women as regards access to employment, vocational training, promotion and working conditions, significantly facilitates the position of complainants and creates more favourable conditions insofar as a complainant is not obliged to obtain documents or any other evidence from the person who committed the violation, as such a process is, as a rule, a difficult task. It is in fact the procedure most used in cases of breach of the principle of equal treatment. Surprisingly enough, the implementation of the Act on Equal Opportunities did not generate substantial case law in this field.

The adoption of the *acquis communautaire* in this field is of great relevance to the countries in accession because the promotion of part-time work will bring a reduction of unemployment, facilitate the flexibility of work, and encourage work mobility. In Lithuania, unemployment increased to 14 percent in 1999, while in Bulgaria the official registered level of unemployment was 20 percent for 2000. Another important effect of encouraging part-time work is that it will promote gender equality by allowing for the improved reconciliation of professional and family responsibilities for both women and men. Also, the realisation of women in the labour market and the improvement of their working conditions and retention of benefits, as women comprise the majority of part-time workers in most of the countries (Lithuania is the only country that does not report part-time work as a female phenomenon).

Part-time work is developed to differing extents in the countries in accession. In Lithuania in 1998, part-time employees made up 11.6 percent, compared with seven percent in Poland in 1999. In Bulgaria, flexible forms of work are less developed than in the other countries, and data from 1997 shows that that only one percent of women were employed part-time, while this figure was 10 percent in the Czech Republic, and 18 percent in Romania.[34] Statistics show that in the Czech Republic in 1998, only 2.6 percent of men worked part-time, compared with 9.6 percent of women. In Estonia in 1999, about to two thirds of part-time workers were women, and women made up 66 percent of all part-time workers in Poland in the same period.

Legal framework and employment conditions concerning part-time workers

The overall assessment of the implementation of the Directive shows a low level of compliance on the whole, although there have been some positive developments in some of the countries surveyed. In general there is no clear definition of part-time work and no conditions for shortening working hours without a significant negative impact on the employees' standard of living. No special provisions in the agreements among the social partners were reported apart from Romania, although such agreements are an important component of implementation.

Nevertheless, the laws in the countries examined do not contain explicitly discriminatory provisions for part-time workers, thus providing a strong basis for future compliance. The main fields of discrimination in practice are the level of remuneration and the opportunities for a transfer from full-time to part-time work or *vice versa*, two areas that are subject to negotiation. The fact that the remuneration is fully negotiable is very often more detrimental to women, who comprise the majority of part-time workers and are effectively obliged to accept any conditions. Another aspect to be considered is the widespread overemphasis on the possibilities for women

---

[34] The average rate in the EU for the period being 32%. Data from the MONEE UNICEF report for 1999.

who are pregnant and/or with small children to take advantage of flexible forms of work. This reasoning only reinforces gender stereotypes in society.

No notion of 'comparable full-time worker' to provide a reference to the definition of part-time worker exists in the countries examined, and the notion of reduced working hours, which was reported as available everywhere for certain categories of work and some employees, is a different form of employment from part-time work.

As a matter of principle, the protection afforded under the labour contract also applies to part-time work. Proportional to the working hours and intensity of work, part-time workers benefit from social security, health insurance, travel allowances, and paid leave. Access to part-time work and transfers, and the opportunities for vocational training, education and career development, remain weak points in all of the countries under review, however.

In the Czech Republic the National Plan on Equality of the Ministry of Labour and Social Affairs envisages the opportunity for variable working hours in order to care for children and the family. In Hungary, a Governmental Decree from 2000 on employment policy guidelines addressed the increased promotion of part-time employment. The purpose of this policy is to harmonise family and workplace obligations and to promote women's employment. Some critics, however, see nuances of furthering the traditional roles in the family. In Lithuania, a Governmental decision on part-time work harmonised the conditions of work for part-time workers, including payment, which will correspond to the working hours and the result of the work. According to the decision, a transfer from full-time to part-time work is possible, and *vice versa*. A positive development has been the amendment of the Labour Code at the request of the specialised Ombudsperson in the direction of gender equality: all fathers will have the opportunity to apply for part-time working schedules, not just single fathers. In Poland, harmonisation has been ensured with the amendments of the Labour Code too, which guarantees non-discrimination and opportunities for part-time workers. The progress in Romania is in line with the Directive due to the inclusion in the Collective Work Agreement for 2000–2001 of the possibility for part-time workers to be employed in a full-time norm if such positions are vacant and if they meet the respective criteria.

4.4 Equal treatment in social security matters

A. *Equal treatment of men and women in the field of social security and compliance with Council Directive 79/7/EEC, Council Directive 86/378/EEC amended by Directive 96/97/EC, Council Directive 86/613/EEC*

General considerations

The main elements of the principle of equal treatment in social security relate to:

- The progressive implementation of the principle of equal treatment for men and women in matters of social security;

- The introduction and definition of the concept of 'occupational social security schemes';

- Non-discrimination in occupational social security schemes;

- Possibilities to declare null and void or amend provisions contrary to this principle;

- Access to courts of justice in case of the violation of the principle of equal treatment;

- Prohibition of dismissal in response to lodging a complaint.

Despite some of the achievements of the previous regimes, especially concerning the social protection of women and maternity, the social security systems were not adapted to the new conditions of a market economy. The process of democratisation brought significant changes to this system, which was based in most of the countries on a paternalistic philosophy and on full contribution from the state budget at the expense of the employees, who were over-employed but underpaid. A recent trend in all the countries examined has been the revision of all social security legislation and the adoption of different models from developed Western European countries. However, this trend has been very little influenced by the EU accession process, and national traditions, and the models on which solutions are adopted, explain why they vary much from one country to another. For example, the development of the social security system for self-employed workers in agriculture in Poland is unique, as is the pension fund for people with special merits in Lithuania.

Changes in the social security system pertain to the system of contributions, of the state budget, and namely the social security budget, and these are all issues dealt with in the countries in accession, which are also countries in transition, in the agreements between the governments and international financial institutions. Therefore, this is an area very much influenced by the restrictive policies and measures, and respective models imposed by these agents. Furthermore, it has been proven already that these institutions do not apply a gender approach in the course of advising and imposing conditions on the respective governments.

The progressive development of legislation in the field of equal treatment in employment in the EU accession process will positively influence the participation of women in the labour market, and improve the balance in family responsibilities between men and women, thus avoiding some negative impact of the otherwise gender neutral social security provisions. Concerns of indirect discrimination in this case have been expressed, though they differ from country to country. These are related to the different retirement ages and early retirement for men and women, and the difference in contributions and benefits that preserve differences in the remuneration for men and women. Some provisions, although gender neutral, do not take into consideration the nature of their occupational activity, marital status or family situation.

In all of the countries examined the legislation guarantees protection and equal treatment in the coverage of risks such as sickness, invalidity, old age, accidents at work and occupational diseases, and unemployment. On the whole, the social protection of maternity and childcare do not constitute grounds for discrimination.

A shortage of research on the gender impact of social security reforms, combined with a lack of policy on equal treatment in social security and the absence of institutional mechanisms for monitoring equal treatment in this field, are all common features of the candidate countries. The overall assessment is that these countries do not yet comply with Directive 96/97/EC, either conceptually or in terms of its concrete development. Not accidentally, in all of the countries under review, harmonisation in the sphere of social security is envisaged for the period 2003–2004.

In Romania, the social security system has undergone over 30 changes in the last 12 years. There are no discriminatory elements in the three-pillar system, and while the retirement age is currently 62 years for women and 65 for men, the transition to a standard retirement age is expected in 13 years. There are no effective mechanisms for monitoring gender equality in social security though, although a Act on Equal Opportunities was adopted and despite the existence of a new independent institution, the National Agency for Equal Opportunities. One positive element is the fact that related to the rights established by the public system of pensions and other social security rights, Act No.19 of 2000 regulates the social security jurisdiction, namely specialised departments or panels of the court. There are no professional social security schemes in Romania, and collective employment agreements only provide few compensations that employers are obliged to pay to their employees, mainly in cash, at the time of old age retirement, in case of dismissal or death.

The new pension system in the Czech Republic has two components: the obligatory system guaranteed by the state, and the voluntary pension additional insurance subscribed to on an individual basis. The retirement age is also gradually increasing to reach 62 years for men and between 57 and 61 years for women, depending on the number of children, by 2007. If women prefer to retire earlier, it is estimated that it will affect eight percent of their income until the end of their lives. Women are disadvantaged as a result of the lower average salaries and a calculation of the old-age pension based on their longer life expectancy. The institutions on gender equality that formulate the policy in this sphere are the Ministry of Labour and Social Affairs, which coordinates the equal opportunities policy, and its Department for the Equality of Men and Women, but no special monitoring institutions and mechanisms are available. The second most important institution in this field is the Section for Equal Opportunities of Men and Women by the Committee of the Government of the Czech Republic for Human Rights, which monitors and evaluates the observance of human rights, and particularly the fulfilment of international obligations. The third central institution is a subcommittee of the Chamber of Deputies Committee for Social Affairs and Healthcare, which deals with the issues of family and equal opportunities.

Council Directive 96/97/EC has not yet been implemented into the Czech legislation. The Act on Occupational Pension Security was drafted and passed by the Czech government, but was not approved by the first chamber of the Parliament in 2001. The draft, although it does not fully correspond with the concept of the Directive, is more in compliance with the principle of equal treatment.

In Lithuania, the retirement age is also being raised to 60 years for women and 62.5 years for men. In October 2000 a new concept of pension reform was adopted with the classical three-pillar system, and the Equal Opportunities Ombudsperson and the Department of Labour and Equal Opportunities at the Ministry of Social Affairs and Labour are monitoring the social security laws with a view to preventing gender discriminatory provisions. A positive trend in the field of gender equality has been the amendment of a discriminatory provision of the Act on Support to Unemployed Persons. As of December 2001, some advantages under this law are applicable not only for mothers with children up to eight years and father raising such children alone, but also to fathers in general of children up to the age of eight. There is no specific legislation on occupational social security schemes in Lithuania.

In Poland, a three-pillar social security system has been adopted (PAYG, a capital pillar and a pillar for voluntary insurance) and a draft law implementing an interesting solution – the so-called 'elastic retirement age' – is being prepared, according to which any working person, irrespective of their sex, may retire between the ages of 62–65 years. The elastic retirement age will also provide additional protection for workers. The Act on the System of Social Security explicitly provides that the insured person, if he/she believes that the principle of equal treatment has not been applied to them, may pursue the claim before a social security court with special and speedier procedures. It is valid for all first pillar litigation and it is recommended that it be made explicitly valid for the second pillar too. It is clear that persons insured within the workers' retirement programs (third pillar) may appeal to common civil courts on a general basis. It is considered that the newly appointed Governmental Plenipotentiary on Equal Opportunities shall undertake the function of monitoring the observance of the principle of equal treatment in social security. Despite these opportunities, traditionally, the function of monitoring the observance of the principle of equality, also in this field, was fulfilled by the Commissioner for Civil Rights, and discriminatory provisions on grounds of sex were abolished under the influence of the case law of the Constitutional Tribunal. This is an important characteristic in Poland that brings it closer to EU standards.[35]

In Estonia, a three-pillar pension insurance system exists and the equalisation of the retirement age, at 63 years, for men and women is envisaged for 2016. There is no legislation on occupational social security schemes, and the monitoring institution for the principle of equal treatment in social security is the Gender Equality Bureau at the Ministry of Social Affairs. Great hopes have been placed in the Gender Equality Act of Estonia, whose adoption is hoped to be forthcoming.

In Hungary, full pension reform was carried out in the 1990s, and the social security acts in force since 1998 were meant to bring compliance with the EU standards. Formerly, there was a different retirement age for women (55 years) and men (60 years). Discontinuing this practice, the Pension Acts of 1997 (social insurance pension and mandatory private pension) introduced the uniform retirement age of 62 years. Today, the only discriminatory regulation that exists related to the early retirement pension. There are no provisions on occupational social security schemes in accordance with the concept of Directive 96/97/EC.

In Bulgaria, a new code on obligatory social insurance was adopted in January 2000 introducing the gradual equalisation of the retirement age for men and women from 60 years for men and 55 for women in 2000 to 60 years for men and 59 and 6 months for women in January 2009. A three-pillar system was introduced, the second pillar of which is additional obligatory pension insurance, a guarantee for early retirement for certain categories of labour. It remains to be seen in the long term whether the formally equal qualifying conditions for pensions under the obligatory second pillar will

---

[35] Thus, the Commissioner for Civil Rights attacked the Act on Employment and Unemployment of 1991 as discriminatory towards women because it deprived persons whose spouse received twice the average salary from benefits. In 1993 the Act on the System of Health Benefits was attacked for discriminating against men, as the health benefit was provided for wives who were unemployed, but only for husbands if they were disabled. In addition, the Constitutional Tribunal considered that in certain situations the privileged treatment of women was admissible, but that it was forbidden to transform these 'equalising rights' into such a differentiation of obligations, which in practice limited women's professional chances.

constitute indirect discrimination against women. Women in the second pillar shall have to rely fully on their employment history in order to qualify for a pension, and each period of unemployment shall influence the eligibility and the amount of the future pension. Given the longer period of unemployment among women compared to men, this system may be deemed to have an indirectly discriminatory effect. Gender equality in the social security system is not part of any kind of gender equality strategy or policy of the government, and no monitoring mechanisms for the respect of the principle of equal treatment exist. The present occupational social security schemes in Bulgaria are set by law and are not part of a collective agreement or individual contract. The two types of occupational schemes used in the EU countries (part of the concept of Directive 96/97/EC) and in Bulgaria are not comparable and differ to the extent that the Bulgarian occupational scheme is based on defined contributions and covers pension risks. The European occupational scheme is based on defined benefits and covers numerous risks, including but not limited to pensions.

B. *Compliance with Council Directive 96/613/EC on the principle of equal treatment between men and women engaged in an activity, including agriculture, in a self-employed capacity, and on the protection of self-employed women during pregnancy and motherhood*

General considerations

The main standards on equal treatment in self-employment relate to:

- The guarantee of the principle of equal treatment for self-employed workers and their spouses who are not employees or partners;

- Ensuring the elimination of all provisions contrary to the principle of equal treatment concerning the establishment, equipment or extension of a business or the launching or extension of any other form of self-employed activity, including financial facilities;

- Ensuring that the conditions for the formation of a company between spouses are not more restrictive than those for unmarried persons;

- Enabling the spouses of self-employed workers who are not protected under the self-employed worker's social security scheme to join a contributory social security scheme voluntarily;

- Encouraging the recognition of the work of the spouses of self-employed workers;

- Examining the conditions for protecting female self-employed workers and the wives of self-employed workers during pregnancy or motherhood in order for them to benefit from services supplying a temporary replacement or existing national social services, or from cash benefits under a social security scheme or other public social protection system;

- Enabling persons wronged by the failure to apply the principle of equal treatment to pursue their claims by judicial process, possibly after recourse to other competent authorities;

- Bringing the relevant provisions in this field to the attention of bodies representing self-employed workers and vocational training centres.

The phenomenon of self-employed workers and the guarantees for their protection is not unheard of in accession countries and their legal systems. With the exception of Romania, where this category of workers was not regulated because self-employment was not allowed during the communist regime, all the other countries have developed self-employment in a number of forms. Poland is a good example of this trend, with its corresponding thorough regulation. Agriculture was a traditional sector of self-employment in this country, where only 20 percent of the agricultural lands were made the object of collectivisation.

A common trend was for new forms of self-employment to emerge following democratisation in 1989 (entrepreneurships, individual and in-business associations); they developed quickly initially and then, in the mid-1990s, due to the hardships of economic transition, decreased in percentage. The main reasons given for this include high taxation and social security contributions. Despite the relatively high number of women in agriculture, especially in countries such as Romania and Poland, the invisibility of their work was a common feature. In Poland, a country very close to accession, the number of self-employed women was 18 percent of all women employed in the national market and 37 percent of all self-employed persons in the second half of 2000. In Hungary, in 2001, men in business comprised 16.2 percent and compared with 8.6 percent of women. Men comprised 0.4 percent of contributing family members, compared with one percent of women. In Bulgaria, men consistently prevail among the employers and entrepreneurs too. An important general consideration is that the social protection of self-employed workers and their spouses has not been a process driven by EU accession so far, and full compliance with the Directive will require more concentrated efforts inline with the recommendations outlined below.

Level of implementation of the directive in the accession countries

The countries under review generally comply with the Directive, despite the major shortcoming that in providing social protection for self-employed workers and their spouses no specific mention of equal treatment of men and women is made. In fact, the principle of equal treatment, which already characterises the employment legislation, has not yet been extended explicitly to self-employed persons and their spouses. Notwithstanding, no discriminatory provisions or obstacles to the formation of a business by one of the sexes or to common businesses were found in the countries examined.

A positive aspect to be noted is that in most countries self-employed workers and their spouses are protected by the social security schemes, through obligatory insurance in many cases, or at least by the opportunity for voluntary contributions. In most cases, female self-employed workers and contributing spouses are subject to optional contributory insurance for maternity protection, which is in line with the Directive.

However, the fact that there are no clear definitions of 'self-employed workers', except for the purposes of social security and taxation laws, is a serious shortcoming. Definitions of self-employed workers in agriculture are, logically, most developed in Poland. The category of 'contributing member' is still an invisible category, and a lack of recognition of the work of the contributory member, which in most cases is a gender issue, is common to all candidate countries.

No substantive research has been conducted on this important issue, and no data on the status of common businesses or the status of contributing member is available. Furthermore, the countries examined all suffer from a lack of specific judicial means for protection against a breach of the principle of equal treatment, and a dearth of information and awareness campaigns. No specific compliance with Article 8 of the Directive, concerning the replacement opportunities and participation in other public social protection systems, was reported.

Specific examples illustrate these trends and certain concrete solutions

In Poland, the Act on Systems of Social Security of 1998 established the principle of equal treatment in social security. This Act, along with the Act on Social Security of Farmers of 1990, forms the framework for the social protection of self-employed workers and their contributing family members. The total social security contributions are paid by the persons running the activity and cover old age and disability pensions, sickness and maternity insurance, insurance against accidents at work and occupational diseases. Of particular interest are the provisions of the Polish Act on Economic Activity of 1999, which contain an obligation for the state to create favourable conditions for medium and small-size enterprises, including for women.

In Lithuania and Hungary, the main principles of the Directive have been implemented and self-employed persons and their contributing family members can join voluntary social security schemes, guaranteeing sickness and maternity social insurance.

There is no independent system of social security for self-employed workers in the Czech Republic. Self-employed workers, together with their cooperating spouses, participate in the general social security system on the basis of registration.

In Estonia, again, all hopes for the regulation of equal treatment to be extended to the field of self-employment lie with the forthcoming Gender Equality Act. During the discussions of this Act, the need to protect the spouses of self-employed workers was raised as an important issue. Self-employed persons must pay social taxes in order to provide themselves and their spouses with coverage under the existing schemes of social security (in the case of labour contracts, this obligation falls on the employer). For example, in this way they are covered by the sickness fund. The medical insurance coverage also extends to the spouses of self-employed workers, as well as to pregnant women and women raising children up to three years of age. The unemployment social security scheme does not extend to self-employed persons.

In Bulgaria, female self-employed workers are subject to obligatory insurance against disability caused by general disease, old age, and death. If they wish, they can pay other contributions for the coverage of all risks, except for unemployment, employment injury or occupational disease. Spouses may join a voluntary social insurance scheme that exists for pensions only. Accordingly, further steps need to be taken in order to ensure compliance with the Directive.

The practice is once again most developed in Poland with the existence of labour and social security courts, but also through the pertinent practice of the Commissioner for Human Rights, who brings cases to the constitutional court, some of them related to the breach of the principle of equality before the law. In the other countries examined, regular civil or administrative procedures can be used, but with limited chances for success due to the lack of substantive gender equality provisions in the field. The Equal Opportunities Ombudsperson in Lithuania and the future Gender Equality Commission in Estonia will develop the practice of settling disputes in issues concerning equal treatment of men and women, including in the field of self-employment.

5. Conclusions and recommendations

OSI's EOWM reports demonstrate that EU accession has generated positive changes in social standards, and particularly standards on gender equality. The process has primarily influenced legislation in the field of employment, especially regarding equal pay and access to employment, and has ushered in the establishment of gender equality institutions and specialised legislation in Lithuania, Romania, and Estonia. The shift in the burden of proof in countries such as the Czech Republic is a clear, and positive, result of the accession process. The influence is visible also in the adoption of parental leave provisions in some countries such as Romania, as well as in the removal of certain discriminatory 'special protective' measures for women. Finally, and perhaps most importantly, the emphasis placed on equal opportunities issues by various EU institutions and leaders during the accession process has led to a growing awareness of gender issues in the societies of candidate countries.

The Opinion of the European Parliament from April 2002 commends candidate countries, including the Czech Republic and Hungary, and to some extent Poland, Lithuania, and Estonia, for the progress they have made. Bulgaria and Romania still lag behind the standards in many respects, although the recent adoption of the Act on Equal Opportunities in Romania will certainly be viewed favourably, at least from the perspective of formal legal harmonisation.

Nevertheless, as of June 2002 all of the countries under review had already closed Chapter 13 "Employment and social policy" of the negotiation process, although the Commission dictated certain conditions for these countries, including in the field of gender equality. The fulfilment of these conditions must be thoroughly monitored by the European Commission, the European Parliament and candidate state NGOs.

In order to promote further progress, EU bodies and, in particular, the European Commission, which is responsible for overseeing the enlargement process, should monitor the implementation of the Directives under review around the critical issues presented in OSI's EOWM national reports and in this overview. Pressure should be exerted on governments specifically, to ensure the following:

Full compliance with the EU Directives under review, including through:

- The explicit introduction of the principle of equal treatment;
- The introduction of a legal definition of indirect discrimination;
- The introduction of a provision for the shift in the burden of proof;
- The adoption of the possibility for introducing positive action;

- The introduction of special mechanisms to ensure that gender equality is not 'lost' among broader non-discrimination considerations, such as the establishment and strengthening, through financial and personal resources, of special institutional mechanisms for gender equality.

In addition, the OSI's EOWM reports all collectively underline the following points:

- The adoption of special gender equality legislation should be strongly encouraged.

- There should be a special focus on supporting the elimination of gender stereotypes through broad educational campaigns, and new educational programs.

- There should be explicit mention throughout the entire negotiation process (and beyond), of the integration of a gender approach into other aspects of the negotiation process with the EU. Gender equality standards should accordingly be emphasised as an obligation of EU membership, which will apply up to and beyond accession.

- The implementation of the commitments made during the negotiation process should be thoroughly observed and monitored, with a special focus on the gender issues raised in the OSI EOWM reports.

- Special attention should be paid and resources should be allocated for the establishment and strengthening of institutional gender equality structures, and for the development of respective policies by the governments.

- The increased role of civil society, namely of NGOs, in the process of accession should be taken into consideration and a permanent mechanism to ensure regular and structured dialogue with EU bodies should be established.

- Dialogue between the governments of the candidate countries and civil society should be strongly encouraged, including through the establishment of formal consultation mechanisms.

- Financial resources should be allocated towards raising gender awareness and the implementation of the EU gender equality standards at the local level in the accession countries.

- Financial resources should be allocated for programs and projects of NGOs, as well as government programs with NGO assistance, in the field of research, awareness raising of EU standards, training of professionals and the judiciary on gender legislation and issues, and pilot initiatives to support the fulfilment in letter and in practice of the *acquis communautaire*.

6. A COORDINATED EFFORT: TOWARDS BROADENING THE EU STANDARDS ON GENDER EQUALITY

The EU Member states, EU women's NGOs and NGOs in the accession countries, as the main actors in the accession process, are conscious of the limitations of EU standards on gender equality. At this stage in the development of the EU, it is clear that existing standards related to labour and social security cannot cover all other forms of discrimination against women, or all areas in which gender policy and gender mainstreaming is needed.

As a matter of fact, EU legislation has given shape only to formal equality for women employed in full-time standard work. This result is a consequence of both the restricted nature of the scope of the Community at its inception, and of limited juridical competence in the matter of equality for women and men. Without underestimating the role of soft law standards in modern times, the demonstrated influence of secondary EU law in other areas suggests that this could be an effective means of exerting pressure on the accession countries for further improvements in the situation of women and men, including in fields other than employment.

Because the EU is primarily an economic union, issues concerning family life are not often addressed, making it difficult to raise important issues such as violence against women. The division of society into public and private spheres is maintained in the EU space, with the public sphere addressed by well-articulated state regulation and intervention in the employment area. However, a link between violence against women and women's economic and social development can certainly be developed and argued, not least through problems such as low productivity and missed workdays.

Gender differences are recognised insofar as they relate to women's economic participation and the way in which it is affected by family responsibility. Even if the EU emphasises that Member States face an unacceptable level of unemployment, disparities between women and men,[36] poverty and social exclusion, its approach still does not take into account the significant consequences of violence against women in maintaining women's social subordination and affecting their social performance.

A crucial impetus for the adoption of broader gender equality standards is provided by Article 13 and the impact of the two Directives. In addition to the influence on the amendment of the Equal Treatment Directive 76/207/EC, the Article 13 Directives

---

[36] Even 27 years after the adoption of the first Directives on equal pay and on equal access to work, we observe that women in the EU countries earn less than men, especially highly qualified women. Women still earn 14% less than men, the gap is more pronounced in the private sector (19 versus 10%); the activity rate of women is around 10% lower than men's. (According to data from 2002 presented by the ILO representation in Brussels.)

are likely to have continuing consequences for gender equality. In the Commission Communication on Gender "Towards a Community Framework Strategy on Gender Equality" (2001–2005) the Commission announced that it would develop another directive based on Article 13 of the Treaty to ensure equal treatment for women and men in matters other than occupation and employment. The adoption of more general anti-discrimination standards in the Treaty clearly underpins the idea that equality is a fundamental principle. By the same token, women's equality within the development of this social dimension is something that ought not to be questioned.

Related to the aforesaid is the issue of the procedure that should be followed for the adoption of broader gender equality legislation. There is a legal question as to what extent the new legislation can be regarded as dealing with matters of occupation and employment (the scope of Article 141(3) of the Treaty). In this case the decision will be taken by a qualified majority of the Council. In the case of legislation under Article 13, the unanimous approval of the Council of Ministers is needed. These considerations are very important when considering appropriate lobbying strategies in the interest of broadening the standards at hand.

In fact, the European women's NGOs in the coalition of the European Women's Lobby support the practical realisation of the principles set forth by the EU bodies through their activities. The need for broadening EU standards beyond labour standards and beyond the 'border' of the public sphere is constantly emphasised as a necessary and distinct priority for EU policy in primary law, as is the need for a separate directive on gender discrimination that would cover all the potential fields of discrimination. For example, the prohibition of violence against women is an explicit standard in the Treaty.

The EU Commission's progressive openness to these new issues is expressed through its response to these appeals. For example, while some years ago the Commission considered that it had no competence in matters such as violence against women and trafficking in women more specifically, these issues currently do receive substantial attention.

The European Parliament has been the strongest advocate for gender equality and its recent initiatives also show a clear trend for broadening the standards. In early July 2002, the Parliament voted in favour of the Report of the Committee on Women's Rights and Equal Opportunities on Sexual and Reproductive Health and Rights in Europe.[37] This was in response to increasing attention to the issue in EU countries and institutions and constitutes an explicit statement of the position of Europe against the anti-choice movement. The report is addressed to the candidate countries as well. A positive argument for the process of broadening of the gender equality standards is further offered by the changes to institutional mechanisms after the Treaty was signed

---

[37] Document A5–0223/2002.

in Nice in December 2000. In addition to marking a new step in the enlargement process, one of the major contributions of the Treaty of Nice is the adoption of the so-called 'co-decision' procedure and the 'consultation' procedure. The 'co-decision' procedure is applicable for the issues of the internal market of the EU, transports, environment policies, and research programs. As mentioned before, it is valid also for the Directives under Article 141(3). In all other cases the decisions are taken through a 'consultation procedure' with the unanimous decision of the Council. The Commission makes a proposition, and all the other bodies are consulted. This is the procedure for decisions in the field of fiscal policy, but also in matters of anti-discrimination. Due to the considerations made above and based on these rules for decision-making in the field of discrimination, adopting the 'co-decision' procedure for these issues will further ensure the adoption of the broader gender equality standards.

The Convention for the Future of Europe is another opportunity to create the conditions and environment for stronger standards, and to elaborate rules for the equal representation of women and men in all the bodies and institutions of the EU. This could also make a difference at the national level, both in member states and in the candidate countries. Moreover, it will have the effect of broadening the EU standards both at the EU level, including through the suggestion for 40 percent representation of women in all committees in EU bodies, and in terms of influencing the substantive law of the Union.

In conclusion, all of the tools identified here should be employed to reach a broader objective: the breakthrough of the 'co-decision' procedure and the possibilities of its extension, the positive influence of the Article 13 Directives, discussions in the Convention for the Future of Europe, as well as the partnership of EU-based NGOs and NGOs from the accession countries, to exert influence on the decision-making process within the EU and in their respective countries. The results of such collaborative efforts and resources will surely go a long way in ensuring that gender equality becomes a *de facto* reality for women and men, not only as a requirement of the accession process, but also beyond it.

OPEN SOCIETY INSTITUTE 2002

Equal Opportunities for Women and Men in Bulgaria

Table of contents

Executive summary 61

Country report: Introduction 69

1. The principle of equal pay for work of equal value 72
   1.1 National legal framework: General provisions 72
   1.2 Legal foundations and institutional structures 73
   1.3 Job classification 74
   1.4 Available legal procedures 75
   1.5 Means of informing employees of their rights 76
   1.6 Out of court alternatives 76
   1.7 Role of trade unions 76
   1.8 Women's factual situation 77

2. Equal treatment for women and men as regards access to employment, vocational training and promotion, and working conditions 79
   2.1 National legal framework: General provisions 79
   2.2 The concept of discrimination on grounds of sex: Definition and legal sanctions 82
   2.3 Access to employment, vocational training and promotion 84
   2.4 Protective measures for women in the labour market 86
   2.5 Prohibition of dismissal 87
   2.6 Women's and men's jobs 87
   2.7 Legal status of sexual harassment 87

3. Protection of pregnant women from the inherent risk of certain activities and related employment rights 90
   3.1 Legal and conceptual framework 90
   3.2 Risk assessment and employers' obligations 90
   3.3 Case law 92

3.4	Night work	93
3.5	Maternity leave	93
3.6	Prohibition of dismissal and employment rights	94

4. The burden of proof in cases of discrimination based on sex 96

    4.1 Legal and conceptual framework concerning indirect discrimination 96

    4.2 The burden of proof and rules of evidence 96

5. Non-discrimination against part-time workers 98

    5.1 National legal framework and employment conditions concerning part-time workers 98

6. The principle of equal treatment for self-employed workers and their assisting spouses 101

    6.1 National legal framework: General provisions 101

    6.2 Social rights of spouses 102

    6.3 Related research and statistics 103

    6.4 Legal means of redress 104

7. The framework on parental leave 106

    7.1 National legal framework: General provisions 106

    7.2 Social security during parental leave 108

    7.3 Parental leave and equal opportunities policy 109

    7.4 Research on sharing family and professional responsibilities 110

8. The principle of equal treatment in occupational social security schemes 114

    8.1 National legal framework: General provisions 114

    8.2 Legal means of redress 118

    8.3 Implementation of the principle of equal treatment 119

Executive summary for Bulgaria

INTRODUCTION

In its Regular Report on Bulgaria's progress towards accession, the EU noted with concern that much of the *acquis communautaire* in the field of equal treatment for women and men has yet to be transposed and that the process until now has not been a speedy one. Despite positive developments that have occurred in the Labour Code, the draft Act on Equal Opportunities for Women and Men, which was a complex undertaking aimed at resolving issues related to gender equality in Bulgaria and which would have ensured compliance with EU Directives, was rejected in April 2002.

The draft Act on Equal Opportunities for Women and Men, which was put forth in June 2000 under the aegis of the Ministry of Labour and Social Policy, provided *inter alia* guarantees for non-discrimination in the fields of employment, political participation and participation in decision-making, education and gender stereotypes, and establishes a national mechanism for equal opportunities, the institution of the Ombudsperson on Equal Opportunities. It was rejected alongside arguments that comprehensive anti-discrimination legislation, which would include the best provisions of the draft Act on Equal Opportunities, would be elaborated. However, NGOs and experts in the field of gender equality are critical of such an approach, fearing that this would preclude the possibility of creating effective gender equality mechanisms, as well as risk marginalising gender issues and further delay the implementation of equal treatment and the Directives. Such arguments are strengthened by the fact that European law itself distinguishes between sex-based and other forms of discrimination.

Two areas in which Bulgaria cannot boast compliance with the EU Directives include part-time work and the burden of proof in cases of sex discrimination, although both topics are dealt with under the draft Act on Equal Opportunities. One particular sphere in which discrimination against women is most apparent is that of remuneration: the latest available data from a private survey carried out in the public sector in 1997, when Bulgaria had one of the largest gender pay gaps among the Eastern European countries, showed that women only earned 69 percent of men's pay.[1]

The adoption of a comprehensive Act on Equal Opportunities and the monitoring and implementation mechanisms for which such an Act would provide is a condition *sine qua non* for the full transposition of the *acquis communautaire,* as well as the most effective means of ensuring that equal opportunities and equal treatment are social and

---

[1] UNICEF (1999).

political goals that will become a *de facto* reality in Bulgaria. The government's genuine commitment to gender equality may therefore remain in question as long as such an Act is not adopted, and there is no training of representatives of the institutions or awareness campaigns to educate the general public on the need for, and value of, an expansive strategy on equal opportunities.

Summary of key points

Defining principles

Bulgarian legislation does not define 'discrimination on the grounds of sex'. The notion of indirect discrimination was introduced with the latest amendments to the Labour Code, but it is framed broadly and does not refer explicitly to sex-based discrimination. The principle of equal pay for women and men was introduced with the amendments to the Labour Code, which came into force on 31 March 2001. There is no explicit prohibition of sexual harassment in the workplace in Bulgarian legislation, although there was clear progress in this direction with the ratification of the European Social Charter, the recent changes of the Labour Code, and the research work of NGOs and official research institutes.

Protective measures

Bulgarian legislation provides special protection for women, especially pregnant women and mothers, and adheres to a significant extent to the requirements of the Directive in this regard. Until very recently, Section 310 of the Labour Code contained the absolute prohibition for an employer to send a pregnant woman or a woman with a child under the age of three on a business trip. The Labour Code still contains an absolute prohibition for night work not only pregnant women, but also for women workers or employees with children up to the age of three. The Labour Code prohibits overtime work for pregnant employees and mothers with children up to the age of six, as well as mothers raising handicapped children irrespective of the latter's age, except with their own consent. The right to time off for antenatal examinations is not explicitly provided for by law, but female workers are entitled under the Labour Code to paid leave for urgent medical examinations or tests. There are no protective measures envisaged in Bulgarian law against dismissals effected in reaction to complaints based on the principle of equal treatment.

Burden of proof

Bulgarian legislation does not comply with Directive 97/80/EC concerning the reversal of the burden of proof, as the general rule of evidence in accordance with Section 127(1) of the Code of Civil Procedural provides that "Each party must establish the circumstances that form the basis of her/his claims or objections [...]". This is also a general principle in Bulgarian legislation and the reversal of the burden of proof in cases of the non-application of the principle of equal treatment would therefore be an exception that should be established by special legal provisions.

Part-time workers

The legal definition of part-time work in Bulgaria is based on the term 'statutory working time', which has important legal consequences. There is no discrimination concerning part-time workers, and if the working time is at least one half of the legally established working hours for the day there are no different legal consequences related to the length of service and hence the right to social security. Bulgarian legislation does not provide any possibility for a part-time worker to request a transfer to full-time work or vice versa if such a position is available, and any transfer is subject to a written agreement between the worker and the employer. Since the beginning of the transition process, flexible and part-time work have been increasingly seen as factors contributing to the reduction of unemployment, and employers are encouraged to employ unemployed persons in part-time work.

Self-employed workers

There is no explicit definition of self-employed workers in Bulgarian legislation. At the same time, there are no directly discriminatory rules contrary to the principle of equal treatment in the existing legal framework, and the Commercial Act and other commercial legal regulations are gender neutral. Unmarried couples are not discriminated against in law or in practice regarding the formation of companies. The main forms of self-employment in which women are engaged are in trade, services, manufacturing, transport, and communications. There are no measures to enable all persons who consider themselves wronged by the failure to apply the principle of equal treatment in self-employed activities to pursue their claims by judicial process, possibly after recourse to other competent authorities.

Parental leave

Bulgarian legislation is in full compliance with the international standards related to maternity leave, but there is no specific definition of the term parental leave. According to the National Programme for the Adoption of the *Acquis* (NPAA), this will be introduced with the drafting (undertaken jointly with social partners) of the amendment to the Labour Code in 2004. Existing provisions, although they do not provide for parental leave in line with the Directive, do give fathers the opportunity to participate in childcare, depending on the decisions of individual families. Despite this however, the recently adopted Act on Employment Promotion (in force as of 1 January 2002) foresees incentives for employers who hire single mothers and mothers with children up to three years, with no mention of fathers who could be in the same position. The potential risk of such provisions is that prejudices will be reinforced rather than challenged, and fathers will be even more reluctant to take advantage of the right to childcare leave. Currently, the father may only take childcare leave if the mother has relinquished her right to leave and given her permission. It is common practice for grandparents to take advantage of this leave instead of the father though, for economic reasons.

Social security schemes

Women in Bulgaria currently have a lower pension age than men, but a consensus is beginning to emerge in favour of a common pension age. Unfortunately though, this issue is not expected to be formally addressed before 2009. Indirect discrimination results from measures which, although often defined without reference to gender, in practice do affect women and men differently because of the nature of their occupational activity, marital status or family situation. Certain conditions, such as long periods of qualification, also penalise women. There is no discrimination on the basis of gender, either directly or indirectly, by reference in particular to marital or family status, especially as regards the scope of schemes and conditions of access to them or the obligation to contribute and calculation of contributions. The progressive implementation of the principle of equal treatment in matters of social security, although not part of the official policy on gender equality, will hopefully be considered with the adoption of the draft Act on Equal Opportunities for Women and Men.

RECOMMENDATIONS RELATED TO EACH SPECIFIC DIRECTIVE

Council Directive 75/117/EEC of 10 February 1975 *on the approximation of laws of the Member States relating to the implementation of the principle of equal pay for women and men*

- The Labour Inspection should develop its expertise to be able to identify cases of sex-based discrimination.
- Provisions should be adopted to ensure compliance with the scope of the Directive and specifically with Articles 2, 6 and 7. To that end, it is recommended that the new Act on Civil Servants, as a special code for this category of workers, should include the principle of equal pay for women and men.
- Comprehensive gender equality legislation should be adopted.
- Effective mechanisms for monitoring and implementing the principle of equal pay need to be provided for in law and implemented in practice.

Council Directive 76/207/EEC of 9 February 1976 *on the implementation of the principle of equal treatment for men and women as regards access to employment, vocational training and promotion, and working conditions*

- Legal guarantees for access to vocational and further training and special measures ensuring such training for women during and after maternity leave should be provided.
- Clear legal provisions on the principle of affirmative action in women's access to employment should be developed.
- Sexual harassment should be prohibited as a form of gender discrimination, and punishment should be stipulated beyond the penal law.

Council Directive 92/85/EEC of 19 October 1992 *on the introduction of measures to encourage improvements in the safety and health at work of pregnant workers and workers who have recently given birth or are breastfeeding*

- Research studies should be conducted to determine how the laws are applied and identify legal and/or practical shortcomings.
- Research should be carried out to determine whether the enforcement of health and safety regulations for the workplace is adequate.
- Absolute prohibitions on overtime work for pregnant women and mothers with children between the ages of three and six, etc. should be reconsidered.

Council Directive 97/80/EC of 15 December 1997 *on the burden of proof in cases of discrimination based on sex*

- The notion of indirect discrimination on grounds of sex should be explicitly defined.

- The principle of the reversal of the burden of proof should be included in Bulgarian legislation, and a broad public awareness campaign on this principle should be carried out, as well as trainings for lawyers, the judiciary, and government officials, to ensure the practical implementation.

- Officers and the judiciary should be trained to identify direct and indirect discrimination and to apply the principle of equal treatment, to study examples from the practice of other European countries more advanced in this field, and to create the conditions for developing theory in this field.

Council Directive 97/81/EC of 15 December 1997 *concerning the framework agreement on part-time work concluded by UNICE, CEEP, and the ETUC*

- Employers should consult the representatives of the workers concerned on the introduction or extension of part-time work on a broad scale and on the protective and promotional measures that may be appropriate.

- The role of trade unions should be emphasised, since they could negotiate workers' right to the transfer from full-time to part-time work (and *vice versa*), which is particularly important for women, in collective labour contracts. However, strict control must be exercised with regard to the actual hours of work to avoid a decrease in pay in the event of overtime work.

- Opportunities for the application of flexible work schemes and the respective protection of part-time workers should be extended through labour legislation.

Council Directive 86/613/EEC of 11 December 1986 *on the application of the principle of equal treatment between men and women engaged in an activity, including agriculture, in a self-employed capacity, and on the protection of self-employed women during pregnancy and motherhood*

- Further developments in the legislation are needed to ensure a clear-cut, transparent system with a view to the harmonisation of Directives covering the self-employed. To this end, a legal definition should be adopted to provide the criteria for defining self-employed persons as a specific group with a flexible status.

- The prohibition of discrimination and the principle of equal treatment should be included in relevant legislation, such as the Code for Obligatory Social Insurance and the Act on Employment Promotion.

- The category of 'contributing family member' should be extended, and self-employed workers should be encouraged – including by positive action of the government – to register contributing family members, since this is a precondition for legally insured status and eligibility for provisions.

- More detailed statistics and research in the field of the application of the directive should be carried out.

Council Directive 96/34/EC of 3 June 1996 *on the framework agreement on parental leave concluded by UNICE, CEEP, and the ETUC*

- Social policy, including legislation, should be developed to improve the quality of women's contribution to the labour market, including equal treatment for women and men, equal pay, flexible conditions for hiring employees, financial and other incentives for employers to support the reconciling of family and professional life.

- Parental leave should be provided for on a non-transferable basis.

- Amendments to the Constitution, Labour Code and the Code for Obligatory Social Insurance are required in order to transpose the Directive 96/34/EC.

- Legal provisions on parental leave and affirmative action should be introduced, as should incentives for men to take paternal leave. The Act on Employment Promotion should be amended to forego the need for the mother's permission in cases of paternal leave.

- Data and research on the roles of men and women in the family should be collected on a regular basis, including research on the taking of parental leave.

- Special provisions should be introduced to protect workers against dismissal on the grounds of applying for or taking parental leave.

- Measures should be taken to encourage public debate on the issue of individual parental leave in order to raise social awareness on gender issues.

Council Directive 96/97/EC of 20 December 1996 *amending Directive 86/378/EEC on the implementation of the principle of equal treatment for men and women in occupational social security schemes*

- Legislation should be adopted to bring the provisions on occupational schemes in line with EU standards.

- The Directive should be taken into account when setting up insurance funds and companies and transposed into the internal regulations of the insurance companies.

- Since the Government envisages introducing amendments in the Code for Obligatory Social Insurance and the Act on Voluntary Social Insurance, it would be appropriate to take into account Directive 96/97/EC and to introduce explicitly gender-neutral rates.

- Pension payments should be analysed to reveal the true gender impact of so-called 'occupational schemes' in the Bulgarian social security system.

Country reports: Bulgaria

INTRODUCTION

According to the 2001 Regular Report on Bulgaria's Progress Towards Accession,[2] "much of the *acquis* in the field of equal treatment for women and men remains to be transposed [...] and no progress has been made in adopting detailed and effective anti-discrimination legislation. Further efforts are needed to ensure alignment with the *acquis* on anti-discrimination based on Article 13 of the EC Treaty [...]." The general assessment of the Government itself does not differ much from that of the European Commission, aware that formal compliance with EU standards, especially in the field of employment, is not sufficient, and there are no implementation mechanisms or consistent legal practice on the issue of gender equality. As a result, legislation, where it does exist, is ineffective.

Outstanding issues were meant to be transposed through the draft Act on Equal Opportunities for Women and Men, which was submitted to the 39th National Assembly, and in the legislation to be adopted in the medium term.

Based on the negotiation positions, the Bulgarian government adopted a strategy for the acceleration of the negotiations for accession in 2001. As priorities under Chapter 13, it provides for the rapid adoption of comprehensive and effective anti-discriminatory legislation and of legislation in the area of equal treatment of women and men, as well as the establishment of a National Council of Equal Opportunities of Women and Men and the appointment of an Ombudsperson.

Although formal compliance is stated with respect to Directives 75/117/EEC and 76/207/EEC, an analysis shows that recent changes to the Labour Code and the new Act on Employment Promotion are not sufficient for the real implementation of EU standards *de jure* and *de facto*.

The following Directives are envisaged to be transposed in the medium term: Council Directive 79/7/EEC concerning the progressive implementation of the principle of equality between men and women in social security; Council Directive 86/378/EEC on the application of the principle of equal treatment for men and women in occupational social security schemes, as amended by Council Directive 96/97/EC; Council Directive 86/613/EEC relating to the implementation of the principle of equal treatment for men and women engaged in an activity, including agriculture, in a self-employed capacity,

---

[2] See European Commission (2001: 61–62).

and on the protection of self-employed women during pregnancy and motherhood; Council Directive 96/34/EC relating to the framework agreement on parental leave, as amended by Council Directive 97/75/EC. The introduction of parental leave, as prescribed by Council Directive 96/34/EC is scheduled to be introduced in the National Programme for the Adoption of the *Acquis* in 2003.

Despite government efforts, no substantial progress was achieved during the preparation of this report and fields such as part-time work and the burden of proof in cases of sex discrimination are areas of full non-compliance. Although there are no provisions in Bulgarian legislation which contradict the principle of equality of treatment of women and men in social security, there are no specific provisions promoting the principle either. Furthermore, the requirements of Directive 86/378/EEC related to occupational pension schemes have yet to be fully transposed.

Due to the specific nature of social security and to the specific subject of Council Directives 86/613/EEC and 86/378/EEC, according to Negotiation Document No. CONF-BG 54/01, it was considered preferable as a first step to establish the institutional framework on gender equality and legal protection in the fields of occupation and employment, education and training, political life and governance and the removal of negative stereotypes for the respective roles of women and men, whereas equal treatment in the field of social security, independent economic activity and agriculture should be dealt with by the newly established institutions and in a more detailed way in other pieces of legislation.

The Bulgarian government shared the opinion of the European Commission that the leave envisaged in Section 164 and 165 of the Labour Code is different from parental leave in the sense of the Directive, which has not been fully transposed.

At the policy level, it must be noted that the implementation of Directives 86/613/EEC and 96/34/EC is fundamental to the National Employment Strategy's aim to realise the principle of equal treatment of women and men.

As a result of the above, the adoption of the draft Act on Equal Opportunities for Women and Men was, and still is, crucial for ensuring compliance with the Directives under review. The Act was drafted in June 2000, as part of the implementation of the government's legislative program, under the aegis of the Ministry of Labour and Social Policy. It represents a complex approach towards resolving gender equality issues in Bulgaria and creates guarantees for non-discrimination in the fields of employment, political participation and participation in decision-making, in the field of education and gender stereotypes, provides guarantees for implementation, and establishes a national mechanism for Equal Opportunities, the institution of the Ombudsperson on Equal Opportunities, etc. The draft Act transposes many of the Council Directives under review and was approved by the Council of Ministers at the end of March 2001 for submission to the National Assembly.

After being rejected once by the Parliamentary Commission on Human Rights and Religious Denominations, this body revised its decision and at the end of January 2002 the draft Act was finally sent before Parliament for the first reading. Concurrently, the government made a decision affecting the implementation process with the drafting of a new general Anti-Discrimination Act, according to which gender equality is to be included among other forms of discrimination (religion or belief, disability, age and sexual orientation). The advantages of such a solution are being discussed, but NGOs and experts in the field of gender equality have focused on the disadvantages, such as the impossibility of creating effective gender equality mechanisms, the risk of marginalising gender issues, and the further delay of the implementation of equal treatment and the Directives. The fact that the issue of equal opportunities for women and men is dealt with separately from other grounds of discrimination in European law provides a strong argument in favour of separate regulation.

At the same time, instead of adopting the draft Act the government tried to use different laws to regulate the matter of equal opportunities together with other forms of discrimination, thus taking concepts from the draft Act and reproducing them in the amendments of the Labour Code enacted at the end of March 2001 and in the Act on Employment Promotion in force since January 2002.

The Bulgarian Parliament actually rejected the draft Act on EOWM, which was only supported by the opposition, on 3 April 2002, with the leading political party arguing that a comprehensive Anti-Discrimination Act would be elaborated and would encompass the 'best provisions' from the draft Act on Equal Opportunities.

Regrettably, dialogue with civil society representatives, which began when the Act on Equal Opportunities was elaborated, broke down after the failure to establish the National Council for Equal Opportunities. In addition, the Government failed to organise a large public campaign or inform the public about the important change in its negotiation position (Document No. CONF-BG 8/02).

Although positive trends can be identified, these legislative measures cannot replace a comprehensive Act on equal opportunities or the mechanisms for which it provides, the adoption of which is a condition *sine qua non* for the transposition of the *acquis* in the fields of employment and social security.

1. THE PRINCIPLE OF EQUAL PAY FOR WORK OF EQUAL VALUE

Council Directive 75/117/EEC of 10 February 75 *on the approximation of laws of the Member States relating to the application of the principle of equal pay for men and women*

1.1 National legal framework concerning the principle of equal pay for work of equal value: General provisions

The principle of equal pay for women and men was introduced for the first time with the amendments to the Labour Code in 2001, thereby establishing the legal grounds on which to bring a claim of discrimination in this field. There are no discriminatory provisions in Bulgarian legislation that are contrary to the principle of equal pay for men and women and Bulgaria complies fully with Article 3 of Directive 75/117/EEC.

Until 1992, a general clause existed in the Labour Code providing for equal pay for work of equal value, but it was subsequently abolished as incompatible with the principles of a market economy and reminiscent of socialism and socialist labour. As a result, women were put at a greater disadvantage during transition, since the gender gap is particularly evident in the field of remuneration. The only provisions that could be applied for protection against discrimination in this field were, and still are, the general anti-discrimination clauses in Article 6 of the Constitution and Section 8(3) of the Labour Code, which prohibit, *inter alia*, discrimination based on sex. The Constitutional principle of equality is directly applicable and takes precedence over any contradictory provisions.

The Labour Code

The newly amended Section 243 provides that women and men have the right to equal pay for the same work or work of equal value, and this principle is valid for all the payments related to labour relations. While the amendment represents clear progress, it is not as broad as the legal wording of Directive 75/117/EEC, either in scope or in its specification of the remuneration. The anti-discrimination clause contained in Section 8(3) has been broadened to prohibit both direct and indirect discrimination on the basis of sex, which is defined in Article 67 of the Transitional and Conclusive Provisions.

The Act on Civil Servants

The 2000 Act on Civil Servants does not regulate the principle of equal pay for women and men, although as a special 'code' for this category of workers it should include the principle.

The Draft Act on Equal Opportunities for Women and Men

The draft Act on Equal Opportunities for Women and Men (hereinafter the AEOWM) provides for the principle of equal pay for equal work or work of equal value in Article 21(1) and contains the main elements envisaged by Directive 75/117/EEC. It also envisages the application of the principle to public servants.

Relevant international provisions[3]

Under Article 5(4) of the Constitution, international instruments signed and ratified by Bulgaria form part of the domestic legislation.

The ILO Convention 100 on Equal Remuneration is part of the domestic legislation and provides that the principle of equal pay for men and women should be expressly declared in the national legislation and enforced in each and every system of remuneration established and recognised by law.

In 2000, Bulgaria ratified the Revised European Social Charter, Article 4(3) of which obliges the government to recognise the right of women and men to equal pay and turns to the domestic legislation for the recognition, concrete guarantees and implementation of this principle of equal opportunities.

These international documents do, however, require the explicit transposition of the principle into the national legislation and this has only been done very recently through the latest amendments to the Labour Code.

1.2 Implementation of the principle of equal pay for work of equal value: Legal foundations and institutional structures

The legal provisions on protection from sex-based discrimination in employment relations do not differentiate between the public and private sectors, but daily practice and research reveal considerable differences between the two. In particular, the economic constraints of the private sector lead women to suffer inequalities in employment conditions, including in relation to pay.

---

[3] See also Section 2.1 below.

Section 399 of the Labour Code charges the Labour Inspection with the overall control of the implementation of labour law in both sectors. Under Ordinance No.92 of 2000 of the Council of Ministers, the Labour Inspection has the status of an Executive Agency under the Minister of Labour and Social Policy. According to Article 4 of the Regulations on the Structure of the Labour Inspection, its control functions primarily cover the safe and healthy working conditions and the implementation of labour relations. To this end, the Inspection can give information and advice where necessary to employers and workers, and cooperates with other institutions, employers' organisations, workers' organisations and with NGOs, and can undertake scheduled or unscheduled inspections (at the discretion of the Minister of Labour and Social Policy and upon signals or complaints from the workers or in connection with media publications).

Under Section 402(2) of the Labour Code, trade unions are also granted the right to exercise the control functions of the Labour Inspection, and Section 406 provides that trade unions can refer a case involving a violation of the labour legislation to the Labour Inspection and request the respective compulsory administrative sanctions.

The draft AEOWM provides a control mechanism for cases of discrimination in labour relations, including the principle of equal pay for men and women. Articles 57 and further envisage the Labour Inspection as the main body with control functions, and the authority to impose fines on persons and entities for violating the law. In addition, under Part 3 of the draft, the independent ombudsperson will play an active role in this process.

There have been no complaints concerning the principle of non-discrimination in remuneration between women and men, and the Labour Inspection has not been particularly active in identifying such discrimination in either sector, and is known primarily for its inspections with respect to work safety. Instead of focusing on inequalities, the inspections related to pay focus more on identifying cases involving the employer's evasion of social security contribution payments.

The State Administration Commission at the Council of Ministers issues rulings in cases involving the violation of the rights of civil servants, but the system of control is unclear and relies too much on the executive power.

1.3 Job classification

There is no unified classification system used for determining pay in the public or private sectors. However, the rules applicable to state-owned and budget-subsidised enterprises are quite clear and the law does not create the conditions for sex-based inequality with regard to remuneration.

There is a salary scale for every job position and its size depends on a set of criteria, including both personal and professional characteristics. The level of remuneration for a specific position is still determined by the employer and is based on the job description. Salaries are updated on the basis of regular personal performance evaluations and an increase depends on the extent to which the above-mentioned set of criteria have been met and will be raised by an amount within the range of the adjustment scale envisaged for that position.

The Act on Civil Servants and the Act on Public Administration determine the size of civil servants' pay, and Ordinance 35 of 2000 of the Council of Ministers establishes strict criteria for hiring a person and determining their pay. The Regulation on the application of a uniform catalogue of administrative positions determines the amount of the basic remuneration for each position and the respective allowances and benefits, which are linked to the job grade and type of the administration, and are also strictly defined in this Regulation. This system allows for the staff's promotion and gradual career growth, accompanied by an appropriate salary increase. The process is linked to demonstrated individual qualities, which are assessed by an evaluation committee, and makes no provision for discretionary practices.

The salary formation rules are not binding for the private sector, where the rules of free negotiation apply.

1.4 Available legal procedures in cases involving the violation of the principle of equal pay for work of equal value

Workers who consider themselves discriminated against in terms of remuneration have the right to initiate court proceedings according to Chapter 18 of the Labour Code.[4]

There are no special measures protecting an employee from dismissal in reaction to court proceedings as required by Article 5 of Directive 75/117/EEC. However, such a provision is envisaged in Article 30 of the AEOWM.

Workers do no benefit from any free legal aid, and such a system is lacking in Bulgaria. However, Article 35(1) of the Act on Attorneys-at-Law gives lawyers the possibility to take the case *pro bono* if the worker is financially disadvantaged. This does not constitute real legal aid provided by the state though, and is simply a possibility.

---

[4] Under Section 359 of the Labour Code, workers must not pay a court fee in cases of labour litigation. This is the only provision so far that assists the worker, but it has been questioned by the Association of Foreign Investors in Bulgaria (BIBA), who believe this clause puts the employer and the worker in unequal positions.

Some trade unions, such as the *Podkrepa* Labour Confederation, have undertaken initiatives to provide free legal aid, but their practice so far has not been related to gender issues. Research shows that lawyers' fees often constitute a barrier for workers to claim their rights.

1.5 Means of informing employees of their right to equal pay for work of equal value

As there are no explicit provisions concerning the principle of equal pay for men and women, no special mechanisms exist for informing the workers. The existing guarantees on non-discrimination are not brought to their attention, and they are expected to know their rights and not rely on the state *(ignoratia legis neminem excusat)*. The perception emerged during the transition period that people tend to make too high demands on the state, which is reminiscent of socialist times.

As a result, the right of workers to be informed of her/his rights by the state and the employer, as developed in European standards, is a totally new concept that needs to be discussed, explained and disassociated from the past.

The AEOWM contains this principle though, and Article 28 specifically obliges the employer to publicise the Act.

1.6 Out of court alternatives

There are no provisions yet in the Bulgarian legal system for settling individual labour disputes related to equal pay out of court. With the recent amendments to the law regulating collective labour disputes, as of 31 March 2001, if no agreement between the representatives of the employee and the employer is reached, each party has the right to look to mediation and/or the voluntary arbitration of unions and employers' organisations, and/or the newly established National Institute for Conciliation and Arbitration. The Institute is a legal entity under the Minister of Labour and Social Policy and has the status of an executive agency.

1.7 Role of trade unions

Under the Labour Code, trade unions have a large competence in the protection of labour rights, in equality matters included in the tripartite cooperation, in the process of collective bargaining and in court proceedings in cases of labour disputes. At the request of the workers, trade unions can represent them in court proceedings and undertake certain legal actions if they have an explicit mandate. This right of trade unions is also stipulated in Section 20(2) of the Code of Civil Procedure, and Article 63 of the AEOWM explicitly mentions this function with regard to disputes involving violations of this Act.

There are no provisions in the Labour Code to render void provisions of collective agreements that contradict the principle of equal pay. Articles 15(3) and 15(4) of the AEOWM, however, do provide for this possibility and would ensure Bulgaria's compliance with Article 4 of Directive 75/117/EEC.

Collective agreements play a very important role in the regulation of labour relations in Bulgaria, but they do not contain provisions concerning equal pay and anti-discrimination yet. These will hopefully be introduced and gradually developed with the implementation of the new amendments to the Labour Code and with the adoption of the AEOWM.

In its 'Black Book' of the violations of labour and syndicate rights, the Confederation of the Independent Trade Unions in Bulgaria does not mention any instances of discrimination with regard to pay.

1.8 Women's factual situation with regard to the principle of equal pay for work of equal value

According to a recent national representative survey on the issue of equality between the sexes (November 2000) conducted by the National Centre for the Study of Public Opinion, 'equal pay' was identified by 41 percent of female and 39 percent of male respondents as one of the main areas of discrimination against women. Still, it is difficult to assess the actual gender pay gap in Bulgaria because there are no official statistics. The programme and practice of the National Statistical Institute (NSI) do not include the collection of disaggregated data in this field, but Article 13 of the AEOWM delegates special responsibilities to the NSI in the area of gender equality statistics.

The latest available data is from a private survey carried out in the public sector in 1997, when Bulgaria had one of the largest gender pay gaps among Eastern European countries. The survey showed that women only earned 69 percent of men's pay.[5] The private sector, by contrast, is very difficult to control and monitor due to its large fluctuation and major economic constraints.

---

[5] UNICEF (1999).

On the whole, the problem of equal pay is hidden due to the economic constraints of the transition period and because it is part of a series of major problems characteristic of this period, including unemployment, delayed payments, tax and social security evasion, etc.

2. Equal treatment for women and men as regards access to employment, vocational training and promotion, and working conditions

Council Directive 76/207/EEC of 9 February 1976 *on the implementation of the principle of equal treatment for men and women as regards access to employment, vocational training and promotion, and working conditions*

2.1 National legal framework concerning the principle of equal treatment for women and men: General provisions

The principle of equal 'rights' for men and women and non-discrimination is incorporated in the legal framework, but giving priority to equality *de jure* and overestimating it is a tradition in Bulgaria. As a result, the declaration of equal rights between the sexes is mistaken for the principle of equal treatment for women and men, which is not in fact guaranteed in practice. This perception is inherited from socialist times and still dominates the philosophy of the legislature, institutions and the public.

It is worth noting though, that according to the study referred to in Section 1.8, for 55 percent of Bulgarian citizens, discrimination on the basis of sex means discrimination against women (57 percent of interviewed women and 53 percent of interviewed men held this view). For 58 percent of those interviewed, women and men in Bulgaria have equal rights, which are set forth in the Constitution. Although 83 percent of persons who stated that they read the Constitution believe that equality has been provided for in it, 48 percent of those interviewed support the idea of special legislation regulating equality between women and men.

The concepts of 'affirmative action' and 'direct' and 'indirect' discrimination are crucial to an understanding of the difference between the principle of equal rights and the principle of equal treatment. Both concepts are new to legal doctrine, the legislature, and legal and social practice in Bulgaria, and were only introduced for the first time through the draft AEOWM. Consequently, it will take some time before they are understood, accepted and implemented in practice.

Article 6 of the Bulgarian Constitution declares that women and men have equal rights, and also prohibits discrimination based on a series of grounds, including sex. No privileges or restrictions can be based on, *inter alia*, sex, or personal or social status. Article 46(2) stipulates that spouses have equal rights and equal obligations in matrimony and the family. According to Article 47(1), the upbringing of children until they reach the age of majority is both the right and obligation of parents, who must be assisted by the state. The principle of giving priority to the protection of women as mothers is further developed in the labour legislation and has been perceived so far as a major component in ensuring the equal treatment of men and women. However, there are examples of the adverse effects of the protective clauses, which have been detrimental to the rights of women in the labour market.

Equal rights for women and men are also guaranteed by international human rights instruments,[6] and the fact that the principle of equal treatment of women and men must be explicitly expressed in domestic legislation, separately from the guarantee of non-discrimination on other grounds, was one of main arguments for the need for a specific Act on Equal Opportunities in Bulgaria.

The main international instrument in the field of equality of men and women is the UN Convention on the Elimination of All Forms of Discrimination against Women (CEDAW), ratified by Bulgaria and in force since 1982, but not yet promulgated.[7]

The understanding and the adoption of the principle of affirmative action has been very difficult for Bulgarian institutions and society, and the UN Committee for the Elimination of Discrimination against Women in its Recommendations (18th session of CEDAW) to the Bulgarian Government in 1998 explicitly noted that, unfortunately, the Government had no understanding of the concept. This reluctance to adopt affirmative action is due in part to the willingness to abandon reminiscences of the socialist past, when women were encouraged to have an equal share in public life and for this purpose were given, allegedly, too many rights and privileges. Rights and privileges related to maternity are often identified with affirmative action by the Bulgarian institutions.

The adoption of the AEOWM, which provides for the introduction of affirmative action where necessary, would permit the full incorporation of the principle of equal treatment of women and men into Bulgarian legislation. A Constitutional Court Ruling No.14 of 1992 (Const. Case 19/92) on Article 6 of the Constitution stressed the equality of all citizens before the law but also held that "[…] the restriction of rights and rendering of privileges to certain social groups shall be admissible under the Constitution whenever such privileges are justified in society." The Constitutional Court ruling could therefore serve as a good entry point for affirmative action.

---

[6] For example, the Universal Declaration of Human Rights; the International Covenant on Civil and Political Rights; the International Covenant on Economic, Social and Cultural Rights (ICESCR).

[7] The fact that this Convention has not been promulgated gives it special status with respect to the domestic legislation. According to the Constitutional Court Ruling No.7 of 1992, it is made part of Bulgarian legislation but does not supersede contradictory legislation.

Bulgaria has also ratified the ILO Convention 111 on Discrimination (Employment and Occupation, 1958), which defines discrimination in Article 1 as "[…] any distinction, exclusion or preference made on the basis of race, colour, sex, religion, political opinion, national extraction or social origin, which has the effect of nullifying or impairing equality of opportunity or treatment in employment or occupation." The Convention obliges the states to adopt national policies for promoting equality and non-discrimination in the field, including legislative measures for implementing such policies. The terms employment and occupation according to the Convention encompass access to employment, vocational training and equal working conditions. Thus, it is another instrument that refers to state polices and legislation in the field of equal treatment.

In 2000, Bulgaria ratified the Revised European Social Charter and is bound under Article 20 to recognise the right of equal opportunities and equal treatment of men and women in the field of employment and occupation (including access to employment, protection against dismissal, professional reintegration, professional orientation, improvement of qualifications, hiring conditions, working conditions, professional development and promotion), and to ensure its implementation by all necessary measures.

The Bulgarian legislation adopted so far refers to equal rights and non-discrimination on the basis of sex in Section 8(3) of the amended Labour Code, Article 2 of the Act on Unemployment Protection and Employment Promotion; Article 7(4) of the Act on Civil Servants of 1999 provides that appointments to civil servant posts must be free of any discrimination, privileges or limitations, notably based on sex or personal and social status. Section 4(2) of the Code of Civil Procedure provides that the court shall recognise the equal rights of parties and is obliged to apply the law equally with respect to everyone. Nevertheless, real mechanisms for the implementation of the rights guaranteed, and namely of the principle of equal treatment, are required and the lack of legal practice shows that such mechanisms still do not exist in Bulgaria. It also confirms that the principle of equal treatment is still not fully incorporated in the Bulgarian legal system.

The aim of the AEOWM is to provide the missing link between equal rights and equal treatment in Bulgarian law, bringing a new concept of equal treatment and equal opportunities, of affirmative action, and of direct and indirect discrimination (Article 3).[8] The AEOWM is unique in that it encompasses the employment and occupation relations of persons with a labour contract and civil servants. It is also very progressive

---

[8] "Article 3(1) Direct and indirect discrimination based on sex is prohibited. (2) Sexual harassment shall be considered a form of discrimination. (3) The following shall not be considered discrimination: 1. Special measures provided for in law with regard to protection in cases of pregnancy, childbirth and breastfeeding; 2. Incentive measures provided for in law in regard to women or men; 3. Qualification requirements for activities in which sex is a determining factor."

insofar as it prohibits employers from putting questions to the applicants, orally or in writing, related to their family or parental status or duties. Furthermore, Article 22(2) encourages the employer to create conditions for maintaining and improving the professional qualifications of employees on leave to raise a child. Article 26 stipulates that the employer shall encourage and facilitate women and men to reconcile professional and family or parental responsibilities.

The Act also provides the mechanisms for the implementation of this principle through a governmental institutional mechanism ensuring gender mainstreaming and supervision of the implementation of the Act, and the independent institution of the ombudsperson.

2.2 The concept of discrimination on grounds of sex: Definition and legal sanctions

Discrimination on the grounds of sex is not defined in Bulgarian legislation, but the draft AEOWM, along with prohibiting discrimination based on sex and defining the measures that are not discriminatory, defines both direct[9] and indirect[10] discrimination in Article 1 of the Additional Provisions. Following the practice of some European countries more advanced in the field of equal opportunities, the AEOWM, without giving a strict definition of discrimination, will open a large field for legal practice and the practice of the ombudsperson.

In cases of sex-based discrimination, the victim has the opportunity to initiate court proceedings based on Section 8 of the Labour Code. According to Section 357, the term 'labour litigation' encompasses all disputes between the worker and employer concerning the commencement, implementation and termination of labour relations, including disputes concerning the implementation of collective agreements.

Persons who consider themselves discriminated against on the grounds of sex in the field of education and vocational training and retraining can invoke the general anti-discrimination provisions contained in the laws mentioned above.

---

[9] "'Direct discrimination' shall mean the placement of a person into a disadvantaged or advantaged position on the grounds of his/her sex," according to the Act on Equal Opportunities for Women and Men, Additional Provisions.

[10] "'Indirect discrimination' shall mean the application of apparently legal provisions in a manner that leads to the *de facto* placement of persons from one sex into a disadvantaged or advantaged position in comparison to the persons from the opposite sex," according to the Act on Equal Opportunities for Women and Men, Additional Provisions.

Article 124 of the Act on Civil Servants provides that all disputes concerning the commencement, content and termination of their functions shall be referred to the court according to an administrative procedure after recourse to the relevant authority.

Persons who consider themselves discriminated against in the field of labour rights can address the controlling institutions, who can impose administrative injunctions and financial sanctions on an employer who violates the labour legislation (Chapter 19 of the Labour Code).

In case of violations of the rights guaranteed under Article 20(4) of the Social Charter, Article D of the Charter provides the procedure of collective complaints whereby organisations representing the workers can denounce the violations before a special control mechanism, the Committee of Experts. It is not an individual complaint mechanism and is still new to Bulgaria.

The draft AEOWM provides an effective complaint procedure for those who seek redress for the violation of the principle of equal treatment before the court, and a complaint procedure is available before the ombudsperson according to Article 62.

Related research

According to the report "The Impact of Privatisation on Women during the Economic Transition in Bulgaria" (1999) of the Bulgarian Gender Research Foundation (BGRF), interviews with judges, lawyers, legal counsel and experts working in the field of labour and social rights (a non-representative survey conducted in the framework of the research) revealed both the reluctance of women victims of discrimination to seek redress in court due to the slow and cumbersome procedure and the scepticism of representatives of the legal profession to initiate and pursue the equal treatment cause before an insensitive court with ineffective mechanisms.

Although nearly half of the persons interviewed confessed that they had come across cases of gender discrimination, not a single concrete case was mentioned. The question: "Do you think there are sufficiently effective mechanisms to protect women's rights?" was answered negatively by all respondents. The respondents were also unanimous about the need for more information among the legal community on the principle of equal treatment and for changes in the legislation.

Furthermore, a recent interview by representatives BGRF with a judge from the Supreme Court of Cassation (Labour Division) showed that there has been no case law so far concerning the violation of the principle of equal treatment of men and women in the field of employment and occupation. The need for improved mechanisms for protection and for additional information and training of judges was also identified.

2.3 National legal framework concerning the principle of equal treatment as regards access to employment, vocational training and promotion, and working conditions

The guarantees listed above could be supplemented with the provision of Articles 11(1)(b) and (c) of CEDAW, according to which states must ensure the right to the same employment opportunities, including the application of the same criteria for selection in matters of employment, the right to free choice of profession and employment, the right to promotion, job security and all benefits and conditions of service and the right to receive vocational training and retraining, including apprenticeship, advanced vocational training and recurrent training.

In addition to the lack of real mechanisms for the application of the principle of equal treatment, some provisions are contrary to the guarantees declared. For example, Chapter 11 "Professional qualification" (amended in 1992) provides that this basic right of the worker shall be exercised only under the conditions of a contract with the employer. Therefore, in Bulgaria this right depends on the discretion of the employer.

Despite the new provisions of Sections 67 and 68 of the Labour Code, created to ensure stability in the duration of contracts, these measures are not effective enough to regulate the disadvantaged situation of women in the labour market.

There is no mention of the protection necessary in the recruitment procedure, where women face humiliating interviews and tests. Although labour rights are not regulated differently in the public and private sectors, women encounter much more severe problems in the private sector, where they are discriminated against in the selection procedure and are deprived of employment security. According to the National Statistical Institute, as of September 2000 half of all working women were still employed in the public sector. The switch from public to private is a difficult one for both men and women, and this is characteristic of transition, but women are particularly vulnerable. Furthermore, the state control of employment conditions has been weaker in the private sector during the transition period.[11]

The proposed AEOWM envisages the implementation of the principle of equal treatment in the field of employment and occupation in a very detailed manner: Part 2

---

[11] The following is a reflection of a woman interviewed in the course of the research of the BGRF: "[...] Women accept lower salaries. It seems that suddenly, after the privatisation, low qualification labour became the more valuable labour. Inexplicably, women turned out to be more suitable for low-qualified labour. Production in the privatised enterprises is feminised." (Sofia, the private sector, higher education).

Chapter 2 covers a wide range of employment conditions and Chapter 4 deals with equal opportunities in education and training, where gender discrimination is subject to monitoring and sanctions.

Related research

Practice and research show that, in addition to the gender pay gap and sexual harassment, other violations of the principle of equal treatment include: discriminatory selection criteria, job advertisements, the terms of employment and problems faced by women after maternity leave and with small children, and limited access to jobs for women over 40. In addition, statistics show that by the end of 2000 women prevailed among the registered unemployed (according to the National Employment Office, they comprised 53 percent), among the long-term unemployed and in all age groups of unemployed persons, except in the age groups of below 24 and above 55 years.

Research further reveals that women are clearly and openly discriminated against in the selection procedure, and employers themselves confess that they apply different criteria in the selection procedure in general and specifically when women are involved. Although the general qualities they seek in an applicant include professional qualifications, education, professional experience, personal qualities, computer literacy, foreign language proficiency, etc., the criteria applied to women include education, ability to work overtime, ambition and future plans, family obligations, ability to travel, marital status, age and health conditions of the children, pregnancy and plans to have children, etc.

Research shows that women are among those most affected by the widespread practice of employers to propose short-term contracts, substitute unlimited term contracts with short-term contracts, or to thoroughly avoid labour contracts in order to evade tax and social security contributions. This is because women face more severe economic constraints, they are often heads of the family and are inclined to take any kind of job.

Another serious problem that has been identified relates to women's status after maternity leave: they are discriminated against in the labour market because of the higher social price and benefits the employer must pay if they are appointed and the need for additional training and qualification after the leave.

Discriminatory job advertisements are another way in which the principle of equal treatment is violated, according to research conducted by the Media Research Group and Gender Project for Bulgaria Foundation in 1998. Additional data from the latter shows that this discrimination still continues in the press.

According to aforementioned study of the National Centre for the Study of Public Opinion, 35 percent of the men interviewed consider that women are discriminated against in terms of their choice and access to a job.

2.4 Protective measures with regard to women's participation in the labour market

Women benefit from special protective measures in Bulgarian legislation that are justified by women's biological specificity and motivated by concern about their reproductive functions. These measures correspond in principle to the requirements of international instruments, including ILO Conventions on Underground Work and Maximum Weights.

Chapter 15 Section 2 of the Labour Code is dedicated to the special protection of women at work, and Section 307 prohibits those hard and harmful work operations that can be detrimental to the health of women and their reproductive functions.

The activities prohibited (in addition to the work prohibited in relation to pregnancy and breastfeeding) are divided into two categories: the first category implies an absolute prohibition for all women, and the second only concerns women up to the age of 35. Although the prohibition of such work is absolute, there are still cases in practice where women work in harmful conditions. Trade unions collect information about the working conditions and have pointed to some cases of the violation of the prohibitions mentioned, especially in some privatised and feminised enterprises. (For example, the 'Black Book' of violations of the labour rights).

Section 308 of the Labour Code requires employers with 20 or more women workers to equip rooms for the their personal hygiene and for the relaxation of pregnant women, according to rules issued by the Minister of Health. This obligation is further developed in Regulation No.11 of 1987 of the Minister of Health.

It should be noted that some provisions of the Labour Code, instead of being protective, risk becoming detrimental and even discriminatory for women. For example, until very recently, Section 310 of the Labour Code contained the absolute prohibition for an employer to send a pregnant woman or a woman with a child under the age of three on a business trip.[12]

The provisions concerning night work for women were not revised or amended and Section 140(4)(2) of the Labour Code still contains an absolute prohibition for night work concerning not only pregnant women, but also women workers or employees

---

[12] With the recent amendment to the Labour Code, the provision of Section 310 reads: "1) An employer cannot send a pregnant woman on a business trip. 2) An employer cannot send a woman with a child under the age of three on a business trip except with her written consent." The arguments in favour of women's choice and chances for professional development prevailed and the legislature revised the absolute prohibition, signifying a further step towards harmonisation with Directive 76/207EEC. However, such an opportunity should also be available for women in early and normal pregnancy.

with children up to the age of three. As a result, women with small children cannot exercise their own choice and are deprived of chances for promotion and higher remuneration. They are also more unsuitable candidates in the process of hiring for certain jobs and positions.

2.5 Prohibition of dismissal

There are no protective measures in Bulgaria against dismissals effected in reaction to complaints based on the principle of equal treatment. However, according to Article 30 of the draft AEOWM, the employer may not undertake any disciplinary measures towards an employee in reaction to a complaint about the violation of his/her rights under Chapter 2 ("Equal opportunities in the field of employment and occupation").

2.6 Women's and men's jobs

There are no additional guarantees in Bulgarian legislation to prevent the classification of jobs as specifically women's jobs and men's jobs, and only the general guarantees for non-discrimination on the basis of sex are valid here. There are no restrictions against women occupying any specific positions except where 'sex' is a determining factor for the fulfilment of activities; for example, in cases where the completion of military service is a precondition for occupying the position. Article 3(3) of the draft AEOWM states that qualification requirements for activities for which sex is a determining factor shall not be considered as discrimination.

There are no jobs that are clearly prohibited for women or for men, except those connected with protecting women's biological specificity and reproductive functions. For example, according to ILO Convention 45 on Underground Work it is forbidden to hire women for underground work in the mines. The prohibition is absolute concerning physical work in the mines. The above mentioned Ministry of Labour and Social Policy Regulation No.7 of 1993 extends the list of the jobs forbidden for women and, in addition to physical work in the mines, includes jobs in industries dealing with non-ferrous metals, lead, and other harmful substances and materials, for example, are forbidden and closed for women.

2.7 Legal status of sexual harassment

Sexual harassment in the workplace is not explicitly prohibited in Bulgarian legislation, although there was clear progress in this direction with the ratification of the Revised

European Social Charter, the recent amendments to the Labour Code, the draft AEOWM, and the research work of NGOs and official research institutes.

The State's obligation to protect workers and employees from sexual harassment is envisaged in such international instruments as the International Covenant on Economic, Social and Cultural Rights (ICESCR) and CEDAW. This obligation has been transposed in Bulgaria through the amendments to the Labour Code and introduced in an additional paragraph: Section 127(2). Although progressive, the provision is general and requires further development to take into account the gender component of sexual harassment and the principle of equal treatment of men and women. In addition, there is currently no explicit prohibition of sexual harassment as a violation of dignity at work in the Labour Code or in any other law. Furthermore, since the Labour Code does not apply to civil servants, they are not protected with a special provision for respect of dignity at work.

Except for cases of rape, the only other provision for protection in severe cases of sexual harassment is envisaged in Section 153 of the Penal Code, whereby a person who takes advantage of his superior position to force a female subordinate to have sexual intercourse with him faces possible imprisonment of up to three years. As such circumstances are very difficult to prove, there is no relevant practice under this article of the Penal Code.

The draft AEOWM contains a special provision prohibiting sexual harassment and obliges employers to prevent and prosecute sexual harassment in the workplace (Article 27[13]). The Act extends protection against sexual harassment to include schools and universities, and is defined in the Additional Provisions.

Research shows that sexual harassment in the workplace is widespread, and has been exacerbated in the period of transition and transformation of property.

The lack of public awareness and of legal and administrative measures to combat the phenomenon was identified by the research of Minnesota Advocates for Human Rights in their 1999 report entitled "Sex Discrimination and Sexual Harassment in the Workplace in Bulgaria," and by the 1999 BGRF report entitled "The Impact of

---

[13] "Article 27(1) Sexual harassment in the workplace by the employer or other employee is prohibited. (2) An employer who received a complaint from an employee who considers himself harassed sexually by another employee shall carry out an investigation and undertake measures for its prevention. (3) The employer must not put in a disadvantaged position or take disciplinary measures against an employee as a result of his actions to oppose or complain of sexual harassment. (4) An employee who has testified or is supposed to testify for sexual harassment is entitled to the same protection." Draft Act on Equal Opportunities for Women and Men.

Privatisation on Women during the Economic Transition in Bulgaria." The following excerpts can be provided:

- "[…] in the private sector this [sexual harassment] takes place in about 90 percent of the firms";
- "I can only say that I […] changed 12 employers until I found someone who did not make a hint like this at all. Since the age of 16, when I started to work, this was one of the main reasons that made me give up and jump from one job to another […]."

According to the two nationally representative surveys of the National Centre for the Study of Public Opinion (conducted in September 2000 and February 2001 respectively), approximately 81 percent of respondents perceive discrimination as physical harassment and more than half of the interviewees would like to see the state take more severe measures and sanctions against sexual harassment.

3. Protection of pregnant women from the inherent risk of certain activities and related employment rights

Council Directive 92/85/EEC of 19 October 1992 on the introduction of measures to encourage improvements in the safety and health at work of pregnant workers and workers who have recently given birth or are breastfeeding

3.1 Legal and conceptual framework

Bulgarian legislation envisages the special protection of women, especially pregnant women and mothers, and meets the requirements of Directive 92/85/EEC to a significant extent. The Labour Code provides a number of privileges for women in relation to preserving their health and that of their children, some of which (such as paid maternity leave) also aim at stimulating the birth rate.

There are a number of legal regulations related to the protection of pregnant women or nursing mothers, the most important of which are contained in the Labour Code, the Act on Health and Safety, and Regulation No.7 of 1993 of the Ministry of Labour and Social Policy and Ministry of Health on work that is heavy or hazardous to women's health and maternal functions, etc.

However, Bulgarian legislation does not contain any legal definitions corresponding to Article 2 of the Directive; for example, for employers to be informed by workers of their specific situation (pregnancy, birth, breastfeeding).

3.2 Assessing the risk to the safety or health of a pregnant worker and employer's obligations

Section 275 of the Labour Code obliges the employer to ensure safe and healthy working conditions in order to eliminate any danger to the life and health of the employee. Under the Act on Health and Safety at Work, the employer is obliged to assess the health and safety risks, taking into consideration the working processes and equipment, premises, working places, organization of work, use of raw materials and other external factors. Moreover, the employer must envisage appropriate measures in accordance with the assessment to protect workers and employees.

The employer, jointly with the health authorities, shall annually designate positions and jobs suitable for pregnant women and nursing mothers,[14] and under the Act on Health and Safety at Work shall provide workers or their representatives with the necessary information about the risks related to their safety and health, as well as the measures undertaken for the elimination, reduction or monitoring of such risks.

Data on the safe and healthy conditions of work must be established annually in accordance with individual indices and through a procedure to be determined by the Ministry of Labour and Social Welfare and the Ministry of Health. Employers are obliged to record occupational injuries and general and professional illnesses in a manner to be determined by the Minister of Labour and Social Welfare and by the Chairman of the National Statistics Institute.

The Labour Code stipulates a number of fines to be imposed on an employer who violates the regulations for the provision of a safe and healthy work environment, and the amount depends on the violation, whether it is repeated, whether the employer failed to meet his obligations or implement a mandatory instruction from the controlling bodies or unlawfully obstructed their work.

Bulgarian legislation fully corresponds with the meaning of Article 5 of Directive 92/85/EEC, and is also in line with CEDAW and the ILO Convention 183 on Maternity Protection (2000).

Transfer to suitable work

A pregnant woman or nursing mother employed in a job unsuitable for her condition shall be reassigned to another appropriate job or to the same job with alleviated conditions upon the prescription of the health authorities, which is mandatory for the pregnant or nursing woman and for the employer.[15]

If the remuneration in the new position is lower than the previous work, she is entitled to the difference in cash compensation.[16] The conditions for the above protection are given in detail in the Ordinance on the Reassignment, according to which the cash compensation should be paid for the period between the date of reassignment and the date of the beginning of the paid maternity leave.

According to the Labour Code, pregnant or breastfeeding women working in unhealthy conditions are entitled to reduced working hours, while keeping their basic monthly salaries. Regardless of the working conditions, mothers with children up to six years of age are entitled to work at home.

---

[14] Labour Code, Section 209, Work-Term Liability (1994).
[15] Labour Code, Section 309, Job Reassignment for Pregnant and Nursing Mothers (1994).
[16] Compulsory Social Security Act, Article 11, Article 48.

Overtime work is not permitted for pregnant employees, mothers with children under three years of age, mothers with children between three and six years of age, or mothers raising handicapped children irrespective of the latter's age, except with their own consent.[17] In addition, the employer may not send pregnant women and mothers of children under three years of age on business travel.

3.3 Cases in which exposure is prohibited for pregnant workers and workers who are breastfeeding

According to Section 307 of the Labour Code, work that is heavy or hazardous to health and maternal functions is prohibited for women. The list annexed to Regulation No.7 of 1993 specifies that heavy or hazardous work prohibited for women and contains three sections: the first section includes work that is prohibited irrespective of the women workers' age; the second section includes work prohibited for women under the age of 35 years; and the third section relates to work not permitted for women who are pregnant or breastfeeding.[18]

Bulgarian legislation provides greater protection to women than required by the Directive and employers do not have the discretion to decide on the level of risk and possible effect on the pregnancy, which is also the case with bans of work with hidden sources of ionised irradiation, work with particular chemical agents, work related to vibration, noise, super-sound, radio frequency waves, electrical magnetic fields over the permissible maximum of the hygiene norms, etc.

---

[17] Labour Code, Section 147, Inadmissibility of Overtime Work (1994).

[18] "Article 3. Work prohibited for pregnant or breastfeeding women: Work involving the liberation of toxic chemical substances in concentrations over the acceptable hygiene norms; vibration, noise, super-sound, radio frequency waves, electrical magnetic fields over the permissible maximum hygiene norms; production and other types of work where the temperature is over the permissible hygiene norms; work linked with physical overburden exceeding the admissible norms of 2.4 kcal/min and work related to lifting and carrying loads exceeding 5 kgs, work with hidden sources of ionised irradiation; work related to inducers of infections, fungi and parasitic diseases."

A number of other relevant laws and regulations provide for the protection of health and safety at work, some of which deal in particular with the protection of women workers (pregnant workers and breastfeeding women).[19]

3.4 Night work

The Labour Code defines night work as work performed between 10.00 p.m. and 6.00 a.m. In the course of night work the employer is obliged to provide employees with hot food, refreshments and other facilities. Night work is prohibited for specified categories of workers, including pregnant employees, mothers with children under three years of age; and mothers of children aged between three and six years of age, as well as mothers raising handicapped children irrespective of the latter's age, except with their own consent.

3.5 Maternity leave

Bulgarian legislation fully complies with international standards related to maternity leave, and Bulgaria has ratified ILO Convention No.3 on Maternity Protection. The Labour Code grants certain rights to women related to maternity leave and the relevant texts fully correspond with the Directive. In addition, Bulgaria has a modern Compulsory Social Security Code (CSSC), which regulates the provision of social security compensations in case of maternity leave.

Pregnant women and mothers are among the categories of employees who are entitled to an extended annual paid leave.

---

[19] Act on Protection against the Negative Effect of Chemical Agents, Substances and Products; Regulation No.7 of 1999 of the Ministry of Labour and Social Policy and Ministry of Health on the Minimum Safety and Health Requirements at the Workplace and the use of Work Equipment; Regulation No.25 of 1999; Regulation No.0-35 of 1974 on Work with Radioactive Substances and Other Sources of Ionised Emissions; Regulation No.3 of 1987 on Compulsory Preliminary and Periodical Medical Examinations of Workers; Regulation No.16 of 1999 on Physiological Norms and Rules for Manual Work with Heavy Loads; Regulation No.41 of 1995 on Unified Rules for the Provision of Health Working Conditions; Regulation No.8 of 1996 on the Hygienic Requirements in Working Places for Work with Screen Equipment.

The Labour Code provides for the following types of leave:

- leave for pregnancy, birth and adoption;
- paid leave for raising a young child;
- unpaid leave for raising a young child;
- leave for breastfeeding and feeding a young child;

Under the Compulsory Social Security Code, social security compensation in case of leave for pregnancy and birth amount to 90 percent of the salary, and no less than the legally specified minimal salary. During paid leave for raising a young child mothers receive monthly cash compensation amounting to the legally specified minimal salary. In addition, according to the Decree of Birth Promotion, women are entitled to benefits for each child that is born.

Antenatal examinations

The right to time off for antenatal examinations is not explicitly provided for by law. Nevertheless, female workers are entitled under Section 162 of the Labour Code to paid leave for urgent medical examinations or tests. This provision fully covers the right under Article 9 of the Directive. Such leave is subject to permission by the medical authorities, and for the duration of the leave the employee shall be paid a cash compensation under the Compulsory Social Security Code.

3.6 Prohibition of dismissal and employment rights

The provisions of the Bulgarian Labour Code preventing the dismissal of pregnant workers or workers who have given birth from the beginning of pregnancy to the end of maternity leave do not provide complete protection for female workers. Nevertheless, they comply with Article 10 of the Directive as such a dismissal is allowed only in exceptional cases and with the prior consent of the competent authority. Employers are permitted to dismiss employees who are pregnant or have children under three years of age under the following circumstances: partial closing down of the enterprise or staff cuts; reduction of the volume of work; if an employee lacks the qualities for efficient work performance; if the requirements for the job have changed and the employee no longer qualifies; in case of disciplinary dismissal.

The recent amendments to the Labour Code will provide for the full protection of women during leave for pregnancy and birth, but will not cover cases where it is impossible to implement the contract of employment due to objective reasons.

Because some of the cases in which dismissal is permitted are open to interpretation, employees can be put in an unfavourable position.

Protection against dismissal is also extended to workers who are socially and economically disadvantaged; for example, workers with family, material or health problems if qualifications and performance are equal; workers with an unemployed spouse; and workers who are sole family providers, given there are equal qualifications.

Proceedings in labour cases are free of charge for employees, and employees are entitled to contest the legal grounds for dismissal before the employer or in a court and can demand: recognition that the dismissal was unlawful and its repeal; reinstatement to the previous position; compensation for the period of unemployment due to dismissal; revision of the grounds for dismissal entered in the employee's service record or other documents. At his or her own initiative an employer may revoke the dismissal before the employee takes the action to court.

Due to the considerable social effect of labour disputes resulting from dismissals, the law stipulates relatively short terms in which such disputes must be resolved by the courts: within three months following the receipt of the claim by the regional court and within one month following the receipt of the appeal by the district court. If the court orders the reinstatement of the employee to his or her previous position s/he may assume the position provided s/he reports to work within two weeks of receiving the reinstatement notice, unless this term is exceeded for valid reasons.

4. THE BURDEN OF PROOF IN CASES OF DISCRIMINATION BASED ON SEX

Council Directive 97/80/EC of 15 December 1997 *on the burden of proof in cases of discrimination based on sex*

4.1 Legal framework concerning indirect discrimination: specific legal means to implement the principle of equal treatment for women and men

Bulgarian legislation does not yet fully comply with this Directive, but the relevant concepts have been incorporated in the draft AEOWM.

Although the notion of indirect discrimination was introduced with the latest amendments to the Labour Code, there is no notion of indirect discrimination based only on sex in Bulgarian legislation, as required by Directive 97/80/EC. The definition in Bulgaria must be made more specific for those cases where the indirect effect is appropriate and necessary and can be justified by objective factors unrelated to sex and therefore does not constitute discrimination.

4.2 The burden of proof procedure in litigation concerning the violation of the principle of equal treatment for women and men and rules of evidence

As mentioned previously, there are no specific legal means for real protection in cases of the violation of the principle of equal treatment for women and men in terms of working conditions, including vocational training. For this reason, there is no relevant practice related to the implementation of Section 8 of the Labour Code with respect to discrimination on the grounds of sex.

There are no 'out of court' procedures for ensuring the application of the principle of equal treatment, and since mediation and conciliation are relatively new concepts in Bulgaria, only a small number NGOs are trying to introduce them in other areas, although it has been suggested to officially introduce mediation at the level of labour relations.

Bulgarian legislation does not comply with Directive 97/80/EC concerning the reversal of the burden of proof, as the general rule of evidence in accordance with Section

127(1) of the Code of Civil Procedure provides that each party must establish the circumstances that form the basis of her/his claims or objections.

The only provision that can be applied to the advantage of the plaintiff is Section 128(2) of the Code of Civil Procedure, which provides that: "In view of the circumstances of the case, the court could accept facts as proved (corroborated) if the party [respondent] created obstacles to the collection of evidence admitted by the court." Still, the respondent is not obliged to prove the non-violation of the principle of equal treatment.

Article 32 of the draft AEOWM envisages the reversal of the burden of proof for several cases of discrimination based on sex in employment and occupation.

5. NON-DISCRIMINATION AGAINST PART-TIME WORKERS

Council Directive 97/81/EC of 15 December 1997 *concerning the framework agreement on part-time work concluded by UNICE, CEEP and the ETUC*

5.1 National legal framework and employment conditions concerning part-time workers

Provisions regulating part-time work are contained in the Bulgarian Labour Code[20] and in the Act on the Protection against Unemployment and Employment Promotion.[21] There are no provisions containing the term 'comparable full-time worker', although a comparison between part-time and full-time workers could be made on the basis of job descriptions, which are mandatory for every working place. The legal definition of part-time work in Bulgaria is based on the term 'statutory working time', which has important legal consequences.

When assessing the status of part-time workers, a distinction must be made between 'part-time work' and 'work at reduced working hours': While part-time work is agreed voluntarily between parties to an employment contract, employment at reduced working hours is introduced only in cases explicitly stipulated by law, for example for youths under 18 years of age and for work in unhealthy conditions or under special conditions. The introduction of reduced working hours favours workers as it aims to protect their health and is obligatory for employers. The concept of 'reduced working hours' also falls within the wide scope of the EU definition.

Proposals for the introduction of reduced working hours may be submitted by employers or representative branch employees' organizations to the Ministry of Labour and Social Policy and Ministry of Health Care. Once the reduced working hours are introduced, workers keep their basic monthly salaries.

The latest amendments to the Labour Code reintroduce the concept of a 'Working Contract for up to Five Days a Month', and this type of employment contract is well-known in Bulgaria. Under such a contract a person works for one employer for no

---

[20] Labour Code, Section 138, Part-time: "Parties to an employment contract may negotiate work for a part of the statutory working hours (part-time work). In this case they shall specify the duration and allocation of the working hours."

[21] Act on the Protection against Unemployment and Employment Promotion, Additional Provisions, Article 1(2), definition of "a person working part-time: any person party to a labour contract working fewer than statutory working hours for the respective job or profession."

more than five working days or 40 hours a month in total, whether continuously or in broken succession. Major legal consequences for the worker are related to the length of service (the time worked is not included), and to the compulsory social security (the worker is only entitled to insurance accidents during work and professional illness).

Employment conditions for workers with employment contracts for reduced working hours are the same as those conditions for workers employed for the full statutory hours.

There is no discrimination concerning part-time workers, and if the working time is at least one half of the legally established working hours for the day there are no different legal consequences related to the length of service and hence the right to social security.

Determination of the amount of remuneration

According to the Labour Code, the amount of remuneration in any employment contract shall be determined in accordance with the duration of work or the results of work. Workers employed under the conditions of Section 137 of the Labour Code (reduced working hours) receive remuneration as for a full working day.

Social security and health insurance

Workers employed for more than five working days or 40 hours per calendar week shall be insured against all social risks. Health insurance contributions must be made on the basis of monthly remuneration, and the amount of the due contribution is set in accordance with a legally defined ratio.

Length of service

One day's length of service shall be recognised whenever an employee has worked for at least one half of the legally established working hours for that day under one or several employment relationships. The same principle is valid for social security relationships.

Paid leave

Bulgarian legislation provides that part-time employees are entitled to annual paid leave proportional to the time acknowledged as the length of service. Workers and employees working under unhealthy conditions or doing work under special conditions are entitled to an extended annual paid leave if their working hours are no less than half of the statutory working hours.

In general, there are no differences concerning the treatment of part-time workers in the public and private sectors, and remuneration in the public sector is calculated in accordance with various Council of Ministers Decrees.

Bulgarian legislation does not provide the possibility for a part-time worker to request a transfer to full-time work or *vice versa* if such a position is available, and any transfer is subject to a written agreement between the worker and the employer. Moreover, part-time work is merely a possibility for employees, and if the employer does not want such a type of labour contract, the employee has no legal means to convince him/her to conclude one.

Flexible working hours may be established in enterprises where the organisation of work allows it, and the details shall be specified by the employer. Depending on the nature of work and the labour organisation, the working day may be divided into two or three parts. For some categories of employees, due to the special nature of their work, the Ministry of Labour and Social Policy may establish open-ended working hours and such employees shall, if necessary, perform their duties even after regular working hours. Overtime on working days shall be compensated by additional annual paid leave; and work on legal holidays shall be compensated by increased remuneration for overtime work.

Since the beginning of the transition process, flexible and part-time work has been increasingly seen as contributing to the reduction of unemployment, and employers are encouraged to employ unemployed persons in part-time work.[22]

The benefits for unemployed persons who worked part-time is proportional to the working time agreed.[23] If an unemployed person began work as a part-time worker, he/she is entitled to receive 50 percent of the unemployment benefit if the salary is below the minimum statutory salary of the country.

In November 2000, the National Employment Office began a new active labour market measure entitled 'Flexible forms of employment', which is pursuant to the provisions of the Act on the Protection against Unemployment and Employment Protection and aims to prevent unemployed persons from becoming unemployed long-term. In December, 422 persons participated in this programme (65 percent more than in the previous month), including 270 women.

---

[22] Act on the Protection against Unemployment and Employment Promotion, Article 61: "For every unemployed person hired under a contract for part-time work for a period of at least 3 months the employer is entitled to receive from the Professional Qualification and Unemployment Fund sums amounting to up to 50% of the minimum salary plus contributions due for the Social Security Fund and Professional Qualification and Unemployment Fund for every unemployed person hired."

[23] Act on the Protection against Unemployment and Employment Promotion, Article 69.

6. The principle of equal treatment to self-employed workers and their assisting spouses

Directive 86/613/EEC of 11 December 1986 *on the application of the principle of equal treatment between women and men engaged in an activity, including agriculture, in a self-employed capacity, and on the protection of self-employed women during pregnancy and motherhood*

6.1 National legal framework on self-employment: General provisions

Self-employment, which has not been excessively regulated, was a relatively stable phenomenon in Bulgaria prior to the political changes in the country, and has remained so. The new group to have emerged in the economy as self-employed persons include sole entrepreneurs, and owners or partners in commercial companies. Their status is regulated by the Commercial Act.

Definition of self-employed workers

There is no explicit definition of self-employed workers in Bulgarian legislation. For the purposes of social security, however, Section 4 of the Code for Obligatory Social Insurance (hereinafter COSI) lists the groups that are defined as self-employed. The social insurance regulations covering self-insured persons contain a definition of persons exercising freelance professions and/or trades, but no definition of a contributing family member. The jobs and occupations that can be practiced by self-insured persons include sole proprietors or partners in commercial companies; agricultural producers; and persons active in freelance professions or trades.

Laws and regulations related to the directive

The legal instruments related to self-employed workers and their assisting spouses are the COSI, the Regulation on Social Insurance of Self-Insured Persons and Bulgarians Employed Abroad, the Decree on Birth Promotion,[24] and the Social Assistance Act. There are no rules that run counter to the principle of equal treatment or which are directly discriminatory in the existing legal framework.

---

[24] Replaced by the new Family Assistance Act of 2002.

Acceptance of the directive

There is no available information on public awareness, due to the lack of research conducted on this matter. However, because opinion polls show that public awareness in EU accession-related questions is only moderate, it can be assumed that public awareness of specific questions will be low due to the technical character of these instruments.

A greater proportion of self-employed women than men are viewed as 'forced' entrepreneurs, due to external circumstances. The ILO report indicates that whereas self-employed women are more likely than their male counterparts to be highly educated, they tend to believe they lack the skills needed to become entrepreneurs. Women also tend to view entrepreneurship as an inappropriate role for them, thus highlighting the importance of raising awareness among young women regarding the benefits, opportunities and challenges of the private sector and of entrepreneurship in general.

6.2 Social rights of spouses of self-employed workers

Section 13(1) of the COSI provides that persons insured for disability due to general ill-health, old age and death shall have the right to:

- pension for disability on grounds of general ill-health;
- pension for insured practice and old age;
- financial support for injury-related auxiliary or technical help.

Section 13(2) provides that upon the death of the insured person, the husband (or wife), children and parents shall have the right to lump sum assistance amounting to the full extent of two minimum salaries and to one survivor's pension.

Right to survivor's pension

According to Section 80(1) of the COSI, it is possible for personal pensions to be transferred into survivor's pensions, except those pensions covered by Sections 87, 89, 90, 91 and 92 (pensions not related to labour/employment activity). Under Section 80(2), the children, surviving spouse and the parents shall have the right to a survivor's pension.

Determining the survivor's pension

Section 81(1) of the COSI provides that the survivor's pension shall be determined as a percentage of the personal pension due to the deceased insured person as follows:

- for one survivor, 50 percent;

- for two survivors, 75 percent;
- for three and more survivors, 100 percent.

Addition to the pension of a widow/widower

According to Section 84 of the COSI, the pensioner shall have the right to an additional 20 percent of the pension or sum of pensions of the deceased spouse. The addition cannot be received together with a survivor's pension from the same source.

Formation of companies by unmarried persons

The Commercial Act of 1991 and other commercial legal regulations are gender neutral, and there are no legal or practical differences concerning the formation of companies by unmarried persons. None of the provisions are contrary to the Directive under review. Most female-owned companies are registered as having sole proprietors, followed by limited liability companies and partnerships.

The rights of self-employed workers whose operational activity is interrupted owing to pregnancy or motherhood

According to the COSI, self-employed women who voluntarily insured themselves against all social risks, excluding industrial injury and occupational illness and unemployment, shall enjoy the rights stemming therefrom.

Benefit for raising a small child

According to Section 53(1) of the COSI, after the elapse of the term of eligibility for maternity benefits during additional paid leave for raising a small child, the mother (or adoptive mother) shall be paid a monthly benefit in an amount determined by the Act on the Budget of the State Public Insurance. If the additional paid leave for raising a small child is claimed by the father (or adoptive father) or legal guardian, this shall be paid as a monthly benefit in an amount determined by the same law.

Spouses and self-employed women who have not insured themselves voluntarily are covered by the general system of social benefits. Voluntary social insurance pension schemes have only recently been introduced and they are open to everyone in a position to pay the contributions.

6.3 Related research and statistics

The main forms of self-employment in which women are engaged include in trade, services, manufacturing, transport, and communications.

Research on women in agriculture

According to the Labour Force Survey of November 1999, 252,800 persons were employed in agriculture, forestry and fishing, of whom 33.6 percent were women. The only research available on this subject is the report *Bulgarian Rural Women Today*,[25] which deals with the sociological aspects of the equality/inequality of rural women in Bulgaria, with the gender aspects of the division of labour in Bulgarian agriculture and with the values and ethnic differentiation in Bulgarian villages. The research, however, does not deal with social security rights.

Past and recent trends in self-employment

Fewer women than men occupy managerial positions in private businesses, the area in which they could expect higher wages. It may be that women do not feel confident enough to take on the risks and obstacles associated with organising and managing a private business, despite their generally high level of education. Other factors affecting their decision include: the difficult economic situation and general lack of business experience in the country, legislative difficulties, criminality, the effects of a shadow economy, lower prices of imported goods as a result of smuggling, etc. Furthermore, women with families face difficulties coping with the longer than average working hours required to manage a private business.

Men comprise the majority of employers and self-employed persons, whereas women with higher and secondary education are better represented in the public sector. Men are also preferred within the private sector, making it more difficult for women to obtain well-paid employment and pay equal to men's.

There are no statistics or research concerning self-employed married couples, but the consistant decline in the number of women in business associations suggests that the proportion of women running an enterprise with their spouses is not rising.

Research results on the status and rights of self-employed women

Unfortunately, no comprehensive survey or study has been published in this area, but the report issued by the InFocus Programme on Boosting Employment through Small Enterprise Development[26] has concluded that women are less likely than men to consider going into business and that those who do are more likely to fail than men. Currently, only six percent of Bulgarian women manage or own their own company. Enterprises run by men are on a larger scale, both in terms of sales revenue and the labour force. Among enterprises run by women, the report described more individual enterprises and fewer business associations.

---

[25] Fotev ed. (2001).
[26] Stoyanovska (2001).

6.4 Legal means of redress

There are no measures to enable all persons who consider themselves wronged by the failure to apply the principle of equal treatment in self-employed activities to pursue their claims by judicial process, possibly after recourse to other competent authorities. Nor are there any measures requiring the measures adopted pursuant to this Directive (together with the relevant provisions already in force) to the attention of bodies representing self-employed workers and vocational training centers.

7. THE FRAMEWORK ON PARENTAL LEAVE

Council Directive 96/34/EC of 3 June 1996 *on the framework agreement on parental leave concluded by UNICE, CEEP, and ETUC*

7.1 National legal framework on parental leave: General provisions

The Bulgarian Constitution reflects traditional concepts of gender roles and does not contain the terms 'paternal' or 'parental' leave. The Labour Code and Act on Civil Service do not contain a specific definition of parental leave as distinct from maternity leave. According to the National Programme for the Adoption of the *Acquis* (NPAA), this will be introduced with the drafting (undertaken jointly with social partners) of an amendment to the Labour Code in 2004.

According to the draft AEOWM, an employer may not select a job applicant only on the basis of his/her gender. The employer may not ask questions, orally or in writing, related to family o parental status or duties, and may not refuse to employ a person for reasons related to pregnancy, maternity or raising a child.

During socialism, the state created favourable legal and economic conditions enabling women to combine different roles. For example, in the 1970s a right to long-term and well-paid maternity leave was introduced. In addition to the special protection of women, especially pregnant women and mothers, the Labour Code (1986) provided a number of privileges for fathers in order to facilitate them taking an active role in raising children. The Labour Code stipulated that with the mother's consent, after the period of leave for pregnancy, childbirth or adoption had elapsed and in case the child is not placed in a child-care establishment, additional leave could be granted to the father (or adoptive father) for raising a first, second and third child until they reach two years of age, and up to six months for each subsequent child. After taking the leave allowed for raising a child up to two years of age, the mother (or adoptive mother) or father (or adoptive father), at their request, could be granted further unpaid leave until the child reaches three years of age. In addition, the State provides that if the mother (or adoptive mother) is a student or post-graduate student, parental leave for raising a child shall be granted to the father (or adoptive father), according to the Decree for Birth Promotion. The Labour Code (Section 160, amended in 2001) further provides that every employee is entitled to unpaid leave pf one month per year to be counted as a period of service.

Although these provisions do not provide for parental leave in line with Directive 96/34/EC, they do give fathers the chance to participate in childcare. However, certain recently adopted legislation goes against the concept of the Directive. For example, Article 53 of the Act on Employment Promotion (in force since 1 January 2002) grants advantages for employers who hire single mothers and mothers with children up to three years, with no mention of fathers who could be in the same position. This risks further reinforcing prejudices and making fathers even more reluctant to take advantage of the right to child-care leave.

Under current Bulgarian legislation, the father may only take childcare leave if the mother has relinquished her right to leave and given her permission. It is common practice for grandparents to take advantage of this leave instead of the father, for economic reasons. Another important factor in deciding who will take parental leave in the family is the inherited traditional stereotypes on the roles of women and men, which do not favour the father. Furthermore, there are very few cases where the woman has the higher salary and it is economically more effective for her to continue her job, and for him to take care of the children. There is a lack of affirmative action encouraging men to take parental leave, especially a lack of financial incentives. The government does not collect data on this issue.

Conditions of access and detailed rules relating to parental leave applications

A father has equal rights with the mother to be granted parental leave for raising a child or in case of illness (Sections 162, 164 and 165 of the Labour Code). The parents have the right to take sick leave in case of a temporary disability or urgent medical examinations or to care for a sick or quarantined child, and this right is granted with permission from by the medical authorities.

The mother has the right to parental leave of two years for her first, second and third children and of six months for each subsequent child. An employer may not refuse the application for parental leave, regardless of whether it is taken immediately following maternity leave.

The mother (or adoptive mother) may relinquish her right to leave at any time in the form of a written declaration addressed to the enterprise in which she works. She may also end the agreement that another family member takes the parental leave and use it herself.

According to Bulgarian legislation, there are no circumstances in which an employer is entitled to postpone the granting of parental leave. Nevertheless, since 1998 there is a trend among foreign investors to claim that fathers' leave should be subject to the discretion of the employer.

Legal protection against dismissal on the grounds of an application for, or taking of, parental leave

There is no specific protection in this field apart from the general protection against dismissal. There is no legal practice relating to such cases, because prior consent for the dismissal is required from the Labour Inspectorate in cases involving a pregnant woman or a woman with a child up to three years of age. Full protection is provided only for women on maternity leave, but exceptions may be made in cases of closure of an enterprise. The protection available is therefore short-term and does not cover the father on parental leave.

Legal entitlement to return to the same, equivalent or similar job

There are no legal guarantees that workers may return to the same, or an equivalent or similar job after parental leave. The proposed draft AEOWM provides such a guarantee though by introducing incentives for employers to support the mother or father during or after parental leave.

7.2 Social security during parental leave, especially related to healthcare

In principle, the social security rights acquired before parental leave are maintained, but many benefits must be reapplied for after the leave, since the conditions change after a certain period of time.

A six-month contribution is the general condition for eligibility benefits according to the COSI. Persons on parental leave are insured against all social risks, and have the right to financial remuneration.[27]

Healthcare

The amount of the contribution is defined according to the Health Insurance Act and the respective rights are regulated in the COSI. The national insurance institution pays benefits for sick leave on the basis of a sickness certified by a general practitioner.

Workers are entitled to leave for reasons of *force majeure* as follows:

- paid leave for raising a young child up to two years of age (Section 164 of the Labour Code);

---

[27] COSI, Section 11(1), Item 1e.

- unpaid leave for raising a young child up to three years of age (Section 165 of the Labour Code);
- leave in case of temporary disability:
  - 10 days per year per insured family member;
  - 60 days per year commonly for all family members;
  - for the duration of the illness or quarantine.

There are no differences based on who takes the leave, i.e., whether it is the mother, father, adoptive parent, or an older family member.

7.3 Parental leave and equal opportunities policy

The general aims of the Directive to set minimum requirements on parental (as distinct from maternity) leave and the importance of reconciling work and family life are accepted by the Government of Bulgaria.

After developing the draft Act on EOWM, the Ministry of Labour and Social Policy was entrusted with developing equal treatment policies, which resulted in the establishment of a National Employment Action Plan (NEAP) and National Employment Strategy (NES) according to the Act on Employment Promotion to plan programmes and measures for combining work activity with family life. Such measures include the creation, application and promotion family-oriented policies and holiday schemes for parents and other workers, incentives for employers to adopt flexible labour arrangements as well as for helping women return to work after a long break in employment.

In February 2002 the Council of Ministers approved the NEAP, which aims to offer professional training in 2002 for 50,000 unemployed persons, largely women seeking work after maternity or childcare leave, who require re-training to meet the new demands of the labour market. The training could also help such persons start their own businesses.

The draft Act on EOWM also offered equal opportunities for job training, and requires employers to create the conditions for maintaining and improving the professional qualifications of employees on leave for raising a child.

Initiatives to encourage the introduction of new flexible ways of organising work

The economic situation in Bulgaria has necessitated a legally approved possibility for additional or second employment, enabling parents to contribute more to the family budget. This measure is also aimed at curbing unemployment. The Act on the Protection against Unemployment and Employment Promotion enables unemployed persons to work part-time and receive 50 percent of their unemployment benefit, at a level less than or equal to the legally specified minimal salary. This provision was not reproduced in the new Act on Employment Promotion, and despite the opportunities provided for in the Labour Code, employers' financial difficulties have hindered this from working in practice.

7.4 Research on the reconciliation of family and work responsibilities and on sharing responsibilities between men and women

In the transition towards a market economy, Bulgarian family life has been characterised on the one hand by the preservation of traditional values, and on the other hand by a rapid adaptation to new conditions. A study by the National Centre for the Study of Public Opinion from 1995 on the family and value systems among Bulgarians showed that the material conditions of the family are regarded as crucial to its stability (according to 88 percent of persons polled). Other factors, in order of importance, included childcare (52 percent), harmony in the family (39 percent), moral issues (24 percent), and religion (20 percent).

The 1992 national census[28] showed that both spouses were employed in fewer than half of all families, while in 2.5 percent of families both spouses were unemployed. Data from the most recent census (2001) will be available towards the end of 2002, but preliminary results show a trend toward an increase of spouses' activities.[29]

In the 1970s and 1980s, the employment rate for women almost reached the demographic maximum (i.e., in 1989, 84.7 percent of women of working age were employed). However, although women were encouraged to participate in all areas of the economy during socialism, this did not guarantee their equal status with men. Women prevail in low-paid occupations, such as technical staff (75.5 percent), retail trade and services (64.1 percent), clerks and administrative personnel (56.1 percent), and the tendency to pay women less for their labour than men has persisted.[30] Other areas where women are traditionally employed include agriculture, textile work, clothing and knitwear production, and the food and tobacco industries. In all these sectors the payment is low and working conditions allow for little professional development. Much of this work involves shift work, including night shifts, which place a particular strain on family life. The feminisation of the education and healthcare workforce (over 75 percent

---

[28] National Statistical Institute (1993).
[29] National Statistical Institute (2001: 36).
[30] National Statistical Institute (2001: 36).

of whom are women) had led men to withdraw in response to the corresponding low income and at least two generations of young persons have hardly encountered a male teacher at school. Currently, there is a higher number of women working in the fields of manufacturing, wholesale and retail, hotels and restaurants, education, health and social work, and other community, social and personal service activities.[31]

Despite their relatively low pay, Bulgarian woman share the burden of providing financially for the family equally with men. Figures show that compared with other countries, Bulgarian women contribute proportionally among the most to the family budget. This reflects the general low level of pay for all employees in Bulgaria. A comparative evaluation shows that the relative share of unpaid labour carried out by women in the GDP of Bulgaria is among the highest in the world.[32] Also compared with other countries, more Bulgarian woman are engaged in professional and family duties.[33]

The working hours of Bulgarian men, which equal the global average for male employees, are 14 hours less per week than that of Bulgarian women, who have among the longest working hours in the world, while men undertake only half the unpaid domestic labour that women carry out. Nearly half the women in Bulgaria (48 percent) believe that they carry an unfair burden of the housework. 88.6 percent of women and 85.1 percent of mensurveyed believe that both men and women should contribute to the family budget. The contribution of the men to unpaid housework was considered insufficient not only by 72 percent of the women asked but also by 52.2 percent of the men. 83.3 percent of the women and 71.1 percent of the men believe that men should also play a greater role in the care and education of children.

The socio-economic transformation of family life in Bulgaria in the past ten years has led to the isolation of the father in intra-family relationships and the mother is traditionally expected to maintain the emotional balance of the family. The ability of the mother to make the family feel secure under conditions of external insecurity is crucial and the withdrawal of the father from family life has made this task difficult. Thus the economic crisis curbs the resources for personal self-fulfilment and development of family members, and has a negative impact on the quality of care for the next generation.

The high labour burden, both paid and unpaid, shouldered by Bulgarian women limits their opportunities for improving education and professionalism, and for fulfilling their own needs, all of which hinders their social development and competitive power in the labour market.

---

[31] National Statistical Institute (2001: 50).
[32] Kirova ed. (1995).
[33] European Community (1992); ILO (1985).

Statistics and research on the number of women who return to work after giving birth and men who take parental leave

There is little social understanding of the importance of this topic, and no research on the number of women who return to work after giving birth and the number of men who stay at home to care for their children has been publicly funded. In families where both parents work, it is common for the mother to take parental leave, generally in its full amount. In families where one of the parents is unemployed, the father may care for the children, but figures on this phenomenon are lacking.

The data in the table below relates to only ten percent of registered cases but is indicative of the overall rate of parental leave taken by mothers and fathers. The data is gathered from the statistics available for the different major towns in Bulgaria for 1998.

Table 1. Pregnancy and maternity leave, and childcare leave in case of sickness

	number of cases		number of days		average length of leave	
	men	*women*	*men*	*women*	*men*	*women*
Sofia						
pregnancy		5		462		92.4
maternity		1,041		56,539		54.3
sick child care	764	9,269	4,739	55,162	6.2	6
Plovdiv						
pregnancy		16		912		57
maternity		1,428		72,895		51
sick child care	599	7,519	3,495	36,513	5.8	4.9
Vidin						
pregnancy		3		378		26
maternity		211		10,751		51
sick child care	63	1,722	604	10,099	9.6	5.9
Varna						
pregnancy		9		211		23.4
maternity		889		46,007		51.8
sick child care	543	3,993	2,992	21,368	5.5	5.4
Bourgas						
pregnancy		3		38		12.7
maternity		203		9,804		48.3
sick child care	65	427	411	2,298	6.3	5.4

Note: This is the only available data on the gender division of sick and childcare leave.

Demographic, social or cultural considerations affecting the reconciliation of professional and family responsibilities

Families without children whose members are of employment age enjoy better financial status, while those with three or more children face the worst economic situation. In 90 percent of families, the income of only one spouse is insufficient to provide normal living conditions for the family.[34]

Another obstacle to combining working and family commitments is the lack of flexible working arrangements that would help parents to contribute to the domestic budget albeit with a lower income. A small minority of the working population has been able to take part-time work and this number increased in 2001 compared with 1996, when only 8.7 percent of women were employed in this manner.[35]

A survey by the National Centre for the Study of Public Opinion, commissioned by the Ministry of Labour and Social Policy while developing the AEOWM, showed that a large proportion (40 percent) of persons polled believed that men seldom take parental leave because of the family traditions in Bulgaria. Only 17 percent blamed legislative problems. Another 17 percent of respondents believed that fatherhood was undervalued by society, and that it was more appropriate for women to take parental leave. Furthermore, more women than men believed that paternal leave went against tradition, since childcare and education were seen as primarily the mother's activities, connected with her skills and natural procreative functions. It is also considered preferable for the parent with greater chances to find work, or better paid work, to do so.

---

[34] MLSP and NSI (2001: 54).
[35] National Statistical Institute (2001: 60).

8. THE PRINCIPLE OF EQUAL TREATMENT OF MEN AND WOMEN IN OCCUPATIONAL SOCIAL SECURITY SCHEMES

Council Directive 96/97/EC of 20 December 1996 amending Directive 86/378/EEC on the implementation of the principle of equal treatment for men and women in occupational social security schemes

8.1 National legal framework on social security schemes: General provisions

A radical reform of the pension system in Bulgaria was introduced with the promulgation of the Code for Obligatory Social Insurance (COSI). Previously, the Act on Pensions of 1957 was in force with several major modifications introduced in 1975 and in *ad hoc* reactions to the changing economic environment after the political changes in 1989.

According to the Act on Pensions, the retirement age for men and women differed according to the category of job performed.[36] Before the reforms in January 2000, the Bulgarian social insurance system was based on a defined benefit approach with universal coverage including employees from the private and public sectors, self-employed workers, members of cooperatives and professional associations. Insurance cover remained the same from 1990.

The COSI introduced a second pillar to the social insurance framework, which came into existence in 2001. The aim of the additional obligatory pension insurance is to ensure pension income and an opportunity for early retirement for those employed in categories I and II. The main principles of this second pillar are defined contributions pension schemes and individual accounts for each insured person and a fully funded system. The second pillar pension funds may also be established by employers, employer organizations, trade union structures, and pension insurance companies.

All individuals insured in the second pillar are entitled to a life pension for old age and a limited period pension for early retirement. In case of disability or death, the insured person has the right to withdraw the funds accrued in the individual account as a lump sum, and in case of death this right is acquired by the dependants of the insured person. The insured persons are also entitled to receive information, to lodge appeals and to notify the respective bodies of poor management of the fund in which they are

---

[36] Category III workers perform 'normal' work from the point of health and safety. Category II workers perform jobs judged to be arduous and unhealthy. Category I jobs are the most difficult and detrimental to health.

insured. The level of the pension shall be determined on the basis of the accumulated sums in the individual file from the payments made and the incomes from their investment, minus the fees and the deductions provided for in the COSI, and depending on life-expectancy after retirement.

An analysis of the second pillar reveals that it is not fully comparable with the occupational social security schemes employed in EU countries, the main differences being the risks covered (old age and death) and the defined contributions versus the defined benefits in the EU Directive 86/378/EEC, as amended by 96/97, on occupational social security schemes and all social security risks mentioned therein. There is no published data on the impact of the reform of the social security system on the status of women in Bulgaria after 1999.

The COSI provides for obligatory social insurance, including the state public insurance covering general ill-health, occupational disease, industrial injury, maternity, unemployment, old age and death as well as the additional pension insurance.

The state public insurance concedes benefits and pensions upon:

- temporary inability to work;
- temporary reduced ability to work;
- disability;
- maternity;
- unemployment;
- old age;
- death.

The principles of the state public insurance are:

- obligatory and comprehensive insurance;
- solidarity of the insured persons;
- equality of the insured persons;
- social dialogue in the management of the insurance system;
- a fund organisation of the insurance payments.

Further provisions related to insured persons are contained in Articles 4(1) to (7) of the COSI.

Direct and indirect gender-based discrimination in social security schemes

The lower pension age for women constitutes formal discrimination against men, and while a consensus is beginning to emerge in favour of a common age, there is still much heated debate about what that age should be. This question is now to be addressed after 2009.

Indirect discrimination results from measures which, although often defined without reference to gender, in practice do affect women and men differently because of the nature of their occupational activity, marital status or family situation. Certain conditions, such as long periods of qualification, also penalize women. It remains to be seen in the long term whether the formally gender-equal qualifying conditions for pensions under the obligatory second pillar do not in fact constitute indirect discrimination against women. However, it is too early to offer an assessment at this stage.

There is no discrimination on the basis of gender, either directly or indirectly, by reference in particular to marital or family status, especially as regards:

- the scope of schemes and conditions of access;
- the obligation to contribute and calculation of contributions;
- the calculation of benefits, including supplementary benefits due in respect of a spouse or dependants, and the conditions governing the duration and retention of benefit entitlement.

There is a risk that the generation of women born before 1959 will not to be able to comply with the pension conditions under the new COSI, as those women aged 50 who lose their employment have no chance of finding a another job given the high national unemployment rate (official figures put unemployment at over 18 percent).

Provisions contrary to the principle of equal treatment with regard to the social security scheme

There are no provisions contrary to the principle of equal treatment, particularly in terms of:

- determining the persons who may participate in an occupational scheme;
- defining the compulsory or optional nature of participation in an occupational scheme;
- establishing different rules regarding the age of entry into the scheme, the minimum period of employment, or membership of the scheme required for obtaining the benefits thereof.

Consideration of the principle of equal treatment by scheme management bodies

The concept of an occupational scheme in the COSI differs from the prevailing pattern in EU countries. The present legislation preserves the difference in the years of insured employment and ages for men and women until 2009.

As mentioned above, according to the Act on Pensions, the retirement age for men and women differs according to the category of job performed (see Table 2.).

Table 2. Eligibility conditions for old-age pensions under the Act on Pensions in force since January 2000

	Category of job		
	I	II	III
Years of employment	15	20	25 for men 20 for women
Retirement Age			
Men	52	57	60
Women	47	52	55

The COSI introduced new eligibility conditions for retirement, and Section 68(1) provides that the right to old age and insurance practice pension shall be acquired upon reaching 60 years and six months for men and 55 years and six months for women.

The previous Act on Pensions envisaged a special retirement scheme for teachers and other staff with the same status. To this end a special public Teachers' Fund was set up providing resources for teachers' early retirement. The new COSI preserves the more favourable retirement regime for teachers up to the end of 2009. Beyond this date, teachers will be covered by the general rule of Section 68. Up to and including 31 December 2009, teachers shall acquire the right to retirement pensions based on 30 years' service for men and 25 years for women and having reached an age three years younger than the age stipulated under Section 68. The insurance installments for the Teachers' Pension Fund is to be determined annually by the Act on the Budget of the Social Security Fund.

In 2000, 2,031 teachers (527 men and 1,504 women) were provided with early retirement pensions. The average number of months the retired teachers lacked in order to qualify for normal retirement pensions under category III was reported by the National Social Security Institute (NSSI) to be 29.6.

There is no provision for the suspension, retention or acquisition of rights during maternity or parental leave which are granted by law or agreement and are paid by the employer. There are not different levels of benefit or worker contributions, except insofar as may be necessary; and no different standards apply only to workers of a specified gender.

The granting of benefits is not left to the discretion of the management bodies.

Legal mechanisms to declare null and void any discrimination

The present occupational schemes are defined by law and are not part of a collective agreement or individual contract. If regulations introduce texts that run contrary to the principle of equality, the person affected may take a case to the Supreme Administrative Court as the appropriate body. Should the Supreme Administrative Court repeal the regulations, its decision must be published in the State Gazette for the repeal to have force of law. Persons affected by this act may then turn to the competent authorities to demand new regulations in compliance with the principle of equality.

It is possible for persons who consider themselves wronged by the failure to apply the principle of equal treatment to sue in tort, but there have not been any cases so far.

8.2 Legal means of redress

Protection against dismissal in the case of complaint of non-compliance with the principle of equal treatment

Protection against dismissal in case of a complaint based on the principle of equal treatment is not specifically envisaged, but there is a general possibility to lodge an appeal in court against unjustified dismissal.

Monitoring mechanisms

The control mechanisms and the rights of control bodies in this area are set out in the COSI. The monitoring of the legislation on state public insurance, as well as the payment of insurance payments for health insurance and the additional obligatory pension insurance, shall be carried out by the control bodies of the NSSI.

These control bodies have the right, *inter alia,* to check the activities of all individuals and corporate bodies concerning state public insurance and the payment of health insurance and additional obligatory pension insurance and undertake measures to hold persons guilty of violating the law accountable.

According to Section 108(2) of the COSI, individuals and corporate bodies are obliged to present to the control bodies of NSSI when required to do so the documents, data, information, declarations, explanations and communications connected with the implementation of state public insurance, the payment of health insurance and of additional obligatory pension insurance, and to offer all cooperation to fulfil their official obligations.

8.3 Implementation of the principle of equal treatment in matters of social security and equal opportunities strategies

Progressive implementation of the principle of equal treatment in matters of social security, although not part of official policy on gender equality, is considered through the draft AEOWM.

Perceived protection of women concerning maternity and social security

The protection of women in maternity is not considered to be an obstacle to the implementation of equal treatment in social security or a factor in the *de facto* discrimination against women. The draft AEOWM establishes an institutional mechanism for equal opportunities, which would also monitor gender equality in matters of social security.

REFERENCES

Bibliography

Bulgarian Gender Research Foundation (1999) "The Impact of Privatisation on Women during the Economic Transition in Bulgaria." BGRF Report.

European Commission (2001) *Regular Report on Bulgaria's Progress Towards Accession.* Brussels: European Commission.

European Community (1992) *Women in the European Community.* Brussels, Luxembourg: The Statistical Office of the EC.

Fotev, Georgiy (ed.) (2001) *Bulgarian Rural Women Today.* Sofia: LIK Publishers.

International Labour Organisation (2001) *World Employment Report 2001.* Geneva: ILO.

Kirova, Krassimira (ed.) (1995) *Women and the family in Bulgaria,* SOFIA, Project BNZ/91 POI.

Ministry of Labour and Social Policy (2001) *Survey of Household Incomes.* Sofia: MLSP and NSI.

National Statistical Institute (1993) *Unemployment in Bulgaria.* Census as of 4 December 1992.

National Statistical Institute (1999) *Employment and Unemployment,* 3/1999. Sofia: National Statistical Institute.

National Statistical Institute (2000) *Employment and Unemployment,* 4/2000. Sofia: National Statistical Institute.

National Statistical Institute (2001) *Employment and Unemployment,* Sofia, 3/2001.

Stoyanovska, Antonina (2001). *Jobs, Gender and Small Enterprises in Bulgaria.* Job Creation and Enterprise Department of the ILO, ILO.

UNDP (2001) *Early Warning Report:* March 2001. Sofia: UNDP.

UNICEF (1999) *Women in Transition.* UNICEF MONEE Report.

United Nations (1985) *Women in Economic Activity: A Global Statistical Survey, 1950–2000.* New York: ILO, INTRAW, UN.

List of Legislation

Acts

Act on Protection against the Negative Effect of Chemical Agents, Substances and Products.

Civil Procedural Code.

Code for Obligatory Social Insurance, in force since 1 January 2000, last amended January 2002.

Compulsory Social Security Code.

Constitution of the Republic of Bulgaria.

Draft Act on Equal Opportunities for Women and Men, 2001.

Employment Promotion Act, in force since 1 January 2002.

Family Code.

Higher Education Act.

Labour Code, in force since 30 March 2001, last amended January 2002.

Act on Civil Servants.

Act on the Attorneys-at-Law.

Act Regulating Collective Labour Disputes.

Penal Code.

Public Administration Act.

Public Education Act.

Social Security Code.

The Unemployment Security and Employment Promotion Act, substituted by the new Employment Promotion Act.

Decrees and Ordinances

Decision No.731 of 1999 of the Council of Ministers with List of Bulgarian State Standards.

Ordinance No.322 of 1994 of the Council of Ministers.

Ordinance No.35 of the Council of Ministers of 20 March 2000 on the adoption of a uniform catalogue of administrative positions, and of a Regulation on the Application of the Uniform Catalogue of Administrative Positions.

Ordinance of the Council of Ministers on Reassignment.

Regulation No.0-35 of 1974.

Regulation No.3 of 1987.

Regulation No.11 of 1987 of the Minister of Health.

Regulation No.7 of 1993 of the Ministry of Labour and Social Policy and the Ministry of Health.

Regulation No.41 of 1995.

Regulation No.8 of 1996.

Regulation No.16 of 1999.

Regulation No.25 of 1999.

Regulation on the Social Insurance of Self-insured Persons, in force since 1 January 2000, last amended January 2002.

The Decree on Birth Promotion substituted by the Family Assistance Act, 2002.

International documents ratified by Bulgaria

European Social Charter.

U.N. Convention on the Elimination of All Forms of Discrimination Against Women.

International Convention on Economic, Social and Cultural Rights.

International Covenant on Civil and Political Rights (ICCPR).

ILO Convention 45 on Underground Work/Women (1935).

ILO Convention 81 on Labour Inspection (1947).

ILO Convention 100 on Equal Remuneration (1951).

ILO Convention 111 on Discrimination (Employment and Occupation) (1958).

ILO Convention 127 on Maximum Weight (1967).

ILO Convention 177 on Home Work (1996); not ratified by Bulgaria.

ILO Convention 183 on Maternity Protection (2000).

ILO Recommendation 182 on Part-Time Work (1994).

Equal Opportunities for Women and Men in the Czech Republic

Table of contents

Executive summary 127

Country report: Introduction 133

1. The principle of equal pay for work of equal value 137
    1.1 National legal framework: General provisions 137
    1.2 Legal foundations and institutional structures 138
    1.3 Job classification 139
    1.4 Available legal procedures 139
    1.5 Means of informing employees of their rights 140
    1.6 Out of court alternatives 141
    1.7 Role of trade unions 141
    1.8 Women's factual situation 142

2. Equal treatment for women and men as regards access to employment, vocational training and promotion, and working conditions 144
    2.1 National legal framework: General provisions 144
    2.2 The concept of discrimination on grounds of sex: Definition and legal sanctions 144
    2.3 Access to employment, vocational training and promotion 145
    2.4 Protective measures for women in the labour market 146
    2.5 Prohibition of dismissal 146
    2.6 Women's and men's jobs 147
    2.7 Legal status of sexual harassment 147

3. Protection of pregnant women from the inherent risk of certain activities and related employment rights 148
    3.1 Legal and conceptual framework 148
    3.2 Risk assessment and employers' obligations 149
    3.3 Case law 149

		3.4	Night work 149

3.4	Night work	149
3.5	Maternity leave	150
3.6	Prohibition of dismissal and employment rights	151

4. The burden of proof in cases of discrimination based on sex 152

    4.1 Legal and conceptual framework concerning indirect discrimination 152

    4.2 The burden of proof and rules of evidence 152

5. Non-discrimination against part-time workers 155

    5.1 National legal framework and employment conditions concerning part-time workers 155

6. The principle of equal treatment for self-employed workers and their assisting spouses 158

    6.1 National legal framework: General provisions 158

    6.2 Social rights of spouses 159

    6.3 Contributory social security system for self employed workers 160

    6.4 Related research and statistics 160

    6.5 Legal means of redress 162

7. The framework on parental leave 164

    7.1 National legal framework: General provisions 164

    7.2 Social security during parental leave 165

    7.3 Parental leave and equal opportunities policy 166

    7.4 Research on sharing family and professional responsibilities 167

8. The principle of equal treatment in occupational social security schemes 168

    8.1 National legal framework: General provisions 168

    8.2 Legal means of redress 172

    8.3 Implementation of the principle of equal treatment 172

Executive summary for the Czech Republic

INTRODUCTION

Czech legislation is not yet fully harmonised in the field of equal opportunities for women and men, but important steps have been taken towards this end, and in recent decades a broad range of secondary EU legal acts connected with equal opportunities and equal treatment for men and women has been passed.

Although discrimination on grounds of sex is prohibited and efforts have been made to reduce the phenomenon, legislators did not define the concept of discrimination itself, a fact that may preclude effective identification and redress in certain cases.

There is relatively low public awareness in the Czech Republic on equal opportunities for women and men, as well as other gender issues and their enforcement. Despite a general acknowledgement that inequalities do exist, there is little understanding of the need to reinforce the specific protection of rights based on gender. This attitude has endured since the communist era, and is changing only gradually.

One particular area in which traditional stereotypes are manifested is the reconciliation of work and family responsibilities, where dicta such as 'the man at work, the woman at home' and 'children belong to their mother, the father works and makes money' are common. Approximately one sixth of the population adheres fully to the conventional image of a male breadwinner in the family, and roughly every fourth man considers himself to be the family's real breadwinner.[1] Such views are nurtured by other factors such as a lack of part-time work options, insufficient childcare provisions, costly domestic services and prejudices that are taught and learned from an early age.

While the Czech government has made significant efforts with regard to gender mainstreaming,[2] the *de facto* implementation of equal opportunities in the Czech Republic will depend largely on the extent to which the government also fulfils its commitment to raising public awareness on equal opportunities for women and men and gender equality more broadly, and improving the quality of legal protection and institutional mechanisms to facilitate the exercise of individual rights concerning gender equality.

---

[1] Hana Maríková (1999).

[2] For example through the creation of the Department for the Equality of Men and Women, the Section for Equal Opportunities for Men and Women under the Committee of the Government for Human Rights, and a subcommittee of the Deputies' Committee for Social Affairs and Healthcare.

Summary of key points

Defining principles

The January 2001 amendments to the Labour Code introduced significant changes based on Directive 75/117/EEC, and employers are now obliged to secure equal treatment for all employees concerning their working conditions, including remuneration for work and other financial rewards, professional training and the possibility to achieve a professional or other career. "Any discrimination based on race, colour, sex, sexual orientation, language, belief or religion, [...], health status, age, marital or family status or obligations towards the family is prohibited. Conduct by an employer that causes discrimination in its consequences only is also prohibited." The Act on Wages, Work Emergency Compensation and on Average Remuneration provides for the principle of equal pay for equal work or work of equal value. The concept of discrimination based on sex is not explicitly defined in the legislation. Indirect discrimination is not explicitly defined either, but could be deduced by analogy from provisions in the Labour Code. As of 1 January 2001, sexual harassment is defined in Czech legislation under Section 7(2) of the Labour Code.

Protective measures

Employers are obliged under the Labour Code to secure the safety and health protection of employees at work with regard to the risk of possible threat to their life and health. This is a general provision and applies to all employees, including pregnant, breastfeeding women and women up to nine months after giving birth. Employers are also obliged to inform pregnant and breastfeeding women and mothers up to nine months after giving birth of the risks and their possible impact on pregnancy or breastfeeding.

If a pregnant woman or woman caring for a child younger than 15 asks for a shorter work time or other modification of the set weekly work time, the employer is obliged to satisfy her request. Pregnant women and women caring for a child under the age of one cannot be employed in overtime work. Night work was generally forbidden for women until May 1994, with an absolute ban for pregnant women and women caring for a child under the age of one. The amendment of the Labour Code[3] introduced a new concept of night work of women in line with ILO Convention No.171 on Night Work.

---

[3] Act No.74 of 1994, amending the Labour Code, published in the Collection of Laws.

Burden of proof

The general legal principle stipulates that the burden of proof lies with the plaintiff; however, the newly amended Code on Civil Procedure shifted the burden of proof in the cases of discrimination based on sex in employment matters. As a result, the defendant (employer) must prove that there was no breach of the principle of equal treatment of women and men. Unless otherwise ascertained in the course of proceedings, the court shall consider direct or indirect discrimination based on sex as proved.

Part-time workers

Czech legislation does not explicitly define the concept of 'part-time work', but the Labour Code authorises an employer to negotiate shorter working hours than normal (40 hours per week) with the employee in the employment contract. Part-time work is not governed by any special legal or contractual regulations, and the employment conditions do not differ from those of full-time work. With respect to the social security system, the difference between full-time and part-time work lies in the amount of the guaranteed entitlement (which is proportional to the income of the particular employee). Research shows that part-time employment is not often offered in the Czech Republic and is primarily taken up by women over 50 years of age, who see it as an opportunity to avoid unemployment prior to retirement, or to make some extra money after they retire. In 1998, only 2.6 percent of men and 9.6 percent of women worked part-time in the Czech Republic, and the percentage has been falling over the last few years.

Self-employed workers

The term 'self-employed person' is defined in the Commercial Code, but there are only general provisions in Czech legislation referring to the social rights of the assisting spouses of self-employed workers. There is no independent system of social security for self-employed workers: self-employed workers, and their assisting spouses, participate in the general social security system on the basis of registration.

Parental leave

Parental leave is granted to a worker (male or female) upon request, and may be granted to the mother from the end of maternity leave and to the father from the birth of a child. Parental leave can only be taken until the child reaches the age of three. The

Labour Code also stipulates maternity and parental leave in the case of an adopted child: maternity leave is granted up to eight months of the age of a child at maximum, and parental leave is granted until the child reaches the age of three. In the Czech Republic, maternity leave is an entitlement, and not an obligation. An employer is not allowed to dismiss a pregnant worker, worker on maternity leave or worker (female or male) caring for a child up to the age of three except in legally prescribed situations.

Social security schemes

Czech legislative provisions defining and regulating social security schemes have implemented only Directive 79/7/EEC, meaning that only statutory social security schemes exist in the Czech Republic. There is no direct discrimination on the basis of sex contained in the laws regulating social security. The legislation does not distinguish between male or female participants of the scheme concerning either access to the schemes or calculation of contributions. However, one example of significant discrimination is the lower amount of pensions payments that women receive compared with men. The retirement age has been rising since 1996, so that as of 1 January 2007 it will be 62 years of age for men and 57 to 61 years of age for women, depending on the number of children she has. The planned increase will hit the female population the hardest, since they will work four years longer than at present.

RECOMMENDATIONS RELATED TO EACH SPECIFIC DIRECTIVE

Council Directive 75/117/EEC of 10 February 1975 *on the approximation of laws of the Member States relating to the implementation of the principle of equal pay for women and men*

- Although the legislative measures to support the principle of equal pay for women and men are satisfactory in principle, it is necessary to improve the mechanisms for ensuring they are observed in practice.

- Women should be encouraged to bring cases to court regarding the violation of the principle of equal pay.

- National information campaigns should be carried out to change the overall attitude of Czech society towards the equality of women and men and to change existing stereotypes that prescribe men as breadwinners, thereby deserving of higher salaries than women.

- Employers should be trained on the relevant labour law provisions and on how to ensure their proper application.

- Employees should be informed of their rights in writing and offered assistance in the protection and promotion of those rights.

- Related training programmes should be organised for the judiciary and lawyers on how to handle such cases, encouraging the latter to bring such cases to court and to develop expertise in this field.

Council Directive 76/207/EEC of 9 February 1976 *on the implementation of the principle of equal treatment for men and women as regards access to employment, vocational training and promotion, and working conditions*

- The concept of 'discrimination', both direct and indirect, should be legally defined.

- Legal provisions on sexual harassment should be made known to employees.

- Awareness-raising activities should be carried out in the workplace and in society in general on gender relations and discrimination based on sex, including sexual harassment.

Council Directive 92/85/EEC of 19 October 1992 *on the introduction of measures to encourage improvements in the safety and health at work of pregnant workers and workers who have recently given birth or are breastfeeding*

- The legal means of safeguarding a woman's right to employment in case she has to care for children should be improved either by amending the existing legislation, or, preferably, by introducing the Act on Equal Opportunities for Women and Men.

- Media campaigns and NGOs should play a more significant role in awareness raising in this area, and public money should be made available for this purpose.

- Provisions should be adopted to include compulsory maternity leave of at least two weeks allocated before and/or after confinement in accordance with Article 8 of the Directive.

- Provisions should be adopted to ensure that pregnant workers within the meaning of Article 2(a) of the Directive are entitled to time off, without loss of pay, in order to attend antenatal examinations, if such examinations must take place during working hours.

Council Directive 97/80/EC of 15 December 1997 *on the burden of proof in cases of discrimination based on sex*

- Specialised training should be made available for judges and lawyers during the law school and afterwards, based on European Court of Justice case-law.

- Nationwide information campaigns should be developed to encourage women and NGOs to bring cases on discrimination to the courts.

Council Directive 97/81/EC of 15 December 1997 *concerning the framework agreement on part-time work concluded by UNICE, CEEP and the ETUC*

- The National Action Plan on equality should be implemented as soon as possible, introducing the means to enable part-time jobs and other flexible arrangements to be explicitly included in the Labour Code.

- It is necessary to create an environment in which social partners could negotiate the modification of work organisation and working arrangements, find solutions that would respond to their needs and enable the companies to face market pressures, fill vacancies by offering part-time jobs and eliminate the disadvantage of those employees who would prefer to work part-time.

- Part-time work should be encouraged, not only for women but also for men, as a means of redistributing the workload within families, which currently falls primarily on women.

Council Directive 86/613/EEC of 11 December 1986 *on the application of the principle of equal treatment between men and women engaged in an activity, including agriculture, in a self-employed capacity, and on the protection of self-employed women during pregnancy and motherhood*

- The Act on Equal Opportunities should be passed.

- The government, with the assistance and expertise of NGOs and professional associations of self-employed women, should map the situation of self-employed female workers.

- Campaigns on equal opportunities for women and men should also focus on equal opportunities and treatment for self-employed women and the spouses of self-employed workers (currently only women employees are considered).

Council Directive 96/34/EC of 3 June 1996 *on the framework agreement on parental leave concluded by UNICE, CEEP, and the ETUC*

- The Labour Code should be amended to include a new article requiring an employer to grant an employee modified working hours upon request in order to care for a child aged up to 15 years.

- The Government and the Parliament should legislate for an increase in women's wages, as a crucial factor in facilitating the taking of parental leave in practice.

- The Ministry of Labour and Social Affairs, with the assistance of NGOs and media, should develop strategies to encourage men to take parental leave.

Council Directive 96/97/EC of 20 December 1996 *amending Directive 86/378/EEC on the implementation of the principle of equal treatment for men and women in occupational social security schemes*

- The Act on Occupational Pension Schemes should be passed in order to allow employees to save for their pensions, with the contribution of their employer.

- The discriminatory calculation of pensions, whereby women receive less than men, should be reconsidered.

- The system of health insurance should be reformed as the current system is extremely complicated and preserves an excessive dependence upon and linkage of the system to the state.

Country report: Czech Republic

INTRODUCTION

After change of the political system in November 1989, the Czech Republic began building a democratic system of government and a liberal market economy. Czech society experienced a fast and intensive change of opinions, views and approaches to life and individuality. At the same time, human rights became more publicly discussed and visible, including women's rights and their equal opportunities with men.

The Convention on the Elimination of All Forms of Discrimination against Women was approved by the Czech Parliament and incorporated into domestic law in 1987. The Czech Government responded to the conclusions of the Fourth World Conference on Women held in Beijing in 1995, among other things, by joining the international trend towards systematic policy development regarding equal opportunities for women and men at the beginning of 1998.

The screening of Czech legislation began on 3 April 1998. As of 25 June 2002, the Czech Republic had closed 25 out of 31 chapters, including Chapter 13 on "Employment and social policy". A whole range of secondary legal acts connected to equal opportunities and the equal treatment of men and women was passed in the last decade, and the Accession Agreement[4] obliges the Czech Republic to implement these instruments within domestic legislation. The Minister of Labour and Social Affairs was entrusted by a Governmental Resolution[5] with coordinating action on equal opportunities and developing a national action plan, and all other government ministers were obliged to cooperate with women's rights NGOs.

The process of harmonisation in this area began with the approval of the amendments to the Act on Employment and the Labour Code, and it is clear that the transposition of the *acquis communautaire* will strengthen the level of legal guarantees in the field of human rights, and especially those developing equal opportunities for women and men. Although Czech legislation is not yet fully harmonised in the field of equal opportunities of women and men, some legal institutes and the level of the protection in the Czech Republic are more generous than in some EU member states.

---

[4] Association Agreement between the European Communities and the Czech Republic, signed on 4 October 1993 in Brussels.

[5] Governmental Resolution No.236 of 1998 on the Governmental Programme of Actions and Priorities in Promotion of Equal Opportunities for Men and Women, from 8 April 1998, published in the Collection of Laws.

The Government's Programme of Action and Priorities in the Promotion of Equal Opportunities for Men and Women was approved in April 1998 and identifies seven major areas where difficulties enforcing gender equality persist: in governmental policy; with regard to legal guarantees of gender equality and awareness of such legal provisions; guarantees of equal opportunities for women and men in the economic sphere; the equal social status of women and men caring for children and family members in need; women's reproductive function and biological differences; in the prevention of violence against women; and in monitoring and evaluating equal opportunities for women and men in practice. The National Action Plan is reviewed every year and adjustments are made where necessary to reflect the social conditions.[6]

Three institutions for implementing the equality of women and men were created at the beginning of 1998: first, the Department for the Equality of Men and Women opened, which ensured the establishment of an inter-sector commission for the equal opportunities of men and women. This Department produced the "Priorities and Procedures of the Government When Enforcing the Equality of Men and Women," a proposal for the governmental resolution.

Second, according to the Statute of the Committee of the Government of the Czech Republic for Human Rights, one of the eight departments is the Section for Equal Opportunities of Men and Women, the second most important institution in this field which is authorised to monitor and evaluate the observance of human rights, and in particular the fulfilment of international obligations.

The third institution is a subcommittee of the Deputies' Committee for Social Affairs and Healthcare, which was established at the initiative of the female deputies. This committee deals with the issues of family and equal opportunities.[7]

The Czech Government is currently focused on the following:

- increasing public awareness regarding the substance and content of the principle of equal status of women and men, creating equal opportunities for women and men, and the exercise of rights related to gender equality between women and men;
- improving the quality of legal protection of the equal status of women and men and the quality of the institutional mechanisms facilitating the exercise of individual rights concerning gender equality;
- mainstreaming the principle of equality into all fields of practical policy.

---

[6] Last update: Governmental Decree No.456 of 9 May 2001.
[7] Čermáková *et al.* (2000).

There is relatively low public awareness of the substance and content of the principle of equal status of women and men and equal opportunities for women and men, as well as rights related to gender issues and their enforcement. Despite a general acknowledgement that inequalities exist, there is little understanding of the need to reinforce the specific protection of rights based on gender. This attitude has endured since the communist rule, and is changing only gradually.

The quality of institutional mechanisms through which individual rights to equality are exercised needs to be improved, since the current system of protection through the courts does not guarantee efficient protection of relevant rights, mainly because of time factors and the procedural complexity of court proceedings, and the high costs are associated with this procedure. There is no option to settle out of court, for example through arbitration with the participation of trade unions or state control bodies, although a solution to this problem is expected in 2003.

Mainstreaming is another means for improving the status of women that has not been fully exploited, largely because of the relatively low understanding among policy-making bodies and civil servants of the substance of the principles of equal opportunities and equal treatment. Social partners lack professional representation that would see the relevant principles of equality for women enforced in programme documentation and collective bargaining agreements. Another issue is the ongoing reform of local government. Despite these problems, however, mainstreaming was built into the employment policy framework based on EU recommendations. This framework at least acknowledges mainstreaming as a natural and logical measure for the development of gender equality.[8]

---

[8] *National Report on the Fulfilment of the Beijing Platform for Action,* Ministry of Labour and Social Affairs of the Czech Republic, 3 January 2002.

1. THE PRINCIPLE OF EQUAL PAY FOR WORK OF EQUAL VALUE

Council Directive 75/117/EEC of 10 February 1975 *on the approximation of the laws of the Member States relating to the application of the principle of equal pay for men and women*

1.1 National legal framework concerning the principle of equal pay for work of equal value: General provisions

The Czech legal order does not contain any provisions contrary to the principle of equal pay for women and men, and contracts that are contrary to the law shall be null and void *ab initio*.

The Constitution
The principal of equal pay for women and men is not a direct part of the Constitution in the Czech Republic. The Charter of Basic Rights and Freedoms, which is an integral part of the constitutional order, only sets forth a very general principle in Article 28.

Amendment to the Labour Code No.155 of 2000
The Amendment to the Labour Code entered into force on 1 January 2001 and introduced significant changes based on Directive 75/117/EEC, obliging employers to secure equal treatment for all employees concerning their working conditions, including remuneration for work and other financial rewards, professional training, etc. Article 1(4) prohibits any discrimination against employees based on race, colour, sex, sexual orientation, language, belief or religion, health status, age, marital or family status or obligations towards the family, including conduct by an employer that causes discrimination in its consequences only.

Act on Wages[9]
Article 4(a) of Act on Wages stipulates the principle of equal pay for equal work or work of equal value.

---

[9] Act No.1 of 1992 on Wages, Work Emergency Compensation and Average Remuneration, and the Act No.143 of 1992 on Salaries and Work Emergency Compensation in Organisations Financed by the State Budget, and Other Organisations and Bodies.

Relevant international provisions

In accordance with Article 10 of the Constitution, the following relevant international instruments are a part of the Czech legal order:

- The UN Convention on the Elimination of All Forms of Discrimination against Women;

- ILO Convention No.100 of 1951 on Equal Remuneration for Men and Women Workers for Work of Equal Value;

- ILO Convention No.111 of 1958 on Discrimination (Employment and Occupation);

- The International Convention on Economic, Social and Cultural Rights.

1.2 Implementation of the principle of equal pay for work of equal value: Legal foundations and institutional structures

The Labour Code regulates relations between employees and employers irrespective of the sector (i.e. both public and private). The principle of equal pay is governed in the private sector by Article 4(a) of the Act on Wages, while the Act on Salaries determines remuneration in the public sector. It does not explicitly provide for equal pay for women and men, but Article 25(1) states that in all other issues not regulated by this law, the Labour Code shall be binding.

The institutional framework enforcing the principle of equal pay for women and men is led by the Ministry of Labour and Social Affairs and at the local level by the District Labour Offices, which monitor the observance of generally binding labour regulations by individual employers, including those on equal pay. The Labour Office is authorised, as is the Ministry of Labour and Social Affairs, to impose a fine on an employer of up to 250,000 CZK (approximately €8,289) in case of a violation of a labour regulation, and up to 1 million CZK (approximately €33,157) in case of a repeated violation.

Individual conflicts arising from labour relationships shall be considered by the courts. According to Article 4 of the Constitution, rights and freedoms shall be protected by the courts and the justifiable protection of the rights and legitimate interests of all parties in court proceedings is secured through procedural provisions, which are applied equally to women and men and guarantee the constitutional principle of independence of the judiciary at the same time. The Charter of Basic Rights and Freedoms states in Article

36(1) that "Everyone can demand his rights through a set procedure at an independent and impartial court and in defined cases at another body."

The monitoring of respect for the principle of the equality falls under the general supervision of respecting the labour legislation as a whole. If an infringement of this principle is discovered, the Labour Office is obliged to impose a fine according to the Act No.9 of 1991 on the Employment and Jurisdiction of the State Bodies of the Czech Republic in the Field of Employment.

1.3 Job classification

Czech legislation includes a job classification system for both public and private sectors, and the Ministry of Labour and Social Affairs has established a regulation stating the means of assessing the value of jobs, including tools designed to ensure the implementation of the principle of equal remuneration for equal work and for work of equal value.

Article 4 of the Act on Wages provides for minimum salary tariffs and the categorisation of employees into salary groups in accordance with the respective requirements for each salary group. The respective government orders define catalogues of jobs according to which employees are categorised into salary groups. For the purpose of distinction between the salary groups, the following criteria are used: complexity, responsibility and physical and/or mental efforts needed for the individual job. An analytical method of evaluating the work has been proposed to classify jobs into the salary groups in the Act on State Service (currently under preparation); the same method is enforced in the private sector.

The selection and definition of individual criteria are based on recommendations contained in international conventions signed and ratified by the Czech Republic, as well as on the experience derived from past assessments of jobs in connection with the determination of salary groups.

1.4 Available legal procedures in cases involving the violation of the principle of equal pay for work of equal value

In accordance with the Constitution, every citizen of the Czech Republic has the right to legal protection. The Charter of Basic Rights and Freedoms further provides that "Everyone has the right to enforce his rights through set procedures at an independent and impartial court and in prescribed cases at another body."

There are no special courts to decide disputes arising from an employment relationship; such disputes are subject to ordinary civil proceedings. Consequently, there are no special protective measures for workers who initiate court proceedings against an employer apart from Section 7(3) of the Labour Code. The measures that enable employees to pursue a claim of discrimination before a court are set forth in Section 7(3) and (4) of the Labour Code, which were introduced by the latest amendments, thus harmonising the Czech Labour Code with the *acquis communautaire*.

In theory, the possibility of filing a petition in litigation connected to an employment relationship and access to justice are not at all complicated. However, the lack of concrete provisions implementing the principle of equal pay makes the legal motivation and proof of facts very complicated.

1.5 Means of informing employees of their right to equal pay for work of equal value

The Ministry of Labour and Social Affairs did not prepare an adequate campaign to inform employees about the changes and new possibilities of enforcing the principle of equality following the amendments to the Labour Code. As a result, public awareness on this issue is quite low.

Employees should be informed of the relevant legal provisions, enforcement measures and availability of grievances and claims through the trade unions. However, many firms do not have trade unions, and if they do exist, not many employees are members. Other places from which to obtain the relevant information include the District Labour Offices or the Ministry of Labour and Social Affairs itself.

According to the report of the Ministry of Labour and Social Affairs, the Labour Offices do take part in the process of making information on equal opportunities for women and men public, especially through the local media, regular press conferences and seminars.

Some public awareness-raising activities are carried out by NGOs, and women's NGOs organise seminars, workshops and other educational activities about the new legislation. The Czech Women's Union runs a project called "Towards Equal Opportunities," whose aim is to empower women and contribute to the elimination of discrimination against women in the labour market.

1.6 Out of court alternatives

According to Article 9 of the Act on Employment and Jurisdiction of the State Bodies of the Czech Republic, the District Labour Offices can impose a fine on employers of up to 250,000 CZK (approximately €82.89) for violating an obligation, and up to one million CZK (approximately €33,157) in case of a repeated violation.

Apart from the possibility of filing a petition with the court or informing the Labour Office, the employee can file an action with the Ombudsperson in cases where the principle of equal pay was violated by the state or local administration authority. This possibility does not concern disputes between employees and employers. The institute and function of the Ombudsperson, as the public protector of rights, is relatively new in the Czech Republic; the first one was only assigned in November 2000. The Ombudsperson acts only at the initiative of the individual or legal personality, and everyone has the right to address the Ombudsperson with a complaint. If the Ombudsperson discovers a violation or other wrong, the administrative office is called upon to comment on his findings within 30 days. The Ombudsperson can propose a solution, but has no power to enforce it.

1.7 Role of trade unions

In accordance with Section 18/B(2) of the Labour Code, trade unions have the right to be informed in particular with regard to the development of wages, the average wage and its components, including the articulation of job classifications, etc. According to Section 22 of the Labour Code, trade unions should monitor observance of the Labour Code and other labour regulations, including the regulation of wages. By analogy, trade unions should also monitor the observance of the principle of equal pay for women and men. Trade unions have the right to propose improvements in working conditions; to insist that employers or their control bodies order the elimination of any discovered defects; to require employers or their control bodies to impose relevant measures against the managers violating the labour regulations; and to demand reports from employees on what measures were accepted in order to eliminate the existing defects.

Under Section 26 of the Code on Civil Procedure, trade unions can represent their members in court, excluding complaints in commercial cases. If the trade union intervenes, a delegate of the trade union shall represent the plaintiff in court. However, trade unions cannot initiate proceedings in equality matters themselves.

The Act on Collective Mediation establishes in Article 4(2) that those parts of a collective agreement that are contrary to the law shall be invalid. Collective agreements in the Czech Republic do not stipulate the principle of equal pay and there are no legal means to enforce such a regulation in collective agreements.

1.8 Women's factual situation regarding the principle of equal pay for work of equal value

Although the principle of equal pay of women and men is clearly provided for in Czech legislation, it is not reflected in practice, and the preferential treatment of men in terms of income is among the basic gender differences that exist in the labour market. Given the level to which wage differentiation has been investigated, it is not possible to determine to what extent discrimination against women is to blame for the difference in average salaries and to what extent it may be explained by the different professional and sector structures of female and male labour forces. Most authors believe it is likely that discrimination exists, but that it is difficult to prove.[10]

The Government Programme of Actions and Priorities in Promotion of Equal Opportunities for Men and Women entrusted the Minister of Labour and Social Affairs and the President of the Czech Statistical Office with "taking measures to regularly issue publications containing gender specific statistical data, including on remuneration." The publication *Women and Men in Figures*[11] is the first step in this process, and is issued annually. Other relevant research is carried out by the Sociological Institute of the Czech Academy of Sciences and by the Research Institute of Labour and Social Affairs, which is connected to the respective Ministry.

According to surveys carried out by the Czech Statistical Office, women earn approximately 73.2 percent of men's income (the latest data in 1999). This shows a four percent decrease compared with 1996.

The labour market in the Czech Republic is segregated into female and male professions, with men dominating in the categories of 'management' and 'craft,' while women predominate among 'specialised employees' and in the category of 'technical employees'. The income structure is further differentiated by education, and women with higher education earn considerably greater salaries. For example, the salary of a female university graduate with scientific education is 173 percent of women's average wage and 299 percent of the average wage of women with incomplete elementary education. When compared with men's salaries, however, women earn comparatively less in all educational categories: women with vocational training, women without

---

[10] Institute of Sociology (2000).
[11] The Czech Statistical Office (2000).

education, and, surprisingly, even female university graduates, who on average receive 68 percent of the salary of male university graduates.

Although legislation on the principle of equal pay for women and men does not differentiate between the public and private sectors in the Czech Republic, differences certainly exist in the application of the law. According to the survey carried out by Stepan Jurajda, entitled "Wage differences and segregation of men and women in the Czech Republic,"[12] "the segregation of women to lower wage groups, firms and work groups is significant in the Czech Republic and creates approximately one third of the entire wage differences between the sexes. Large differences still exist between men and women in the same workplace and such differences are […] twice as high in the business sphere. As a result of discrimination, women lose nearly one fifth of their wage."

---

[12] Jurajda (2000).

2. EQUAL TREATMENT FOR WOMEN AND MEN AS REGARDS ACCESS TO EMPLOYMENT, VOCATIONAL TRAINING AND PROMOTION, AND WORKING CONDITIONS

Council Directive 76/207/EEC of 9 February 1976 *on the implementation of the principle of equal treatment for men and women as regards access to employment, vocational training and promotion, and working conditions*

2.1 National legal framework concerning the principle of equal treatment for women and men: General provisions

Article 1 of the Charter of Basic Rights and Freedoms provides that persons are free and equal in their dignity and rights, and that basic rights and freedoms are inherent, inalienable, unlimited and irrevocable, irrespective of sex, social origin, nationality, religion, political opinions, etc. Article 3 prohibits discrimination.

The amended Labour Code introduces special provisions on the principle of equal treatment for women and men in Sections 1(3) and (4).[13] The Act on Employment also contains provisions on the equal treatment of women and men and grants each person the right to employment regardless of sex, social origin, marital and family status and family duties, etc. It also prohibits employment proposals that violate the principle of equal treatment of women and men.

2.2 The concept of discrimination on grounds of sex: Definition and legal sanctions

The concept of sex-based discrimination is not explicitly defined in the legislation. In the process of harmonising Czech legislation with EU law, the prohibition of discrimination

---

[13] "(4) Discrimination of employees based on race, colour, sex, sexual orientation, language, belief and religion, political or other opinion, membership or activity in political parties or movements, trade unions or other associations, nationality, ethnic or social origin, property, health, age, marital and family status or family duties is prohibited in employment. Employers are prohibited to take any actions that are discriminatory directly or in their consequences. Conduct that would otherwise be considered discriminatory but represents an exception to the above stated rule is specified in the Labour Code and other laws. Conduct that reflects the special nature of work performed by an employee and is essential for performing such work shall not be considered discriminatory."

on the basis of sex and efforts to reduce the phenomenon were introduced. However, because legislators did not define the concept itself, doubts have arisen as to whether the newly introduced concept can be effectively prohibited. The general concept of discrimination is defined in the Labour Code and the Act on Employment.

An employer's behaviour which, though legally neutral, is in fact discriminatory towards an employee in its consequences is considered indirect discrimination. Behaviour that is based on the specific nature of work essential for the performance of a job, or taking into account safety regulations and health protection at work, is not considered discriminatory.

Cases of sex-based discrimination are subject to the general legal provisions and penalties. Such cases are arbitrated by the courts in accordance with Section 207 of the Labour Code, but it is not yet possible to ascertain whether such cases received judicial protection because the appropriate items (types of discrimination) were not entered into the statistical classification list of disputes or into the statistical penal register of the Ministry of Justice until 1999.

There have only been very few cases of discrimination handled by the courts so far. The first ever case in the Czech Republic occurred in 1995, when the manager of a branch of Komercní bank in Kroměříž was accused of verbally sexually abusing his subordinate. His behaviour was qualified as a violation of Article 10(1) of the Charter of Basic Rights and Freedoms,[14] but the court did not find enough evidence.

2.3 National legal framework concerning the principle of equal treatment as regards access to employment, vocational training and promotion, and working conditions

Czech legislation does not include any discriminatory provisions as regards access to employment, vocational training and promotion, and working conditions. The right to free access to employment and equal working conditions is guaranteed in the Charter of Basic Rights and Freedoms and applies both to public and private sectors.

Apart from the general principle of non-discrimination, Section 1(2) of the Act on Employment explicitly introduces a ban on discriminatory employment offers. This provision enables everyone to enforce his/her right to employment without discrimination in court or through the relevant Labour Office.

---

[14] "Everyone has the right to the preservation of his human dignity, personal credit, reputation and good name."

District Safety and Health Protection bodies (managed by the Czech Office of Safety and Protection of Health at Work) are entrusted with observing the regulations on safety and protection of health at work and the working conditions of employees. In case of a violation, they can impose a fine on the employer of up to 500,000 CZK (approximately €16,564), and in exceptional cases of up to one million CZK (approximately €33,129). Section 1(4) of the Labour Code provides for 'extenuating circumstances' in which discrimination would not occur. Although the law guarantees a person's right to employment, it is important to note that employers have the right to choose the required number and structure of employees.

2.4 Protective measures with regard to women's participation in the labour market

Women are afforded greater protection in labour relations because of their role as mothers, as stipulated in Article 32(2) of the Charter of Basic Rights and Freedoms. The Labour Code regulates working conditions for women according to biological factors (i.e. their physiological differences) and social factors (i.e. their role as mothers).

The Labour Code prohibits women from *inter alia* underground mining work, and labour that is physically excessive or detrimental. The Ministry of Health provides a list of work and workplaces forbidden to breastfeeding women, pregnant women and mothers with a child under nine months of age. In accordance with the ordinance, such women cannot perform work that is hard and strenuous, work connected with transferring loads, work performed in hard positions, etc.

2.5 Prohibition of dismissal

According to Section 7(3) of the Labour Code, employers may not harm or handicap in any way an employee who seeks to legally enforce his/her rights in an employment relationship. Protection against dismissal is further incorporated in Section 44 of the Labour Code, stating that the employer can only give notice to an employee in legally defined cases.[15]

---

[15] For example, liquidation, redundancy, serious breach of discipline, etc.

2.6 Women's and men's jobs

There are no legal measures in the Czech Republic to prevent the classification of jobs as specifically for men or women, and such divisions do exist in practice. The basic problems related to such classification are the stereotyped, fixed ideas on what women and men are capable of doing. The consequences of this are most visible in the labour market, where women are not given equal opportunities from the beginning, and are considered unable to compete with men because of their possible maternity and household obligations. The same stereotypes are applied if women enter the labour market: they are not treated similarly to men, have lower salaries, fewer possibilities for promotion, etc. All of these factors ensure the 'glass ceiling' phenomenon.

The Ministry of Education, Youth and Physical Education refers to the ordinance mentioned above in establishing the academic disciplines (more than 100) forbidden to girls. The Government Programme of Actions and Priorities in the Promotion of Equal Opportunities for Men and Women proposed the revision of this Ordinance in order to allow girls to study the listed disciplines.

In addition, the Ministry of Interior issued an ordinance regulating certain details of service in the police force. Annex 3 of the ordinance provides a list of activities forbidden to female members of the police, pregnant members of the police and mothers up to the ninth month after giving birth. The forbidden activities are similar to those mentioned in the Ordinance of the Ministry of Health.

Article 41 of the Act on Servicemen provides that pregnant soldiers cannot be appointed to activities that threaten pregnancy; they can only be appointed night shifts, shifts beyond the basic week shifts and emergency shifts with their consent. A pregnant soldier and soldiers caring for a child up to the age of eight can only be dispatched or sent on a service trip with their consent.

2.7 Legal status of sexual harassment

The concept of sexual harassment has quite a pejorative meaning in Czech society and the opinion that this problem should be resolved by legal means and enforced by the state is not yet pervasive.

As of January 2001, sexual harassment is defined in Section 7(2) of the Labour Code, which provides that: "It is prohibited to abuse the rights and obligations stemming from labour relations to the detriment of the other party, or to humiliate their human dignity. Undesirable behaviour of a sexual nature in the workplace that is unwelcome, undue or offensive, or which could rightly be perceived by the other party in labour relations as a determining factor influencing the performance of rights and obligations stemming from labour relations shall be considered the humiliation of human dignity."

3. Protection of Pregnant Women from the Inherent Risk of Certain Activities and Related Employment Rights

Council Directive 92/85/EEC of 19 October 1992 *on the introduction of measures to encourage improvements in the safety and health at work of pregnant workers and workers who have recently given birth or are breastfeeding*

3.1 Legal and conceptual framework

The concepts of 'pregnant worker', 'worker who has recently given birth' and 'worker who is breastfeeding' are not defined in Czech legislation, although the laws regulating the protection of these workers do refer to them. In order to prove a pregnancy, women must obtain a medical certificate, and there is a legal presumption that women breastfeed their babies until the age of nine months.

3.2 Assessing the risk to the safety or health of a pregnant worker and employer's obligations

According to Section 132(a) of the Labour Code, employers are obliged: to create a safe and non-life threatening working environment; to identify any risks, determine their roots and sources and accept the relevant measures for their elimination; to regularly check the level of security and health protection at work; to evaluate and accept measures to limit risks that cannot be eliminated in order to minimize the threat to employees' safety and health; and to adapt the measures to changing conditions, monitor their effectiveness and observance, and develop the working conditions.

Employers are further obliged to inform pregnant and breastfeeding women and mothers up to nine months after giving birth of the risks and their possible impact on pregnancy or breastfeeding. The employer is obliged to accept measures, including those concerning a decreased risk of mental and physical fatigue connected to the performed work, during the entire period necessary for their protection and health.

Risk factors include physical conditions (such as vibrations and noise); chemical agents (such as carcinogens); biological agents (such as viruses, germs, moulds); and unfavourable microclimatic conditions (such as extreme cold, heat or humidity). Only authorised employees may work under these conditions.

3.3 Cases in which exposure is prohibited for pregnant workers and breastfeeding workers

The list of work forbidden to pregnant and breastfeeding women and women up to nine months after giving birth is established in the Ordinance of the Ministry of Health No.261 of 1997. The Labour Code does not provide any special sanctions for the violation of the provisions on safety at work, and the general rules therefore apply.

If a pregnant or breastfeeding woman, or mother up to ninth months after giving birth performs work that is forbidden by law or which, according to medical reference, threatens the pregnancy, the employer is obliged to temporarily move her to another suitable job with the same remuneration. Employers are obliged to accept a request to be transferred from night work to day work. If the position to which she is transferred to is less well paid, the difference shall be reimbursed to her according to the provisions on health security. Section 154 of the Labour Code establishes a ban on trade routes for pregnant women and women caring for children up to eight years, unless the woman agrees. This provision also applies to single women caring for a child up to 15 years. It is prohibited to terminate an employment relationship with a pregnant worker and worker caring for a child under the age of three except in legally prescribed case.

Pregnant women and women caring for a child under the age of 15 can request a shorter working time or other modification of the set weekly working time, and the employer is obliged to do this. Pregnant women and women caring for a child under the age of one cannot be employed in overtime work. Breastfeeding women are entitled to additional breaks, and employers are obliged to adapt a resting area for them and pregnant women in the workplace.

3.4 Night work

Night work was generally forbidden for women until May 1994 and the ban was absolute for pregnant women and women caring for a child under the age of one. The amendment of the Labour Code introduced a new conception of night work for women in line with ILO Convention No.171 on Night Work.

The legal regulation of a transfer of pregnant workers, breastfeeding workers and workers who have recently given birth to another work, was described above, in Section 3.3. Czech legislation does not provide for the possibility of leave from work or the extension of maternity leave in case such a transfer is not technically feasible.

3.5 Maternity leave

Women are entitled, but not obliged, to take maternity leave in the Czech Republic. The Labour Code provides that maternity leave connected with childbirth may be no less than 14 weeks and may completed or interrupted within six weeks of the birth.

The right to maternity leave is stipulated in the provisions of the Labour Code, and the financial contributions during maternity leave are stipulated by Act No.88 of 1968 on the Extension of Maternity Leave, Benefits in Maternity and Contributions to Children from the Health Security and by the Act on State Social Security. There is no need to stipulate the right to maternity leave in an employment contract; the mandatory content is set forth in Section 29 of the Labour Code.

Pregnant women and women on maternity leave have the right to contributions in maternity, the details of which are established in the Act on the Extension of Maternity Leave, Benefits in Maternity and Contributions on Children from the Health Security and contributions based on the Act on State Social Security. The financial contributions in pregnancy and maternity offered by health security include the compensatory contribution in pregnancy and maternity, and financial assistance in maternity. The compensatory contribution in pregnancy is granted in accordance with Section 153(3) of the Labour Code if a pregnant woman is transferred to other work where she receives less remuneration than previously. The same applies to mothers up to the end of the ninth month after giving birth.

The financial assistance in maternity is granted to a female employee if she participated in the health security for at least 270 days in the last two years prior to giving birth. This contribution is offered during 28 weeks of maternity leave, beginning with the sixth week before the anticipated date of birth. Special assistance in maternity is provided in the case of multiple births or for workers who are unmarried, widowed, divorced or otherwise single even after the period of 28 weeks, for a maximum of 37 weeks.

The Act on the State Social Security further stipulates a one-off birthing benefit and continual parental contribution during maternity/parental leave. The parental contribution is granted to a parent caring for a child of up to four years of age, or up to seven years of age in case the child is handicapped, in accordance with the prescribed conditions.

Antenatal examinations

Czech legislation does not provide for or prohibit time off without loss of pay in order to attend antenatal examinations that must take place during work hours. In general, visits to medical doctors are to be agreed between the employer and the employee in each individual case.

3.6 Prohibition of dismissal and employment rights

An employer may not dismiss a pregnant worker, worker on the maternity leave or a worker (female or male) caring for a child up to the age of three except in situations strictly set forth in Section 155 of the Labour Code. In the event of an unlawful dismissal, there are no special means available for pregnant workers or workers who have recently given birth, but they may enforce their rights according to the general provisions of the Labour Code.

The District Court in Brno upheld a claim of unlawful dismissal in a case involving a woman caring for a child under the age of three. After completing two years of maternity leave, the worker did not return to work, against the appeal of the employer, because she could not put the child in a nursery or in the care of another person. The employer had accused her of seriously violating the work discipline, which is grounds for dismissal in accordance with the Labour Code.[16]

---

[16] Decision of the District Court in Brno, No.31 C 246/75.

4. THE BURDEN OF PROOF IN CASES OF DISCRIMINATION BASED ON SEX

Council Directive 97/80/EC of 15 December 1997 *on the burden of proof in cases of discrimination based on sex*

4.1 Legal and conceptual framework concerning indirect discrimination and specific legal means to implement the principle of equal treatment for women and men

The general legal principle stipulates that the burden of proof lies with the plaintiff. In cases of discrimination based on sex in the employment relationship, it was very difficult for a person alleging discrimination to collect and present the relevant evidence of the discriminatory behaviour. The newly amended Code on Civil Procedure,[17] however, shifted the burden of proof in the cases of discrimination based on sex in employment matters. As a result, the defendant must prove there was no breach of the principle of equal treatment. Unless otherwise ascertained in the course of proceedings, the court shall consider direct or indirect discrimination based on sex as proved. It is an exception in the Czech legal framework for the defendant to present evidence that his/her behaviour was not discriminatory, and this provision is expected to speed up the work of the courts in disputes arising from the violation of the mentioned principle, and to improve the resolution of disputes in cases of discrimination based on sex.

The Czech legal system does not explicitly define the concept of indirect discrimination, but it could be deduced by analogy from Section 1(4) of the Labour Code, described earlier.

4.2 The burden of proof procedure in litigation concerning the violation of the principle of equal treatment for women and men and rules of evidence

The legal means to implement the equal treatment for women and men are incorporated in the Code of Civil Procedural, and Section 133(a) regulates the burden of proof in cases of discrimination based on sex.

---

[17] See Article 133(a) of Act No.99 of 1963, Code on Civil Procedure, as amended, published in the Collection of Laws.

Out of court procedures to implement the principle of equal treatment are provided for in Sections 7(4) to (6) of the Labour Code. In cases of the violation of the principle of treatment the employee has the right to demand that the violation be ceased, its effects are eliminated and he/she be granted adequate compensation. In case the employee's dignity or reputation in the workplace was harmed, and the redress according to the Section (4) was not satisfactory, the employee has the right to financial compensation for non-material damage, the amount of which shall be decided by the court.

In addition, administrative sanctions can be imposed by the District Labour Offices or the Ministry of Labour and Social Affairs.

Trade unions should play a more important role in the out of court settlement of disputes; for example, they should achieve a conciliatory agreement and settle disputes between an employee and employer without initiating civil court proceedings. Unfortunately, in practice the role of the trade unions is not significant.

Prior to the amendment introducing the reversal of the burden of proof, many articles were published in the media by lawyers expressing concern that women would exploit this provision and wrongfully accuse employers of discrimination, blackmail them, etc. Most criticism was aimed at Section 133(a) of the Code of Civil Procedure concerning sexual harassment, and lawyers stated it is inconceivable that the wrongfully accused employer should have to prove his innocence. However, women in the Czech Republic are not aware of the provision or how to use it, and it will probably be some time before the possibilities and progress of the new legislation are realised.

Public institutional and social mechanisms that may contribute to changing gender differences and help publicise the legal regulations for bringing cases involving the violation of the principle of equality to court were activated only recently through the policy of EU accession and the related requirements to harmonise Czech law EU standards. The weak public response and support of such activities is due to differences in the value system and the social climate in the Czech Republic.

Czech NGOs struggle with women's ignorance of their activities and even existence and, aware of this fragmentation, sought to overcome it by creating an umbrella organization in 1998 called the Association for Equal Opportunities. The proclaimed will to create a national female representation is, for the time being, a formality and no resolutions or mechanisms to fulfil such resolutions have been adopted yet.[18]

So far, no cases involving the violation of the principle of equal treatment for women and men as regards employment, vocational training, remuneration, social protection

---

[18] Čermáková *et al.* (2000).

and promotion, and working conditions have been handled by the courts in the Czech Republic.

Other obstacles that women experience in practice include:

- stereotypical ideas about the lower competence of the female labour force as a result of their social roles;
- the double standard for women and men and the fact that the market often uses and exploits the lower price of female labour;
- the fact that forms of discrimination are veiled by social and economic mechanisms.

Surveys also reveal a strong tendency for women to under-estimate themselves, to give up hope for equal treatment and yet to refuse to see their own labour situation as unequal, although the inequality exists according to a number of indices. The willingness of women to work under discriminatory conditions also attests to the shortcomings of trade unions and law enforcement.[19]

---

[19] Čermáková *et al.* (2000).

5. NON-DISCRIMINATION AGAINST PART-TIME WORKERS

Council Directive 97/81/EC *concerning the framework agreement on part-time work concluded by UNICE, CEEP and the ETUC*

5.1 National legal framework concerning part-time workers and employment conditions concerning part-time workers

Czech legislation does not explicitly define the concept of 'part-time work', but Section 86 of the Labour Code authorises the employer to negotiate shorter working hours than normal (40 hours per week) with the employee in the working contract, either for operational reasons or due to the health, etc. of the employee. The shorter working hours need not be allocated to all the working days, and the employee is entitled to remuneration proportional to the shorter working hours. For this reason, women do not want to work shorter hours and try to better arrange and harmonise their work and family duties. Families with two, full incomes are prevalent in the Czech Republic, as in most families this is the only way to guarantee an average standard of living.

In practice, an employee is not entitled to shorter working hours; such an arrangement is made in cases connected to health protection or the need to care for family members. The National Action Plan on Equality for Women and Men[20] requires the Minister of Labour and Social Affairs to facilitate, by amending the existing legislation, the creation of variable working hours enabling employees caring for children and family members to combine employment with family responsibilities.

Since part-time work is not governed by any special legal regulations, the provisions promoting the principle of equality with regard to employment conditions apply to part-time work as well. With regard to the social security system, the difference between full-time and part-time work lies in the amount of the guaranteed entitlement (which is proportional to the income of the particular employee). The Czech National Employment Plan proposes measures to create the preconditions for building a dynamic and flexible labour market, aimed at modernising work organisation and working time arrangements, and encouraging the adaptability of businesses and their employees.

Present forms of work organisation in most enterprises, in particular working time arrangements and the use of working time, do not fully meet either the needs of the

---

[20] Priorities and Procedures of the Government in Promotion of Equal Opportunities for Men and Women.

employer or the employees. In particular, employees have little opportunity to reconcile their professional and family responsibilities. Compared with developed European economies, diversified working arrangements (such as part-time work, workplace sharing, placing the company employees at the disposal of other employers by means of labour contract arrangements) could not develop properly in the absence of conditions for shortening working hours without a significant impact on the employees' standard of living.

The Ministry of Labour and Social Affairs is trying to raise a debate on the issue of part-time work with the social partners. However, the pace of introducing these arrangements into practice will depend on establishing a proper balance between the employers' need to maintain the necessary competitive advantage by means of new work patterns and work organisation, and efforts made by trade unions to safeguard an adequate level of employees' security and protection.

From a legal point of view, there are no differences in the treatment of workers in the public or private sectors. In practice, however, given that part-time work is not often offered to employees in the Czech Republic, there are some differences between the treatment of part-time workers in the public and in private sectors. For example, there is a greater chance of finding part-time work in the public sector than in the private sector due to the competitive nature of the latter.

Transfer to part-time work

There is a possibility to request a transfer from full-time to part-time work if such a position becomes available. There are no statistical data available on this issue, but it can be presumed that only a small number of employees request such a transfer, mainly for economic reasons, for the reasons mentioned above.

There are no legal or administrative measures to facilitate or restrict access to part-time work at all levels of the enterprise, including skilled and managerial positions, or requiring concrete measures to facilitate part-time workers' access to vocational training to enhance career opportunities. The Czech National Employment Plan proposes to provide incentives to employers in order to encourage them to organise training for their employees. This measure may be applied to part-time workers also; but most employers have limited possibilities and motivation to train full-time as well as part-time workers, which reflects the relatively low standards of personnel management in a number of companies. Frequently, employers have only limited time and funds available for upgrading their workers' skills. Therefore, one of the objectives of Czech social policy is to create legal prerequisites for human resource investment. The target groups are especially small and medium-sized enterprises with fewer than 250 workers.

The enactment of tax laws enabling employers to include a certain percentage of money spent on training and retraining their employees in their operational costs has been proposed.[21] Labour Offices would then have the opportunity to provide subsidies to employers for training or retraining their workers in specified situations. An ordinance that would define the conditions for the provision of this type of support and subsequent control of approved training measures is due to be issued soon.

Related research

Statistic data regarding the percentage of women engaged in part-time work is available in two sociological studies: the survey of the Research Centre of Labour and Social Affairs (established in the framework of the Ministry of Labour and Social Affairs) entitled "Equal opportunities for women and men" (2000), and the research of the Sociological Institute of the Academy of Sciences of the Czech Republic entitled *Relations and changes in gender differences in Czech society in the 1990s* (2000).

According to the above research, part-time employment is not often offered in the Czech Republic, and is primarily taken up by women over the age of 50 since they see it as an opportunity to avoid unemployment prior to retirement or to make some extra money after they retire. In 1998, only 2.6 percent of men and 9.6 percent of women worked part-time in the Czech Republic, and the percentage has been falling over the last few years. Some women do prefer part-time work because of childcare duties, which they are primarily responsible for.

Women are not usually hired if they request part-time work, and Czech employers do not realise the potential positive benefits of meeting the family needs of their employees. Approximately one third of employers declare a willingness to modify the working hours of women who care for school-age children and about half of employers are willing to offer the modification of working time to women who care for children of pre-school age.

---

[21] Act No.586 of 1992 on Income Tax published in the Collection of Laws.

6. THE PRINCIPLE OF EQUAL TREATMENT TO SELF-EMPLOYED WORKERS AND THEIR ASSISTING SPOUSES

Council Directive 86/613/EEC of 11 December 1986 *on the application of the principle of equal treatment between men and women engaged in an activity, including agriculture, in a self-employed capacity, and on the protection of self-employed women during pregnancy and motherhood*

6.1 National legal framework on self-employment: General provisions

Definition of self-employed workers

According to Section 2(2) of the Commercial Code, an entrepreneur is defined as:

a) a person entered in the Commercial Register,

b) a person conducting business on the basis of a Trade License,

c) a person conducting business on the basis of a license other than the Trade License, according to special laws,[22]

d) a natural person involved in agricultural production, entered in the Commercial Register according to a special law.

According to the Act on Pension Insurance, a self-employed person for the purpose of the pension security is defined as a person who conducts independent profit-making activity, or who cooperates in the conduct of independent profit-making activity. A corresponding definition is contained in Article 145(2) of the Act on Social Security for the purposes of health insurance.

Acceptance of the aim of the directive

Although Czech legislation contains the principle of equal treatment and there are no provisions contrary to Directive 76/207/EEC, a clear and precise statement of the principle of equal treatment in the Commercial Code and the Act on Trade License, the crucial legal acts regulating self-employment activities, is lacking.

---

[22] Freelance work, for example, as architects, attorneys etc., with each field regulated by a special law.

The principle of equal treatment and self-employed workers

There are no regulations specifically relating to self-employed women, thus there is no mechanism to enforce equal opportunities for self-employed women. The principle of equal treatment is enshrined in the Labour Code, but neither the Act on Trade License nor other legislation regulating self-employment contains similar provisions.

6.2 Social rights of spouses

Czech legislation contains only general provisions referring to the social rights of the cooperating spouses of self-employed workers.[23] Several special laws refer to the rights and especially obligations of the spouses of self-employed workers. For example, the Act on Income Tax regulates the division of business incomes between spouses for tax purposes. The Act on Social Security and Contribution to State Employment Policy defines obligations regarding social security payments for self-employed workers and their cooperating spouses, including those relating to health insurance (Article 3[2]).

Formation of companies by unmarried persons

The Commercial Code, which regulates the basic conditions for forming a company, does not make reference to the marital status of partners forming a company.

If one spouse becomes a partner in a company during the marriage, the other spouse does not automatically become a partner of the company as well, with the exception of housing associations. Section 148(2) of the Civil Code provides that a court may reduce the common property of spouses upon the proposal of one of the spouses if one spouse obtains a business license or becomes an unlimited partner. Furthermore, if the business activity is conducted by the entrepreneur together with or with help from the other spouse who is not an entrepreneur, following a court decision, the income resulting from the activity shall be divided between both of them at a rate set by a written contract; if no contract was concluded, the income shall be divided into equal shares.

Recognition of the work of spouses

There is no independent system of social security for self-employed workers in the Czech Republic; self-employed workers and their cooperating spouses participate in the general social security system on the basis of registration. The same applies to the spouses of self-employed workers. The Act on Social Security specifically mentions self-employed workers in the group of insurance ratepayers, and regulates the health insurance of self-employed workers.

---

[23] Section 2 of the Civil Code, and Section 1 of the Commercial Code.

There is no available research on the working conditions and remuneration of the spouses of self-employed persons.

The rights of self-employed workers whose operational activity is interrupted due to pregnancy or motherhood

Article 145(c) of the Act on Social Security regulates the cash benefits to which self-employed workers and cooperating spouses are eligible, for example, sickness pay and maternity benefits. The maternity benefits include a one-off birth benefit and a continuing parental contribution.

6.3 Contributory social security schemes for self-employed workers and spouses

Self-employed women are subject to the same legal regulations as the rest of the population in this regard, since there is no special legislation for self-employed workers.

6.4 Related research and statistics

Persons wishing to set up a viable business, whether male of female, require a great deal of time, effort and money. Nevertheless, the number of self-employed persons is increasing year by year. The table below shows the development of self-employment in the Czech Republic[24] (data from 2000 and 2001 were not available):

Table 1. Status of self-employed persons in the Czech Republic

	1993	1995	1997	1998	1999
Total (thousands)	634.4	687.6	687.4	727.1	739.9
% of total workforce	013.2	013.9	014.1	015.1	015.8
Males					
Thousands	425.6	470.8	482.4	509.9	521.3
% of all working men	015.9	017.2	017.6	018.8	019.7
Females					
Thousands	208.7	216.9	205.1	217.2	218.6
% of all working women	009.8	009.9	009.5	010.4	010.5

---

[24] The Czech Statistical Office (2000).

Research on women working in agriculture

The rural economy has suffered serious decline since 1989, bearing the marks of fundamental changes connected to property restitution, the transformation of agricultural production and the restructuring of farms into viable economic units. Limits placed on agricultural production have either reduced or destroyed employment opportunities in rural areas. Recent years, however, have seen a boom in organic farming and eco-tourism, and the rural tourist industry in particular offers chances for women to find work.

Table 2. Number of women engaged in agriculture, hunting and other related activities in comparison to total workforce and number of men employed.[25]

	1993	1995	1997	1998	1999
Total (in thousands)	21.4	28.6	27.6	27.8	27.1
Of whom men (in thousands)	16.2	21.7	22.2	22.1	21.8
Of whom women (thousands)	05.2	06.9	05.4	05.7	05.3

Social perceptions of self-employed men and women

The Czech Women's Association carried out a survey entitled "Women in Rural Areas" to look at the employment opportunities for women during and after the changes, the situation in rural tourism, etc. Based on this, a priority action list for state and non-governmental bodies was drawn up, including: involving mayors in supporting the self-employment of women in the rural tourist industry; raising awareness among rural populations; more active promotion of successful self-employed women; supporting start-up schemes for unemployed women to start their own businesses; securing real equality of opportunity for both sexes in obtaining financial credit for small- and medium-size enterprises – since women earn less than men it is often difficult for them to obtain credit from financial institutions. Unfortunately, the mechanisms for putting these recommendations into practice remain undeveloped.

Successful women managers or businesswomen attract more criticism than admiration in the Czech Republic, and self-employed women face great problems of social acceptance. Rather than being seen as a positive example of what women are capable of, many are shunned in their immediate social circle. According to research conducted in the beginning of 2001,[26] every second man in the Czech Republic has reservations

---

[25] The Czech Statistical Office (2000).
[26] Research by the DEMA agency, published by the *Pravo* daily, 7 March 2001.

about their partner obtaining higher education, a higher income or higher position at work than himself. Over 90 percent of women did not see this as a problem.

According to NGOs and the Ministry of Labour and Social Affairs, the level of public awareness of this Directive remains low, partly due to the general limited awareness of EU legislation among the Czech population, but also partly because of the reluctance of women to campaign for equal treatment themselves. Women's NGOs and professional associations, such as the Czech Women's Association and the Association of Businesswomen and Managers, do run training workshops and publish information on equal opportunities, as does the Ministry of Labour and Social Affairs.

Past and recent trends on self-employment

According to the Association of Women Entrepreneurs and Managers, although women are involved in all areas of business, they are mainly engaged in tax consultancy, accountancy, translation, public relations and consultancy work. The success of women in managerial or self-employed positions depends upon their high level of education, acquired possibly in other countries, knowledge of foreign languages as well as changes in social attitudes towards women in independent and managerial work situation.

Research on the status/rights of self-employed women

There are no figures available concerning married couples who run a business or women who assist their spouses. Surveys consistently show though that women lack self-confidence in setting up businesses, and that they are reluctant to fight for equal treatment or indeed to identify inequalities even when evidence exists.

During the 2002 election campaign, the Czech weekly *Týden* carried out a survey on "How Czech women view their position in society." The results showed that 13 percent of women felt women's position was satisfactory, 31 percent felt it was unsatisfactory and the remainder expressed no opinion. When men were asked about women's position in society, 38 percent felt it to be satisfactory and 10 percent felt it to be unsatisfactory. Only 21 percent of all respondents agreed that positive discrimination for women was acceptable, although in Prague 31 percent of men and 49 percent of women agree with positive discrimination.

6.5 Legal means of redress

Czech legislation contains the measures necessary to enable all persons who consider themselves wronged by the failure to apply the principle of equal treatment in self-employed activities to pursue their claims by judicial process.

Bringing measures adopted pursuant to the directive to the attention of representative bodies

The Act on the Collection of Laws and Collection of International Treaties contains the sole, generalised, provision on publishing the constitutional laws, other laws, Senate legal measures, government decrees and legal regulations of the Ministries, Czech National Bank and other bodies of the central administration. There are no other provisions to bring measures adopted pursuant to this Directive to the attention of bodies representing self-employed workers and vocational training centres.

7. THE FRAMEWORK ON PARENTAL LEAVE

Council Directive 96/34/EC of 3 June 1996 *on the framework agreement on parental leave concluded by UNICE, CEEP, and ETUC*

7.1 National legal framework on parental leave: General provisions

This Directive was implemented in stages in the Czech Republic. Provisions on parental leave were introduced by the amendments to the Labour Code, replacing the so-called additional maternity leave (which could only be taken by women after the expiration of maternity leave). According to Section 158 of the Labour Code, parental leave may be taken either by women following maternity leave or by men after the birth of the child.

Conditions of access and detailed rules for applying for parental leave

Employees – men and women – have an individual right to parental leave after childbirth or when caring for a child up to the age of three. The employee is entitled to receive state social support benefits during this period and the employer is obliged to offer the employee the same or a corresponding position on his/her return to work. If the parent stays with a child until the child is four years of age, this is classified as additional leave, for which the parent is entitled to state social benefits, but the employer is not obliged to offer him/her the same or equivalent post when he/she wishes to return to work.

Parental leave is granted on a full-time basis, and is not dependent on a period of work qualification or length of service qualification. The Labour Code guarantees the same rights and conditions for taking parental leave to adoptive or foster parents or legal guardians after the death of natural parents. Parental leave is granted from the day responsibility for the child is assumed until the child reaches three years of age. Employers may not postpone granting permission to take parental leave.

Female workers are entitled to 28 weeks of maternity leave, or 37 weeks in the case of multiple births. Maternity leave may be no less than 14 weeks and may not in any case terminate or be interrupted until six weeks after childbirth. The female worker must apply for parental leave before the maternity leave expires, stating clearly that the leave is required for childcare and the period claimed. The maternity and parental leave entitlements of female and male employees can be taken simultaneously.

Legal protection against dismissal on the grounds of application for, or taking of, parental leave

In accordance with Article 2(4) of the Directive, the employee taking the parental leave is protected against dismissal if caring for a child under the age of three.

Applicability of rights on return from parental leave

All labour rights in place before exercising the right to parental leave remain valid after the leave expires, and Czech legislation complies with the requirements of Article 6 of the Directive.

7.2 Social security during parental leave

The Act on State Social Support enables the parent who personally cares for at least one child up to four years of age full-time to draw on the parental contribution. If the parent cares for the child after three years of age and still draws on the parental contribution, there must be an agreement with the employer. The employer can grant unpaid work leave to the employee, but is not legally obliged to meet this request.

The right to parental leave can be transferred from the mother to the father and *vice versa* according to for any length of time until the child reaches the age of three. While men can take parental leave *de jure*, the opportunity for them to exercise this right in practice depends on an agreement between the partners. Since women generally have lower incomes than their partners, they are usually the ones who benefit from the parental leave.

According to the Act on State Social Support, a parent who cares for a child under the age of four at home is eligible for parental social support, which is a monthly benefit calculated on the basis of the minimum amount of standard of living set by the Governmental Decree No.333 of 2001, which is currently 3,230 CZK per individual per month (approximately €107). The parent loses benefit if he/she carries out income-generating work beyond a certain amount per month. The highest monthly income permitted while receiving the benefit is currently 3,480 CZK (approximately €115).

Health insurance coverage for employees on parental leave is provided by the state through public funds. State pension contributions are covered for persons on leave to care for a child until the age of four.

The right to time off from work on grounds of *force majeure* for urgent family reasons (for example, sickness or accident) is provided for by Section 127 of the Labour Code.

Financial support during leave to care for a family member is granted for a maximum of nine calendar days in accordance with the Act on Employees' Health Insurance. A single parent is granted financial support for 16 calendar days.

Currently, a new term for granting benefits begins when a new medical certificate of the child's illness and the consequent need for care is issued. In the absence of a medical certificate, an employee may take unpaid leave from work.

7.3 Parental leave and equal opportunities policy

Initiatives to encourage the introduction of flexible work

While one third of women and six percent of men in the EU worked part-time in 1998, only 9.6 percent of women and 2.6 percent of men did so in the Czech Republic, and these numbers have been falling in recent years.[27] Approximately only half of employers in cases involving pre-school children, and one third of employers in cases involving school-age children, declared a willingness to comply with female employees' wishes to modify their work hours.[28]

The amended Governmental Programme of Actions and Priorities in the Promotion of Equal Opportunities for Men and Women from May 2001 upholds the right to part-time work and aims in Item 4.2 to "enable […] the creation of variable working regimes that could support the employment of persons taking care of children and the family." Regrettably, this statement is far from a reality.

Another form of employment that could facilitate the reconciliation of work and family responsibilities is private businesses, but there have not been any programmes supporting women in private business in the Czech Republic so far. Approximately 2.3 percent of economically active women have their own company, which is approximately 24 percent of all employers. An additional 6.4 percent of women work with a personal business license, comprising 29 percent of all those engaged in this form of business activity.[29]

The option of working from home, which has been slowly emerging in Western Europe, also offers flexible working hours. However, it is unlikely that Czech employer–employee relations will change sufficiently to make this possible for many in the short to medium term.[30]

In any case, the 'targeted expansion' of part-time jobs only for women with small children could lead to deepening gender segregation in the labour market, have a negative effect on the prestige of feminised professions and their remuneration, which would, in the end, increase female poverty and employment insecurity.

---

[27] Hana Maríková (1999).

[28] Ibid.

[29] Czech Statistical Office (1999).

[30] Čermáková *et al.* (2000).

7.4 Research on the reconciliation of family and professional responsibilities and on sharing responsibilities between men and women

Research from 1999[31] showed that it is characteristic in Czech society for both partners to work, and also for there to be an asymmetric division of labour in the family "which is the result of a social contract between the partners and is accepted by both sides." It is not expected that the current family situation will change significantly in the near future. However, in order to minimise gender inequalities between men and women in the family, certain legislative measure have been approved, including the introduction of parental leave and the relevant parental contribution; the 1998 Governmental Resolution concerning the priorities and procedures of the Government in affirming the equality of men and women in the public as well as the private sphere; and a 1998 amendment to the Family Act which introduces the significant concept of alternating care.

Demographic, social, and cultural considerations affecting the reconciliation of women and family responsibilities

The reconciliation of work and family responsibilities is certainly affected by common stereotypical notions, such as "the man goes to work and the woman stays at home" and "the father is the breadwinner and the mother takes care of the children." About one sixth of the population adhere fully to the conventional image of the male breadwinner in the family, and approximately every fourth man considers himself to be the real breadwinner of his family. Approximately 32.7 percent of men and 24.9 percent of women agree that it is inappropriate for men to care for the children and for women to work.[32] Other obstacles to reconciling work and family responsibilities is the fact that employers are not willing to grant women with children the possibility of part-time work, childcare provisions are insufficient and paid help in the home is too expensive for most of Czech families to consider. It should also be noted that Czech men still consider contributing to housework to be humiliating; a prejudice relating to the previous regime and also to the stereotypes according to which boys are raised.

According to the Czech Statistical office website, in most families it is the woman who takes care of the household and the children, and only a small proportion of men help with this.

---

[31] Hana Maríková (1999).

[32] Hana Maríková (1999).

8. THE PRINCIPLE OF EQUAL TREATMENT OF MEN AND WOMEN IN OCCUPATIONAL SOCIAL SECURITY SCHEMES

Council Directive 96/97/EC of 20 December 1996 *amending Directive 86/378/EEC on the implementation of the principle of equal treatment for men and women in occupational social security schemes*

8.1 National legal framework on social security schemes: General provisions

The principle of equal treatment of women and men in matters of social security is laid down in the Charter of Basic Rights and Freedoms.[33] Article 30 provides that:

(1) Citizens have the right to adequate material security in old age and when unable to work, as well as upon the loss of the breadwinner.

(2) Everyone in material need has the right to such help as is essential for securing basic living conditions.

The paternalist social policy in place before 1989 was based on a completely different type of economy and social doctrine from the current practice in the Czech Republic. The totalitarian system eliminated the principles of merit, reciprocity and subsidiarity from social policy, while artificially enforcing egalitarian principles. With the exception of the state, other institutions were excluded from social policy. This model approached a redistributive model of the welfare state, with negative political modifications. The social security system was not transparent and, given the (continuing) economic and social transformation of Czech society, no longer adequate. The move to a market economy brought with it new social needs (for example, related to unemployment), which existing tools of social policy were ill-suited to deal with. New measures were therefore needed in the fields of employment, social security, pension security, wage regulation, etc.

Early developments after 1989 aimed to gradually replace paternalist principles using mechanisms that took account of economic reform while preserving state regulation in key areas. A liberalized and pluralist social security system, privatisation and democratisation were considered the main principles of social reform. Citizens were supposed to consider their future needs and assume full responsibility for them – hence the need to pluralise institutions and forms of social security, as well as to define social solidarity anew, in the form of a guaranteed minimum standard of living.

---

[33] Act No.2 of 1993.

In Czechoslovakia, women's presence in the labour market was seen as the principal element of female emancipation. However, the state supported women's rights only at the institutional level, especially in the field of social security, which ultimately preserved traditional gender relations. Provisions such as guarantees of work or support during maternity enforced the model of a dual role for women as an employee and mother. The state intervened in all spheres of life – legislative, economic, educational and social – ostensibly to promote the emancipation and equal status of women. Social development in private life did not reflect the pace of political and economic change and cultural stereotypes changed only very slowly.

At the beginning of the 1990s, social security regulations were covered by the Act on Social Security. This regulation was not satisfactory, as the system according to the law was static, and did not take account of the value of the benefits already awarded in the light of economic development, while the pensions system did not take into account significant factors such as future demographic development.

Changes in the field of social security had, from the start, both short- and long-term aspects. In order to compensate for income differentiations, the new system was designed to motivate citizens to achieve increased incomes from paid employment, thus decreasing their dependence on social benefits. A new, targeted system was therefore established to respond to concrete social events and situations. At present, women are forced to determine how to combine motherhood and work without losing their position in the labour market. Sometimes, they opt not to take their full entitlement to maternity leave, and only take the period for which their job is guaranteed by law. In this respect, the legislation does not treat women and men equally.

Crucial problems still exist concerning the pensions system because women are put at disadvantage in relation to men as a result of their lower average salaries and calculation of the old-age pension based on their longer life expectancy.

Council Directive 96/97/EC has not been implemented in Czech legislation yet. A draft Act on Occupational Pension Schemes was presented by the Czech government, but was not approved by the first chamber of Parliament before the June general elections in 2002. Therefore, only statutory social security schemes exist in the Czech Republic.

The Czech social security system includes pension insurance, health insurance, state social support benefits, and state care provisions. The sickness insurance system of benefits includes four benefits, namely sickness benefit, family member care benefit, maternity benefit, and pregnancy and maternity compensation benefit. These benefits are fully provided to employed persons, members of producer cooperatives, and cooperative farmers. Self-employed workers do not receive the family member care benefit or the maternity and pregnancy compensation benefit. Job applicants do not receive the family member care benefit, maternity and pregnancy compensation benefit, or the sickness benefit.

Social care benefits and services include care for family and child, care for citizens with a reduced capacity to work, care for senior and severely handicapped citizens, care for citizens requiring special help, and care for socially ill-adapted citizens. They include, for example, community care services, catering for pensioners, etc.

The Czech Government prepared and approved the draft Act on Occupational Pension Schemes, promoting the equal access and treatment of women and men in occupational pensions schemes in 2001. However, the law was rejected by the Chamber of Deputies and no other attempts were made before the June 2002 general elections.

Direct and indirect discrimination on the basis of sex in social security schemes

There is no direct discrimination on the basis of sex in the laws regulating social security. The legislation does not distinguish between male or female participants in the scheme either in relation to access to the schemes or calculation of contributions.

However, indirect discrimination arises from the lower pensions payments paid to women. According to statistics,[34] the average old-age pension for men in December 1998 amounted to CZK 6,174 (approximately €204), compared with only CZK 5,087 (approximately €168) for women.

Provisions contrary to the principle of equal treatment with regard to social security schemes

The reform of the pension scheme has not brought about dramatic changes. The new law defined a transition period during which citizens are guaranteed the basic contributory system. Meanwhile, the retirement age will gradually increase. The retirement age has been rising since 1996, so that as of 1 January 2007 it will be 62 years for men and between 57 and 61 years for women, depending on the number of children. The planned increase will hit the female population the hardest, as women will work four years longer than at present.

In connection with the increase of the retirement age, a problem may appear in the future for women who will not want or be able to accept this prolongation and will choose early retirement instead. This will lead to a cut in their post-retirement income of up to 8 percent (CZK 400 less per month – approximately €13.25 – on average).

A similar situation concerns the calculation of unemployment benefits. All citizens of the Czech Republic are entitled to unemployment benefits according to the Act on

---

[34] Czech Statistical Office (1998).

Employment. Self-employed workers are entitled to a proportion of their contribution to the pensions scheme and to the state employment policy. The unemployment benefit is granted for a period of six months.

Consideration of the principle of equal treatment by scheme management bodies

The draft Act on Occupational Pension Schemes, which was rejected by Parliament, prohibits discrimination based on *inter alia* sex in Article 3(3). Article 3(4) obliges employers to secure the equal treatment of all employees in the occupational pension schemes.

In accordance with other laws regulating social security, the draft does not distinguish between male and female participants. Article 2 defines a participant of the occupational scheme as an individual older than 18 years who is on a permanent employment contract or a contract worker, or who is a member of cooperative, or who engaged by the cooperative as a contract worker. Participation in the occupational scheme is voluntary. The minimum period of employment or membership in an occupational pension scheme required to obtain the benefit differs.

The conditions for granting the benefits from the occupational pension scheme are generally set equally for women and men, although pensions payments are different for women and men. Article 3(3) of the draft Act states that shall not be considered discrimination if relative longevity expectations are used for calculating the pension and result in different values for men and women. Although Directive 86/378/EEC contains a similar adjustment, this provision may still be considered discriminatory. It should be noted that the draft Act grants employers the possibility to grant higher contributions to women in order to adjust the amount of benefits according to actuarial calculation tables.

The draft Act sets the same retirement age for men and women at least 60 years, but the retirement age laid down in the Act on Pension Security differs for men and women, as mentioned above.

Article 5 of the draft Act on Occupational Pension Schemes specifies persons whose pension contributions are covered by the state, including women on maternity leave and a parent on parental leave caring for a child under four years of age.

The level of workers' contributions to occupational pension scheme is set in Articles 5 and 6 of the draft Act, based on a baseline assessment for the social security and contribution to the state employment policy per month. The contribution cannot be lower than two percent of the baseline assessment, but can be higher. The upper limit is set in the articles of the particular pension fund.

The calculation of the contributions according to the current Act on Pension Security is based on a similar principle but is more complicated. It does not distinguish between female or male participants, but is based on individual income. This is also true for health insurance contributions. The only specific benefit pertaining to women is maternity leave.

8.2 Legal means of redress

Protection against dismissal in the case of complaint of non-compliance with the principle of equal treatment
Section 7 of the Labour Code provides that an employer cannot harm or disadvantage in any way an employee seeking to legally enforce his/her rights stemming from the employment relationship.

Monitoring mechanisms
As the respective Directive has not yet been implemented into the Czech legislation, no special monitoring mechanisms are provided for apart from the general mechanisms monitoring observance of equal opportunities of women and men. In addition to the three key institutions noted in the introduction, the regional and local employment offices, local authorities and women's NGOs play a role in monitoring the observance of equal opportunities.

8.3 Implementation of the principle of equal treatment in matters of social security and equal opportunities strategies

Although implementation of the principle of equal treatment of women and men in matters of social security should be considered a fundamental prerequisite of gender equality, it is not clearly mentioned in any official document. The Government Programme of Actions and Priorities in Promotion of Equal Opportunities for Men and Women approved in May 2001 does not mention the need to promote equal treatment in this field, nor do any special laws regulating social security.

Perceived protection of women in maternity and social security
The protection of women in maternity is not considered an obstacle to the implementation of the equal treatment in social security, nor is it considered a factor in the *de facto* discrimination of women.

REFERENCES

Bibliography

Čermáková, Marie (1997) *Family and Changing Gender Roles – Social Analysis of the Czech Family, Working Papers*. Prague: Institute of Sociology, Czech Academy of Sciences.

Čermáková, Marie *et al.* (2000) *Relations and Changes of Gender Differences in the Czech Society in the 1990s,* Prague: Institute of Sociology, Czech Academy of Sciences.

Czech Statistical Office (2000) *Women and Men in Figures,* Prague: Czech Statistical Office and the Ministry of Labour and Social Affairs.

Czech Statistical Office (1999) *Statistická ročenka, 1999* (Annual Statistic, 1999). Prague: Czech Statistical Office.

Czech Statistical Office (1998) *Vybrané údaje o sociálním zabezpečení* (Selected Data on sScial Security). Prague: Czech Statistical Office.

Czech Women's Association (2001) *Nedej se – rozhoduj za sebe.* Prague.

Czech Women's Association (2001) *Woman of the third century,* Press Release, June 2001. Prague.

DEMA (2000) *Signal Information from Research "A Chance of Success on the Labour Market".* Prague: DEMA.

Equal Opportunities for Women and Men in the European Union, Annual Report 1999.

Family Module 1994 – sociological research into changes in gender roles in the family carried out within the ISSP program (N = men 503, women 521), funded by the Institute of the Academy of Sciences of the Czech Republic. Prague: Rodina.

Foundation Gender Studies (1998) *Pravni postaveni zen v Ceske republice.* Prague.

Gender Centre of the Faculty of Social Sciences, Masaryk University (2001), *Rovne prilezitosti zen a muzu ve vybranych ceskych podnicich 2000–2001,* Brno.

Institute of Sociology (2000a) *Gender, Rovné příležitosti, Výzkum,* 1/2000, 2-3/2000, 4/2000. Prague: Sociologický ústav AV ČR.

Institute of Sociology (2000b) *Relations and Changes in Gender Differences in the Czech Society in the 1990s.* Sociologický ústav AV ČR.

Institute of Sociology (2000, 2001) *Gender – Equal Opportunities – Research,* 1–4/2000, 1–3/2001. Prague: Sociologický ústav AV ČR.

Jakubka, J. (2000) "Obecné poznámky k novele ZP." In *Práce a mzdy* 7–8. pp. 2–7.

Jurajda, Stepan (2000) *Platove rozdily a segregace muzu a zen v CR.* Gender, rovne prilezitosti, vyzkum, 2–3/2000, Prague.

Komentář k novele zákoníku práce, *Sociální politika,* 11/2000: I–XXIV.

Kuchařová, V., L. Zamykalová (2000) *Rovnost příležitostí žen a mužů.* Prague: VÚPSV.

Kuchařová, V., L. Zamykalová (1998) *Aktuální otázky postavení žen v ČR.* Prague: VÚPSV.

Machonin, P., M. Tuček (1996) *Česká společnost v transformaci.* Prague: Slon.

Hana Maríková, *Muz v rodine: demokratizace sféry soukromé. Pracovni texty,* (Man in the family: democratisation of the private sphere. Working texts). Sociological Institute of the Czech Academy of Sciences, 1999.

Ministry of Labour and Social Affairs (2000) *National Employment Plan 2000.* Prague: MPSV ČR.

Ministry of Labour and Social Affairs (1998) *National Report on the Fulfilment of CEDAW.* Prague: MPSV ČR.

Ministry of Labour and Social Affairs (2002) *National Report on the Fulfilment of CEDAW.* Prague: MPSV ČR.

Ministry of Labour and Social Affairs (1998) *Pekingská akční platforma, Shrnutí závěrů 4. světové konference o ženách v Pekingu.* Prague.

Ministry of Labour and Social Affairs (1998) *Plnění Úmluvy o odstranění všech forem diskriminace žen (CEDAW),* Interní material, MPSV ČR, Úsek pro evropskou integraci. Prague.

Ministry of Labour and Social Affairs (1998) *Princip rovného postavení mužů a žen v právu Evropské unie.* Interní material, MPSV ČR, Úsek pro evropskou integraci. Praha.

Ministry of Labour and Social Affairs (2000) *Princip rovného zacházení s muži a ženami v zaměstnání.* Interní material, MPSV ČR, Úsek pro evropskou integraci. Praha.

Ministry of Labour and Social Affairs (2000) *Principal of Equal Treatment of Men and Women at Work.* Prague: MPSV ČR.

Musilová, M. (1999) *Vývoj politiky rovných příležitostí mužů a žen v České republice v kontextu evropské integrace,* Working Papers, 99:5. Prague: Sociologický ústav AV ČR.

Overview of the Administrative Structure in Charge of Application and Enforcement of EC Legislation in Equal Opportunities in the Czech Republic, Ministry of Labour and Social Affairs, 1998.

Nadace Gender Studies (1998) *Právní postavení žen v České republice.* Prague: Nadace Gender Studies.

Priorities and Procedures of the Czech Government in Promoting the Equality of Men and Women (1998–2000).

Rothová, E. (2000) "Úplné znění novelizovaného zákona o platu s komentářem k provedeným změnám." *Práce a mzdy* 9–10; pp. 22–37. Praha.

Second Periodical Report on the Fulfilment of CEDAW by the Czech Republic from the period of 1995 to 31 June 1999.

Steinichová, L. (2000) "Výklad novely zákona o zaměstnanosti." *Právo a zaměstnání* 3–4; pp. 9–21. Praha.

Tomší, I. (2000) "Úplné znění novelizovaného zákona o mzdě s komentářem k provedeným změnám." *Práce a mzdy* 9–10; pp. 3–21, Praha.

Trestr, Pavel (2000) *Law on Social Security.* Prague: C. H. Beck.

Troester, P. (2000) "Zákoník práce po pětatřiceti letech." *Právo a zaměstnání* 7–8; pp. 3–18. Praha.

Tucek, Milan (1998) *The Czech Family in Transformation – Stratification, Role Division and Value Orientation,* Working *Papers.* Prague: Institute of Sociology, Czech Academy of Sciences.

United Nations (2000) *Report of the Ad Hoc Committee of the Whole, of the 23rd special session of the UN General Assembly.* New York: United Nations.

List of Legislation screened

Acts

Act No.54 of 1956, on Sickness Benefit Security of Employees, as amended, adopted on 30 November 1956, in effect from 1 January 1957.

Act No.140 of 1961, Criminal Code, as amended, adopted on 29 November 1961, in effect from 1 January 1962.

Act No.94 of 1963, the Family Law, as amended, adopted on 4 December 1963, in effect from 1 April 1964.

Act No.99 of 1963, Code of Civil Procedure, as amended, adopted on 4 December 1963, in effect from 1 April 1964.

Act No.40 of 1964, the Civil Code, as amended, adopted on 26 February 1964, in effect from 1 April 1964.

Act No.65 of 1965 Coll., Labour Code, as amended, adopted on 16 June 1965, in effect from 1 January 1966.

Act No.71 of 1967, Code on Administrative Procedure, adopted on 29 June 1967, in effect from 1 January 1968.

Act No.88 of 1968, on Extension of Maternal Leave, Benefits in Maternity and Contributions on Children from Health Security, as amended, adopted on 27 June 1968, in effect from 1 July 1968.

Act No.174 of 1968, on the State Technical Supervision of the Safety at Work, adopted on 20 December 1968, in effect from 1 January 1969.

Act No.100 of 1988, on Social Security, as amended, adopted on 16 June 1988, in effect from 1 January 1988.

Act No.100 of 1988, on Pension Security, as amended, adopted on 30 June 1995, in effect from 1 January 1991.

Act No.120 of 1990, Regulating Relations between the Trade Unions and Employers, adopted on 23 April 1990, in effect from 23 April 1990.

Act No.1 of 1991, on Employment, adopted on 4 December 1990, in effect from 1 February 1991.

Act No.2 of 1991, on Collective Mediation, adopted on 4 December 1990, in effect from 1 February 1991.

Act No.9 of 1991 on Employment and Jurisdiction of the State Bodies of the Czech Republic in the Field of the Employment, adopted on 19 December 1990, in effect from 1 February 1991.

Act No.455 of 1991, on Trade License, as amended, adopted on 2 October 1991, in effect from 1 January 1992.

Act No.513 of 1991, the Commercial Code, as amended, adopted on 5 November 1991, in effect from 1 January 1992.

Act No.1 of 1992, on Wage, Work Emergency Compensation and Average Remuneration, adopted on 10 December 1991, in effect from 16 January 1992.

Act No.143 of 1992, on Salaries and on Work Emergency Compensations in Organisations Financed from the State Budget and Some Other Organisations and Bodies, adopted on 13 March 1992, in effect from 1 May 1992.

Act No.586 of 1992, on Income Tax, as amended, adopted on 20 November 1992, in effect from 1 January 1993.

Act No.589 of 1992, on Social Security and Contribution to the State Employment Policy, adopted on 20 November 1992, in effect from 1 January 1993.

Act No.1 of 1993 Coll., Constitution of the Czech Republic, adopted on 16 December 1992, in effect from 1 January 1993.

Act No.2 of 1993, the Charter of Basic Rights and Freedoms, as amended, in effect from 1 January 1993.

Act No.42 of 1994, on Pension Reinsurance, adopted on 16 February 1994, in effect from 21 March 1994.

Act No.74 of 1994, amending the Labour Code, adopted on 23 March 1994, in effect from 1 June 1994.

Act No.117 of 1995, on State Social Security, adopted on 26 May 1995, in effect from 1 October 1995.

Act No.118 of 1995, amending the State Social Support Law, adopted on 26 May 1995, in effect from 1 October 1995.

Act No.155 of 1995, on Pension Security, as amended, adopted on 30 June 1995, in effect from 1 January 1996.

Act No.48 of 1997, on Public Health Insurance, as amended, adopted on 7 March 1997, in effect from 1 April 1997.

Act No.75 of 1997, on Social Benefit, adopted on 19 March 1997, in effect from 1 July 1997.

Act No.221 of 1999, on Servicemen, amended by 155 of 2000, adopted on 14 September 1999, in effect from 1 December 1999.

Act No.309 of 1999, on the Collection of Laws and Collection of International Treaties, as amended, adopted on 11 November 1999, in effect from 1 January 2000.

Act No.155 of 2000, amending the Labour Code, adopted on 18 May 2000, in effect from 1 January 2001.

Draft proposals

Draft Act on Occupational Pension Schemes.

Decrees

Government Decree No.3 of 1995, on the Minimum Wage, adopted on 6 December 1995, in effect from 1996.

Government Decree No.236 of 8 April 1998 updated by the Government Decree No.452 of 10 May 1999, and the Government Decree No.565 of 7 June 2000, "Priorities and Procedures of the Czech Government in Promotion of Equality of Men and Women".

Government Decree No.198 of 2001 Report on possible measures to eliminate discrimination, adopted on 5 June 2001, in effect from 1 July 2001.

Ordinance of the Ministry of Health No.261 of 1997 Coll., which indicates works and working places forbidden to all women, pregnant women, mothers till the end of the ninth month after the childbirth and juveniles and conditions under which juveniles can exceptionally do this work in order to undergo professional training, adopted on 6 October 1997, in effect from 1 January 1998.

Ordinance of the Ministry of Interior No.161 of 2000, Regulating Details on Service of the Members of Police, adopted on 5 June 2000, in effect from 22 June 2000.

Equal Opportunities for Women and Men in Estonia

Table of contents

Executive Summary 183

Country report: Introduction 191

1. The principle of equal pay for work of equal value 193
   1.1 National legal framework: General provisions 193
   1.2 Legal foundations and institutional structures 194
   1.3 Job classification 194
   1.4 Available legal procedures 194
   1.5 Means of informing employees of their rights 195
   1.6 Role of trade unions 195
   1.7 Women's factual situation 196

2. Equal treatment for women and men as regards access to employment, vocational training and promotion, and working conditions 197
   2.1 National legal framework: General provisions 197
   2.2 The concept of discrimination on grounds of sex: Definition and legal sanctions 198
   2.3 Access to employment, vocational training and promotion 198
   2.4 Protective measures for women in the labour market ... 199
   2.5 Prohibition of dismissal 200
   2.6 Women's and men's jobs 200
   2.7 Legal status of sexual harassment 201

3. Protection of pregnant women from the inherent risk of certain activities and related employment rights 202
   3.1 Legal and conceptual framework 202
   3.2 Risk assessment and employers' obligations 203
   3.3 Case law 205
   3.4 Night work 205

	3.5	Maternity leave	205
	3.6	Prohibition of dismissal and employment rights	206

4. The burden of proof in cases of discrimination based on sex 207
    4.1 Legal and conceptual framework concerning indirect discrimination 207
    4.2 The burden of proof and rules of evidence 208
    4.3 Case law 209

5. Non-discrimination against part-time workers 210
    5.1 National legal framework and employment conditions concerning part-time workers 210

6. The principle of equal treatment for self-employed workers and their assisting spouses 212
    6.1 National legal framework: General provisions 212
    6.2 Social rights of spouses 213
    6.3 Contributory social security system for self employed workers 214
    6.4 Related research and statistics 215
    6.5 Legal means of redress 218

7. The Framework on parental leave 219
    7.1 National legal framework: General provisions 219
    7.2 Social security during parental leave 220
    7.3 Parental leave and equal opportunities policy 220
    7.4 Research on sharing family and professional responsibilities 222

8. The principle of equal treatment in occupational social security schemes 224
    8.1 National legal framework: General provisions 224
    8.2 Legal means of redress 226
    8.3 Implementation of the principle of equal treatment 227
    8.4 Related research and statistics 228

Executive summary for Estonia

INTRODUCTION

The European Commission's 2000 Regular Report on Estonia's Progress Towards Accession, while recognising that the requirements for accession had been partially met, emphasised that further progress is needed in order to bring national legislation on gender equality into compliance with the *acquis communautaire*. Since the publication of that report, the government in Estonia has demonstrated a growing overall commitment to guaranteeing equal opportunities for women and men by approving the draft Gender Equality Act, the second reading of which is expected to take place in Parliament in the autumn of 2002.

The Gender Equality Act is essentially a roadmap towards securing equal opportunities for women and men and, once adopted, will constitute an essential step towards meeting the requirements of the various international documents to which Estonia has acceded, including *inter alia* the Revised European Social Charter and the UN Convention on the Elimination of All Forms of Discrimination of Women, as well as bringing Estonian legislation in line with the EU Directives. The process of harmonisation has also spurred the enactment of several other laws regulating labour relations, including the Working and Rest Time Act, the Unemployment Insurance Act, the Holidays Act, and the Wages Act.

Despite these positive legal trends and substantial general progress in implementing the accession criteria, however, Estonia will retain a number of discriminatory provisions until the actual adoption of the Gender Equality Act. Moreover, the *de facto* implementation of these new regulations will require continuous concrete efforts to ensure that the real meaning and substance of gender equality and sex-based discrimination are understood as social and political objectives to be implemented, and not simply legal requirements.

SUMMARY OF KEY POINTS

Defining principles

The principle of equal treatment for women and men is only partially and vaguely incorporated in the Estonian legal framework and it is not *expressis verbis* established by any legal act regulating the field of employment. For the first time in Estonian law, the requirement of equal pay for equal work or work of equal value for women and men was established in the new draft Wages Act. The notions of direct or indirect discrimination are not specified by law, nor have there been any court precedents that defined discrimination. There is no provision on the prohibition of sexual harassment in Estonian legislation and there is no legal definition of 'sexual harassment'. The draft Gender Equality Act, once adopted in the terms described in the report, will, however, rectify these shortcomings and bring Estonian legislation in line with the respective EU Directives.

Protective measures

Employers are obliged to assess the nature, degree and duration of exposure to the agents and work processes involving specific risks to the health and safety of female workers, including any possible effect on pregnancy or on breastfeeding, and to inform female workers and their representatives about the results of any risk assessment and measures that must be taken with regard to their health and safety. In accordance with the above, pregnant women cannot be discharged for pregnancy-related reasons or forced to work, if this will damage their health. Pregnant workers are not obliged to perform night work.

Employers are required to ensure that pregnant workers are entitled to time off without loss of pay in order to attend antenatal examinations if such examinations must take place during working hours. It is prohibited for an employer to terminate an employment contract with a pregnant woman or a woman raising a child under three years of age, except in legally prescribed cases.

Burden of proof

The rules of evidence and the burden of proof in civil court proceedings are the same in litigation concerning a violation of the principle of equal treatment for women and men as in any other litigation. The *actori incumbit probatio* principle applies as the general legal principle, meaning that each party must prove the facts on which her/his claims are based. However, the draft Gender Equality Act contains a provision on the reversal of the burden of proof in cases of the violation of the principle of equal treatment of women and men as regards access to employment, vocational training and promotion, and working conditions.

Part-time workers

There are few legal provisions regulating part-time work in Estonia, although in practice the working conditions of part-time workers can often be discriminatory compared with full-time workers. Estonian legislation does not explicitly contain the concept of 'part-time worker', but part-time work is defined by 'part-time working time' which means "working time that is less than the established standard for working time at the place of employment and which is applied upon the agreement of an employee and employer."[1] There are several differences in definitions provided by the EU Framework agreement and the relevant provisions of Estonian national legislation. At the legislative level, no distinction is made between full-time and part-time workers with regard to working conditions. At the same time, there is no explicit requirement that would prohibit discrimination against part-time workers. Due to a lack of research in this area, there is no satisfactory data on the real situation of part-time workers in Estonia.

Self-employed workers

There are no legal provisions on the equal treatment of self-employed men and women, although the draft Gender Equality Act will apply to all fields of social life, with the exception of family and private life and certain aspects of religious practices. Statistics show that there are nearly two times fewer women working in their own enterprise, and fewer women working on self-owned farms or involved in other forms of self-employment. At the same time, more women than men are working in subsidiary housekeeping. There have been programmes to encourage women to become self-employed in the rural areas, including one in 1996 aimed at supporting self-initiatives and small businesses. Women's organisations have been very active supporters and implementers of the projects.

Parental leave

The Holidays Act stipulates that a mother or father shall be granted parental leave at his or her request for raising a child of up to the age of three. It is up to the parents to choose which of them shall take the leave. According to the draft Gender Equality Act, a father

---

[1] Article 18(1) of the Working and Rest Time Act (RT* I 1994, 2, 12) stipulates the following: "Part-time working time is working time that is less than the established standard for working time at the place of employment and which is applied upon the agreement of an employee and employer."

shall be entitled to additional childcare leave of 14 calendar days during a mother's pregnancy and maternity leave or for a period of two months after the birth of a child.

In cases where there is the most housework, i.e. in families with underage children, the division of chores between working parents is rarely equitably distributed. The most equal division occurs in those families with working parents where there are no children or the children have already left home. However, despite relatively conservative public opinion on the matter, there has apparently been a shift in the movement towards equalising the distribution of home duties between men and women. This is in contrast with the start of the 1990s, when, many families responded positively to slogans encouraging women to return to the home.

Social security schemes

There are no provisions in Estonian legislation that directly violate the principle of equal treatment of men and women in social security schemes. The different retirement age for men and women has been changed, although the transition period to equalising the retirement age will continue until 2016 and discrimination will exist in practice until that time. In practice, problems remain in concrete situations where employers with certain obligations in connection to the protection of the maternity of their employees do not act in accordance with their responsibilities. It is usually difficult to initiate court action in such cases and the problem remains largely invisible to the public eye.

RECOMMENDATIONS RELATED TO EACH SPECIFIC DIRECTIVE

Council Directive 75/117/EEC of 10 February 1975 *on the approximation of laws of the Member States relating to the implementation of the principle of equal pay for women and men*

- A professional qualification system should be created.
- The basis for evaluating jobs should be analysed.
- Individual employment contracts and collective agreements should be analysed.

Council Directive 76/207/EEC of 9 February 1976 *on the implementation of the principle of equal treatment for men and women as regards access to employment, vocational training and promotion, and working conditions*

- The principle of equal treatment should be fully incorporated into the Estonian legal framework, setting forth a clear prohibition of direct or indirect discrimination on grounds of sex, in particular by reference to marital or family status. In addition, the necessary definitions of 'discrimination on grounds of sex' as well as 'direct discrimination' and 'indirect discrimination' should be provided for by law.

- The principle of equal treatment with regard to access to all types and to all levels of vocational training should be incorporated into the present Adult Education Act or set forth explicitly in the new Gender Equality Act.

- Better access to all jobs or posts should be ensured by establishing the basis for positive treatment in the legislation and introducing positive measures with the aim of eliminating discrimination in access to employment and decreasing horizontal and vertical segregation on the labour market.

- In order to ensure the implementation of the principle of equal treatment as regards to access to employment, 'job applicants', as well as 'employees', should have the right to bring a case before the Labour Dispute Committees.

- In order to improve the possibilities for employees whose rights have been violated to file a complaint, a competent authority should be set up as an alternative to the court and the Labour Dispute Committee. Furthermore, the necessary legal measures ought to be introduced in order to protect employees against dismissal as a reaction to their complaint.

Council Directive 92/85/EEC of 19 October 1992 *on the introduction of measures to encourage improvements in the safety and health at work of pregnant workers and workers who have recently given birth or are breastfeeding*

- Scientific and epidemiological studies on hazardous chemicals capable of causing genetic damage affecting the fertility of the male or the female worker, and which are hazardous to the unborn child or to pregnancy, should be taken into consideration as the basis for the re-evaluating chemicals in the workplace and their exposure levels.

- Guidelines on the assessment of the chemical, physical, and biological agents and industrial processes considered hazardous to the safety and health of pregnant workers and workers who have recently given birth or are breastfeeding, prepared by the Commission of the European Communities in 2000, should be introduced and translated into the Estonian language.

Council Directive 97/80/EC of 15 December 1997 *on the burden of proof in cases of discrimination based on sex*

- A reversal of the burden of proof should be established in cases concerning the principle of equal treatment of men and women.

- Information should be made available to employees in the workplace on the legal regulations for bringing a case of discrimination case to the court.

- Administrative capacity should be improved, primarily by training judges, but also lawyers, to improve the acceptance of the reversed burden of proof when a violation of equal treatment of women and men reaches a court.

Council Directive 97/81/EC of 15 December 1997 *concerning the framework agreement on part-time work concluded by UNICE, CEEP and the ETUC*

- Research should be conducted in order to identify the current situation of part-time workers and their working conditions compared to full-time workers, as well as the key problems that are to be addressed by further measures.

- A general clause on the prohibition of discrimination against part-time workers should be included in the Estonian legal framework as the basis of special provisions on the equal treatment of full-time and part-time workers that are to be incorporated into the Estonian legal system.

- A special provision should be included in the Wages Act on the prohibition of discrimination of part-time workers, unless there are other relevant objective criteria on which the differences of wages are based.

- Part-time workers should have access to vocational training that would provide them with opportunities to pursue a career. Such access should be promoted on the legal and administrative levels.

- Possibilities should be introduced for part-time workers to request a transfer from full-time to part-time work, and *vice versa*, if/when such a position becomes available in the enterprise.

- Social dialogue between the state authorities and social partners, e.g. trade unions, should be enhanced regarding issues of non-discrimination of part-time and full-time workers unless differentiated treatment is justified on objective grounds.

Council Directive 86/613/EEC of 11 December 1986 *on the application of the principle of equal treatment between men and women engaged in an activity, including agriculture, in a self-employed capacity, and on the protection of self-employed women during pregnancy and motherhood*

- Data should be collected on the factual situation of self-employed workers and their spouses, particularly on the self-employed activities that women are engaged in and with a particular focus on rural areas.
- The principle of equal treatment for men and women should explicitly apply to self-employed workers.
- The term 'self-employed worker' should be clearly defined in Estonian legislation.
- Information campaigns on the rights of self-employed workers should be made for the general public.
- The participation of self-employed women in social security schemes should be investigated, including their protection during pregnancy and motherhood.

Council Directive 96/34/EC of 3 June 1996 *on the framework agreement on parental leave concluded by UNICE, CEEP, and the ETUC*

- Statistics and research should be collected with regard to which parent takes parental leave or sick leave in practice and why.
- Flexible working hours should be encouraged for both women and men.
- There should be a legal possibility for both parents to share the period of parental leave.
- Campaigns should be carried out to encourage a more equitable distribution of responsibilities in the home, and to encourage men to take a more active role in the home, specifically with regard to taking parental leave.

Council Directive 96/97/EC of 20 December 1996 *amending Directive 86/378/EEC on the implementation of the principle of equal treatment for men and women in occupational social security schemes*

- A monitoring system should be set up, for example under the anticipated Gender Equality Commission, to ensure that the principle of equal treatment of men and women is respected with regard to social security schemes.

- Research and data should be collected to assess the situation in practice and the possible indirect discriminatory impact of the social security schemes.

Country report: Estonia

INTRODUCTION

In April 2000, the Estonian Government adopted a concept paper on gender equality to serve as the basis for transposing the *acquis communautaire*, including in the fields covered by the Directives under review. A draft Gender Equality Act was also elaborated by the Ministry of Social Affairs setting forth the principles, definitions and legal measures necessary for the implementation of the principle of equal treatment. The objective of the Act is to promote equal opportunities for men and women and prevent gender discrimination, whether direct or indirect, as well as to establish equality in the labour market, education, social security schemes and other spheres.

The draft Gender Equality Act was approved by the Government and passed the first reading in Parliament; the second reading is scheduled for autumn 2002. Its adoption is critical to meeting the requirements of the various international documents that Estonia has acceded to (including the UN Convention on the Elimination of All Forms of Discrimination against Women and the Revised European Social Charter), and to harmonising Estonian legislation with the *acquis communautaire*.

Since June 2000, several new labour laws have been drafted and submitted to the Government, several of which entered into force in early 2002, including the Working and Rest Time Act, the Unemployment Insurance Act and the Holidays Act. The Wages Act has been amended in accordance with Directive 75/117/EEC, and the draft Employment Contracts Act has passed the second reading in Parliament.

In its Regular Report on Estonia's Progress towards Accession in 2000, the European Commission considered that further progress is needed in order to bring legislation on gender equality in line with the *acquis communautaire*. Indeed, the principle of equal treatment for women and men has not been sufficiently recognised in Estonia, either legally or conceptually. Furthermore, Estonian legislation does not comply with a number of Directives, including those on the burden of proof, part-time workers, and the principle of equal treatment for men and women as regards access to employment, vocational training and promotion, and working conditions. The laws are generally gender neutral, but the substantive meaning of gender equality and the spirit of the Directives, including the principle of equal treatment for self-employed men and women and discrimination on grounds of sex, are rarely understood. In the long term, this risks hindering social acceptance of the relevant legislative measures once they are adopted.

No research has been conducted to determine why persons who suffer discrimination in relation to equal opportunities do not bring the case to court, but it is largely attributed *inter alia* to the lack of protection for employees against dismissal by the employer in reaction to a complaint alleging a violation of the principle of equal treatment, and the traditional burden of proof model, which renders it difficult for persons alleging discrimination to collect evidence to support their claims. It is hoped that this situation will improve with the adoption of the draft Gender Equality Act, which provides for the reversal of the burden of proof. As no cases explicitly concerning gender equality have been brought before the court or the Legal Chancellor, the awareness of people in Estonia regarding these issues, including persons who have been discriminated against on grounds of sex, is very low.

There are no legal measures to protect part-time workers from discrimination, except with regard to holidays. Since women comprise two thirds of part-time workers, they are more vulnerable to discrimination in this area.

Although there is no sociological data or research on the actual working conditions of part-time workers compared with full-time workers, it is generally recognised that part-time workers are at a comparatively disadvantaged position. It is hoped that the measures necessary to improve this situation will be included in the future Employment Contracts Act, which is currently under reform.

The lack of research also applies to the actual situation of self-employed workers, although by law they are entitled to the same social protection (for example, social security schemes) as salaried workers provided that they pay social tax in accordance with the law. The last directly discriminatory provision in social security schemes was removed with the new State Pension Insurance Act, which equalises the age at which persons are entitled to receive an old-age pension.

While the adoption of the draft Gender Equality Act, together with amendments to other relevant legal acts, is vital to ensuring that Estonian legislation complies with EU Directives in the field of gender equality, its successful implementation will require a commitment to raising social awareness of the standards it encompasses, as well as trainings for judges, lawyers, the media, and government officials.

1. THE PRINCIPLE OF EQUAL PAY FOR WORK OF EQUAL VALUE

Council Directive 75/117/EEC of 10 February 1975 *on the approximation of laws of the Member States relating to the application of the principle of equal pay for men and women*

1.1 National legal framework concerning the principle of equal pay for work of equal value: General provisions

Estonia has adopted and amended a number of laws with a view to transposing the *acquis communautaire* and harmonising Estonian legislation with EU standards on equal opportunities, including the principle of equal pay.

The Wages Act

According to Article 5 of the Wages Act[2] it is prohibited to increase or reduce an employee's wages on the grounds of sex, nationality, colour, race, native language, social origin, social status, previous activities, religion, political or other opinion, or conscientious objection. It is prohibited to reduce wages on the grounds of *inter alia* marital status and family obligations.

Following amendments to the Wages Act, it is now prohibited to establish unfavourable conditions of remuneration for employers of the opposite sex for the same work or work of equal value. This is the first time that the principle of equal pay for equal work or work of equal value for women and men is established in Estonian law, thereby giving women a legal basis on which to claim equal standing in the labour market.

The Collective Agreements Act

The Collective Agreements Act stipulates that terms and conditions of a collective agreement which are less favourable to employees than those prescribed under other laws shall be invalid. There is currently no special provision on equal pay in collective agreements.

---

[2] The Wages Act regulates remuneration for persons with an employment contract, the granting of guarantees and the payment of compensation in relation to remuneration.

1.2 Implementation of the principle of equal pay for work of equal value: Legal foundations and institutional structures

The legal foundations in this area are rather weak, and consequently there are no special measures to enable employees who feel wronged by a violation of the principle of equal pay to pursue their claims before a court. Furthermore, there is no special protection for such workers or legal assistance/support from the state.

The Labour Inspectorate, a government agency operating within the structure of the Ministry of Social Affairs, oversees state supervision of the legislation regulating labour relations.

1.3 Job classification

There is currently no job classification system in the private sector to determine pay, but it is regulated in the public sector by the State Public Servants Official Titles and Salary Scale Act, whose purpose is to establish uniform titles of office and support staff positions, and a uniform salary scale in state administrative agencies.

1.4 Available legal procedures in cases involving the violation of the principle of equal pay for work of equal value

The Individual Labour Dispute Resolution Act regulates the procedure and conditions for resolving individual labour disputes between employees and employers, both of whom have the right to recourse to labour dispute committees or to the courts in order to resolve such disputes.

The Confederation of Estonian Trade Unions (Eesti Ametiühingute Keskliit, EAKL) and its affiliates provide free legal aid for trade union members, and the Labour Inspectorate is obliged to inform workers of their rights, although they do not represent them in proceedings. In labour dispute resolution, a committee worker is not entitled to free counsel, although according to Section 83(3) of the Code on Civil Procedure, the court may appoint a lawyer at the state's expense if the interests of a person may be insufficiently protected due to insolvency. In practice, a person need not be declared insolvent to benefit from this provision, it is normally sufficient if the person is unemployed and has no savings. There is no precise data available on the granting of free legal aid to persons who were employed at the time the complaint was submitted.

No discrimination on the basis of sex has been ascertained regarding individual labour disputes.

1.5 Means of informing employees of their right to equal pay for work of equal value

According to the Wages Act, employers must inform employees of the legal framework concerning the principle of equal pay at the start of the employment relationship. This provision is significant not only because it serves an informative function for employees, but also because it places responsibility for imparting such information with the employers themselves.

1.6 Role of trade unions

Trade Unions play an important role in the following:

- giving opinions on draft laws or bylaws on equal pay;
- in collective labour relations, trade unions can represent all workers, not only their members;[3]
- collective bargaining (promoting equal pay in collective agreements);
- information and consultation in the workplace;
- representing members before employers, labour dispute resolution committees and in court;
- drawing the attention of state supervisory bodies' to the violation of the principle of equal pay;[4]
- education within the trade union system about equal pay (for example, the EAKL established an Equal Treatment Commission [formerly the Women's Issues Commission], which takes an active part in educational projects on gender equality).

In terms of collective labour relations, trade unions can initiate proceedings in equality matters. Article 24(2) of the Trade Unions Act stipulates that if an employer violates a legal provision and a worker who is a member of a trade union accordingly submits a complaint

---

[3] Article 16(1) of the Trade Unions Act.
[4] Article 24(1) of the Trade Unions Act.

to the union, then the union can order that the violation be stopped and inspect all relevant documents and data. According to the Individual Labour Disputes Resolution Act, a trade union that represents workers may submit an application to the Labour Dispute Committee in individual proceedings, but this provision is interpreted in practice as requiring an initial petition from a worker to the trade union. As a result, the trade union can only initiate individual proceedings if the worker applies in writing for the trade union's assistance in the first place.

1.7 Women's factual situation regarding the principle of equal pay for work of equal value

Women's average wage has been approximately one quarter less than men's average wage since Estonia regained independence, but the difference has grown in recent years. For example, while women earned 80 percent of men's wages in 1992, the rate dropped to 72 percent of men's average wage in 1997.

Men's average hourly wage rose at a significantly quicker pace in the 1990s than it did for women (4.3 and 3.9 times respectively), and this applied to nearly all spheres of activity, except for civil servants, where due to a considerable decline in wage differential for men and women in 1997, a somewhat larger increase in women's average wage was noted. The greatest differences in the growth rates of wages for men and women were observed among service workers, salespersons and top specialists.[5]

The national minimum wage is fixed by way of trilateral negotiations between the government, employers' representatives and employees' organisations.

---

[5] Vöörmann (1999).

2. EQUAL TREATMENT FOR WOMEN AND MEN AS REGARDS ACCESS TO EMPLOYMENT, VOCATIONAL TRAINING AND PROMOTION, AND WORKING CONDITIONS

Council Directive 76/207/EEC of 9 February 1976 *on the implementation of the principle of equal treatment for men and women as regards access to employment, vocational training and promotion, and working conditions*

2.1 National legal framework concerning the principle of equal treatment for women and men: General provisions

The principle of equal treatment for women and men is only partially and vaguely incorporated into the Estonian legal framework and it is not *expressis verbis* established by any legal act regulating the field of employment.

There is a general provision on equality in the Constitution,[6] but specific regulations are needed to ensure the implementation of the Constitutional requirements and to combat existing inequalities. Unfortunately, such regulations are lacking in Estonia.

No cases explicitly concerning gender equality have been brought before the Legal Chancellor, who supervises the compliance of legislative acts with the principles set forth in the Constitution (including the principle of gender equality).

The Employment Contracts Act prohibits giving preference to employees or restricting employees' rights on the basis of their sex. Because this provision refers to the 'rights of employees', it does not cover access to employment and important aspects of the principle of equal treatment are thus actually left unaddressed. Furthermore, the Act does not use the term 'equal treatment'. There is an additional clause in Article 10 of the Employment Contracts Act that prohibits the restriction of the rights of employees or employers on the grounds of marital status or family obligations.

In this context it is important to note that according to Article 3 of the Constitution, generally recognised principles and rules of international law are an inseparable part of the Estonian legal system and the international conventions ratified by Estonia take precedence over national laws. Estonia has ratified the UN Convention on the Elimination of All Forms of Discrimination against Women and the Revised Social

---

[6] Article 12(1) of the Constitution (RT 1992, 26, 349) sets forth the following: "(1) Everyone is equal before the law. No one shall be discriminated against on the basis of nationality, race, colour, sex, language, origin, religion, political or other opinion, property or social status, or on other grounds."

Charter of the Council of Europe, both of which are incorporated in the Estonian legal system. However, no studies have been carried out to determine the extent to which the Convention or the Charter have been used to interpret national legislation or whether the norms of the Convention have been applied directly, and there is no relevant case law in this field.

2.2 The concept of discrimination on grounds of sex: Definition and legal sanctions

Estonian legislation is mostly gender neutral and there are few provisions that can be seen as directly discriminatory, although discrimination does exist in practice. The concepts of 'discrimination on grounds of sex', and 'direct' and 'indirect' discrimination have not been defined by law or through court practice, and this is a serious shortcoming.

There are no express legal ramifications for discrimination on grounds of sex in the Estonian legal system, although the draft Gender Equality Act does rectify this. It is possible to bring a case before a Labour Dispute Committee or a court within a period of four months in case of a violation of the Employment Contracts Act. This procedure is again only open to employees, and not to job applicants, and access to employment is therefore not included in the ambit of the Act. Unions representing employees and, where provided for by law, associations representing employers in labour disputes may also have recourse to labour dispute committees. There is no case law associated with discrimination on grounds of sex.

2.3 National legal framework concerning the principle of equal treatment as regards access to employment, vocational training and promotion, and working conditions

The application of the principle of equal treatment for women and men as regards access to employment, vocational training and promotion, and working conditions is poorly regulated and not ensured in practice in Estonia.

The field regulated by the Employment Contracts Act is currently under legal reform, and one of the aims of the new draft act, which will form a part of the new Civil Code, is to bring Estonian legislation in line with Directive 76/207/EEC.

The current Employment Contracts Act and other labour laws do not contain a clearly defined legal norm establishing the right to equal access to employment and the application of non-discriminatory selection criteria. Nevertheless, it is prohibited to take into account the sex of an employee in hiring or assigning duties, unless this is unavoidable due to the nature of the work or working conditions, although the provision is general in nature and compliance must be assessed by the court in individual cases. Unfortunately, there is no research on the effect of this provision or whether it has been abused in practice. The new Employment Services Act lists the equal treatment of women and men among the principles that must be obeyed when providing employment services.

The Advertisement Act prohibits all offensive and discriminatory advertising, and although it does not refer specifically to job advertisements,[7] it has been suggested that job advertisements which refer to the grounds listed in the provision on non-discrimination would violate the law. It has further been suggested that job applicants could be granted the same rights as employees by analogy, although this is a question of legal theory and has not been tested in practice. As of yet, no complaints have been filed with a court on this matter and so they have not been called upon to interpret these provisions.

Vocational training is regulated by the Adult Education Act, which does not contain any provisions establishing or implementing the principle of equal treatment, although the draft Gender Equality Act does address this area as well as promotions.

In terms of the implementation of the principle of equal treatment in employment, there is no difference between the public and private work sectors on a legislative level.

2.4 Protective measures with regard to women's participation in the labour market

According to the Employment Contracts Act it is prohibited to hire and employ women for heavy work, work that poses a health hazard or underground work. The list of work that is prohibited for women is determined by Government regulation and contains over 40 jobs. As all labour legislation is being harmonised with EU standards, this list will also be reviewed.

---

[7] Article 5 of the Advertising Act (RT I 1997, 52, 835) stipulates the following: "An advertisement is offensive if it is contrary to good morals and customs, calls on people to act unlawfully or to violate prevailing standards of decency, or if it contains such activities. An advertisement is considered offensive in particular if the advertisement presents, incites or endorses discrimination on the grounds of nationality, race, colour, sex, age, language, origin, religion, political or other opinion, and financial or social status or other circumstances."

There are no positive measures to increase the participation or access of women in the labour market and there is no express provision in Estonia that sets a basis for positive treatment. The draft Gender Equality Act, however, provides the necessary legal basis for such measures, and also establishes the promotion of equal treatment as an obligation of the state and the administration.

There has been an ILO (International Labour Organisation) programme in Estonia since 1999 entitled "More and Better Jobs for Women" in Estonia, and its main aim is to shape a favourable business climate for women and to provide business training. Lecturers have included leading Estonian specialists as well as experts from Finland. As of the end of 2000, approximately 1,000 women had participated in the training. Further training and re-training programmes for women have been supported through several foundations, including a programme to support women in rural areas that is financed by the Regional Development Fund.[8]

2.5 Prohibition of dismissal

There are no legal measures to protect employees against dismissal by the employer in reaction to a complaint or any legal proceedings initiated by an employee seeking compliance with the principle of equal treatment.

In practice, rather wide possibilities are given to employers to dismiss an employee, and some of the reasons for termination are rather vague by nature. For example, an employer may terminate an employment contract upon the unsuitability of an employee for his or her work (suitability is to be assessed by the employer) or upon loss of trust in an employee.

Protection of employees against dismissal for the reasons described above is provided for in the draft Gender Equality Act.

2.6 Women's and men's jobs

Although in practice strong horizontal and vertical job segregation can be seen in Estonia, there are no legal measure that prevent jobs from being classified as specifically for women or men. The law itself does not prohibit access to any jobs for women or for men, except for the prohibition noted above to hire or employ women for heavy work, work that poses a health hazard or underground work.

---

[8] Estonian Ministry of Social Affairs (2001).

2.7 Legal status of sexual harassment

Sexual harassment is not defined or prohibited in Estonian legislation, although this is an area covered by the draft Gender Equality Act.

3. PROTECTION OF PREGNANT WOMEN FROM THE INHERENT RISK OF CERTAIN ACTIVITIES AND RELATED EMPLOYMENT RIGHTS

Council Directive 92/85/EEC of 19 October 1992 *on the introduction of measures to encourage improvements in the safety and health at work of pregnant workers and workers who have recently given birth or are breastfeeding*

3.1 Legal and conceptual framework

The notion of preventing reproductive hazards in the workplace has been integrated into Estonian legislation in two ways: First, the Occupational Health and Safety Act obligates the employer to ensure that working conditions are not likely to cause genetic damage to the worker and are not harmful to the unborn child or to the reproductive health and pregnancy of the worker. Second, the Holiday Act allows women who are exposed to agents considered harmful to pregnancy or to the offspring to request a transfer to safe work from the beginning of the pregnancy. If such a task cannot be offered, the woman may not be entitled to a specific maternity leave and benefits, and a special maternity allowance is paid by the Social Insurance Institution.

The risk is assessed by an occupational physician who is acquainted with the workplace and the level of exposure to any hazards. Improvements in working conditions and work organisation and the selection of the safest possible materials are recommended as primary methods of prevention. Agents that are considered capable of causing generic damage, affecting the fertility of the male or female worker, and which are hazardous to the unborn child or to pregnancy are listed in accompanying regulations.

According to Article 10 of the Occupational Health and Safety Act:

> "(1) An employer shall create suitable work and rest [conditions] for pregnant women, women who are breastfeeding, minors and disabled workers.
>
> (2) Upon assigning work to pregnant women, women who are breastfeeding, or minors, employers shall observe the restrictions provided by legislation to ensure their safety. […]
>
> (6) The occupational health and safety requirements for the work of pregnant women and women who are breastfeeding shall be established by the Government of the Republic."

Regulation No.50 of the Government of Estonia stipulates that an employer shall ensure full compliance with the occupational health and safety requirements according to the regulation where a female worker informs the employer of her condition and provides a certified medical certificate.

There is no concrete definition of 'pregnant worker', 'worker who has recently given birth' or 'worker who is breastfeeding' in Estonian legislation.

3.2 Assessing the risk to the safety or health of a pregnant worker and employers' obligations

The Occupational Health and Safety Act lists the occupational health and safety requirements for a working environment, the duties of employers and workers in creating a working environment that does not present health risks, the organisation of occupational health and safety in enterprises and agencies and at the state level, the procedure for resolving corresponding disputes, and liability for non-compliance with the occupational health and safety requirements.

Employers are obliged to ensure compliance with the occupational health and safety requirements in every aspect related to the work:

- conduct regular internal controls of the working environment to plan, organise and monitor the occupational health and safety situation in the enterprise;
- review the organisation of internal control of the working environment annually and analyse its results and, if necessary, adjust measures;
- ascertain the risk factors present in the working environment, measure their parameters and assess the effect of the risk factors on workers' health;
- based on the risk assessment of the working environment, prepare a written action plan designating measures to prevent or reduce health risks;
- notify the workers of the risk factors, the results of risk assessments and of the measures to be implemented in order to prevent damage to health through working environment representatives, members of the working environment council and workers' representatives;
- arrange for the health surveillance of workers and provision of other occupational health services either through the occupational health service of the enterprise or based on a contract with an occupational health service or occupational health doctor, and to cover the expenses relating thereto;
- at the request of a worker and at the decision of a doctor, transfer the worker to another position temporarily or permanently or ease his or her working

conditions temporarily, pursuant to the procedure provided for by Acts regulating employment and service relationships.

According to Article 2 of the Government Regulation No.50, an employer is obliged to:

- assess the nature, degree and duration of exposure to the agents listed in Article 6 and work processes involving specific risks to the health and safety of female workers, including any possible effect on pregnancy or on breastfeeding;
- inform the female worker and workers' representative of the results of the risk assessment and measures that must be taken with regard to their health and safety.

Article 28 of the Occupational Health and Safety Act stipulates *inter alia* that a fine of up to 50,000 Kroons shall be imposed for concealing an occupational accident, or in the case of an occupational disease, for failure to investigate or prepare a report, involve a work environment representative in the investigation, conduct the health surveillance of a worker, or for non-compliance with the restrictions on the work of female, minor or disabled workers.

According to Article 3 of the Government Regulation No.50:

"(1) An employer should implement the following measures in order to protect health and safety of female workers:

- temporarily adjust working conditions;
- change the organisation of work, including the reduction of working hours and enabling sufficient breaks;
- make work temporarily easier;
- transfer the worker to a more suitable job;
- temporarily transfer the worker to daytime or night work."

If the adjustment of working conditions is not technically and/or objectively feasible, the employer is obliged to temporarily transfer the female worker to easier work or another job, taking into account the capacity and professional experience of the worker. If the labour inspector establishes that it is not possible for the employer to temporarily ease the working conditions of the female worker or temporarily transfer the female worker to another job, the female worker is released from work for the period prescribed at the decision of a doctor. For that period the female worker shall receive compensation from medical insurance funds.

In accordance with the above, pregnant women cannot be discharged for pregnancy-related reasons or forced to work, if this will damage their health.

3.3 Cases in which exposure is prohibited for pregnant and breastfeeding workers

According to Article 4 of the Government Regulation No.50, pregnant workers are not obliged to perform work involving a hyperbaric atmosphere, the Rubella virus, toxoplasma, lead and lead derivates, underground mining work, night work and the manual handling of heavy loads. Breastfeeding workers are not obliged to perform duties when the work involves lead and lead derivates or underground mining work.

3.4 Night work

As noted above, pregnant workers are not obliged to perform night work. According to Article 3(4) of the Government Regulation No.50, if night work may affect the health of a worker who is breastfeeding or the health of a breastfeeding child, an employer is obliged to temporarily transfer the worker to daytime work. If the labour inspector of the employer establishes that it is not possible for the employer to temporarily transfer the worker to daytime work, the worker concerned is released from work for the period prescribed by a doctor.

3.5 Maternity leave

Issues related to maternity leave are governed by law, and there is no need for additional agreements in the employment contract.

According to Article 28 of the Holidays Act, on the basis of a certificate, a woman is granted pregnancy leave of 70 calendar days prior to giving birth and maternity leave of 56 calendar days after giving birth. In the case of multiple births or a delivery with complications, maternity leave of 70 calendar days is granted. Pregnancy leave and maternity leave are combined and granted in full, regardless of the date of birth of the child.

Compensation for the period of pregnancy leave and maternity leave is paid pursuant to Article 4(10) of the Health Insurance Act.

Antenatal Examinations
According to Article 2(5) of the Government Regulation No.50, employers are required to ensure that pregnant workers are granted time off without loss of pay in order to attend antenatal examinations if such examinations must take place during working hours.

3.6 Prohibition of dismissal and employment rights

According to Article 92 of the Employment Contracts Act:

"(1) It is prohibited for an employer to terminate an employment contract with a pregnant woman or a woman raising a child under three years of age, except in cases specifically provided for by law.
"(2) The termination of an employment contract with an employee specified in paragraph (1) of this Article on the bases prescribed in clauses 86(1)–(2) and (5)–(8) is only permitted with the consent of the labour inspector at the location of the employer.
According to Article 87, the employer is required to justify the need terminate the employment contract when giving written notice.

According to Article 87 of the Individual Labour Dispute Resolution Act, if the termination of an employment contract is declared unlawful, an employee has the right to reclaim his or her former position. In such a case, a labour dispute resolution body shall issue a decision on the reinstatement of the employee to his or her former job or position. If an employee contests the lawfulness of the termination of his or her employment contract but does not request reinstatement, a labour dispute resolution body shall, upon declaring the termination of the employment contract unlawful, deem the employee to have left employment upon his or her own initiative as of the date that the decision of the labour dispute resolution body is made public.

In addition to the Occupational Health and Safety Act, the health and safety of pregnant workers and workers who have recently given birth or are breastfeeding are protected by the legal provisions according to the above-mentioned Government Regulation in full compliance with Directive 92/85/EEC.

4. THE BURDEN OF PROOF IN CASES OF DISCRIMINATION BASED ON SEX

Council Directive 97/80/EC of 15 December 1997 *on the burden of proof in cases of discrimination based on sex*

4.1 Legal framework concerning indirect discrimination and specific legal means of implementing the principle of equal treatment for women and men

There is no definition of indirect discrimination in Estonian legislation, although the draft Gender Equality Act does provide that an apparently neutral provision, criteria or practice that puts a substantially higher proportion of members of one sex at a disadvantaged position compared to members of the opposite sex shall constitute indirect discrimination. The exceptions to this general norm outlined in the Directive are introduced separately by the draft Gender Equality Act in the list of notions that do not constitute discrimination.

The legal means for implementing the principle of equal treatment for women and men as regards access to employment, vocational training and promotion and working conditions are regulated by the Code of Civil Procedure and the Code of Administrative Procedure, as well as the Individual Labour Disputes Act and the Collective Labour Disputes Act. These legal instruments contain no special provisions or procedures whereby employees can lodge a complaint specifically relating to equal treatment.

Individual labour disputes are resolved by the labour dispute committees or the courts; there is no special authority to resolve cases arising from violations of the principle of equal treatment. Accordingly, improving the legal mechanisms for implementation is among the objectives of the draft Gender Equality Act. The procedures of mediation and conciliation have been established by the law as 'out of court' procedures for individual labour disputes. Mediation aims to achieve an agreement between the employee and employer with the aid of a representative of a directing body of a union or federation of employees. In the conciliation procedure, the employer establishes a conciliation committee in coordination with a representative of employees or a directing body of a union or federation of employees.

Attempts to resolve disputes by agreement do not deprive parties of the right of recourse to labour dispute resolution bodies if they discover that the labour dispute cannot be resolved by mediation or conciliation. Conciliation, which draws on impartial experts to help the parties in labour disputes reach a mutually satisfactory solution, is also established for collective labour disputes.

In civil court proceedings, the conciliation of parties is one of the objectives of pre-trial court proceedings, in the course of which a court may require parties to appear before an impartial person (conciliator) appointed by the court. The court is obliged to first determine whether a settlement can be reached in each case and to explain the consequences of terminating proceedings by a settlement; for example, the same parties cannot file a new action on the same basis.

4.2 The burden of proof procedure in litigation concerning the violation of the principle of equal treatment for women and men and rules of evidence

The burden of proof and rules of evidence are the same in cases involving a violation of the principle of equal treatment as in other civil court proceedings and the *actori incumbit probatio* principle applies as the general legal principle, meaning that each party must prove the facts on which her/his claims are based. This principle is established in the Code of Civil Procedure,[9] as well as by the Individual Labour Disputes Act and the Government Regulation on Labour Dispute Committees. The court has a rather passive role in the civil proceedings (unlike in administrative proceedings) and the case is decided only on the basis of evidence produced by the parties.

In practice, the regulation of the burden of proof and the rules of evidence are among the main reasons for the lack of any case law concerning the implementation of the principle of equal treatment in civil and administrative matters, including in the field of employment.

Considering the position of the person who suffered the discrimination, and the difficulties she/he might have collecting evidence and thus proving the discrimination that took place, the present regulation is not effective in ensuring just adjudication. As a rule, it is firstly incumbent upon the complainant who filed a claim to produce evidence supporting the claim; the respondent can either admit or contest the evidence,

---

[9] Section 91 of the Code of Civil Procedure (RT I 1998, 43/45, 666) stipulates the following on the burden of proof and submission of evidence:

"(1) Each party shall prove the facts on which the claims and objections of the party are based.
(2) Evidence shall be submitted by the parties and other participants in proceedings. A court may propose that the parties and other participants in proceedings submit additional evidence. A court may collect evidence at its own initiative for the protection of the public interest."

and is entitled – but not obliged – to submit additional evidence. The respondent's failure to produce evidence does not lead to an inference of discrimination.

The draft Gender Equality Act contains a provision on the reversal of the burden of proof in cases of the violation of the principle of equal treatment of women and men as regards access to employment, vocational training and promotion, and working conditions.

In terms of informing persons of the legal regulations for bringing a case involving the violation of the principle of equal treatment to court, according to the Constitution all legal acts must be published in the special official journal *Riigi Teataja*.

4.3 Case law on the violation of the principle of equal treatment for women and men

There is no information available on cases concerning the violation of the principle of equal treatment as regards employment, vocational training, remuneration, social protection and promotion, or working conditions in Estonia and the county and city courts have not rendered any decisions in this area.

5. NON-DISCRIMINATION AGAINST PART-TIME WORKERS

Council Directive 97/81/EC *concerning the framework agreement on part-time work concluded by UNICE, CEEP and the ETUC*

5.1 National legal framework concerning part-time workers and employment conditions

The percentage of part-time workers increased at the beginning of the transition period in Estonia, and while this was a matter of choice for some people, it was inevitable for certain categories, including pensioners (who wanted to retain a full pension) and young people (who wanted to reconcile work and studies).

There are few legal provisions regulating part-time work in Estonia, and in practice the working conditions of part-time workers can often be discriminatory compared to full-time workers. Due to a lack of research in this area, however, there is no satisfactory data on the factual situation of part-time workers in Estonia.

The Estonian legislation does not explicitly contain the concept of 'part-time worker', but 'part-time working time' means 'working time that is less than the established standard working time at the place of employment and which is applied upon the agreement of an employee and employer'.

There are several differences in the definitions provided by the EU Framework agreement and the relevant provisions of Estonian national legislation. First, Estonian legislation does not introduce the notion of a 'comparable full-time worker' that would clarify the ways of determining what is meant by 'part-time work.'

Second, in Estonia there is no legal norm for situations where there is no comparable full-time worker in the same establishment, and comparison can be made with regard to any standard-time worker in the same establishment.

At the legislative level, no distinction is made between full-time and part-time workers with regard to working conditions. At the same time, there is no explicit requirement that would prohibit discrimination against part-time workers. For example, *expressis verbis* it is only stated that regarding holidays, the duration of a holiday is not shortened in the case of part-time employment. Other working conditions are to be agreed upon by the parties in individual or collective labour agreements.

From a legal point of view, there are almost no restrictions on the content of labour agreements with regard to working conditions for part-time workers, with the exception of the duration of holidays. The principle of non-discrimination of part-time workers with regard to employment conditions has not been set forth by any legal act and its implementation is not assured by the law either. In practice, this often leads to employment contracts that do not respect the rights of part-time workers.

Discrimination against part-time workers with regard to working conditions is most likely to occur in connection with remuneration because the law stipulates that the wage rate of an employee shall be determined through the agreement of the parties upon entering into an employment contract and in practice this means less favourable wage rates are often applied to part-time workers.

In cases of less favourable treatment, the national legislation does not provide adequate remedies since protection is only established with regard to holidays. Again, this contributes to the lack of case law and there is no information regarding any claims concerning discrimination against part-time workers that have been brought to a court or labour dispute committee in Estonia.

In practice, the equal treatment of part-time and full-time workers is better protected in the public sector where the situation is also easier to control, although differential treatment is not provided for by law.

In general, it is not possible to request a transfer from full-time to part-time work, or *vice versa,* if a respective position becomes available in the workplace, and there is no legal norm regulating this. However, the Working and Rest Time Act stipulates that persons raising children under 14 years of age or disabled children under 16 years of age are entitled to work part-time. The same advantages are enjoyed by pregnant women.

Employers do have the right to establish part-time working time pursuant to the procedures and conditions prescribed by law, for example in the event of a temporary decrease in work volume or orders.

There are no legal or administrative procedures stipulating requirements for concrete measures to facilitate access to part-time work at all levels of the enterprise, including skilled and managerial positions or to facilitate part-time workers' access to vocational training to enhance career opportunities.

According to statistics from 1999, seven percent of employed persons worked part-time (currently less than 35 hours a week). About one third of those working part-time wanted and were ready to work longer hours, but could not find suitable work. According to the available statistical data, women comprise approximately two thirds of all part-time workers.[10]

---

[10] Estonian Ministry of Social Affairs (2001).

6. THE PRINCIPLE OF EQUAL TREATMENT TO SELF-EMPLOYED WORKERS AND THEIR ASSISTING SPOUSES

Directive 86/613/EEC of the 11 December 1986 *on the application of the principle of equal treatment between men and women engaged in an activity, including agriculture, in a self-employed capacity, and on the protection of self-employed women during pregnancy and motherhood.*

6.1 National legal framework on self-employment: General provisions

Definition of self-employed workers

There is no specific definition of self-employed workers in Estonian legislation. Section 3 of the Commercial Code provides that any natural person may be self-employed and shall be entered into the commercial register at his or her request.

Laws and regulations related to the directive

There is no legislation directly governing the equal treatment of self-employed workers and/or their spouses, although the Constitution does contain a general provision on equality. The Action Plan of the Government of the Republic states that this Directive will be transposed into national legislation with the adoption of the Gender Equality Act.

There are no provisions contrary to the principle of equal treatment as defined in Directive 76/207/EEC, especially with regard to the establishment or extension of a business or the launching or extension of any other form of self-employed activity, including financial facilities.

Acceptance of the aim of the directive

The general aim of the Directive is accepted by the authorities in Estonia responsible for the elaboration of social policy in general, and for the elaboration of the draft Gender Equality Act in particular.

In general, the level of awareness of this Directive is low among self-employed workers and their spouses and there have not been any information campaigns on its content. There has not been any ongoing debate and no arguments have been raised against the philosophy of the Directive, although this does not in itself indicate an understanding of the principles enshrined in it.

The Estonian authorities and relevant organisations are currently in the process of raising awareness of the principle of equal treatment in society as a whole and several information booklets have been published in order to increase awareness on issues related to equal treatment.[11] However, there has not been any awareness raising on such concrete issues as the equal treatment of self-employed workers and there is still a strong need for more substantial steps in this area for the different sectors of the population as well as the relevant authorities in all aspects of gender equality.

The principle of equal treatment of self-employed men and women

There are no provisions on the equal treatment of self-employed men and women in Estonia, and while the draft Gender Equality Act does not contain any specific reference to self-employed men and women, they are included in its ambit.

6.2 Social rights of spouses

The Health Insurance Act provides that the spouses of self-employed workers shall be covered by medical insurance if the self-employed worker pays social taxes.

Formation of companies by unmarried persons

The formation of companies is regulated by the Commercial Code, which does not stipulate any special conditions for married couples; they have the same possibilities as unmarried persons. Estonian rules concerning the establishment of companies between spouses do not restrict the rights of women *de jure*. There is no concrete numerical data on the situation of spouses who are not in an employment relationship or who are not partners but who participate on a regular basis in business activity, fulfilling the same or additional duties as the other family member.[12]

Recognition of the work of spouses

No concrete steps or initiatives have been taken by the government or interest groups/organisations so far to encourage the recognition of the work of spouses referred to in Article 2(b) of the Directive. However, there has been some debate in public fora in connection to the elaboration of the draft Gender Equality Act, whereby the need to improve the position and work of spouses has been raised.

---

[11] For example: *Tegevusjuhis naiste ja meeste võrdseks tasustamiseks võrdväärse töö eest*. Sotsiaalministeerium, Phare, Tallinn, 1999; *100 mõistet naiste ja meeste võrdõiguslikkuse kohta*. Sotsiaalministeerium, Phare, Tallinn, 1999.

[12] Estonian Ministry of Social Affairs (2001).

The draft Family Law Act also touches upon this issue, Article 28 of which sets forth the rights of women to claim a share of the income corresponding to their contribution. This draft law has led to large-scale discussions within society, raising issues related to the position of spouses in the family and the new arrangements concerning common property have been debated in the press and over the internet.[13] One of the central issues has been whether the draft act is more or less favourable for the spouse in the 'weaker' position (which in most cases is the housewife). On the one hand, it has been claimed that the draft provides the possibility to keep one's belongings and earnings as separate property. On the other hand, it is argued that the draft would prohibit transactions of property used in the everyday life of the family (for example, selling the house where the family resides if it is the separate property of one spouse).

The rights of self-employed workers whose operational activity is interrupted owing to pregnancy or motherhood

There are no services providing temporary replacements for female self-employed workers or the wives of self-employed workers during interruptions in their occupational activity owing to pregnancy or motherhood.

They are entitled to cash benefits under the health insurance schemes, and social security is guaranteed on a uniform basis both for women in both rural and urban areas.

6.3 Contributory social security system for self-employed workers

There is no special contributory social security system for self-employed workers in Estonia; they must pay social taxes in order to provide themselves and their spouses with coverage under the existing schemes of social security (where a labour contract exists, this obligation falls on the employer). The social tax must be paid in accordance with the Social Tax Act.

Health insurance is one of the social security schemes in Estonia and operates through a compulsory scheme under which employers are obliged by law to pay social tax for their employees. Self-employed persons pay this social tax themselves. Both categories are then deemed to be insured and members of the Sick Fund.

The following persons are also treated equally with the insured and are members of the Sick Fund:

---

[13] There is a special site created as a citizens' forum for debate on draft legislation: TOM (*Täna Otsustan Mina* – Today I Decide, <http://tom.riik.ee/>) where the draft Family Law Act has been under discussion.

- dependent family members;
- non-working persons raising a child up to the age of three;
- pregnant women.

In order to become a member of the Sick Fund, self-employed persons must present a personal application, a certificate of registration for advance payments issued by the local tax board covering their place of residence, proof of their permanent or main place of residence and proof of payment of social tax on their income.

Both self-employed workers and their spouses can voluntarily join certain social security schemes, for example the accumulative pension scheme, but the unemployment social security scheme does not extend to self-employed workers.

6.4 Related research and statistics

The main source of statistics related to the labour force is the quarterly Estonian labour force surveys prepared by the Statistical Office.[14] Although this facilitates an analysis of the situation of men and women in the labour market, the status and situation of self-employed persons in this regard has not been researched thoroughly enough, and no special studies have been conducted on this topic.

Research on women in agriculture

The tentative percentage of women in working in the primary sector (including agriculture, hunting and forestry and fishing) is 4.2 percent, compared with 10.3 percent of men (see Table 1).

---

[14] All the surveys referred to below are available on the internet site of the Statistical Office: <http://www.stat.vil.ee/l-market/indexi.htm>.

Table 1. Employed persons by sex, place of residence and sector of the economy
(3rd quarter of 2001)

Place of residence, sector of economy	Males		Females		Total	
	thousands	*%*	*thousands*	*%*	*thousands*	*%*
Town and countryside						
Primary sector	32.7	10.3	12.9	4.2	45.6	7.3
Secondary sector[15]	132.9	41.7	66.3	21.6	199.1	31.8
Tertiary sector	153.1	48.0	228.3	74.3	381.3	60.9
TOTAL	318.7	100.0	307.4	100.0	626.1	100.0
Town						
Primary sector	(6.6)	(3.1)	...	...	(8.0)	(1.8)
Secondary sector	97.6	45.8	52.9	23.2	150.5	34.1
Tertiary sector	109.1	51.1	173.3	76.2	282.4	64.1
TOTAL	213.2	100.0	227.6	100.0	440.8	100.0
Countryside						
Primary sector	26.1	24.8	11.5	14.4	37.6	20.3
Secondary sector	35.3	33.5	13.3	16.7	48.7	26.3
Tertiary sector	44.0	41.7	54.9	68.9	98.9	53.4
TOTAL	105.4	100.0	79.8	100.0	185.2	100.0

Source: Labour force survey, 3rd quarter of the year 2001.

In rural areas, there is a higher number of men who are self-employed or working in their own enterprise.

Social perceptions of self-employed men and women

There is unfortunately no research on how self-employed women, including women in agriculture, are viewed in Estonia. It is generally regarded as normal, and there is no discussion or debate in public forums on this issue.

Special attention should be paid to women in rural areas, however, as an important reason why women miss out on productive resources and training in rural areas is their invisibility and limited awareness of their rights. Women's work in the agricultural sector is often composed of unpaid work on a family farm or enterprise, work for

---

[15] The secondary sector includes mining, manufacturing, electricity, gas and water supply, and construction. The tertiary sector is the service sector.

means of subsistence, part-time or seasonal work. This work has been underestimated to a large extent. Such activities are not reflected in official statistics and are viewed as housework, the level of recognition for which is not sufficient. Some women's groups have formed to support self-employed women, for example in rural areas, at their own initiative.

Percentage of self-employed men and women

According to statistics, approximately 5 percent of workers are self-employed, and the percentage of unpaid family workers, which includes spouses (usually women) who help their self-employed spouses and housewives, is approximately one percent. There is no data related to the main kinds of self-employed activities that women are engaged in.

Past and recent trends on self-employment

Because gender disaggregated statistics on self-employed persons is a rather new phenomenon in Estonia that has been increasingly included in statistics since the second half of the 90s, it is difficult to compare the number of self-employed women now with the number in the years prior to independence.

Estonia is a society of salaried workers, and men have been much more active in enterprises than women. For example, in 1997, the number of entrepreneurs was much higher among men (9.1 percent) than among women (3.0 percent) and the proportion has not changed much during the past decade.[16] In terms of women's general situation in the labour market, the tendency was for young women to leave the labour market at the end of the 1980s and early 1990s. This was due in part to an increased birth rate and the prolongation of parental leave, which meant that many women did not re-enter the labour market.

Approximately 83 percent of both women and men working in agriculture were salaried workers in 1999. 6.34 percent of women and 7 percent of men worked on self-owned farms; 2.4 percent of women and 4.2 percent of men worked in self-owned enterprises; 6.46 percent of women and 4.5 percent of men worked in subsidiary housekeeping and 0.93 percent of women and 1.71 percent of men were self-employed.

There have been programmes to encourage women to become self-employed in rural areas and a national regional policy programme to support village movement has been implemented since 1996. The programme further aims to support self-initiative and small businesses, and women's organisations have been very active supporters and implementers of the projects. A database of women entrepreneurs in South-Eastern Estonia has been created, a network of women's organisations is developing, and business plans and marketing strategies have been developed. The situation of rural

---

[16] Vöörmann (2000).

women and strategies for guaranteeing their economic capabilities are issues that have featured on the agenda.

There is no data on the tendency for married couples to form businesses or companies together, nor is there any information on the percentage of businesses run by self-employed married couples.

Research results on the status and rights of self-employed women

No research has been conducted on the status or rights of self-employed women, such as women assisting their spouses and women during pregnancy or motherhood. It is therefore difficult to estimate whether they are discriminated against in practice or whether self-employed work is less favourable for these women than other forms of work.

6.5 Legal means of redress

The Estonian national legislation contains the measures necessary to enable persons who consider themselves wronged by the failure to apply the principle of equal treatment in self-employed activities to pursue their claims by judicial process. Self-employed workers cannot turn to individual labour dispute commissions as employees can; they must present their claims directly to the court in accordance with the Civil Procedure Act. With regard to seeking recourse from other competent authorities, all persons who consider themselves wronged by the failure to apply the principle of equal treatment in self-employed activities also have the opportunity to file a complaint with the Legal Chancellor.

In practice it would be very difficult to make a strong case only upon the constitutional principle of equality before the law. The absence of concrete provisions is clearly among the main reasons for the lack of case law on this issue so far.

Estonian national legislation does not contain any provisions requiring the measures adopted pursuant to this Directive to be brought to the attention of the bodies representing self-employed workers and vocational training centres.

7. THE FRAMEWORK ON PARENTAL LEAVE

Council Directive 96/34/EC of 3 June *1996 on the framework agreement on parental leave concluded by UNICE, CEEP, and ETUC.*

7.1 National legal framework on parental leave: General provisions

The Holidays Act

The Holidays Act, which is in line with Directive 96/34/EC, entered into force on 1 January 2002 and regulates the duration and organisation of granting holidays for employees and public officials. According to the Act a father is entitled to additional childcare leave of 14 calendar days during a mother's pregnancy and maternity leave or during a period of two months after the birth of the child. The holiday pay for father's additional childcare leave is paid from the state budget. At the request of the employee, the employer is required to grant unpaid leave to an employee raising a child up to fourteen years of age. The new regulation extends the father's right to unpaid leave irrespective of whether he is raising the child alone or not. An adoptive parent of a child of up to four years of age is granted leave of 70 calendar days, starting from the day of adoption (formerly, the age limit was one year).

According to Article 29(1), a mother or father shall be granted parental leave at his or her request for raising a child up to 3 years of age. It is for the parents to decide which one of them takes the leave. Parental leave may be used in whole or in part at any time to raise a child up to three years of age. It is not subject to a period of work or length of service qualification.

The person taking the leave should inform the employer of the beginning and ending dates of the leave, and the employer may not postpone the granting of parental leave under any circumstances.

Legal protection against dismissal on the grounds of an application for or the taking of parental leave

Employment Contracts Act

Article 91(1) provides that an employer cannot terminate an employment contract while an employee is on holiday (including parental leave and unpaid leave). Furthermore, Article 92(1) prohibits an employer from terminating an employment contract with a pregnant woman or a woman raising a child under three years of age, except on the following grounds: 1) upon liquidation of the enterprise, agency or other organisation; 2) upon the declaration of bankruptcy of the employer; 3) due to unsatisfactory results of a probationary period; 4) due to an indecent act by an employee.

7.2 Social security during parental leave, especially healthcare

Social Tax Act
Article 6(1) outlines special cases for paying social tax, including persons who are paid a childcare allowance pursuant to the State Family Benefits Act.

State Family Benefits Act
Article 3(1) provides that childcare allowance is among the state benefits, and Article 6 provides that a monthly childcare allowance shall be paid to one parent raising one or more children up to three years of age or three children up to the age of eight.

Health Insurance Act
Article 8(3) provides that a benefit shall be paid on the basis of a certificate in order to care for an ill child under 14 years of age and the benefit shall be paid in order to care for a child under three years of age (or a disabled child under 16 years of age) if the person caring for the child is ill or is in hospital for childbirth.

In these cases the benefit shall be paid for no more than fourteen calendar days.

7.3 Parental leave and equal opportunities policy

Although equality between women and men has become a very important aspect of Estonian social policy and the public is more willing to discuss the rights and responsibilities of men and women, in its contemporary, internationally recognised meaning it remains a relatively new concept for Estonia.

On basis of the Government Order No.480-k of 27 May, 1996, an inter-ministerial committee was formed and specified the development priorities for Estonia concerning gender equality:

- to establish and strengthen national machinery for gender equality at all levels of government;

- to analyse compliance of Estonian legislation with international standards on equality;
- to ensure the availability of official gender-sensitive statistics;
- to improve the position of women in the labour market and increase their participation in decision-making processes.

In December 1996, a Bureau of Equality Between Women and Men was established in the Ministry of Social Affairs to coordinate the mainstreaming of a gender equality perspective into socio-political development. One of the principles of Estonia's national policy on equality is also the reconciliation of working and family life (and consequently issues of unpaid housework, availability of childcare services, and the possibility for men to take parental leave).[17]

Government of the Republic Act

Another step towards promoting equal opportunities policy is the amendment to the Government of the Republic Act, which adds the promotion of the equality of men and women to the responsibilities of the Ministry of Social Affairs.

Strengthening the policy on equal opportunities for men and women is an important component of Estonia's Employment Action Plan, since the reconciliation of family responsibilities is an inseparable component of gender equality at work. For various reasons women find it difficult to harmonise these two areas and it is therefore necessary to study these issues in greater depth in order to offer more viable solutions.

To account for gender discrepancies in economic status and work productivity, a collection of indicators will be developed based on two aspects:

- different opportunities and positions for men and women in the labour market at the organisational/business level;
- parameters characterising the division of paid and unpaid jobs and time resources between men and women.

The Ministry of Social Affairs will be responsible for implementing this task.

---

[17] Papp (2000).

7.4 Research on the reconciliation of family and professional responsibilities and on sharing responsibilities between men and women

Statistics and research on the number of women who return to work after giving birth and men who take parental leave

According to data from the "Estonia 98" population survey,[18] women and men aged between 18–70 years old have similar 'life values', prioritising children, family and health in that order.

Men and women place almost equal importance on professional work, and this situation has changed substantially compared to the early 1990s, when less value was placed on this area. Data from "Estonia 98" reveals that persons who work, are married and have children, place the highest value on the family.

There are no specific separate statistics or research data about men and women who take parental or sick leave.

Demographic, social or cultural considerations affecting the reconciliation of work and family responsibilities

Despite the similar life values that men and women share, their conditions, opportunities and actual division of labour are quite different. In cases where there is the most housework, i.e., in families with underage children, the division of chores between working parents is rarely equitably distributed. The most equal division occurs in families with working parents where there are no children or the children have already left home, primarily due to the reduction in housework.

Surveys also show that if both spouses agree on the division of household tasks and consider the existing distribution to be fair, they are both more satisfied with family life. If, however, the opinions of the men and women differ greatly, then discord and dissatisfaction are more prevalent. However, despite the relative conservatism of public opinion, it is apparent that in practice there has been a shift towards equalising the distribution of home duties between men and women.

Although the near 100 percent employment rate that was characteristic of the Soviet period has decreased for both men and women, employment in Estonia is still higher than the European average. Estonian women have not adopted part-time work to the

---

[18] The survey was carried out by sociologists from the Institute of International and Social Studies at the end of 1998. The survey covered the population aged 18–70. 2,317 people were surveyed throughout Estonia.

degree favoured by women in many other countries though, and still favour full-time work. According to "Estonia 98," 16–17 percent of both men and women work part-time either because of personal preference or at the employer's request. The same proportion (15 percent) of men and women among the employed population hold more than one job. However, two major differences have remained. First, carrying out household tasks is still considered to be primarily the wife's responsibility even when both spouses work outside the home. Second, although engaged in the same kind of duties, women's average salary is lower than men's and, therefore, men's share of the family income is still generally higher than the women's.

8. The Principle of Equal Treatment of Men and Women in Occupational Social Security Schemes

Council Directive 96/97/EC of 20 December 1996 *amending Directive 86/378/EEC on the implementation of the principle of equal treatment for men and women in occupational social security schemes*

8.1 National legal framework on social security schemes: General provisions

Estonia has been developing a social security system since 1991 that contains all the social security benefits within the meaning of Directive 71/1408/EEC (health, pregnancy, maternity, invalidity, old-age, family and other benefits). Pension reform has nearly reached the stage of completion, and a three-pillar pension insurance system has been established. The first pillar is a mandatory national pension scheme based on the principle of solidarity. The second pillar is a mandatory pension scheme based on the accumulation principle. The third pillar is constituted by optional additional pension schemes based on accumulation principle. The pillars are of a complementary nature. Adding pre-financed private pension schemes has been seen necessary for provision of long-term stability of the pension system.

In general, Estonian legislation does not directly violate the principle of equal treatment of men and women in social security schemes. The different retirement ages for men and women was an example of such a violation, although it has since been amended. Discrimination will continue to exist though until the ages are equalised in 2016.

The Constitution
Article 28 provides that everyone has the right to health protection, and Estonian citizens have the right to state assistance in the case of old age, incapacity for work, loss of a provider, or need. The categories and extent of assistance and the conditions and procedures for receiving assistance are provided for by special laws. Citizens of foreign states and stateless persons who are in Estonia have this right on the same grounds as Estonian citizens, unless otherwise provided by law.

The draft Gender Equality Act

Article 1 provides for the promotion of gender equality in the social sphere.[19]

Health Insurance Act

Health insurance is a state-guaranteed system for the payment of costs related to protecting the health of residents of the Republic of Estonia, costs related to their temporary incapacity for work and their medical treatment as a result of illness or injury, and benefits in the event of pregnancy and childbirth. The Health Insurance Act also applies to persons whose work is interrupted by illness, accident or maternity.

Unemployment Insurance Act

Social security schemes in case of involuntary unemployment are regulated by the Unemployment Insurance Act. Article 1(1) regulates the conditions and rules for paying and determining benefits in the event of the loss of a job, termination of collective agreements and insolvency of the employer as well as the organisation of unemployment insurance.

Social Protection of the Unemployed Act

The rights of unemployed persons are also protected by the Social Protection of the Unemployment Act, which regulates the registration of persons as unemployed and the payment of state unemployment benefits, single benefits and stipends through employment offices.

Employment Service Act

This Act regulates the provision of employment services to persons seeking employment and to employers.

State Pension Insurance Act

The social security schemes for retired and disabled workers are regulated by the State Pension Insurance Act, which provides the legislative framework for old-age pension and pension for incapacity for work, the survivor's pension and the national pension. Pension insurance is also regulated by the Pension Funds Act.

---

[19] Article 1 of the draft Gender Equality Act states "The Act aims at promoting the equality of men and women as a fundamental human right, prohibiting discrimination on grounds of sex and obliging state and local government authorities, education and science institutions and employers to take action to promote gender equality in economic, social, educational, cultural and other fields of social life."

Direct and indirect discrimination on the basis of sex in social security schemes

There is no direct discrimination by reference to marital or family status concerning the scope or accessibility of the schemes, the obligation to contribute or the calculation of contributions or benefits.

As pension reform was just completed in Estonia, there is a significant sphere of new legislation. While these acts do not contain any provisions that would imply direct discrimination, it is nevertheless difficult to estimate the risk of differential and disproportionate impact.

There are no provisions contrary to the principle of equal treatment in terms of the determination of persons who may participate in an occupational scheme; fixing the compulsory or optional nature of participation in an occupational scheme; laying down different rules as regards the age of entry into the scheme or the minimum period of employment or membership of the scheme required to obtain the benefits thereof; laying down different rules for the reimbursement of contributions where a worker leaves a scheme without having fulfilled the conditions guaranteeing him a deferred right to long-term benefits; setting different conditions for the granting of benefits or restricting such benefits to workers of either sex; suspending the retention or acquisition of rights during the period of maternity leave or leave for family reasons which are granted by law or agreement and are paid by the employer; setting different levels of benefit or worker contributions, except insofar as may be necessary or laying down different standards or standards applicable only to workers of a specified sex.

Consideration of the principle of equal treatment by scheme management bodies

If the granting of benefits is left to the discretion of the scheme's management bodies, these bodies must take into account the principle of equal treatment in accordance with the Estonian legislation and the draft Gender Equality Act. However, there is a need for a better monitoring system to ensure this.

Legal mechanisms to declare null and void any discrimination

It is legally possible to declare null and void any legal provisions regulating the pension schemes that are contrary to the principle of equal treatment, as they would violate the relevant norms of the Constitution.

8.2 Legal means of redress

Everyone whose rights are violated by the failure to apply the principle of equal treatment can legally pursue a remedy in court. Complaints can be presented to the

Legal Chancellor and, once the draft Gender Equality Act is adopted, also to the Gender Equality Commission.

Protection against dismissal in case of complaint of non-compliance with the principle of equal treatment

The draft Gender Equality Act will further address the gap in the present legislation and protect workers against dismissal by the employer in response to a complaint aimed at enforcing compliance with the principle of equal treatment

Monitoring mechanisms

There are no control mechanisms under the law to ensure that men and women are treated equally in social security schemes, but the Gender Equality Commission established by the draft Gender Equality Act would cover this area.

8.3 Implementation of the principle of equal treatment in matters of social security and equal opportunities strategies

The policy-makers of the Gender Equality Bureau of the Estonian Ministry of Social Affairs, who are responsible for preparing the strategy of equal opportunities, consider the progressive implementation of the principle of equal treatment in matters of social security essential to achieving the goals of these policies.

Perceived protection of women in maternity and social security

The protection of maternity through positive discrimination is perceived as an integral part of the policy on social security, and there are several provisions aimed at implementing this. Maternity is understood as a natural difference between men and women and the abolition of these protective measures would likely raise arguments, although it does not seem to pose any ideological contradictions in society.

In practice, problems remain in concrete situations where employers with certain obligations in connection to protecting the maternity of their employees do not act in accordance with their responsibilities. It is usually difficult to initiate court action in these cases and the problem usually remains invisible to the public eye. As a result, the rights of women in maternity are often *de facto* violated.

There are also no legal provisions stipulating the basis for positive treatment, although this is to be incorporated into the Estonian legal system through the draft Gender Equality Act.

8.4 Research and statistics on the impact of social security systems on women

In a broader context, attention should be paid to the fact that the number of pensioners rose in Estonia throughout the entire period of Soviet occupation, and the maximum was reached in 1993 when the percentage of pensioners totalled 25 percent.

The former pension system functioned as a redistribution mechanism between, but also within, generations. The redistribution to the benefit of women was due to the shorter life expectancy of men and a higher retirement age. As a result, when women made up 48 percent of the labour force and their salary was on average approximately 72 percent of the average salary for men, in 1996 women comprised 67.6 percent of all pensioners and their average pension was 96.7 percent of that of men.

REFERENCES

Bibliography

Estonian Ministry of Social Affairs (2001) *Report on the Implementation of the UN Convention on the Elimination of All Forms of Discrimination against Women in Estonia.* Tallinn: Sotsiaalministeerium.

Luuk, Mai (2000) *Position of Women in the Labour Market of the Republic of Estonia.* Report to the International Confederation of Trade Unions. Tallinn.

Maimik, Peeter, Kadi Mänd, and Ülle-Marike Papp (eds.) (2000) *Towards a Balanced Society. Men and Women in Estonia.* Tallinn: UNDP Estonia and Estonian Ministry of Social Affairs. Website <http://www.undp.ee/gender/>, accessed on 5 October 2002.

Narusk, Anu (2000) "Professional and Family Life: Combining Paid and Unpaid Work." In *Towards a Balanced Society. Women and Men in Estonia.* Tallinn: UNDP Estonia and Estonian Ministry of Social Affairs. Webpage <http://www.undp.ee/gender/en/6.html>, accessed on 5 October 2002.

Orgo, Inge-Maret (2000) *Resolving Labour Disputes.* Tallinn: Õigusteabe AS Juura.

Orgo, Inge-Maret, Heino Siigur and Gaabriel Tavits (1996) *Employment Contracts Act, Edition with Commentaries.* Tallinn: Õigusteabe AS Juura.

Papp, Ülle-Marike (2000) "National gender equality policy." In *Towards a Balanced Society. Women and Men in Estonia.* Tallinn: UNDP Estonia and Estonian Ministry of Social Affairs. Webpage <http://www.undp.ee/gender/en/11.html>, accessed on 5 October 2002.

Vöörmann, Rein (1999) *Soolised erinevused tööturul in Malle Järve Jagatud õigused ja vastutus. Sooline võrdõiguslikkus Eestis.* Tallinn: Sotsiaalministeerium.

Vöörmann, Rein (2000) "Men and Women on the Labour Market: Wage Ratios." In *Towards a Balanced Society. Women and Men in Estonia.* Tallinn: UNDP Estonia and Estonian Ministry of Social Affairs. Webpage <http://www.undp.ee/gender/en/7.html>, accessed on 5 October 2002.

List of legislation screened

Acts

Employment Contracts Act (RT 1992, 15/16, 241; RT I 1993, 10, 150; 26, 441; 1995, 14, 170; 16, 228; 1996, 3, 57; 40, 773; 45, 850; 49, 953; 1997, 5/6, 32; 1998, 111, 1829; 1999, 7, 112; 16, 276; 60, 616; 2000, 25, 144; 51, 327; 57, 370; 102, 669; 2001, 17, 78; 42, 233; 53, 311).

Constitution of the Republic of Estonia (RT 1992, 26, 349).

Collective Agreements Act (RT I 1993, 20, 353).

Collective Labour Dispute Resolution Act (RT I 1993, 26, 442).

Adult Education Act (RT I 1993, 74, 1054).

Wages Act (RT I 1994, 11, 154; 2001, 50, 287).

General Principles of the Civil Code Act (RT I 1994, 53, 889).

Commercial Code (RT I 1995, 26/28, 355; consolidated text RT I 1998, 91/93, 1500).

Government of the Republic Act (RT I 1995, 94, 1628).

The United Nations Convention on Elimination of All Forms of Discrimination against Women (RT II 1995/5–6/29).

Individual Labour Dispute Resolution Act (RT I 1996, 3, 57).

State Public Servants Official Titles and Salary Scale Act (RT I 1996, 15, 265).

Health Insurance Act (RT I 1998, 40, 611).

Code of Civil Procedure (RT I 1998, 43/45, 666).

Occupational Health and Safety Act (RT I 16.06.1999).

Public Service Act (RT I 1999, 7, 112).

Code of Administrative Procedure (RT I 1999, 31, 425; 96, 846; 2000, 51, 321).

The Revised Social Charter of Council of Europe (RT II 2000, 15, 93).

Employment Services Act (RT I 2000, 57, 370).

Social Protection of the Unemployed Act (RT I 2000, 57, 371).

Trade Unions Act (RT I 2000, 57, 372).

Social Tax Act (RT I 2000, 102, 675; 2001, 50, 285; 59, 359; 79, 480).

Working and Rest Time Act (RT I 2001, 17, 78).

Holidays Act (RT I 2001, 42, 233).

Unemployment Insurance Act (RT I 2001, 59, 359).

State Family Benefits Act (RT I 2001, 95, 587).

State Pension Insurance Act (RT I 2001, 100, 648).

Draft Legislation

Draft Gender Equality Act

Draft Family Law Act

Decrees and Ordinances

Government of the Republic Regulation No.214 of 1992 on the list of heavy work and work which poses a health risk where employment of women is prohibited and the list of underground work of sanitary and common nature where employment of women is allowed (RT 1992, 34, 454).

Government of the Republic Regulation No.186 of 1996 on Labour Dispute Committees (RT I 1996, 55, 995)

Government of the Republic Regulation No.50. of 2001 on Occupational Health and Safety Requirements for the Work of Pregnant Women and Women Who Are Breastfeeding (RT 07.02.2001).

Equal Opportunities for Women and Men in Hungary

Table of contents

Executive summary 237

Country report: Introduction 244

1. The principle of equal pay for work of equal value 246
   1.1   National legal framework: General provisions 246
   1.2   Legal foundations and institutional structures 247
   1.3   Job classification 248
   1.4   Available legal procedures 248
   1.5   Means of informing employees of their rights 249
   1.6   Out of court alternatives 250
   1.7   The minimum wage 250
   1.8   Role of trade unions 250
   1.9   Women's factual situation 251

2. Equal treatment for women and men as regards access to employment, vocational training and promotion, and working conditions 252
   2.1   National legal framework: General provisions 252
   2.2   The concept of discrimination on grounds of sex: Definition and legal sanctions 252
   2.3   Access to employment, vocational training and promotion 253
   2.4   Protective measures for women in the labour market 254
   2.5   Prohibition of dismissal 255
   2.6   Women's and men's jobs 256
   2.7   Legal status of sexual harassment 257

3. Protection of pregnant women from the inherent risk of certain activities and related employment rights 258
   3.1   Legal and conceptual framework 258
   3.2   Risk assessment and employers' obligations 258
   3.3   Case law 259

3.4	Night work	260
3.5	Maternity leave	260
3.6	Prohibition of dismissal and employment rights	262

4. The burden of proof in cases of discrimination based on sex 263

4.1	Legal and conceptual framework concerning indirect discrimination	263
4.2	The burden of proof and rules of evidence	264
4.3	Case law	265

5. Non-discrimination against part-time workers 266

5.1	National legal framework and employment conditions concerning part-time workers	266

6. The principle of equal treatment for self-employed workers and their assisting spouses 269

6.1	National legal framework: General provisions	269
6.2	Social rights of spouses	271
6.3	Contributory social security system for self-employed workers	272
6.4	Related research and statistics	273
6.5	Legal means of redress	275

7. The framework on parental leave 276

7.1	National legal framework: General provisions	276
7.2	Social security during parental leave	278
7.3	Parental leave and equal opportunities policy	279
7.4	Research on sharing family and professional responsibilities	280

8. The principle of equal treatment in occupational social security schemes 283

8.1	National legal framework: General provisions	283
8.2	Legal means of redress	287
8.3	Implementation of the principle of equal treatment	287
8.4	Related research and statistics	288

Executive summary for Hungary

INTRODUCTION

With the exception of Directive 97/81/EC concerning the framework agreement on part-time work (for which the deadline for harmonisation is the end of 2002), Hungary has harmonised its national legislation with the relevant EU Directives on equal opportunities and met most requirements *de jure*.

The trend in Hungary in the past decade, as in other candidate countries, has been to adjust and align the existing legal and political framework to that of countries in the European Union and it is against this background, and within the context of EU accession, that the modification of the Labour Code, which has been in force since 1 July 2001, took place.

The modification of the Labour Code is highly significant in terms of equal opportunities for women and men as it contains the integration of the principle of 'equal pay for equal work or work of equal value' in the Hungarian labour law, and further clarifies and details the rule of reversing the burden of proof in cases related to discrimination. Both of these principles are central to the ideology and implementation of equal opportunities for women and men.

Despite these positive trends however, persistent and pervasive obstacles to the practical realisation of the newly formulated standards include a lack of awareness-raising and positive measures or affirmative action and the absence of institutions or other monitoring mechanisms to ensure the enforcement of the law. A further shortcoming is the tendency for laws on sex-based discrimination to be loosely formulated within the context of a broader definition of discrimination, such that sex is simply one factor among many. In the absence of a greater political commitment to increasing women's opportunities and supporting gender equality more broadly, this risks marginalising women's rights and weakening the potential impact of EU accession on equal opportunities.

Summary of key koints

Defining principles

The principle of 'equal pay for equal work' is defined in the Hungarian Constitution and the Labour Code and can be derived from the general clauses prohibiting discrimination. The Labour Code further stipulates the term 'equal pay for equal work or work of equal value', and includes a definition of indirect discrimination. Hungarian legislation does not contain *expressis verbis* a stipulation and/or prohibition concerning sexual harassment, and there have been no published decisions on cases of sexual harassment. The Labour Code prohibits discrimination in the establishment and termination of an employment relationship, as well as in defining the rights and obligations and in the establishment of liability therein. Following the amendments to the Labour Code, there is also a definition of indirect discrimination that enhances compliance with the relevant Directive.

Protective measures

The entitlement to modify working conditions in the labour contract due to pregnancy is the lawful right of the employee from the time her pregnancy is established, and those cases in which exposure is prohibited for pregnant workers and workers who are breastfeeding are outlined in Decree No.33 of 1998. Women may not be assigned to night work from the time the pregnancy is established until the time the child reaches one year of age. Maternity leave is not obligatory under Hungarian law, and therefore is not in accordance with the respective Directive. Pregnant women can be relieved from work in order to undergo antenatal examinations if such examinations can only be performed during working hours. Although employers are legally prohibited from terminating an employment contract during pregnancy, maternity leave, for three months after giving birth or during unpaid leave to care for a sick child, a 1999 survey revealed that 40 percent of mothers cannot return to their original job and in 80 percent of cases the labour contract is terminated by mutual consent.[1]

Burden of proof

According to the Labour Code, in cases of litigation concerning the violation of the principle of equal treatment, the employer shall bear the burden of proof. Although

---

[1] Magyar Szakszervezetek Országos Szövetsége Női Választmánya (Women's Section of the Hungarian Association of Trade Unions).

there have not yet been any cases on the 'objective justifiability' of the employer's actions, concerns have been raised about what evidence might exculpate an employer, as well as the difficulties inherent in any subjective evaluation of the proof presented.

Part-time workers

The concept of part-time worker is not currently defined in Hungarian legislation, nor is there any legal provision whereby a part-time worker may request a transfer to full-time work or vice versa. The parties are free, however, to mutually modify the labour contract with regard to working times. The number and proportion of part-time workers in 2000 was only four percent, and the gross wage of persons not working full-time did not even reach 40 percent of the gross wage of full-time employees, which may partly explain why there is little interest in part-time employment.[2]

Self-employed workers

The definition of the term 'self-employment' has proved to be a contentious issue and there is considerable uncertainty regarding the proper translation of the expression. Self-employed women are viewed by many as 'forced' entrepreneurs (an assertion which is supported by a survey concluding that women become self-employed due to 'coercive' external circumstances more often than men). There are no regulations that differentiate between persons founding and/or operating an undertaking on grounds of marital status. A 1999 study concluded that the income of women working in agriculture was approximately 15 percent lower than that of men, and that "women were much more exposed to disadvantages due to the unfavourable situation of the sector and their gender."[3] Between 1992 and 2000, there was a constant and significant decrease in the number of female members of business associations, while the number of female entrepreneurs rose continuously between 1992 and 1999, though dropping considerably in the year 2000.[4]

---

[2] OMKMK (2000e: x).
[3] See Hamza *et al.* (2001: 9).
[4] Central Statistical Office, Hungary.

Parental leave

Hungarian law meets the requirements of the Directive with regard to parental leave, but there are no regulations that actually encourage men to apply for parental leave. However, in 2001 the Ministry for Social and Family Affairs organised a conference entitled "To become a man and a responsible father," where the Swedish model on preparation for fatherhood was presented. While the Hungarian government has indicated the political will to address the promotion of better working hours, greater flexibility, an easier return to working life and the division of responsibilities regarding children and the family, no comprehensive governmental measures have been put in place so far. Studies have shown that respondents with lower levels of education and who reside in rural areas tend to be more supportive of traditional divisions of labour in the home.

Social security schemes

The progressive implementation of the principle of equal treatment in matters of social security is considered integral to an effective strategy of equal opportunities at the governmental level, and gender-based discrimination, both direct and indirect, has been removed from most legislative instruments. Major reform of the pension system was undertaken in 1998, whereby a provision equalising the retirement ages for women and men was enacted, abolishing the previously discriminatory provision for women. It is possible to note the progressive implementation of equal treatment in the field of social security, and the prohibition of discrimination (on grounds including but not limited to sex) appears explicitly in legal texts.

RECOMMENDATIONS RELATED TO EACH SPECIFIC DIRECTIVE

Council Directive 75/117/EEC of 10 February 1975 *on the approximation of laws of the Member States relating to the implementation of the principle of equal pay for women and men*

- Hungarian legislation should be amended to include the obligation to inform employees of their rights in accordance with Article 7 of the Directive.

- The Act on Labour Inspection should be modified to enable the investigation of discrimination and of the implementation of the principle of equal pay for equal work or work of equal value *ex officio*.

- Hungarian authorities should consider the adoption of the models or systems of job classification in place in the EU member states.

- Judicial training programs should include information on the comparability of jobs, with a particular focus on European case law.

- The institution of actio popularis should be extended to cases of discrimination on grounds of sex, including the violation of the principle of equal pay.

Council Directive 76/207/EEC of 9 February 1976 *on the implementation of the principle of equal treatment for men and women as regards access to employment, vocational training and promotion, and working conditions*

- The Act on Vocational Training should be amended to include a provision prohibiting discrimination.

- Marital or family status should be included among the impermissible grounds for discrimination in all labour laws and provisions.

- The Labour Code should be amended to include provisions on sexual harassment.

- A 'Parliamentary Committee for Equal Opportunities' or an 'Ombudsman for Equal Opportunities' should be established.

Council Directive 92/85/EEC of 19 October 1992 *on the introduction of measures to encourage improvements in the safety and health at work of pregnant workers and workers who have recently given birth or are breastfeeding*

- Hungarian law should be amended to provide that in workplaces where there is no labour safety representative (i.e., in workplaces with fewer than ten workers), employees should be directly informed of the results of any risk assessments.

- The Labour Code provisions on maternity leave should be amended to ensure compliance with Article 8(2) of the Directive.

- Hungary should introduce provisions and proactive programs to facilitate the fair division of responsibilities between both parents with regard with raising and caring for a child.

- Hungarian law should be amended to stipulate that female workers can choose to perform night work while the child is under one year of age, but cannot be obliged to do so.

Council Directive 97/80/EC of 15 December 1997 *on the burden of proof in cases of discrimination based on sex*

- The definition of 'discrimination' should include 'indirect discrimination' not only in the Labour Code, but also in all substantive laws related to the scope of the Directive (i.e. the Civil Code and the Act on Vocational Training) and the Constitution.

- The procedural rule on the reversal of the burden of proof should be introduced into all laws governing procedures in cases of discrimination.

- Training courses should be organised for all law enforcement officials and lawyers and a training manual including relevant EU case law should be published and used in such training.

Council Directive 97/81/EC of 15 December 1997 *concerning the framework agreement on part-time work concluded by UNICE, CEEP and the ETUC*

- Part-time work should be encouraged by positive means, not solely or primarily for women, but for both sexes. Such programs should link the idea of more equal distribution of responsibilities in the family with the concept of flexible working schedules.

- The existing system of health contributions whereby employers pay a flat fee amount for employees regardless of the working hours of individual employees should be changed to a system whereby the health contribution is proportionate to the employee's working hours, and in this way encourage part-time work.

- The introduction of Point 3 of Clause 5 of the Framework Agreement is recommended to harmonise Hungarian law with the actual aim of the Directive and to encourage work mobility.

Council Directive 86/613/EEC of 11 December 1986 *on the application of the principle of equal treatment between men and women engaged in an activity, including agriculture, in a self-employed capacity, and on the protection of self-employed women during pregnancy and motherhood*

- The definition of the term 'self-employed' should be clarified in Hungarian law in accordance with the definition under Directive 86/613/EEC.

- The prohibition of sex-based discrimination and the principle of equal treatment should be incorporated into related legislation, such as the Act on Social Security Provisions and the Act on the General Rules of Public Administration Procedures.

- The category of 'contributing family member' should be extended to include self-employed workers, since this is a precondition for legal insurance and eligibility for provisions.

- Self-employed persons should also be eligible for unemployment benefits.

Council Directive 96/34/EC of 3 June 1996 *on the framework agreement on parental leave concluded by UNICE, CEEP, and the ETUC*

- Employees should be entitled to unpaid leave to care for a child until the child reaches the age of eight and irrespective of whether the child is chronically sick or severely handicapped.

- Both male and female employees should be able to avail themselves of more flexible working schedules.

- Employers should be given incentives in order to introduce such forms of work.

- Both parents should be entitled to a sickness benefit if the child is under the age of one.

- Positive steps should be taken to encourage men to have a greater share in family responsibilities and to apply for parental leave.

- Non-transferable leave for which fathers would be eligible after the birth of the child should be introduced.

Council Directive 96/97/EC of 20 December 1996 *amending Directive 86/378/EEC on the implementation of the principle of equal treatment for men and women in occupational social security schemes*

- Continuous efforts should be made to annul any existing discriminatory provisions Legal supervisory mechanisms should be developed, and steps should be taken to raise gender awareness within society.

- Professional training for administrators should be organised, as well as training on the importance of equal opportunities.

- Greater steps should be taken to ensure the implementation and enforcement of Hungarian laws on social security.

Country report: Hungary

INTRODUCTION

The accession negotiations on the Chapter on Employment and Social Policy were provisionally closed on 5 December 2000. According to the official Hungarian position, Hungary met the requirements for harmonisation with Directives under review, except for Directive 97/81/EC concerning the framework agreement on part-time work (the deadline for harmonisation with this Directive is the end of 2002). However, the lack of awareness-raising and pro-active, affirmative action and institutions to ensure the implementation of the laws is problematic in all of the areas analysed.

There are certain legal institutions in Hungarian labour law that differ significantly from the regulatory solutions of the EU Member States, although the last decade can be regarded as a decade of adjustment to developed countries, also in the area of equal opportunities. An important element of this adjustment has been the legal harmonisation with a view to accession to the European Union, and it is within this framework that the modification of the Labour Code, which has been in force since July 2001, took place.

The modification of the Code is highly significant in terms of equal opportunities for women and men, as it contains the integration of the principle of equal pay for equal work or work of equal value in Hungarian labour law, and further clarifies and details the rule of reversing the burden of proof in cases related to discrimination. Another significant law in Hungary is the Act on Employment, which contains provisions on job security, the expansion of employment and on statutory provisions for the unemployed, and the Act on Labour Inspection, which relates to the inspection of the employment by means of authoritative measures.

A specific feature of Hungarian labour law is that *vis-à-vis* collective agreements, deviation is possible only to the benefit of the employee, thus quasi-restricting collective autonomy. Legislation in the area of self-employment is a relatively new, inter-disciplinary area that is not yet well established. Analyses in this field are made even more difficult because various pieces of legislation contain different definitions of the term 'self-employed', and no sufficient and relevant statistical data are available.

The institution of parental leave is regulated in the Labour Code, and this is an area that is still influenced most by the prevailing traditional roles of men and women. The reconciliation of work and family responsibilities and the practical division of labour within households operate as further obstacles.

The social security system has undergone significant changes in the past few years, and laws that entered into force in 1998 established a new foundation for the system. Besides the pay-as-you-go system of state pensions, the second (funded) pillar was established. The occupational social security system in terms of the EU criteria, however, does not exist in Hungary.

Legislation on the prohibition of sexual harassment in the workplace is an important legislative process, and draft legislation is currently under preparation at the Ministry of Social and Family Affairs as part of a body of laws aimed at preventing and solving different forms of violence against women.

Among the legislative or preparatory measures taken to promote the equal opportunities of women, mention should be made of the Bill which was submitted in February 2001 by two Members of Parliament, as an individual motion, "On The Promotion of Equal Opportunities for Men and Women." One of several proposals included in the motion aimed to establish a Committee for Equal Opportunities to provide a background and drive towards the *de facto* implementation of equal opportunities. Regrettably, however, the Bill did not receive sufficient support to be submitted to the Parliament for debate.[5]

Although Hungarian law, with the exception of a few concrete regulations, complies with the requirements of the respective EU Directives, most of the laws are concerned with discrimination in general and formulated in such a way that 'sex' is only one factor among many. Accession to the EU can only result in a significant improvement in the quality of life for women and men in Hungary if, in addition to the *de jure* legal approximation, *de facto* changes are prioritised and given the appropriate level of attention. In other words, the spirit of the Directives must play at least an equally important role as the laws themselves.

---

[5] In order to present the characteristics of the Hungarian labour law, we referred to the Introduction of Zoltán Bankó, Gyula Berke and György Kis, eds. (2000) *Munkaügyi Jogszabályok* (Labour Laws). Budapest: KJK Kerszöv.

1. THE PRINCIPLE OF EQUAL PAY FOR WORK OF EQUAL VALUE

Council Directive 75/117/EEC of 10 February 1975 *on the approximation of laws of the Member States relating to the implementation of the principle of equal pay for women and men*

1.1 National legal framework concerning the principle of equal pay for work of equal value: general provisions

The principle of equal pay for equal work is defined in the Hungarian Constitution and in the Labour Code, and it can also be derived from the general clauses prohibiting discrimination.

The Constitution

Article 66(1) contains a general provision on the equality of women and men and Article 70/A(1) provides that the human rights and civil rights of all persons shall be respected without discrimination on the basis of race, colour, gender, language, religion, political or other opinion, national or social origins, financial situation, birth or on any other grounds whatsoever.

Article 70/B(2) provides that everyone has the right to equal pay for equal work without any discrimination whatsoever.

The Labour Code

Section 5(1) prohibits discrimination against employees on the basis of gender, age, family or disabled status, race, national origin, religion, political views or membership in organisations that represent employees' interest or their activities, or any other circumstances not related to employment.

Section 142/A(1) provides that it is prohibited to differentiate on an unfounded basis between workers when defining remuneration for equal work or work considered of equal value.

1.2 Implementation of the principle of equal pay for work of equal value: Legal foundations and institutional structures

The provisions described above apply to both the public and the private sectors. Nevertheless, Hungarian legislation applies a so-called classification system to public employees and civil servants, which makes the practical implementation of the principle more accountable.

Article 32/B of the Constitution established the institution of the Parliamentary Commissioner (Ombudsman) to safeguard citizens' rights *inter alia* by investigating or initiating the investigation of cases involving the violation of constitutional rights, including women's rights.

Special state protection is provided for by Article 3(1)(d) of Act LXXV of 1996 on Labour Inspection, which extends the scope of authority of the Labour Inspection to cases involving the violation of anti-discrimination provisions. The efficiency of this instrument, however, is weakened by the fact that labour inspection is not carried out by the labour inspector *ex officio,* but only on request.

The Council for Women's Issues was established by Government Decree in 1999 and aims to accelerate the legislation and action programs enhancing and ensuring equal opportunities for women and the involvement of social groups representing women's interests.[6] As a consultative body with the right to give opinions, proposals and having a coordinating role regarding action programs, the Council prepares the decisions taken by the Government.

Officially, there are fora that deal with discrimination against women and monitor the practical implementation of the legal regulations pertaining to this field.[7]

---

[6] The Council is comprised of the representative of the Government, six representatives of national women's organisations, five members from the people active in the academic and practical activities related to the equal opportunities of women, further members represent 'women's' civil organisations different from those mentioned above. All the women's representatives are called up for membership or designated by the Minister of Social and Family Affairs. (Under the auspices of the Ministry, a separate Office for Women's Issues has been set up.)

[7] The National ILO Council on the basis of ILO Convention 144 monitors the implementation of the ILO Convention 100 on the Equal Remuneration of Men and Women for Equal Work and the ILO Convention 111 on Discrimination (Employment and Occupation) ratified by Hungary. The ILO Council is comprised of representatives of the Government, the six trade union confederations, and the nine national employers' organisations.

1.3 Job classification

Classification criteria are stipulated under Article 42 of the Act on the Legal Status of Civil Servants, Articles 60–66 of the Act on the Legal Status of Public Employees, the Act on the Legal Status and Remuneration of Judges and the Act on the Public Prosecutors Service Relationship. There is no similar wage classification system in the private sphere, where wages are negotiable.

The Act on the Legal Status of Civil Servants provides a completely objective basis for determining remuneration in the public sphere, but the employer has the discretion to set a higher or lower base salary. Furthermore, classification is based on the qualitative description of employees, which entails a value judgement by the head of the office, who can confer this power to another person.

There are no regulations that put women at a particular disadvantage, but the regulations do provide for the opportunity to differentiate between civil servants with identical performance by ensuring the possibility of individual assessment.

Employees who work in the private sector are covered by Ministry of Labour Decree No.6 of 1992 (VI. 27.), which divides individual workers into different groups and does not assess the jobs or provide any criteria for the evaluation of particular jobs. The decree distinguishes between white-collar and blue-collar workers, and further differentiation within these categories relates to education, qualification and position. There are no regulations that directly address the remuneration of women and men in this regard.

1.4 Court proceedings in cases involving the violation of the principle of equal pay for work of equal value

In addition to the institutional opportunities described above, legal remedy is ensured in Hungarian legislation since any person without restriction can file for court action in questions stipulated by the Directive if she/he believes her/his rights were violated. The legal basis of such a case would either be the 'equal pay for equal work' principle set forth in the Constitution, or Article 142/A of the Labour Code.

In several cases of gender-based discrimination the violation of an individual's rights cannot be proved or be proved easily, and the right to initiate court proceedings depending on the individual grievances makes the initiation of court or out of court proceedings difficult or impossible. This problem is solved in many legal systems by the instrument of *actio popularis*, which did not exist until December 1999 in the post-transitional Hungarian legal system.

Actions can be filed in accordance with the general rules set forth in the civil procedural law and the special rules related to labour law proceedings, but from the point of view of substantive law there is no efficient punishment for a violation of the principle of equal pay in Hungary. Moreover, there is no concrete labour regulation on what the employer is obliged to do if the court were to establish a case of discrimination.

If the claimant is a member of a trade union he/she can be represented in proceedings by the trade union or a lawyer employed or hired by the trade union. Beyond this, an extremely important provision provides that in court proceedings related to an employment relationship parties are exempt from the obligation to pay legal costs, regardless of their income and wealth. Within this framework, an employee is entitled to request that the court appoint legal counsel.

Article 93(1) of Government Decree 218 of 1999 provides that the refusal of an employer to employ a person on account of their gender or discrimination between workers on that ground shall constitute a violation of the regulation, punishable by a fine of up to 100,000 Forints. (approximately €500).

According to Section 8(1) of the Labour Code, an agreement that violates an employment-related or other legal regulation shall be considered null and void.

1.5 Means of informing employees of their right to equal pay for work of equal value

There is no evidence of the obligation for employers to inform employees of their rights, at least not in the spirit and wording of the Directive. However, employees may turn to the trade union and/or the trade union legal advisory service for information. In accordance with the Act on civil proceedings, the court is obliged to provide information on relevant procedural questions.

The Labour Code further provides that "The works council can request information from the employer in any question related to the economic and social interests of employees and the enforcement of regulations on discrimination. The employer may not refuse to provide the requested information." The same obligation to provide information is established for trade unions. Still, the obligation to provide information to the works council (or trade unions) and not directly to employees and the fulfilment of this obligation so not conform with Article 7 of the Directive.

1.6 Out of court alternatives

Section 199/A of the Labour Code stipulates a conciliation (mediation) procedure, and if the matter cannot be successfully resolved this way, court action may be filed within the statute of limitations.

Non-contentious proceedings can be initiated in accordance with the labour inspection described above, and within the framework of this procedure there is an opportunity to impose a fine (on the employer) or to continue legal proceedings.

1.7 The minimum wage

The law does not differentiate between men and women in terms of the minimum wage. However, since there is a legal opportunity to deviate from the minimum wage in part-time work, and given that women make up the majority of part-time workers, indirect discrimination may occur in this way.

1.8 Role of trade unions

Section 19(2) of the Labour Code provides that trade unions should inform their members of their rights and obligations concerning their financial, social, cultural, as well as living and working conditions, and can represent their members against employers and before state agencies in matters concerning labour relations and employment matters. Trade unions can represent their members, with authorisation, before the court or any other authority or agency in matters concerning their living and working conditions.

Before the changes in the political system took place, a trade union legal advisory service, where workers were provided with legal counselling and in certain cases legal representation before court free of charge, had been operational in nearly every workplace. After the political transformation, the majority of these services ceased to exist and are now only rarely provided by trade unions.

The Women's Committee of the National Confederation of the Hungarian Trade Unions recently developed recommendations to promote women's interests, the principle of equal pay and equal treatment in collective agreements. One of the recommendations proposes that a committee be set up by the local trade union organisation and the works council to remedy grievances related to equal opportunities. The composition of this committee would aim to reflect the proportion of men and women in the workplace and would ensure conciliation prior to court proceedings in the case of the violation of Section 5 of the Labour Code. Furthermore, it would monitor the enforcement of the principle of equal pay for work of equal value in performance assessment procedures, as well as the wage classification set forth in Ministry of Labour Decree No.6 of 1992.

1.9 Women's factual situation regarding the principle of equal pay for work of equal value

In accordance with Decree No.9 of 1996 issued by the Ministry of Labour, the Office for Employment collects data on wages, monitors and analyses their changes and registers wage agreements.

The research programme undertaken by the National Research and Methodological Centre for Labour Relations (OMKMK) and completed in 2000 analysed the wage differences between men and women between 1986 and 1996. According to the research, in 1986 women's monthly wage did not reach 75 percent of men's monthly wage, by 1992 this proportion exceeded 85 percent and remained stable at this level. The wage difference is relatively small and stable among young workers, but the gap is significantly wider and constantly increasing among older people, persons with higher education and persons in management positions.[8]

In 1999, women earned 79.04 percent of men's national average monthly way; women earned 77.4 percent of men's average wage in the public sector,[9] and 82.69 percent of men's average wage in the entrepreneurial sector.[10] If the averages base wages in the given period are compared, the proportion is significantly more favourable: 83.28 percent, 83.31 percent and 89.35 percent respectively. The wage gap in Hungary has been 'achieved' in the context of much lower wages than those in European Union Member States.

Statistical data on the breakdown of workers in terms of their wages, sectors and gender in 1999 can be found in the OMKMK individual wage database of 1999.[11]

---

[8] OMKMK (2000f: 7–8).
[9] OMKMK (2000c), Appendix 2.
[10] OMKMK (2000b), Graph 2.
[11] OMKMK (2000d: 4).

2. Equal treatment for women and men as regards access to employment, vocational training and promotion, and working conditions

Council Directive 76/207/EEC of 9 February *1976 on the implementation of the principle of equal treatment for men and women as regards access to employment, vocational training and promotion, and working conditions*

2.1 National legal framework concerning the principle of equal treatment for women and men: General provisions

According to the Labour Code, discrimination is prohibited in the establishment of an employment relationship, in defining the rights and obligations within the employment relationship, in the establishment of liability, and in the termination of the employment relationship. Following the modification of the Labour Code, and specifically Section 5(1) and (2), it is clear that the orders, measures, conditions and practices *prior* to the establishment of the employment relationship and related to the procedure for furthering that relationship shall be construed as related to the employment relationship. It was previously unclear whether the prohibition of discrimination applied, for example, to discriminatory conditions set by the employer before the employment relationship was established.

The Code of Civil Procedure further stipulates that the assertion of a claim based on negotiations prior to the conclusion of a labour contract shall be construed as a labour lawsuit.

2.2 The concept of discrimination on grounds of sex: Definition and legal sanctions

Following its modification, Section 5 of the Labour Code contains a definition of indirect discrimination as a new element in the second paragraph and in this way specifies the legislative intent and enhances compliance with the Directive.[12]

The preamble of the Act on Vocational Training focuses on the acquisition of professional knowledge necessary to establish an employment relationship based on

---

[12] Previously, indirect discrimination could only be inferred by the general clause.

equal opportunities, but it does not contain any provision on discrimination. Accordingly, Hungarian legislation does not meet the requirements set forth in the Directive in this respect. This shortcoming could be overcome though if the Act on Vocational Training were to be supplemented with a provision that prohibits direct and indirect discrimination *expressis verbis* and defines the concept of indirect discrimination.

According to Section 5(1) of the Labour Code, family status is among those particular grounds that cannot be the basis of discrimination.

According to Hungarian legislation, a person who suffers discrimination can claim pecuniary and non-pecuniary compensation. In accordance with Section 8(1) of the Labour Code, an agreement that violates an employment-related regulation or other legal regulation shall be considered null and void. This, however, does not provide sufficient protection for an employee who has been discriminated against on the basis of gender and the employer is not put at a great disadvantage. The fines that can be imposed by the Labour Inspection, which can range from €204–12,215 and are determined on the basis of the duration of the unlawful situation, the damage incurred and the number of workers concerned, may have a more significant deterrent effect though.

2.3 National legal framework concerning the principle of equal treatment as regards access to employment, vocational training and promotion, and working conditions

The principle of equal treatment in access to employment can be derived from the general constitutional provisions on the right to work, freedom to choose employment and the equal rights of men and women, and an interpretation of their interrelated nature. The Act on Furthering Employment and Provisions for Unemployed Persons provides for the principle of equal treatment in the context of promoting employment (i.e. in access to employment) and primary importance is given to affirmative action in this regard.

The Act on Vocational Training does not contain explicit provisions on the principle of equal treatment, but the preamble provides that the acquisition of vocational qualifications contributes to the establishment of equal opportunities in the field of employment.

Section 5(4) of the Labour Code provides that employers shall give employees the opportunity to advance to higher positions without negative discrimination, especially on the basis of professional skills, experience, performance and critical factors regarding job performance.

The Act on the Promulgation of the Employment Policy Convention adopted by the Forty-Eighth Session of the General Conference of the International Labour Organisation in 1964, which was promulgated in Hungary in 2000, provides that "With a view to stimulating economic growth and development, raising standards of living, meeting manpower requirements and overcoming unemployment and underemployment, each Member shall declare and pursue, as a major goal, an active policy designed to promote full, productive and freely chosen employment. 2. The said policy shall aim at ensuring that […] (c) There is freedom of choice of employment and the fullest possible opportunity for each worker to qualify for, and to use his skills and endowments in, a job for which he is well suited, irrespective of race, colour, sex, religion, political opinion, national extraction or social origin." Article 1(2)(c) also contains a regulation on the principle of equal treatment.

2.4 Protective measures with regard to women's participation in the labour market

Section 5(5) of the Labour Code provides that any differentiation clearly and directly required by the character or nature of the work shall not be construed as discrimination.

Hungarian legislation contains a number of provisions providing protection and preferential treatment for women. However, the seemingly favourable, automatic prohibitions (for example, relating to night work) may have a disadvantageous impact on women because they are denied the possibility for increased remuneration and professional advancement.

Section 105(3) of the Labour Code provides that women shall not be required to carry out work at another location without her consent from the time the pregnancy is established until the child reaches the age of one; the same applies to men raising a child alone. This provision requiring the woman's consent could also be applied to the prohibition on overtime work.

Hungarian human resources experts have provided the following analysis:[13] "Legal regulations considering women as a homogeneous social group use this consideration as a basis for prohibiting them from certain jobs which often ensure higher incomes or faster promotion […] Such regulations do not respect the individual's abilities […] Recognising the need for stronger protection for workers in certain conditions that

---

[13] Nemeskéri and Csizmadia (2000: 13).

might pose risks to their health and recognising the fact that such measures should perhaps cover women workers in a larger number, we still have to conclude that measures of this nature are discriminatory. From this point of view, legal regulations allowing for individual decisions of workers and thereby individualising positive differentiation can be considered progressive [...]."

An authoritative ruling of fundamental importance was handed down in the context of discriminatory job advertisements in Hungary in 1997.[14] The case involved a private employer who advertised for an assistant, stipulating that the ideal applicant should *inter alia* be male and aged 25–35 years. The plaintiff, a 51-year-old woman, met all the other requirements listed in the job advertisement, but when speaking by phone the defendant repeatedly stated that the company only accepted applications from men younger than the plaintiff. The plaintiff filed a complaint on the basis of the general anti-discrimination provisions of the Constitution. The court held that there had been a violation of the law and prohibited the defendant from such or similar violations in the future. Although a landmark case, one shortcoming was the fact that the court held that the Labour Code did not apply to the case because the plaintiff had not claimed to establish an employment relationship.[15]

The retirement age will be uniformly set at 62 years for both men and women as January 2009, until which time women can retire before they reach 62. The current ages are 55 years for women and 60 years for men.

Among the positive programmes (affirmative action) implemented and/or coordinated by the Office for Women's Issues within the Ministry of Social and Family Affairs[16] the title "Family Friendly Workplace" is awarded to employers who take concrete measures to harmonise family and employment obligations and duties.

2.5 Prohibition of dismissal

According to the Labour Code, it is unlawful to dismiss an employee in 'retaliation' to legal action or a complaint and such a termination of employment shall be considered invalid and serves as a legal basis for reinstating the employment relationship. This

---

[14] Decision No.3 P. 21.321/1997/13 of the Municipal Court of Monor.

[15] For the detailed analysis of problems and dilemmas with respect to labour law and related to the verdict see Csilla Lehoczkyné Kollonay (1998) "Kezdeti lépések a foglakoztatási diszkrimináció bírósági gyakorlatában (Initial steps in the court case law regarding employment discrimination)." In *Fundamentum* 4/1998, 91–95.

[16] The central government agency responsible for elaborating and implementing women's policy in Hungary.

holds true even if the termination of the employment relationship otherwise complied with all legal and material conditions, and would have been lawful had it not been in reaction to the complaint.

2.6 Women's and men's jobs

The Constitutional Court has held that restrictive reference made to women in the list of jobs and names of occupations is unconstitutional.[17] The Labour Law Council of the Supreme Court has also stated that "any differentiation clearly and directly required by the character or nature of the work, therefore all the differentiation based on essential and lawful conditions that can be considered in the establishment of the employment relationship, shall not be construed as discrimination [...]. Accordingly, the employer can lawfully insist on employing men only in jobs which – due to the character or nature of the work and the working conditions – exclude the employment of women." This interpretation of the law is in full compliance with the requirements of Community law.

According to Section 75 of the Labour Code, women and young employees may not be employed in work that may have detrimental effects on their physical condition or development. The particular jobs for which women or young employees may not be employed, or which they may only perform if specific working conditions are provided or on the basis of a preliminary medical examination, shall be determined by law.

According to Decree No.33 of 1998 issued by the Ministry of Welfare, when examining and evaluating the aptitude of workers for certain jobs, it must be considered that women (especially women of reproductive age and pregnant women, especially in the early stage of pregnancy, women who have recently given birth, breastfeeding mothers and mothers providing mother's milk) are unable to perform work under circumstances described in Appendix 8 which pose risks to their health or impose hazardous burdens on them, or are able to perform such work only on certain conditions.[18]

A number of other Decrees issued by the Ministry of Labour and the Ministry of Welfare denote vocational qualifications that can only be acquired by women.[19] At the

---

[17] Constitutional Court Resolution No.7 of 1998 AB. Examples of related names and occupations include spinning women, knitting women, female textile workers, etc.

[18] "Furthermore, [...] the employer shall implement a risk assessment and take measures to guarantee the health and safety of persons described in subsection 1."

[19] Decree No.7 of 1993 denotes three vocational qualifications that are exclusively for women: midwife, female farmworker I and II. See also Decree No.5 of 1995 on the service of district nurses and Decree No.31 of 1999 issued by the Ministry of Education.

same time, several regulations stipulate that participation in a given vocational training course and/or the acquisition of a vocational qualification is only permitted for men.[20]

2.7 Legal status of sexual harassment

Hungarian legislation does not explicitly prohibit sexual harassment, and there have not been any published decisions in this area. However, sexual harassment could constitute slander, or a violation of the general provision of the Civil Code protecting the rights attached to the person. Furthermore, the Labour Code contains several sections that could be interpreted and cited in concrete cases, including the prohibition of discrimination, provisions on the proper exercise of rights, proper conditions for occupational safety and health, and the performance of work in a manner that does not endanger health, cause financial disadvantage or damage a person's reputation.

---

[20] Decree No.6 of 1987 issued by the Ministry of Health stipulates that caisson operations can only be performed by male workers (Appendix 9.1). See also Decree No.5 of 2001 issued by the Ministry of Agriculture, Decree No.64 of 1994 issued by the Ministry of Agriculture, and Decree No.18 of 1995 issued by the Ministry of Industry and Commerce.

3. PROTECTION OF PREGNANT WOMEN FROM THE INHERENT RISK OF CERTAIN ACTIVITIES AND RELATED EMPLOYMENT RIGHTS

Council Directive 92/85/EEC of 19 October *1992 on the introduction of measures to encourage improvements in the safety and health at work of pregnant workers and workers who have recently given birth or are breastfeeding*

3.1 Legal and conceptual framework

The terms 'pregnant worker' and 'worker who is breastfeeding' are not defined in concrete terms in Hungarian legislation. According to Section 138(1) of the Labour Code, the term 'worker who has given birth' also applies to women who give birth to a stillborn child.

Section 90, Subsection (1)(d) of the Labour Code provides protection for the entire period of pregnancy, irrespective of when it was detected or when the employee reports the pregnancy to the employer.

Employees are entitled to modify working conditions in the labour contract from the time the pregnancy is established upon presenting a medical report related to the employee's suitability to perform the job.

According to the laws on social security, the pecuniary allowances provided for mothers include the benefit for pregnant women and women who have recently given birth, and the childcare benefit, which is payable to either parent, whether natural and adoptive.

3.2 Assessing the risk to the safety or health of a pregnant worker and employer's obligations

Section 102(2) of the Labour Code stipulates that employers should ensure proper conditions for occupational safety and health in the observation of the provisions pertaining thereto. Further labour safety regulations to be respected by the employer are stipulated in Act XCIII of 1993 on Labour Safety and Decree No.5 of 1993 (XII. 26) issued by the Ministry of Labour on the Executive Provisions of the Act.

Section 54 stipulates that employers must respect, *inter alia,* the following general requirements: the avoidance of hazards, an assessment of hazards that are unavoidable and the elimination of hazards where they emerge. It further provides that on the basis of the assessment preventive measures shall be taken to ensure the improvement of working conditions and shall be integrated into the employer's activities at all levels of management.

Section 58(3) provides that employers must guarantee that employees and their labour safety representatives receive the necessary information from the occupational health service in connection with their working conditions, and particularly in the course of exercising their rights provided in Section 61.

Hungarian law does not stipulate an obligation to provide information *vis-à-vis* the employees concerned, and it can be argued that neither the person qualified for occupational safety (and employed by the employer) nor the occupational health service specified under Section 58 can be regarded as the representative of the employee concerned.

It is possible for employees to elect a representative or representatives if their number exceeds 10, and/or 20 if the employers pursue exclusively or decisively non-physical activities. Under Section 71, for the purpose of safe work performance not endangering health, labour safety representatives (the committee) and employers shall cooperate in the course of exercising the rights and fulfilling the obligations.

Since the election of a labour safety representative and committee is only possible for employers employing more than ten people, where there are fewer employees there is no representative to whom the obligation to provide information should be addressed. Consequently, the effective Hungarian legislation is not fully harmonised with the provisions of the Directive, and therefore needs to be adjusted. For example, the text could be amended to provide that "in workplaces without a labour safety representative, the employee concerned should be directly informed about the outcome of the risk assessment."

According to Section 82, the Labour Safety Inspectorate charged with administrative supervision can impose a penalty on an employer who violates the health and safety protection obligations stipulated in the Directive. In addition, under Article 98 of the Governmental Decree No.218 of 1999 (XII. 28), a minor offence punishment can be imposed on natural persons who violate labour safety provisions.

3.3 Cases in which exposure is prohibited for pregnant workers and breastfeeding workers

Annex 8 of Decree No.33 of 1998 provides a long and detailed list of working conditions and factors that are prohibited for pregnant and breastfeeding workers, including, *inter alia,* exposure to ionising radiation, noise, cold and wet working environments, and vibration effecting the entire body.

Annex 9 lists the physical, biological and chemical pathogenic factors[21] that must be subject to a risk assessment before employing pregnant and breastfeeding workers, as well as workers who recently gave birth.

3.4 Night work

Section 121(1) of the Labour Code contains an absolute prohibition of night work for pregnant women from the time the pregnancy is established until the time the child reaches one year of age. Night work is defined as work performed between 10 p.m. and 6 a.m. for at least two hours duration.

3.5 Maternity leave

Maternity leave, which is not obligatory in Hungary, is defined and regulated by the Labour Code, and female workers and students are entitled to maternity leave of 24 weeks. If a labour contract were to prohibit the enjoyment of maternity leave, such a provision would be considered null and void.

Section 138 of the Labour Code stipulates that the period of maternity leave shall be scheduled to commence four weeks prior to the expected birth if possible. If the child is stillborn, the leave ends six weeks following the birth; if the child dies the leave ends 15 days following the death.

Employees are also entitled to an unpaid leave in order to care for the child until the age of three; to care for a child until the age of fourteen if the employee receives a childcare allowance; or, if the child is ill, to provide home care until the child reaches the age of twelve.[22]

Section 138(6) provides that women are entitled to two hours off work each day for the first six months of nursing, and one hour daily thereafter up to the end of the ninth month. In the case of multiple births, the time off for nursing shall be commensurate with the number of children.

---

[21] "Physical pathogenic factors include *inter alia* vibration or movement; lifting heavy weights that cause back and lumbar problems; noise; non-ionising radiation; position of the body, [...] mental or physical exhaustion and other physical burdens. Chemical pathogenic factors include carcinogenic materials listed in the separate decree; medicines inhibiting mitosis; carbon monoxide; known and dangerous materials with percutan resorption."

[22] Section 138(5).

Transfer to suitable work

Section 85(1) of the Labour Code provides that, from the time the pregnancy is established until the child reaches one year of age, women are to be temporarily placed in a position that is medically suitable, or the working conditions in the existing position are to be modified as appropriate on the basis of a medical report pertaining to employment. The employee must consent to the transfer and she cannot receive less than her previous wage. If the employer cannot provide the employee with suitable work, she will be exempt from work and paid the relevant wage during that period.

Statement No.57 of the Labour College of the Supreme Court provides that a woman temporarily transferred to a new job due to pregnancy is entitled to the average wage of the previous job even if the transfer is to a job with fewer working hours; from night work to day work; or from shift work to non-shift work. A pregnant woman can be temporarily transferred to a new job only with her consent. Adoptive mothers are entitled to the same benefits as women who recently gave birth.

Pregnancy and young mother benefits, childcare benefits and sick pay

The 'pregnancy and young mother's benefit' is governed by Article 40 of the Act on Compulsory Health Insurance, and is payable for the term of the maternity leave. It amounts to 70 percent of the average daily wage.

According to Article 42/B of the Act on Compulsory Health Insurance, the childcare benefit is payable from the day following the expiration of the pregnancy and young mother's benefit until the child reaches the age of two. It amounts to 70 percent of the average daily wage, and was forecasted to be 83,000 Ft. (approximately €326) in 2002. From 2003 the maximum monthly amount of the benefit will be determined by the Act on the Annual Budget.

According to Article 43 of the Act on Compulsory Health Insurance, persons entitled to sick pay due to an inability to work include women who cannot perform work due to pregnancy of childbirth and who are not entitled to the pregnancy and young mother's benefit, breastfeeding mothers with a child under the age of one and who are being treated in hospital, and a mother or single father caring for a sick child under the age of one.

Article 50 of the Act provides the opportunity for the General Director of the National Health Insurance Fund to authorise the payment of the pregnancy and young mother's benefit, childcare benefit, sick pay or other type of aid if there is a duly substantiated request and even if the insured person does not meet the necessary insurance requirements.

According to Article 20 of the Act on Family Provisions, parents, foster parents or guardians are entitled to a childcare benefit until the child reaches the age of three. If the child has a long chronic illness or is severely handicapped, the childcare benefit can be paid until the child reaches the age of ten.

Article 29 of the Act on Family Provisions provides that women are entitled to a maternity benefit after the birth of a child if they attended pregnancy consultations at least four times during the pregnancy, or at least once in the case of a premature birth.

Antenatal examinations

Section 107 of the Labour Code provides that employees shall be relieved from the obligation to work for the duration of a compulsory medical examination, including pregnancy tests.[23] Statement No.23 of the Labour College of the Supreme Court provides that the employer must pay the employee if the obligation cannot be performed outside working hours. This is the case unless otherwise stipulated by the collective agreement or labour contract.

3.6 Prohibition of dismissal and employment rights

Section 90(1) of the Labour Code stipulates that employers may not terminate an employment relationship during pregnancy, for three months after giving birth, or during maternity leave or unpaid leave to nurse or care for a child.

Pregnant employees and employees who recently gave birth can benefit from the general legal means available in the case of unlawful dismissal. According to the Labour Code, if the employee does not request reinstatement or if the court waives reinstatement at the employer's request, the court can order, after weighing all the applicable circumstances, in particular the unlawful action and its consequences, the employer to pay no less than two and no more than twelve months' average earnings to the employee.

Furthermore, if the employment is unlawfully terminated the employee shall be reimbursed for lost wages and compensated for any damages arising from that loss.

A survey[24] conducted in 1999 on the situation of women who intend to return to work after childcare leave revealed that more than 40 percent of mothers cannot return to their original job, the labour contract is terminated by mutual consent in 80 percent. In such cases the employer is not obliged to pay severance pay.[25]

---

[23] An antenatal examination shall be regarded as a compulsory medical examination if it can only be performed during working hours.

[24] Comprised of 5,000 questionnaires.

[25] Magyar Szakszervezetek Országos Szövetsége Női Választmánya (Women's Section of the Hungarian Association of Trade Unions).

4. THE BURDEN OF PROOF IN CASES OF DISCRIMINATION BASED ON SEX

Council Directive 97/80/EC of 15 December 1997 *on the burden of proof in cases of discrimination based on sex*

4.1 Legal and conceptual framework concerning indirect discrimination and specific legal means to implement the principle of equal treatment for women and men

Section 5(1) of the Labour Code provides that "indirect discrimination occurs if a concerned group of workers/employees can mostly be considered a homogeneous group on the basis of the features listed in (1) and the orders, measures, conditions and practice related to the employment relationship, which formally prescribes equal conditions for each person or grant equal rights to each person, is disproportionately unfavourable for members of this group, unless it is appropriate and necessary and can be objectively justified."

While several resolutions of the Constitutional Court have addressed the issue of sex-based discrimination, none of them dealt with the term 'indirect discrimination'. Prevailing court practice grants employers discretion in selecting workers; for example:

- In Constitutional Court Decision No.555 of 1998 it was held that unless a concrete provision is stipulated by law in relation to filling a vacant position, the employer is free to set the recruitment criteria, as this is related to his economic and general management practice.

- In Constitutional Court Decision No.227 of 2000 it was held that a legal remedy can be sought against an employer's discretionary decision only if the employer violated the relevant legal provisions when making the decision.

- In Constitutional Court Decision No.329 of 1999 it was held that the examination of the circumstances concerning an employer's decision to terminate an employment agreement does not constitute a labour dispute (Constitutional Court Decision No.453 of 1996 also deals with this point).

4.2 The burden of proof procedure in litigation concerning the violation of the principle of equal treatment for women and men and rules of evidence

Section 5(8) of the Labour Code provides that in an employment-related dispute, the employer is required to prove that his actions did not violate provisions prohibiting discrimination, and complies fully with the Directive.

However, the reversal of the burden of proof can pose a serious problem in the evaluations of judges, who may reject even a well-founded excuse submitted by the employer to avoid having to evaluate the facts of the case. By the same token, a court may accept a superficial excuse based on general statements submitted by the employer. In contrast to the Code of Criminal Procedure, the Code of Civil Procedure does not require that the absence of the violation of law be proved unambiguously and in a way that cannot be challenged.[26] No court decision has been passed so far with respect to the 'objective justifiability' of the employer's action, but most practical problems are likely to stem from what evidence is sufficient to exculpate the employer.

A number of measures have already been taken in Hungary to publicise Community and Hungarian legislation on equal treatment on a wide scale. In the series entitled "I am also concerned" published by the Ministry of Foreign Affairs, a publication was issued and distributed to every Hungarian school to provide information for teachers and students. With the common support of the European Union and the Hungarian Government, several publications, textbooks and leaflets were published under the auspices of the Equal Opportunities Actions Programmes to provide information on these regulations. Civil organisations, trade unions and the National Employment Public Foundation have organised several fora, conferences and seminars on this issue. Nevertheless, experience shows that employees, generally speaking, have little information on labour law and in the event of a labour dispute, it is difficult to have access to specific legal information, and the number of labour law specialists is relatively low.

---

[26] Nacsa (1999: 133).

4.3 Case law on the violation of the principle of equal treatment for women and men

In terms of existing case law, the followings findings can be noted:

- Employment – The landmark decision of the Municipal Court of Monor, described earlier, on discriminatory job advertisements.

- Remuneration – Constitutional Court Decision No.350 of 1994 concerned a public employee on unpaid leave for a longer period of time to nurse her child. The employer refused to pay the salary for the 13th month, which, in line with the relevant legal provision, is payable to a person who in the given year was a public employee for a minimum of six months. The court ruled that, contrary to the reasoning of the employer, the remuneration was payable to the employee even if she did not perform work in the given year.

- Social protection – According to Constitutional Court Decision No.61 of 1992, "A single father raising his child alone is entitled to the same protection concerning the termination of his employment relationship as a single female worker, until his child reaches 18 years of age […]."

5. NON-DISCRIMINATION AGAINST PART-TIME WORKERS

Council Directive 97/81/EC *concerning the framework agreement on part-time work concluded by UNICE, CEEP and the ETUC*

5.1 National legal framework and employment conditions concerning part-time workers

The term 'part-time worker' is not defined in Hungarian legislation, although the Labour Code notes that rules concerning employment or a labour contract concluded between the parties may stipulate working hours that are less than full-time employment. Part-time workers are not subject to different conditions than full-time workers.

According to Section 144(6) of the Labour Code, the Minister of Economy may grant exemptions from the mandatory minimum wage in certain spheres, particularly with regard to young employees, partially disabled and part-time employees, with the agreement of the National Labour Council and if such appears necessary in the interest of promoting employment.

The Labour Code does not explicitly prohibit discrimination on grounds of part-time work, although the general provision on equal treatment in Section 5 of the Labour Code could be invoked in such cases. There was a case[27] where part-time workers did not receive the same travel allowances as full-time workers, and in such cases the court can evaluate the facts of the case with reference to Section 5 of the Labour Code to decide whether any of the listed grounds for discrimination can be established or not.

The Labour Code does not contain discriminatory provisions with regard to part-time workers' entitlement to vacation, although remuneration for the duration of annual leave is payable only for a period commensurate with the working time.

No legal or administrative obstacles could be identified in Hungarian legislation; in practice, however, the Act on Health Care Contributions provides that the itemised health care contribution to be paid by the employer to each employee (which is currently approximately €17.60) does not depend on whether the employer employs the employee full-time or part-time. As a result, part-time employment is less favourable for employers since the payment obligation is the same in both cases. There are no differences between part-time workers in the public and private sectors in Hungary.

---

[27] *Source:* lecture delivered by Dr. Tünde Handó, President of the Municipal Labour Court of Budapest at the conference of the Labour Law TDK, ELTE Faculty of Law.

Transfer to part-time work

Hungarian law does not stipulate that a part-time worker may request a transfer to full-time employment or vice versa, although there is no legal obstacle preventing this. The parties are free to mutually modify the labour contract concluded between them, including in terms of the working time.

There is a need to improve the harmonisation of family and workplace obligations in Hungary, but concerns have been raised about encouraging part-time employment primarily among women workers, since this reinforces the traditional distribution of labour within the family.

Regulations on vocational training do not differentiate between part-time and full-time workers. However, there is no separate regulation that underlines the importance of providing vocational training to part-time workers.

Related research

In January 2000, there were 153,700 part-time workers: the manufacturing industry employed 33,600 persons, the sector of commerce and repair/maintenance employed 26,300 persons, the educational sector employed 13,500 persons, while 13,400 persons worked in the healthcare and social sector.[28]

According to the Central Statistical Office, 30,600 men and 65,900 women worked 1–29 hours a week in 2001 while 1,808,900 men and 1,569,000 women worked 30 hours or more a week. Another breakdown showed that 50,100 men and 124,600 women worked 1–35 hours a week while 1,789,400 men and 1,510,300 women worked 36 hours and more weekly.[29]

The following available data illustrates the actual situation of part-time workers:

- The number and proportion of part-time workers was low in the year 2000: only four percent of respondents considered themselves to be part-time workers, but the proportion of those working less than 36 hours a week on a regular basis is approximately five percent.[30]

- The gross wage of persons not working full-time did not reach 40 percent of the gross wage of full-time workers, and this might partly explain why workers show only little interest in part-time employment.[31]

---

[28] Central Statistical Office (2001d).

[29] *Source:* Labour Force Survey, Central Statistical Office, 2001 (This sample does not include the number of respondents who considered their working time to be variable).

[30] Central Statistical Office (2001e: 46).

[31] Central Statistical Office (2001d: x).

- According to a survey conducted in 2000 by the Central Statistical Office among unemployed persons, 56.6 percent of women would be willing to take up part-time employment, either provisionally or not (the proportion of men is 38.7 percent). Out of this percentage, the proportion of women who want to work exclusively part-time is 8 percent (in the case of men this proportion is 1.7 percent).[32]

---

[32] Central Statistical Office (2001e: 28).

6. The principle of equal treatment for self-employed workers and their assisting spouses

Directive 86/613/EEC of 11 December 1986 *on the application of the principle of equal treatment between men and women engaged in an activity, including agriculture, in a self-employed capacity, and on the protection of self-employed women during pregnancy and motherhood*

6.1 National legal framework on self-employment: General provisions

Definition of self-employed workers

The definition of 'self-employment' has proved contentious in Hungary and there are several uncertainties about the proper translation of this expression. The Hungarian version of several pieces of Community legislation and certain Hungarian laws define 'self-employed' as *'önálló vállalkozó'* (independent entrepreneur).[33] However, the Government Decree on issues related to the employment of foreign citizens in Hungary translates 'self-employed' as *'önfoglalkoztató'* (the verbatim translation of self-employed) and identifies this concept with the individual entrepreneur mentioned in the Act on Private Enterprises.

On the basis of the relevant laws[34] and from the point of view of the application of the Directive, individual entrepreneurs, members of business associations, entrepreneurs pursuing activities for supplementary income, primary agricultural producers, members of cooperatives actively participating in the activities of the cooperative in an entrepreneurial status, those performing work for remuneration in an entrepreneurial type of relationship but not qualifying as individual entrepreneurs, and contributing family members can be considered self-employed in Hungary.

---

[33] The basic principle of Community legislation is that it does not include employers and employees in the category of the self-employed, so an individual who employs others is not self-employed. This is one of the reasons for the uncertainties in Hungarian translations and concepts, as *'önfoglalkoztató'* (verbatim 'self-employed') in Hungarian legislation can cover individual entrepreneurs/sole proprietors, independent entrepreneurs, owners of business associations, etc. Individuals belonging to these categories may and usually do have employees.

[34] Act LXXII of 1998 on the Right of Foreign Citizens to be Established as Independent Entrepreneurs for Economic Purposes, Act V of 1990 on Private Enterprises, the Act on Social Security and Private Pension Provisions, the Act on Cooperatives.

Laws and regulations related to the directive

All individual entrepreneurs/sole proprietors and entrepreneurs in economic partnerships are insured regardless of whether they work part-time or full-time, except for pensioners who pursue entrepreneurial activity at the same time, who are entitled to medical care only in the case of injury.

Any person working within the framework of any other legal relationship for financial compensation, whether as an outworker, contract worker, entrepreneur other than an individual entrepreneur, or contributing family member, is also insured. The precondition for this status is that the monthly income of the person, which serves as the basis of contribution, must reach 30 percent of the minimum wage in effect in the previous month.

The social security regulations cover the social security rights of agricultural workers as well. The Social Security Act stipulates that membership in a cooperative does not automatically lead to insured status; members of the cooperative must personally take part in the operation of the cooperative within the framework of an employment relationship or as an entrepreneur. Family members of the insured person, including the spouse, will be insured automatically. As of January 1997, primary agricultural producers are not obliged to pay social security contributions either to the health care or the pension funds, but they can voluntarily join the system of provisions by means of individual social security agreements.

Since the modification of the Employment Act in 1996, self-employed persons are excluded from the mandatory system and the question of their entitlement to unemployment provisions has not been settled.[35]

Acceptance of the directive

There is no information on the public awareness of new legislation because the relevant surveys have not been conducted. However, because public opinion polls show that awareness of general EU accession-related questions is below 'medium' level,[36] it can be

---

[35] Resolution No.50 of 2000 (V. 26.) of the Parliament ordered the revision of the entitlements for unemployment provisions and initiated that the self-employed should also be entitled to apply for unemployment benefit if they cease to operate as individual entrepreneurs. Therefore, the Parliament in the Resolution called on the government to investigate on what conditions could the duration of work performance of sole proprietors or persons in business associations be taken into consideration from the point of view entitlement to unemployment provisions. The present regulations do not provide any possibilities to this end. Furthermore, the government was requested to define the conditions of providing insured status for the mentioned target group.

[36] See *Az Európai Unió és a magyar közvélemény* (The European Union and Hungarian Public Opinion). (Budapest: Szonda Ipsos, 2000. április)

assumed that public awareness of specific issues, such as Community legislation, is even lower.

There is no information on the acceptance of the general aim of the Directive, although with regard to the acceptance of equal opportunities, there has been a gradual improvement both among professional experts and the general public.

The principle of equal treatment and self-employed workers

No survey or opinion poll has been carried out to gage public opinion with regard to the principle of equal treatment and self-employed workers, and so no data is available.

Self-employed women are viewed by many as 'forced' entrepreneurs, and this is supported by a survey concluding that women become self-employed due to 'coercive' external circumstances more often than men.[37] The survey conducted by the Institute for the Development of Small-Sized Enterprises concluded that there is a difference between men and women in terms of their evaluation of the economic situation and their own position. Men are more optimistic while women evaluate their own position as 'average' and 'stagnating'.[38]

No provisions which are contrary to the principle of equal treatment as defined in Directive 76/207/EEC have been found in Hungarian legislation especially with respect to the establishment, equipment, or extension of a business, or the launching or extension of any other form of self-employed activity, including financial facilities.

6.2 Social rights of spouses

According to social security regulations, a 'contributing family member' is a close relative[39] of the individual entrepreneur/sole proprietor or one who is in a business association with no legal personality who performs work in a private enterprise or a business association, receives financial compensation for this activity, is not a pensioner, and is not in an employment relationship with the individual entrepreneur/sole proprietor or the business association. Contributing family members are insured in accordance with the conditions described below.

---

[37] See footnote 8.

[38] See footnote 9, p. 71.

[39] Close relatives include spouses, relatives in the direct line of descent, an adopted child, a foster child, a step-child, and adoptive, foster or step-parent, siblings, a life-partner, the spouse of the relative in the direct line of descent, fiancees, a direct-line relative or sibling of the spouse, and the spouse of a sibling. Act IV of the Civil Code, Section 685(b).

It should be noted, however, that not all persons considered self-employed can have contributing family members (for example, members of business associations with a legal entity). Although the rules in the Directive are rather lenient, this restriction could be modified to increase the number of insured contributing family members.

Formation of companies by unmarried persons

Hungarian law does not differentiate between persons founding and/or operating an undertaking on grounds of marital status.

Recognition of the work of spouses

According to Article 34(3) of the Act on Social Security Provisions, dependent relatives of an insured person who are not in any other way entitled to health care services can sign an individual contract in order to gain entitlement to health care services. The contract obliges the individual to pay 14 percent as a health insurance contribution.

No initiatives have been taken to examine the recognition of spouses' work, but there have been several positive developments that go beyond the scope of obligations directly deriving from the Directive. In accordance with the social security legislation, the contributing family member of the self-employed persons, including the spouse, shall be insured.

The rights of self-employed workers whose operational activity is interrupted due to pregnancy or motherhood

The Act on Support Given to Families regulates the forms and eligibility criteria for family benefits provided by the State, including the family allowance/schooling benefit, childcare aid, childrearing benefit and maternity allowance. The entitlements are granted regardless of the insurance relationship and income, provided the eligibility criteria stipulated by law are met.

The Act on Mandatory Health Insurance Provisions regulates those provisions that are payable on the legal basis of health insurance, including the pregnancy and young mother's benefit.

6.3 Contributory social security schemes for self-employed workers and spouses

Self-employed workers are covered by the Act on Social Security Provisions detailed above.

6.4 Related research and statistics

Research on women working in agriculture

The National Agricultural Census in 2000 showed that 39.2 percent of female agricultural producers are primary producers, while an extremely small proportion, 0.6 percent, are individual agricultural entrepreneurs. The distortions in the sector are proved by the data regarding the age of agricultural producers: the average age of women in this sector is 60, while that of men is 53.[40]

A comprehensive study on this issue concluded that in 1999, the income of women working in agriculture was approximately 15 percent lower than men's, and that women were "much more exposed to disadvantages due to the unfavourable situation of the sector and their gender."[41]

Social perceptions of self-employed men and women

Setbacks in productive sectors such as agriculture can be observed in the national economy recently, while service sectors have gained ground. Accordingly, the most significant decline in employment was recorded in agriculture.

According to the data issued by the Central Statistical Office, 18 percent of the 548,200 persons pursuing independent activities were engaged in agricultural activities. Women accounted for 25.7 percent of this category.[42]

According to data from 2001, 175,600 women worked as individual entrepreneurs, 29.5 percent of them were engaged in commerce, 16.6 percent in other community services,[43] 14.5 percent in agriculture, and 12 percent in real estate.

In 2001, the proportion of women exceeded that of men in education, health care, and other community and personal service sectors by 56.7 percent, 53.8 percent and 64.7 percent respectively.[44]

Percentage of self-employed men and women

Hungarian legislation does not apply a single concept with respect to self-employed persons, and this is also reflected in statistics, where there is various data according to the different definitions of this category.

---

[40] See Central Statistical Office (2000b: 6., 15).
[41] See Hamza *et al.* (2001: 9).
[42] See *Labour Force Survey,* Central Statistical Office, 2001.
[43] Such as film and video making, work in libraries, archives and museums.
[44] See *Labour Force Survey,* Central Statistical Office, 2001.

According to the Central Statistical Office, in 2001, the majority (82.4 percent) of working men (2,115,600 persons) were employees. 16.2 percent of men were either individual entrepreneurs or members of business, one percent were members of cooperatives, while the proportion of contributing family members was 0.4 percent. Of 1,728,900 working women in 2001, 89.8 percent were employees, 8.6 percent were either individual entrepreneurs or members of business associations, 0.6 percent were members of cooperatives, and one percent were contributing family members.[45]

In conclusion, men and women in Hungary favour employment relationships, and individual entrepreneurs and members of business associations account for hardly more than ten percent of the active population on average.

Past and recent trends in self-employment

According to the Central Statistical Office, between 1992 and 2000 there was a significant and constant decrease in the number of female members of business associations, from 98,700 persons in 1992 to 36,000 in 2000. On the other hand, the number of female individual entrepreneurs increased constantly between 1992 and 1999,[46] but by 2000 it dropped by nearly 8,000 (to 115,600). A constant decline was observed in the number of female contributing family members as well.[47]

There are no available records, statistics, or research findings concerning self-employed married couples. However, as the number of women in business associations is declining, it can be assumed that the proportion of women running an enterprise with a spouse is not increasing either.

---

[45] See *Labour Force Survey*, Central Statistical Office, 2001.

[46] It is important to note that although no surveys have been conducted in this area, recent experience has revealed the trend that a large number of employers prefer alternative ways of employment to the traditional employment relationship. This is primarily due to the high level of social contibutions related to wages. Therefore the number of individual entrepreneurs (working for an employer) has increased. However, a large proportion of these individual entrepreneurs might be considered as 'forced entrepreneurs'.

[47] See Central Statistical Office (2000a: 35).

Research on the status/rights of self-employed women

Unfortunately, no comprehensive survey or study has been published in this area.[48] The report issued by the Institute for the Development of Small-sized Enterprises concluded that between 1997 and 1999, the proportion of women running enterprises increased from 30 to 34.5 percent. Enterprises run by men were of a larger scale in terms of sales revenue and labour force alike. Among enterprises run by women, there were more individual enterprises and fewer business associations. Both women and men identified the high tax and social security contributions, fierce competition, and the unpredictability of economic regulations as the main obstacles to the expansion of their activities.[49]

6.5 Legal means of redress

According to Hungarian legislation, the provisions of the Act on the General Rules of Public Administration Procedures are to be applied.[50] The Act does not contain any provisions that expressly prohibit discrimination based on sex.

As indicated above, the principle of equal treatment is not contained in the related substantive legislation, therefore claims in cases of the violation of the principle of equal treatment principle based on the general anti-discrimination provisions in the Constitution.

Bringing measures adopted pursuant to the directive to the attention of representative bodies

No such reporting obligation towards the representative bodies of the self-employed or vocational training centres is required by law with regard to measures adopted in compliance with the Directive.

---

[48] In the light of experience gathered from surveys among male and female entrepreneurs at the beginning of the 1990s, women set up in business as the result of external circumstances more frequently than men. The size and significance of their enterprises was less than those of ventures established by men. Women had significantly lower revenues and income from these enterprises, and they were underrepresented among the members of business associations. See Nagy (1996).

[49] See *Kis- és közepes vállalkozói konjunktúra-jelentés* (2000: 69–73).

[50] 40 percent of the cases submitted to the labour courts in 2000 requested the court revision of resolutions in social security-related matters. *Source: Magyar Statisztikai Évkönyv (Hungarian Statistical Yearbook).* (Budapest: KSH, 2001), p. 255.

7. The Framework on Parental Leave

Council Directive 96/34/EC of 3 June 1996 *on the framework agreement on parental leave concluded by UNICE, CEEP, and ETUC*

7.1 National legal framework on parental leave: General provisions

According to Section 125 of the Labour Code, employees are entitled to unpaid leave to care for a child up to the age of three; or until the age of eleven if the employee receives childcare aid for the purpose of looking after the child; or until the age of twelve in order to care for an ill child at home for the duration of the illness.

The law does not distinguish between men and women or on the basis of the legal relationship to the child requiring care (for example, if the parents are natural, adoptive, foster parents or guardians). The employer is obliged to permit unpaid leave upon the employee's request.

Employed parents cannot transfer their unpaid leave to another person. However, if they do not take the leave then the benefits allocated to care for and/or nurse a child in the above cases can be transferred to a close relative as defined in Article 22 of Act LXXXIV of 1998.

The law now permits both parents to apply for child-related benefits, whereas previously only mothers and single fathers were entitled to it. There are no regulations encouraging men to apply for parental leave, although in 2001 the Ministry of Social and Family Affairs organised a conference entitled "To become a man and a responsible father," where the Swedish model on preparing for fatherhood was presented.

Conditions of access and detailed rules for applying for parental leave
The duration of childcare leave does not depend on the service time and no advance notification is required. It is the exclusive right of the parent to decide when to take the childcare leave and if so on what date and for how long, in accordance with the legal provisions. The granting of leave can be postponed for justifiable reasons, and the law does not differentiate between full-time and part-time employees in this regard.

The employee is not entitled to remuneration during the period of childcare leave granted by the employer, but a childcare allowance is stipulated. The Act on Assistance Provided for Families contains detailed provisions on the conditions, the scope of eligibility, the degree, the duration of the payment, etc.

In addition, the Labour Code states that the employer is obliged to grant annual supplementary leave to one parent depending on the number and age of the children. During this time the employer pays the employee's wage. The purpose of the supplementary leave is not to attend to an urgent situation but to ensure extra rest for the parent raising a child under the age of 16. The supplementary leave cannot be shared between the two parents and the employer is obliged to record and register the parent who received the supplementary leave.

According to the Labour Code, parents eligible for this leave include biological, adoptive, and foster parents. Part-time employees are entitled to supplementary leave of the same duration as full-time employees, but their wage during the supplementary leave will be proportionally less.

Legal protection against dismissal on the grounds of application for, or taking of parental leave

According to Section 90(1) of Labour Code, an employer may not terminate employment during the period of sick pay or during unpaid leave to nurse or care for a child. The Act on the Legal Status of Public Employees further restricts the termination of employment if the public employee is a single parent and the child is under the age of 18.[51] In such a case, the termination of employment is not prohibited, but can be done only in justified cases that must be proved by the employer. This protection extends to all public employees and civil servants entitled to care for and nurse a child under the provisions of the Labour Code regardless of gender.

Legal entitlement to return to an equivalent or similar job

There is no specific provision providing the possibility to return to the same job after leave. However, after the above-mentioned supplementary leave, the employer is obliged to employ the employee in accordance with the general regulations pertaining to the work contact and employment and other rules of law.[52] The prohibition of discrimination on the grounds of family status is included in the provisions on the prohibition against discrimination in relation to employment.[53]

The Labour Code stipulates that the personal wage of the employee returning to work from childcare or nursing leave must be approximated to that of other employees.

---

[51] Act on the Legal Status of Public Employees Article 32(1)(b).
[52] Labour Code, Section 102.
[53] Labour Code, Section 5(1).

7.2 Social security during parental leave

Childcare allowance

Parents who have been insured for 180 days prior to an application for childcare allowance or prior to giving birth are entitled to a childcare allowance. Parents are defined as biological or adoptive parents, a partner sharing the same household as the parent, a person who intends to adopt the child only if the relevant procedure is already in progress, and the guardian. The allowance can be applied for from the day following the expiration of maternity leave until the child reaches the age of two. Only one parent, where applicable, is entitled to the childcare allowance. Among the conditions to receive the allowance, the beneficiary may not perform any work for remuneration or receive any other regular income.

Childcare assistance

Parents, foster parents, and guardians are entitled to childcare assistance until the child reaches the age of three, or the age of ten if the child is chronically ill or severely handicapped. The parent may not engage in employment for remuneration until the child reaches 18 months, after which time the parent may work up to four hours a day outside the home (there is no limitation if the parent works at home). The Minister of Social and Family Affairs may establish eligibility for childcare assistance in other cases or under different conditions (for example, until the child reaches the age of 14).

It is advisable to apply for childcare assistance if one is not entitled to the childcare allowance because the necessary requirements are not met.

Sickness benefit for the term of caring for a sick child

Parents with no earning capacity who are caring for a sick child at home are entitled to a sickness benefit. The following persons are also entitled to the sickness benefit: mothers breastfeeding a child under one year of age being treated in hospital; mothers and single fathers caring for a child under the age of one; either parent caring for a sick child between the age of one and 12 at home and who does not apply for childcare aid.

The fact that the provision refers to mothers and single fathers caring for a child under the age of one and does not provide for equal entitlement to this benefit is discriminatory and encourages the preservation of traditional roles.

Under Section 138(5) of the Labour Code, an employee is entitled to unpaid leave in the event of a child's illness in order to care for the child at home for the duration of the illness until the child reaches the age of 12.

In other *vis majeure* cases, the employee shall be exempt from his/her obligation to carry out work in accordance with the general rules, i.e. subject to the permission of the employer. The employee shall not receive remuneration during this absence from work.

It is possible to come to an agreement regarding further leave or working time allowances in order to perform parental or family responsibilities in collective agreements or individual labour contracts.

7.3 Parental leave and equal opportunities policy

The Hungarian government has indicated the political will to address the promotion of better organised working hours, greater flexibility hours, an easier return to working life, and the division of responsibilities regarding children and the family. Although no comprehensive governmental measures have been put in place so far, there has been some affirmative action in this respect.

For example, the Office for Women's Issues of the Ministry of Social and Family Affairs has awarded the 'Family-Friendly Workplace Award' each year since 2000 to encourage employers to promote the reconciliation of work and family life. The Office for Women's Issues pays special attention to, among other things, the existence of different working models and regular contact with employees on childcare leave in order to promote their return to working life.

The work and family audit programme has been launched within the framework of community programmes, and objective is to promote human resource management policies that endorse the reconciliation of work and family life.

Initiatives to encourage the introduction of flexible work

Background papers, experts' proposals, and projects have been elaborated on the relatively new concept of flexible work,[54] but there is no information about any governmental initiatives based on the presentation of these new forms.

Recent legislation has reflected a need for stimulating atypical forms of employment. For example, according to the Governmental Decree on the principles of long-term demographic policy, "The possibility of the wider use of part-time employment could be an effective and active measure to promote the reconciliation of individual working career and family responsibilities and childrearing. [...] The establishment of part-time jobs for public employees and civil servants should also be encouraged."

---

[54] For example the transnational pilot project (NeoPraxis) run by the Hungarian Foundation for Women in the framework of the Leonardo Program, whose aim is to make telework widely known in Hungary in all sectors of society, and to encourage its application.

According to the measures set forth by the Governmental Decree on the Medium-Term Action Plan Regarding the Implementation of the National Disabled Programme,[55] "complex programmes should be elaborated to promote atypical employment (teleworking, part-time work, and flexible working hours) and to encourage integrated work performance in the case of disabled persons who need individual assistance both to reach their workplace and to create their special working conditions."

As the regulation and utilisation of concepts of flexible work is underdeveloped in Hungary, the only available statistics are on part-time employment from the fourth quarter of 1999: The rate of part-time work has been the highest in the postal and telecommunication sector (9.3 percent), construction (7.3 percent), real estate, and economic services (5.3 percent) and the agricultural (5.2 percent) sectors of national economy.[56]

A survey on telecommuting in Hungary determined four areas of work that could create opportunities to employ teleworkers for a relatively high number of firms: accountancy, market research, translating and data recording.[57]

7.4 Research on the reconciliation of family and professional responsibilities and on sharing responsibilities between men and women

According to a 1998 survey, the majority of respondents regarded family life as more important than professional life, although respondents with a university degree also gave considerable importance to professional life.[58]

According to a survey on the traditional division of labour within the family, indications show the level of agreement with traditional roles is closely related to educational levels and environment. For example, 43 percent of women and 51 percent of men with only primary education agree with the traditional division of household labour, compared with 11 percent of women and 14 percent of men with a university degree. Additionally, 37 percent of women and 38 percent of men living in villages

---

[55] Government Decree No.2062 of 2000 (III. 24.).

[56] See Central Statistical Office (2001b: 15).

[57] *The chances for teleworking in Hungary* (Research report by psyma Hungary and MONA, March 2000, in the framework of NeoPraxis Project), p. 4.

[58] See Central Statistical Office (2001f: 108).

agree with the traditional division of household labour, compared with 19 percent of women and 18 percent of men living in the capital.[59]

According to another survey carried out in 1999 among persons aged 15–74 to determine time spent on traditional household duties (excluding maintenance, repair and construction, etc.), women spent an average of 172 minutes per day on domestic tasks, whereas men only spent 28 minutes per day on such tasks. Compared with data from 1986 though, the time spent on household chores increased to a small extent for men.[60]

Research on women who return to work after giving birth and men who take parental leave

No surveys have been carried out on this question, but according to the Central Statistical Office, 207,600 women and only 3,500 men took advantage of childcare assistance in 2000, compared with 187,500 women and 4,000 men in 2001.[61]

Data from the National Health Insurance Fund for the first half of 2000 showed that out of the 4,660,000 sickness benefit cases, 172,000 were given to men (37 percent) and 294,000 to women (63 percent). Other data reflects the different rates of participation for women and women childcare; for example, 2.2 percent of cases of sickness benefit to care for a sick child were granted to men, and 25 percent to women.[62]

Demographic, social, and cultural considerations affecting the reconciliation of work and family responsibilities

When women take on greater family responsibilities the loss of income is less than if men were to do the same, because on average women earn less than men. Other obstacles to the reconciliation of family and work responsibilities include the fact that there is no guarantee of women's return to work after giving birth,[63] and the fact that the legal framework for flexible forms of employment has not been elaborated yet. Many women restrict the desired number of children as a final solution[64] or become full-time mothers. It is therefore more appropriate to speak about a choice between work and family life than about reconciliation.

---

[59] See TÁRKI-Omnibusz 2000/3. Quoted in: IBID pp. 46–47.

[60] See Central Statistical Office (2001f: 84).

[61] *Source:* Central Statistical Office, Budapest.

[62] See OEP Former sickness benefit cases – 2001, first half-year preliminary data.

[63] According to the survey of the Women's Assembly of the MSZOSZ, 34.7 percent, more than one third of the respondents, think that having children is a strong disadvantage when finding a job, 41 percent thinks that it is a certain disadvantage.

[64] See Pongrácz and Molnár (2000).

The existence of traditional male and female roles, the lack of efficient governmental measures acting against this model, and regulations strengthening this phenomenon also present obstacles to the reconciliation of work and family responsibilities. An example of the latter is the Governmental Decree in force since 1994 that contradicts the Lisbon criteria according to which: "Economic-policy measures should be used to promote the single-earner family model so that women will not be forced to work, sometimes against their intention. [...] Replacement benefits for families with children [...] would enable more women to choose caring for children or elderly family members as their "full-time profession."[65]

According to a study on the economic activity of women in the 1990s, "While for men raising children the probability of employment increases, the economic activity of women caring for children of pre-school or school-age children is significantly less than for the same women without children or with older children [...] the younger the children are, the greater the decreasing effect on economic activity."[66]

According to another study, the majority of respondents found it difficult to reconcile the increased responsibility of childrearing and household duties with work. These burdens are especially difficult for parents who raise more than one child. Most male respondents indicated that although they could see the mother was overburdened in terms of childrearing and household duties, they thought she could resolve it without any particular problems. Most men also felt that women face no problems in reconciling motherhood with their career opportunities.[67] The study concluded that the modern, non-traditional family concept is linked with an urban environment and higher education level, which is confirmed by the data mentioned above.

---

[65] No.1031 of 1994. (IV. 30.) Gov. decree on the principles of long-term demographics policy.

[66] Nagy (2000: 2).

[67] See Pongrácz and Molnár (2000).

8. THE PRINCIPLE OF EQUAL TREATMENT OF MEN AND WOMEN IN OCCUPATIONAL SOCIAL SECURITY SCHEMES

Council Directive 96/97/EC of 20 December *1996 amending Directive 86/378/EEC on the implementation of the principle of equal treatment for men and women in occupational social security schemes*

8.1 National legal framework on social security schemes: General provisions

Hungarian legislation on social security complies with the provisions of Directive 79/7/EEC. As of January 1998, the previously uniform social insurance legislation is divided into four separate acts and four implementing provisions.[68] Concerning the material scope of the Directive, these acts are accompanied by Act IV of 1991 on Furthering Employment and the Provisions for Unemployed Persons.[69] The Constitutional Court has dealt with these issues in several rulings.[70] The provisions in the Hungarian social security system do not entirely meet the requirements set forth by Directive 96/97/EC concerning occupational social security schemes, and no purely occupational social security system exists in Hungary.

Most persons pursuing work activity, regardless of the type and frequency of the activity, are among the beneficiaries[71] of the social insurance legislation. The system on mandatory state social insurance complies with the provisions of Directive 79/7/EEC.

---

[68] Act LXXX of 1997 on Eligibility for Social Security Provisions and Private Pensions and the Coverage of these Services; Act LXXXI of 1997 on Social Insurance Pension Provision; Act LXXXII of 1997 on Private Pension and Private Pension Funds; and Act LXXXIII of 1997 on Mandatory Health Insurance Provisions.

[69] Unemployment benefits in cash are payable on the legal basis of mandatory insurance but they are not part of the social insurance.

[70] These are the follows: 32/1997 (V. 16.); 7/1998 (II. 18); 39/1999 (XII. 21.); 28/2000 (IX. 28.); 18/2001 (VI. 1.). Further cases include the *Commission of the European Communities v. Hellenic Republic* (C-457/98); *Commission c. Grand-duché de Luxembourg* (C-438/98); *Jean-Marie Podesta v. Caisse de Retrait par répartition des Ingénieurs C:.adres & Assimilés* (CRICA) *and Others; Barber v. Guardian Royal Exchange Assurance Group* (1990); *Commission v. French Republic* (C-354/98); Beune [1994] (C-7/93) ECR I-4471.

[71] Beneficiaries include insured persons; close relatives of insured persons; and persons eligible for certain benefits.

The provisions on the social insurance system can be included in the framework of healthcare and pension insurance, and the state disburses provisions in most cases of social crisis situations determined on the basis of various eligibility criteria.

In general, there has been a strong effort in the development of the Hungarian social security system to replace the enterprise and professional systems (occupational social security systems with the terminology of the Directive) with a uniform mandatory state system. Act 39 of 1955 on Workers' Health Insurance promoted this effort by annulling the former principle of 'company-related insurance' and introducing the principle of 'legal relationship-based' insurance, the so-called 'personal insurance'.

Voluntary mutual insurance funds

Voluntary mutual insurance funds are established by citizens who feel the need to provide for themselves and their families. Employers can become members of a voluntary mutual insurance fund if they partially or fully assume the membership fee for their employees. This instrument does not qualify as an occupational social security system because the employer is not necessarily a member of the fund in the Hungarian system and is not obliged to pay the membership fee in part or in full for the employee; moreover, because the system is, by nature, voluntary, it does not meet the requirements of Article 2(e) of the Directive.

The service relationship of professional members of the armed forces

This system is not completely separate from the mandatory system of social security and social provisions, although it is ostensibly an occupational social security system. According to the Act on the Service Relationship, any professional member of the armed forces is eligible for health insurance provisions on the basis of the Act on Mandatory Health Insurance.

Miners' pension

This system appears to be a typical occupational security system at first glance, but in accordance with the related Government Decree, the regulations of the mandatory state social security system are to be applied. It therefore does not qualify as an independent occupational social security system in line with the requirements of the Directive.

Railroad social insurance directorate and section of journalists

Act XXXIX of 1998 lists the Railroad Social Insurance Directorate and the Section of Journalists among the administration authorities of social security. The regulations of the mandatory state social insurance system only apply to those under the scope of the mentioned authorities. As a result, these formally separate systems, which are still maintained, do not meet the requirements of the relevant Directive.

Direct and indirect discrimination on the basis of sex in social security schemes

There are no discriminatory regulations, related to maternal and family status or otherwise, in the social security legislation. At the same time, indirect discrimination does result from the wage gap between men and women, which primarily affects women. It is difficult to influence this problem in a legal sense, since it is dependent upon one of the most important principles of the mandatory state social security system: that contributions and provisions are adjusted to incomes. Consequently, the person with the lower income (usually the woman) will receive a lower benefit.

The following discriminatory regulations can be identified in the calculation of benefits, including supplementary benefits dependent on conditions related to a spouse or dependants, and the conditions governing the duration and retention of entitlement to benefits:

- Article 44(c) of the Act on Health Insurance only refers to 'mothers' when discussing an infant's care, although fathers are able and should be encouraged to take care of the infant as well. Article 44(d) of the same Act refers to a 'single father', which gives rise to concern because fathers should be able to care for a sick child under the age of one, regardless of whether they are single or not.[72]

- According to the Act on Social Insurance Pension, the proportion of service time and the insurance period are proportional to earnings, which may lead to indirect discrimination, since women frequently take low-income jobs.

- Article 25(1)(d) of the Act on Furthering Employment and Provisions for Unemployed Persons discriminates on the basis of marital status by stipulating that "a workplace is suitable is commuting by public transportation does not exceed three hours and/or two hours in the case of an unemployed women or man raising a child under ten years of age in a single parent family."

In addition to the above, Constitutional Court Ruling 7 of 1998 (III. 18.) (on the discriminatory naming of certain professions) and Constitutional Court Ruling 39 of 1999 (XII. 21.) (on the different retirement ages for men and women) addressed discriminatory regulations concerning the establishment and calculation of benefits.

---

[72] It is worth noting that Article 44(e) already uses the term parent.

Provisions contrary to the principle of equal treatment with regard to social security schemes

The 1997 Pension Act introduced a uniform retirement age of 62 years; previously the age had been 55 years for women and 60 years for men.[73] Currently, the only discriminatory regulation relates to the early retirement pension,[74] whereby in accordance with Article 8 of the Act on Social Insurance Pensions a two-year allowance shall be granted to men who worked for a minimum of ten years in a job that entitles them to early retirement, and to women who worked for a minimum of eight years in such a job. A further year of allowance is to be added after every five years for men, and every four years for women.

There are no discriminatory regulations in terms of continuing or suspending the acquisition of entitlements provided on the basis of maternity leave or related to the period of paid leave for family reasons.

Employers do not pay different levels of contribution; the percentage relates to the level of income. For the social insurance contribution, employers pay 18 percent for the pension insurance fund and 11 percent for the health insurance fund. Employees pay eight percent and three percent respectively. If insured persons are also members of a private pension fund, they may divide their contribution and give two percent to the public pension insurance fund and six percent to the private pension insurance fund.

Consideration of the principle of equal treatment by scheme management bodies

Both types of the mandatory state social insurance (health insurance and pension insurance) provide certain benefits on the principle of equity. The text does not directly refer to the application of principle of the equal treatment, but this is the constitutional obligation of the person making the decision.

Legal mechanisms to declare null and void any discrimination

As ensuring equal opportunities is a fundamental constitutional requirement, claims in this respect can be submitted primarily to the Constitutional Court.

---

[73] The Constitutional Court also tackled the temporary maintenance of the differences referring to the transitional period which resulted from the previous differentiated gender-based retirement age (28 of 2000. (IX. 8.) Constitutional Court Ruling B). The Constitutional Court declared in its ruling that these temporary regulations are not anti-constitutional. Constitutional Court Ruling 32 of 1997 (V. 16.) declared the gender-based difference of service period qualifying for early retirement old age pension on the basis of giving birth and raising child null and void.

[74] The present (discriminatory) regulation on early retirement pensions is scheduled to stay in effect until 1 January 2003.

8.2 Legal means of redress

Judicial remedy is possible in cases involving a violation of the right to equal treatment, but according to available information no definitive judgement has been passed in any case of this nature to date.

Protection against dismissal in the case of complaint of non-compliance with the principle of equal treatment

The Labour Code contains protective measures related to the unlawful termination of the employment relationship. According to Section 100, if the court rules that the employer unlawfully dismissed the employee, at the request of the employee the employment relationship can be continued as prior to the dismissal.

Monitoring mechanisms

Besides the court procedures, there are only rudimentary or universal institutional mechanisms and institutions in place. For example, the National Health Insurance Fund and National Pension Insurance Directorate General as the central official institutions of social insurance are responsible for, among other things, supervision, internal control, and legal remedies in the field; the Parliamentary Commissioner for Civil Rights and Constitutional Court can also play a role.

8.3 Implementation of the principle of equal treatment in matters of social security and equal opportunities strategies

The progressive implementation of the principle of equal treatment in matters of social security is considered integral to an effective strategy of equal opportunities at the governmental level.

Perceived protection of women in maternity and social security

The protection of women in maternity is not considered an obstacle to the implementation of equal treatment at the governmental level, and this is confirmed by the great number of existing protective measures. However, the protection of women in maternity and the traditional division of household labour often serve as obstacles to women themselves in many respects, for example when entering or returning to the labour market. There have been certain professional initiatives to examine possible ways of overcoming these obstacles, but no governmental measures have been taken to tackle this problem (although the Office for Women's Issues has organised some programs and carried out projects in this field). Moreover, there is no monitoring system in place.

8.4 Research and statistics on the impact of social security systems on women

Significant changes have occurred in the field of social security in Hungary recently. In 1993, the Act on Social Administration and Social Provisions was approved, creating the institutional framework for the implementation of social security schemes. A much-needed Act on the Establishment and Management of Voluntary Mutual Insurance Funds was adopted at the end of 1993. In 1995, the Act on Economic Stabilisation tried to curtail universal benefits in a means-tested way. After the 1998 political elections, the amendments aimed at developing family assistance schemes and supporting families were enacted.

A major reform of the national pension scheme was undertaken in January 1998, introducing a mixed pension scheme. The public pension scheme was partially replaced by a mandatory system of privately managed individual savings accounts. New legislation also established an equal retirement age for men and women, abolishing what had previously been a discriminatory provision towards women.

It is therefore possible to trace a progression towards the implementation of equal treatment in the field of social security, and certain pieces of legislation (for example, the Act on Furthering Employment and the Provisions for Unemployed Persons, and the Act on Private Pension Benefits and Private Pension Funds) a prohibition of discrimination, on ground including but not limited to sex, appears concretely in the text.

REFERENCES

Bibliography

Central Statistical Office (2001) *(Family and Career – Values and Concerns after the Political Changeover)* NKI Kutatási Jelentések 62, 2000/1. Budapest: *Központi Statisztikai Hivatal.*

Bankó, Zoltán, Gyula Berke and György Kis (eds.) (2000) *Munkaügyi Jogszabályok.* Budapest: KJK Kerszöv.

Barnard, Catherine (2000) *EC Employment Law.* Oxford: Oxford University Press.

Bitskey Botond (2000) *Az Alkotmánybíróság diszkriminációs gyakorlata, különös tekintettel a férfiak és nők egyenjogúságára, valamint a munka világára vonatkozóan* (The Practice of Constitutional Court in the Field of Discrimination with Special Regard to Equal Rights for Men and Women and the World of Work). Kézirat (Manuscript). Budapest.

Burrows, Noreen and Jane Mair (1996) *European social law.* Chichester: John Wiley and Sons.

Cairns, Walter (1999) *Introduction to European Union Law.* Budapest: Co-NEX.

Central Statistical Office (2000a) *Magyar Statisztikai Évkönyv 1999* (Hungarian Statistical Yearbook 1999). Budapest: Központi Statisztikai Hivatal.

Central Statistical Office (2000b) *Magyarország mezőgazdasága a 2000. évben. Az Általános Mezőgazdasági Összeírás tapasztalatai.* (Hungarian Agriculture in Year 2000. Results of the National Agricultural Census). Budapest: Központi Statisztikai Hivatal.

Central Statistical Office (2001a) *A munkaerő-felmérés idősorai* (Time-series of the Labour Force Survey) 1999–2000. Budapest: Központi Statisztikai Hivatal.

Central Statistical Office (2001b) *A nők munkaerő-piaci helyzete* (The Situation of Women in the Labour Market). Budapest: Központi Statisztikai Hivatal.

Central Statistical Office (2001c) *Legfrissebb Adatok: Foglalkoztatottság és munkanélküliség, 2000. október–december* (Most Recent Data: Employment and Unemployment, October–December 2000). Budapest: Központi Statisztikai Hivatal.

Central Statistical Office (2001d) *Létszám és kereset a nemzetgazdaságban* (Number of workers and wages in the national economy). Budapest: Központi Statisztikai Hivatal.

Central Statistical Office (2001e) *Munkaerő-piaci jellemzők 2000 IV. negyedévében és a 2000. évben* (Labour Market Characteristics in the Fourth Quarter of 2000 and in 2000). Budapest: Központi Statisztikai Hivatal.

Central Statistical Office (2001f) *Nők és férfiak Magyarországon (Women and Men in Hungary),* 2000. Budapest: Központi Statisztikai Hivatal, Szociális és Családügyi Minisztérium.

Ékes, Ildikó (2000) *Az önfoglalkoztatás helyzete Magyarországon* (The Situation of Self-Employment in Hungary). Kézirat (Manuscript). Budapest.

Ellis, Evelin (1998) *EC Sex Equality Law.* Oxford: Clarendon Press.

European Commission (1997) *Assisting spouses of the self-employed, Report of the two round tables organised by the European Commission in Brussels on 7 February and 23 and 24 June 1997.* Brussels: European Commission.

European Commission *(1999) Transformation of labour and future of labour law in Europe, Final Report.* Brussels: European Commission.

European Commission *(2000) Report on Member States legal provisions to combat discrimination.* Brussels: European Commission.

European Community (1997) *Women and work – Report on existing research in the European Union, European Commission Employment and Social Affairs.* Luxembourg: Office for Official Publications of the European Communities.

European Community (1998) *Earning differentials between men and women – Study based on the Structure of earning survey (SES), European Commission Employment & Social Affairs.* Luxembourg: Office for Official Publications of the European Communities.

European Community (2000) *Sexual harassment at the workplace in the European Union, European Commission Employment and Social Affairs.* Luxembourg: Office for Official Publications of the European Communities.

Gyulavári Tamás (ed) (1997) *Egyenlő esélyek és jogharmonizáció* (Equal opportunities and Legal Harmonization), Budapest: Munkaügyi Minisztérium Egyenlő Esélyek Titkársága, Integrációs Stratégiai Munkacsoport.

Gyulavári Tamás (ed) (2000) *Az Európai Unió szociális dimenziója* (The Social Dimension of the European Union). Budapest: Szociális és Családügyi Minisztérium (Ministry of Social and Family Affairs).

Gyulavári, Tamás and Gábor Kardos (eds) (1999) *Szociális jogok az Európai Unióban, Az Európai Bíróság esetjoga* (Social Rights in the European Union, The Case Law of the European Court). Budapest: AduPrint.

Gyulavári, Tamás and Gábor Kardos (eds) (2000) *A nők és férfiak közötti esélyegyenlőség az európai közösségi és a magyar jogban – Jogharmonizációs javaslat* (The Equality of Opportunities between Women and Men in the European Community Law and Hungarian Law – Suggestion forLegal Harmonization.) Budapest: INDOK.

Gyulavári, Tamás and Gábor Kardos (eds) (2000) *Egyenlőbben! A nők és férfiak esélyegyenlősége az Európai Unióban és Magyarországon* (More Equal Way! The Equality of Opportunities of Women and Men in the European Union and Hungary). Budapest: INDOK.

Hamza, Eszter, Krisztina Miskó, and Erzsébet Tóth (2001) *Az agrárfoglalkoztatás jellemzői, különös tekintettel a nők munkaerőpiaci helyzetére* (Employment in the Agricultural Sector with Special Focus on the Labour Market Situation of Women) 1990–2000. Budapest: AKII.

Károlyi, Géza (1994) "Gondolatok az egyéni vállalkozás szabályozásáról (Ideas about the Regulation of Private Enterprise)." In *Magyar Jog* 1994/4.

Kende, Tamás (ed) (1995) *Európai közjog és politika* (European Public Law and Politics). Budapest: Osiris.

Király, Miklós (1998) *A diszkrimináció tilalma az Európai Bíróság joggyakorlatában* (The Prohibition of Discrimination in the Legal Practice of the European Union). Budapest: Akadémiai Kiadó.

Kisvállalkozás-fejlesztési Intézet (2000) *Kis- és közepes vállalkozói konjunktúra-jelentés* (Report on the Situation of Small-and Medium-Sized Enterprises). Budapest: Kisvállalkozás-fejlesztési Intézet (Institute for the Development of Small-Sized Enterprises).

Lehoczkyné Kollonay, Csilla (1998) *Kezdeti lépések a foglalkoztatási diszkrimináció bírósági gyakorlatában* (Initial steps in the court case law regarding employment discrimination). In *Fundamentum*, 4: 91–95.

Lévai, Katalin and István György Tóth (eds) (1997) *Szerepváltozások – Jelentés a nők helyzetéről 1997* (Changing Roles – Report about the Situation of Women 1997). Budapest: TÁRKI, Munkaügyi Minisztérium Egyenlő Esélyek Titkársága.

Lévai, Katalin, Róbert Kiss and Tamás Gyulavári (eds) (1999) *Vegyesváltó – Pillanatképek nőkről, férfiakról* (Mixed Relay – Snapshots about women, men). Budapest: Egyenlő Esélyek Alapítvány.

Lewis, Jackie (2000) "Az út Amszterdamig." In László Mocsonaki and Bea Sándor, eds., *Amszterdam után: A szexuális orientáció az Európai Unióban és Magyarországon* (After Amsterdam: The Sexual Orientation in the European Union and Hungary). Budapest: Háttér.

Ministry for Foreign Relations (2000) *Nők és férfiak közötti esélyegyenlőség az Európai Unióban és Magyarországon* (The Equality of Opportunities between Women and Men in the European Union and Hungary). Budapest: A Magyar Köztársaság Külügyminisztériuma.

Ministry for Social and Family Affairs (1999) *Nők a rendszerváltásban* (Women in the Change of Regime), UNICEF MONEE Project Regionális Monitoring Jelentés (UNICEF MONEE Project Regional Monitoring Report). No.6, 1999. Budapest: Szociális és Családügyi Minisztérium.

Ministry for Social and Family Affairs (2000) *Magyarország IV és V. kormányzati jelentése az ENSZ számára a nőkkel szemben alkalmazott hátrányos megkülönböztetés minden formájának kiküszöböléséről* (Hungary's Joint Fourth and Fifth Periodical Report to the CEDAW Committee). Budapest: Szociális és Családügyi Minisztérium.

Nacsa, Beáta (1999) "A hátrányos megkülönböztetés tilalma a magyar munkajogi gyakorlatban. A jogharmonizáció követelményei és a hazai jogszemlélet" (The Prohobition of Megative Discrimination in the Practice of the Hungarian Labour Law, The Requirements of Legal Harmonization and the Domestic Legal Attitude). In Tamás Gyulavári, Róbert Kiss and Katalin Lévai, eds., *Vegyesváltó* (Mixed Relay). (Budapest: Egyenlő Esélyek Alapítvány, 1999).

Nagy, Beáta (1996) "Üzletasszonyok és üzletemberek: férfi és női vállalkozók az 1990-es évek elején (Business Women and Business Men: Male and Female Entrepreneurs at the Beginning of the 1990s)." In Lengyel György ed. *Vállalkozók és vállalkozói hajlandóság* (Entrepreneurs and the Willingness to Enterprise). Budapest: BKI, pp. 117–145.

Nagy, Gyula (2000) *A nők munkaerő-piaci helyzete* (The Labour Market Situation of Women). Budapest: OMKMK.

Nemeskéri, Gyula and Péter Csizmadia (2000) "Nőkkel szembeni diszkrimináció a munkakörök értékelésén és összehasonlításán alapuló személyzeti rendszerekben (Discrimination against Women in the Staff Systems based on the Valuation and Comparison of Field of Works)." In *Munkaügyi Szemle*, April 2000.

OFA (2000) *Esélyegyenlőség és kollektív alku az Európai Unióban 2. A helyzet feltárása* (Equality of Opportunities and Collective Bargain in the European Union 2, Revealing the Situation). Budapest: OFA.

OMKMK (2000a) *1999. évi létszám-, bér- és kereseti adatok – Nemzetgazdaság összesen* (Staff, Wage and Income Data – National Economy Total of 1999). OMKMK Munkaügyi Adattár, 1/2000. Budapest: Országos Munkaügyi Kutató és Módszertani Központ.

OMKMK (2000b) *1999. évi létszám-, bér- és kereseti adatok – Vállalkozások* (Staff, Wage and Income Data – Enterprises of 1999). OMKMK Munkaügyi Adattár, 2/2000. Budapest: Országos Munkaügyi Kutató és Módszertani Központ.

OMKMK (2000c) *1999. évi létszám-, bér- és kereseti adatok – Költségvetési szféra* (Staff, wage and Income Data – Budgetary Sphere of 1999). OMKMK Munkaügyi Adattár, 3/2000. Budapest: Országos Munkaügyi Kutató és Módszertani Központ.

OMKMK (2000c) *1999. évi létszám-, bér- és kereseti adatok területi feldolgozásai* (Regional Disaggregation of Staff, wage and Income Data for 1999). OMKMK Munkaügyi Adattár, 4/2000. Budapest: Országos Munkaügyi Kutató és Módszertani Központ.

OMKMK (2000e) *A munkaerőpiac keresletét- és kínálatát alakító folyamatok – Munkaerőpiaci helyzetjelentés* (Trends influencing the demand and supply on the labour market – Labour Market Situation Report). Budapest: OMKMK, A "Közösen a Jövő Munkahelyeiért" Alapítvány.

OMKMK (2000f) *Női–férfi kereseti különbségek Magyarországon 1986–1996* (Women–Men Income Differences in Hungary 1986–1996). Budapest: OMKMK.

Pongrácz, Tiborné and Edit S. Molnár (2000) *Család és munka – értékek és aggodalmak a rendszerváltozás után.* (Family and Work – Values and Concerns after the Political Changes). Budapest: KSH-NKI.

Pongrácz, Tiborné and István György Tóth (eds.) (1999) *Szerepváltozások – Jelentés a nők és férfiak helyzetéről 1999.* (Changing Roles – Report about the Situation of Women 1997). *Budapest:* TÁRKI, Szociális és Családügyi Minisztérium Nőképviseleti Titkársága.

Presidency Conclusions. Nice European Council Meeting, 7–9 December 2000, Annex I, European Social Agenda, p.16

Scharle Ágota (2000) "Önfoglalkoztatás, munkanélküliség és családi vállalkozások Magyarországon (Self-Employment, Unemployment and Family Enterprises in Hungary)." In *Közgazdasági Szemle,* No.3.

Schiek, Dagmar (2000) "Positive action before the European Court of Justice – New conceptions of equality in Community law?" In *The International Journal of Comparative Labour Law and Industrial Relations,* 16(3): 254.

Sejal, Parmar (2000) "Az Amszterdami Szerződés (The Amsterdam Treaty)." In László Mocsonaki and Bea Sándor, eds., *Amszterdam után: A szexuális orientáció az Európai Unióban és Magyarországon* (After Amsterdam: The Sexual Orientation in the EuropeanUnion and Hungary). Budapest: Háttér.

Sipos, Katalin (1996) "Az Európai Unió szociálpolitikája. Szociális jogok Maastricht előtt és után (The Social Policy of the European Union. Social Rights before and after Maastricht)." In *Acta Humana,* No.22–23.

Sörös, Éva (2000) *A munkaügyi felügyelő szerepe és lehetőségei a nemek közötti esélyegyenlőség megvalósulásában (The Role and Possibilities of Labour Supervisor in the Realization of Equality of Opportunities between the Sexes).* Budapest: Szociális és Családügyi Minisztérium.

Szonda Ipsos (2000) *Az Európai Unió és a magyar közvélemény (The European Union and Hungarian Public Opinion),* April 2000. Budapest: Szonda Ipsos.

Watson, Philippa (1993) "Social policy after Maastricht." In *Common Market Law Review,* No.30.

List of Legislation screened

Acts

Act XX of 1949, The Constitution of the Republic of Hungary.

Act III of 1952, Code of Civil Procedures.

Act IV of 1957 on the General Rules of Public Administration Procedures.

Act IV of 1959, the Civil Code (with Law Decree No.11 of 1960 on the Enactment and Implementation of the Civil Code, and with Law Decree No.2 of 1978 on the Enactment and Implementation of Act IV of 1977 on the Amendment and Uniform Text of the Civil Code).

Act IV of 1959 on the Civil Code of the Republic of Hungary.

Act V of 1990 on Private Enterprise.

Act IV of 1991 on Furthering Employment and Provisions for the Unemployed.

Act XXII of 1992, The Labour Code.

Act XXIII of 1992 on the Legal Status of Civil Servants.

Act XXXIII of 1992 on the Legal Status of Public Employees.

Act III of 1993 on Social Administration and Social Provisions.

Act LXXVI of 1993 on Vocational Training.

Act LXXIX of 1993 on Public Education.

Act XCIII of 1993 on Labour Safety.

Act XCVI of 1993 on Voluntary Mutual Insurance Funds.

Act LXXX of 1994 Public Prosecutors Service Relationship and Data management of the Public Prosecutors Service.

Act CXVII of 1995 on Personal Income Tax.

Act LXXV of 1996 on Labour Inspection.

Act XLIII of 1996 on the Service Relationship of Professional Members of Armed Forces.

Act XXXI of 1997 on the Protection of Children and Guardianship.

Act LXVII of 1997 on the Legal Status and Remuneration of Judges.

Act LXXX of 1997 on Eligibility for Social Security Provisions and Private Pensions and the Coverage of these Services, with Government Decree No.195 of 1997 (XI. 5.) on its Implementation.

Act LXXXI of 1997 on Social Insurance Pensions, with Government Decree No.168 of 1997 (X. 6.) on its Implementation.

Act LXXXII of 1997 on Private Pension and Private Pension Funds.

Act LXXXIII of 1997 on Compulsory Health Insurance.

Act LXXXIII of 1997 on Mandatory Health Insurance Provisions, with Government Decree No.217 of 1997 (XII. 1.) on its Implementation.

Act CLIV of 1997 on Health Care.

Act XXVI of 1998 on the Rights and Promotion of Equal Opportunities of the Disabled.

Act XXXIX of 1998 on the State Supervision of the Financial Funds of Social Security and of Social Security Authorities (including Rail-road Social Security Directorate and the Section of Journalists).

Act LXVI of 1998 on Health Care Contribution.

Act LXXII of 1998 on the Establishment of Foreign Citizens as Independent Entrepreneurs for Economic Purposes.

Act LXXXIV of 1998 on Family Provisions.

Act LXXXIV of 1998 on Support to Families, with Government Decree No.223 of 1998 (XII. 30.) on its Implementation.

Act C of 1999 on the Promulgation of the European Social Charter.

Act LVII of 2000 on the Promulgation of the ILO Convention No.100 on the Equal Remuneration for Men and Women Workers for Work of Equal Value adopted by the Thirty-fourth Session of the General Conference of the International Labour Organisation in 1951.

Act LXII of 2000 on the Promulgation of the ILO Employment Policy Convention adopted by the Forty-Eighth Session of the General Conference of the International Labour Organisation in 1964.

Act LXXI of 2000 on the Promulgation of the ILO Convention No.144 on the Tripartite Consultation to Promote the Implementation of International Labour Standards adopted by the Sixty-first Session of the General Conference of the International Labour Organisation in 1976.

Draft proposals

T/3468 Draft proposal on the modification of the Act XXII of 1992 on the Labour Code and the related acts due to legal harmonisation.

Decrees

Government Decree No.150 of 1991 (XII. 4.) on Miners' Pension.

Government Decree No.24 of 1994 (II. 25.) on the Employment of Home Workers.

Government Decree No.202 of 1996 (XII. 3.) on the Implementation of Act LXXXVIII of 1996 on Health Care Contribution.

Government Decree No.168 of 1997 (X. 6.) on the execution of Act LXXXI of 1997 on the Provision of Social Security Pensions.

Government Decree No.199 of 1998 (XII. 4.) on the Further Training of Public Servants and Public Administration Management Training.

Government Decree No.218 of 1999 (XII. 28.) on Certain Minor Offences.

Government Decree No.197 of 2000 (XI. 27.) on Mandatory Minimum Wage.

Decree of the Ministry of Labour No. 6 of 1992 (VI. 27.) on the Sectoral Classification System of Workers.

Decree of the Ministry of Labour No.5 of 1993 (X. 26.) on the Execution of Act XCII of 1993 on Labour Safety.

Decree of the Ministry of Labour No.7 of 1993 (XII. 30.) on the National Register of Occupations.

Decree of the Ministry of Labour No.6 of 1996 (VII. 16.) on Allowances Promoting Employment and Grants to Manage Employment Crises Situations from the Labour Market Fund.

Decree of the Ministry of Labour No.9 of 1996 (XII. 20.) on the Management of the Labour Market Organisation, the Scope of Authority of the Particular Bodies Belonging to the Organisation and Certain Organisational Matters.

Decree of the Ministry of Labour No.19 of 1997 (XII. 18.) on the Registration Order of Collective Agreements and the Related Data Provision Obligation.

Decree of the Ministry of Health No.6 of 1987 (VI. 24.) on the Caisson Operations.

Decree of the Ministry of Agriculture No.64 of 1994 (XII. 15.) on the Professional Requirements.

Decree of the Ministry of Agricultural and Regional Development No.5 of 2001 (I. 16.) on the Plan Protection Activities.

Decree of the Ministry of Industry and Commerce No.18 of 1995 (VI. 6.) on the Professional Examination Requirements of Industrial and Commercial Qualifications.

Decree of the Ministry of Justice No.6 of 1986 (VI. 26.) on the Exemption from Paying Costs of Court Proceedings.

Decree of the Ministry of Public Welfare No.20 of 1994 (XI. 15.) on the Professional Requirements of Midwife Training.

Decree of the Ministry of Public Welfare No.5 of 1995 (II. 8.) on District Nurse Service.

Decree of the Ministry of Public Welfare No.24 of 1995 (VII. 25.) on Occupational Health Service.

Decree of the Ministry of Public Welfare No.33 of 1998 (VI. 24.) on the Medical Examination and Reporting of the Professional and Personal Hygienic Aptitude.

Decree of the Ministry of Education No.31 of 1999 (VIII. 13.) on the Qualification Requirements of the Professional Further Training Faculty of Nurses for the Juvenile.

Decree of the Ministry of Education No.45 of 1999 (XII. 13.) on the Conditions of the Commence and Continuation of Vocational Training.

Decisions

Government Decision No.1059 of 1999 (V. 28.) on the Establishment of the Council for Women's Issues.

Government Decision No.1005 of 2000 (I. 18.) on the Tasks of the Transformation of the Advancement System of Civil Servants into Civil Service as a Life Career.

Government Decision No.1040 of 2000 (V. 31.) on the Employment Policy Guidelines for the Year 2000.

Other Legal Sources

Rulings of the Constitutional Court 1992–2000 (cited: 7 of 1998, order of the CC).

Statements of the Labour Law Council of the Supreme Court (cited: MK 19, MK 23, MK 57, MK 97).

Decisions of the Labour Court 1992–2000 (cited: Court Decision 1992.61, 1993.772, 1994.350, 1995.377, 1995.612, 1995.739, 1996.667, 1997.608, 1998.610, 1999.329, 1999.474, 2000.227).

Decision No.3 P. 21.321/1997/13 of the Municipal Court of Monor.

Equal Opportunities for Women and Men in Lithuania

Table of contents

Executive summary 301

Country report: Introduction 309

1. The principle of equal pay for work of equal value 311
   1.1 National legal framework: General provisions 311
   1.2 Legal foundations and institutional structures 312
   1.3 Job classification 312
   1.4 Available legal procedures 313
   1.5 Means of informing employees of their rights 313
   1.6 Role of trade unions 314
   1.7 Women's factual situation 315

2. Equal treatment for women and men as regards access to employment, vocational training and promotion, and working conditions 316
   2.1 National legal framework: General provisions 316
   2.2 The concept of discrimination on grounds of sex: Definition and legal sanctions 316
   2.3 Access to employment, vocational training and promotion 317
   2.4 Protective measures for women in the labour market 319
   2.5 Women's and men's jobs 319
   2.6 Legal status of sexual harassment 320

3. Protection of pregnant women from the inherent risk of certain activities and related employment rights 321
   3.1 Legal and conceptual framework 321
   3.2 Risk assessment and employers' obligations 321
   3.3 Night work 322
   3.4 Maternity leave 323
   3.5 Prohibition of dismissal and employment rights 324

4. The burden of proof in cases
   of discrimination based on sex 325
   4.1 Legal and conceptual framework
       concerning indirect discrimination 325
   4.2 The burden of proof and rules of evidence 327
   4.3 Case law 327

5. Non-discrimination against part-time workers 329
   5.1 National legal framework and employment
       conditions concerning part-time workers 329

6. The principle of equal treatment
   for self-employed workers and their assisting spouses 333
   6.1 National legal framework: General provisions 333
   6.2 Social rights of spouses 334
   6.3 Contributory social security system
       for self employed workers 334
   6.4 Related research and statistics 335
   6.5 Legal means of redress 338

7. The framework on parental leave 339
   7.1 National legal framework: General provisions 339
   7.2 Social security during parental leave 340
   7.3 Parental leave and equal opportunities policy 341
   7.4 Research on sharing family
       and professional responsibilities 341

8. The principle of equal treatment
   in occupational social security schemes 342
   8.1 National legal framework: General provisions 342
   8.2 Legal means of redress 349
   8.3 Related research and statistics 350

Executive summary for Lithuania

INTRODUCTION

According to the 2000 Regular Report from the Commission on Lithuania's Progress Towards Accession, in the field of equal treatment for women and men, Lithuanian legislation is substantially in line with the *acquis communautaire*. The main provisions that have yet to be introduced concern, *inter alia,* the shift in the burden of proof in cases of discrimination based on sex and the introduction of a definition of indirect discrimination.

The Act on Equal Opportunities of the Republic of Lithuania, which entered into force on 1 March 1999, was the first to be passed in the entire region of Central and Eastern Europe. The purpose of this law is to ensure the implementation of the constitutionally consolidated equal rights for women and men; amendmends were passed on 18 June 2002 defining positive discrimination. In order to ensure the work of the Equal Opportunities Ombudsperson, the *Seimas* (Parliament) of the Republic of Lithuania instituted the Office of the Equal Opportunities Ombudsperson, which was given the status of an independent public institution on 25 May 1999.

While the Office of the Ombudsperson has proved to be effective in enhancing the implementation of equal treatment and Lithuania is clearly in the process of achieving gender equality, major efforts are still required in order to achieve full harmonisation with the Directives and real equality *de facto*. Specifically, while the establishment of national equal opportunities machinery, including specific institutions, reveals a certain determination of the state, equal opportunities are far from playing a core role in the negotiation process and are not looked upon with the greatest possible attention. This is due mainly to public attitudes, which prioritise the economic situation or social matters over equal rights for women and men, but it speaks to the need for greater social dialogue and awareness on gender equality, as well as a greater commitment to promoting equal opportunities.

One positive example of the activities of the Ombudsperson took place in the year 2000, when six public agencies and 90 private companies were asked to provide explanations for their discriminatory announcements. Following thorough investigations, three persons were punished with administrative fines for violating the provisions of Article 8 of the Act on Equal Opportunities. In particular, an administrative penalty was incurred by the director of a joint-stock company for publishing an advertisement in which only women were invited to attend special courses for secretaries/referents. A further two cases also related to advertising vacancies in the newspapers.

Differences in the average wages of men and women do exist in Lithuania, and confirm women's disadvantaged position in the labour market. In the first quarter of the year 2000, women received 81.3 percent of men's wages,[1] the ratio for the first quarter of the year 2001 was 88 percent.[2] As in many developed countries, women's average wage in Lithuania is lower than men's, for several reasons, including the fact that women are only exceptionally employed in leading positions. Statistically, the highest level a woman has achieved in employment is the position of an assistant manager. This research is evidence that a legal framework on equal opportunities alone will not guarantee an improved position for women in the labour market, and that the translation of such provisions into real and lasting change for women has yet to be fully seen.

Summary of key points

Defining principles

The principle of equal pay is provided for in a number of legal acts in the Republic of Lithuania, and no discriminatory legal provisions that provide other than the principal of equal pay for women and men can be identified in the legislation. However, while the official translation of the law into English uses the term 'work of equal value', the original Lithuanian version of the law establishes a requirement of equal pay for 'equal work', and does not include 'work of equal value'. It is prohibited for an employer to persecute an employee who filed a complaint because he/she felt discriminated against because of his/her sex, including complaints regarding unequal pay. The definition of equal opportunities in the Act on Equal Opportunities is not concrete, but the legal text allows the use of a wide range of provisions from international human rights documents. The Act on Equal Opportunities defines direct and indirect discrimination, but Lithuanian society perceives the core of direct discrimination better than it perceives indirect discrimination. It also prohibits sexual harassment.

---

[1] Lithuanian Department of Statistics (2000: 106).

[2] Data was provided by the Department of Statistics.

Protective measures

In general, the applicable laws regulating employment provide for many privileges and guarantees for women who are raising small children. Men, as a rule, are only entitled to such privileges if they are raising their children alone. Pregnant and breastfeeding women, as well as women who recently gave birth, are included in the group of individuals with a limited functional capacity. Night work is prohibited for pregnant women and, unless the employee consents, also for women who recently gave birth or are breastfeeding. Pregnant workers have the right to attend antenatal examinations without loss of pay if such examinations must take place during working hours. The Act on Employment Contracts stipulates limitations on terminating the employment contract with a pregnant woman or a woman with a child under three years of age. Under the Criminal Code, criminal responsibility is foreseen for the dismissal or refusal to employ a pregnant or breastfeeding woman.

Burden of proof

According to the statutory provisions in this field, during an investigation into a complaint of sex-based discrimination, the duties of the Office of the Equal Opportunities Ombudsperson include collecting evidence and examining the individual who allegedly committed the violation. Such an investigation procedure for complaints involving the application of the principle of equal treatment for women and men regarding access to employment, vocational training, promotion and working conditions, significantly facilitates the position of complainants and creates more favourable conditions – insofar as a complainant is not obliged to obtain documents or any other evidence from the person who committed the violation, because such a process is, as a rule, a difficult task.

Part-time workers

The terms 'part-time worker' and 'comparable full-time worker' are not legally defined in accordance with the Directive. Part-time work does not lead to restricted social benefits, reduced job security or fewer career opportunities than full-time work, and the hourly rate of pay is not lower for part-time employees than for full-time employees. In Lithuania, the man is still considered to be the family's main breadwinner, while the woman's income is seen as merely supplementary. Despite this stereotype and the fact that the level of unemployment is steadily increasing, it is not yet popular for either women or men to work part-time: only 11.6 percent of employees were occupied in part-time positions in 1998 (and 6.9 percent in 1999).[3]

Self-employed workers

There is no direct definition of a self-employed person in the national legislation. However, legal acts do contain provisions concerning such persons' right to develop a business, and their social insurance. The legal acts regulating self-employed activities consolidate the provisions on equal opportunities for men and women, married and unmarried, to establish a business, register a farm, and to borrow and receive state aid for business development. A self-employed worker alleging sex-based discrimination has the right to appeal in accordance with general legal procedures; however, not a single case has been recorded so far. Social insurance issues for self-employed and contributing family workers are regulated in great detail by legal acts and in general comply with the provisions of the Directive. Lithuania has both compulsory and voluntary social insurance schemes.

Parental leave

In Lithuania, the term 'parental leave' described in the Directive refers to 'leave to care for a child under the age of three'. The legal framework for the right to leave is established under the Act on Holidays. Child-care leave shall be granted to: the mother, or upon her or the family's decision to the father, grandparents, or other relatives raising the child. Parental leave may be taken either in full or in part, and persons entitled to this leave may split the parts between themselves; it is a legal right and not a question of the employment agreement. The employer is not entitled to postpone the granting of parental leave for any reasons. No statistics were available on the gender segregation of parental benefits prior to 2000, but in 2000 parental benefits were received by 36,533 women and 420 men. Thus, women accounted for 98.8 percent of all recipients.[4] Men are not currently encouraged to take parental leave in Lithuania.

---

[3] Lithuanian Department of Statistics (2000: 95).

[4] Lithuanian Department of Statistics (2001: 83).

Social security schemes

The policy of equal opportunities in Lithuania includes the implementation of equal treatment in matters of social security. As set forth in the Constitution and social security legislation, all persons in Lithuania have the right to social security, irrespective of their gender. The social insurance for self-employed persons differs from that of other employees due to their more recent inclusion in social security policy. Different retirement ages (60 years for women and 62.5 for men) are provided for in the Act on State Social Insurance Pensions, but there is no legal provision obliging either women or men to retire from work after reaching the age of retirement.

RECOMMENDATIONS RELATED TO EACH SPECIFIC DIRECTIVE

Council Directive 75/117/EEC of 10 February 1975 *on the approximation of laws of the Member States relating to the implementation of the principle of equal pay for women and men*

- The principle of equal pay for equal work and work of equal value should be explicitly provided for in the Act on Equal Opportunities.

- Research should be carried out to determine whether trade unions are able to initiate and influence arrangements concerning working conditions and social guarantees.

- Research should be carried out on how collective agreements regulate the level of wages, calculate salaries and determine payment.

Council Directive 76/207/EEC of 9 February 1976 *on the implementation of the principle of equal treatment for men and women as regards access to employment, vocational training and promotion, and working conditions*

- The definition of equal treatment as it is set forth in the Act on Equal Opportunities is too vague to be fully implemented in practice, and should thus be amended.

- 'Equal opportunities' should be explicitly defined in the Act on Equal Opportunities.

- The Act on Equal Opportunities should include a definition of 'positive action'.

- There should be clear provisions that provide compensation in cases of discrimination. This is especially important since it gives the clear signal that such behaviour will be punished, and encourages victims of discrimination to bring such cases to court for proper remedy.

- Research should be carried out on a continuing basis to monitor women's access to vocational training and educational opportunities, as well as access to employment and continued professional development.

- Employers should take all necessary measures to inform employees of their rights.

- The gathering and dissemination of reliable statistics on women and men's comparative position in the labour market, e.g. women employers in the private sector, etc. should be improved and followed by appropriate action to remedy the existing discrepancy.

Council Directive 92/85/EEC of 19 October 1992 *on the introduction of measures to encourage improvements in the safety and health at work of pregnant workers and workers who have recently given birth or are breastfeeding*

- The principle of equal opportunities for women and men should be consolidated in the relevant legal acts, providing equal access to labour and social guarantees to both women and men.

- Provisions of an absolute character (i.e. prohibition of night work for pregnant women) should be reconsidered in light of developing equal opportunities and encouraging women to make their own informed decisions with regard to their health and safety as far as possible.

- Women should be encouraged to take cases of discrimination to court, and NGOs should be encouraged to support them in such cases.

Council Directive 97/80/EC of 15 December 1997 *on the burden of proof in cases of discrimination based on sex*

- A shift in the burden of proof should be legally provided for.

- The Supreme Court of Lithuania and the Senior Administrative Court of Lithuania, which are involved in shaping common court practice, should propose that the courts handling civil and administrative cases related to the violation of the principle of equal treatment as regards access to employment, vocational training, promotions and working conditions, lay the burden of proof on the defendant.

- Legislative changes or changes in court practice should be made known to employees, for example through information campaigns and/or training courses.

Council Directive 97/81/EC of 15 December 1997 *concerning the framework agreement on part-time work concluded by UNICE, CEEP and the ETUC*

- A legal definition of 'part-time worker' should be adopted in accordance with the Directive.
- Reliable statistics on the position of women and men in labour relations should be gathered and made accessible to the public. In particular, it is necessary to gather information and statistics on part-time workers, and their factual situation.
- Part-time work for both women and men should be encouraged as a means of equally sharing parental roles in the family.
- Concrete measures should be taken to facilitate part-time workers' access to educational and vocational opportunities.

Council Directive 86/613/EEC of 11 December 1986 *on the application of the principle of equal treatment between men and women engaged in an activity, including agriculture, in a self-employed capacity, and on the protection of self-employed women during pregnancy and motherhood*

- A legal definition of self-employed worker should be adopted.
- The principle of equal treatment and non-discrimination should be consolidated in all legal acts relating to this Directive.
- Research and data should be collected on the comparative numbers of self-employed women and men, including working in agriculture.

Council Directive 96/34/EC of 3 June 1996 *on the framework agreement on parental leave concluded by UNICE, CEEP, and the ETUC*

- Statistics and research in the field regulated by the Directive should be improved.
- Public discussion and debate on the role of both parents should be initiated, and men should be encouraged to take parental leave.

Council Directive 96/97/EC of 20 December 1996 *amending Directive 86/378/EEC on the implementation of the principle of equal treatment for men and women in occupational social security schemes*

- The law should provide for the same retirement age for women and men.

- The establishment of occupational security schemes should be promoted, prompting organisations to set up programmes for the promotion of gender equality, especially in regard to social security schemes.

- Data should be collected on the work of contributing spouses in order to implement a programme and/or policies at the regional or state level to encourage their work.

- Awareness raising, communication, and dialogue within the society should be promoted, as well as active partnership with women's organisations.

- Competent institutions should continue to gather statistical data on self-employed persons in rural and urban areas disaggregated by gender, in order to carry out an analysis of business development problems faced by self-employed persons according to gender.

- More gender disaggregated statistics on statutory as well as occupational security schemes should be collected.

- Employees should be provided with the proper information on their social security rights and how the application of the principle of equal treatment affects these rights.

Country reports: Lithuania

INTRODUCTION

According to the 2001 Regular Report from the European Commission on Lithuania's Progress Towards Accession, "in general, the alignment with the acquis has been particularly good in the area of equal treatment for women and men, and the Ombudsman office has proved to be effective in enhancing the implementation of equal treatment."[5] Although Lithuania is clearly in the process of achieving gender equality, efforts are still needed to ensure complete alignment with the acquis in this field.

While economic and social matters have been prioritised over equal rights for women and men in the accession process, largely due to public attitudes, the establishment of national machinery on equal opportunities does speak to the determination of the State to change the current situation both at the level of officials and the general population.

Equal rights for women and men are enshrined in most national laws, including the Act on Elections, the Act on Referendum, the Act on Employment Contracts, the Act on Wages, the Act on Labour Protection, the Act on Support for Unemployed Persons and a number of other laws, including the national Codes. The new Labour Code, whose norms are in line with the *acquis communautaire*, was passed on 4 June 2002, but will not enter into force until January 2003.

The Act on Equal Opportunities, which entered into force on 1 March 1999, was the first such law in the entire region of Central and Eastern Europe and aims to ensure the implementation of the equal rights for women and men consolidated in the Constitution. Amendments to the Act on Equal Opportunities passed on 18 June 2000 introduced definitions of indirect and positive discrimination. In order to ensure the effectiveness of the work of the Equal Opportunities Ombudsperson, the *Seimas* (Parliament) of the Republic of Lithuania instituted the Office of the Equal Opportunities Ombudsperson, which was given the status of an independent public institution in May 1999.

The Equal Opportunities Ombudsperson *inter alia* supervises the implementation of the provisions on equal rights and opportunities for women and men set forth in the Constitution and the Act on Equal Opportunities; investigates complaints related to discrimination and sexual harassment in cooperation with other office officials, and can conduct such an investigation at his/her own initiative in certain cases; within his/her competence submits recommendations of State government and administration

---

[5] European Commission (2001: 69).

institutions of the Republic of Lithuania on the revision of legal acts and priorities related to equal rights policy; and supervises the mass media in order to prevent the publication of discriminatory advertisements. One of the main powers of the Office is the right of the Ombudsperson to investigate administrative cases and to impose administrative sanctions.

In addition to the Office of the Equal Opportunities Ombudsperson, accompanying institutional structures include the Parliamentary Commission of Family and Child, as well as the Group of Women Members of Parliament, and the Labour Market and Equal Opportunities Department in the Ministry of Social Security and Labour. In March 2000 the Government established an inter-ministerial Commission on Equal Opportunities for Women and Men, aimed at coordinating the activities of State institutions in the implementation of the principle of equal rights and opportunities. Representatives from all ministries and two departments are appointed as members of the Commission, and the Equal Opportunities Ombudsperson and NGO representatives are invited to participate in the Commission's work.

The Government is undertaking to adopt and implement the following three National Programmes that are currently under preparation by the Ministry of Social Protection and Labour and are expected to be adopted in autumn 2002:

- The National Program for Support for Families with Children, which aims to provide favourable conditions for the combination of parental duties and professional activities. The Ministry of Social Affairs is currently making amendments to Lithuanian laws in order to ensure they are gender neutral and give parents the opportunity to decide for themselves which of them will avail of the guarantees provided for and, in this way, encourage parents to share family responsibilities.

- The National Action Plan for Employment will reflect the main EU Employment Guidelines and foresees activities to support women returning to work after childcare leave, etc.

- The National Program for Equal Opportunities for Women and Men will be fully oriented towards the further implementation of a gender mainstreaming strategy. It will encompass new guidelines established in EU directives, as well as other international instruments, and special attention is to be paid to the critical area of 'women and the economy.'

The strategy used to promote gender mainstreaming is meant to increase gender visibility and the knowledge of issues concerning women and men with the active participation of different women's organisations that promote education on gender issues. Lithuanian NGOs are active in raising society's awareness about gender equality, and this is an important aspect in ensuring it is achieved in practice.

1. THE PRINCIPLE OF EQUAL PAY FOR WORK OF EQUAL VALUE

Council Directive 75/117/EEC of 10 February 1975 *on the approximation of laws of the Member States relating to the application of the principle of equal pay for men and women*

1.1 National legal framework concerning the principle of equal pay for work of equal value: General provisions

The principle of equal pay is provided for in a number of legal acts in the Republic of Lithuania, including the Constitution, and there are no discriminatory legal provisions that provide other than the principle of equal pay for women and men.

The Constitution

The Constitution provides that every person may freely choose an occupation or business, and shall receive adequate compensation for work.

The Act on Employment Contracts

The Act on Employment Contracts ensures equal rights for all employees, regardless of their sex and based on their professional qualifications.

The Act on Wages

Article 1(2) of the Act on Wages prohibits the reduction of an employee's wages on grounds of sex, considering that quantity and quality of work are the main grounds for differentiating between employees' pay.

The Act on Collective Agreements

Article 12(4) of the Act on Collective Agreements provides that conditions, provisions and obligations of a collective agreement that are less favourable to an employee than those established by national legislation and employment contracts shall be invalid.

The Act on Equal Opportunities

In the official translation of the Act on Equal Opportunities into English, employers are obliged to respect the principle of equal pay for work of equal value. However, the original Lithuanian version does not contain this term, referring only to 'equal pay for equal work'.

Article 6 of the Act on Equal Opportunities provides that the application by an employer of less (or more) favourable terms of payment to an employee shall be considered discriminatory if this is based on the employee's sex.

It is prohibited for employers to persecute employees who filed a complaint of sex-based discrimination, including complaints regarding unequal pay.

1.2 Implementation of the principle of equal pay for work of equal value: Legal foundations and institutional structures

The Office of the Equal Opportunities Ombudsperson, the Labour Inspectorate, and the courts all have the right to investigate claims regarding a violation of the principle of equal pay. The Ombudsperson has the possibility to investigate cases of discrimination not only in private or public sectors, but also in the non-governmental sector.

According to the Act on Equal Opportunities, the Ombudsperson shall investigate complaints relating to discrimination and is authorised *inter alia* to refer the material to investigative bodies if indications of an offence have been established; to address an appropriate person or institution with a recommendation to discontinue the actions violating equal opportunities or to repeal a related legal act relating; to hear cases of administrative offences and impose administrative sanctions; or to dismiss the complaint if the violations mentioned therein have not been corroborated. All legal and physical persons are obliged to immediately submit the material and necessary explanations upon the request of the Ombudsperson.

Article 5 of the Act on the State Labour Inspectorate empowers the Labour Inspectorate to deal with equal pay as a part of labour matters and to monitor the implementation of labour laws, as well as monitor legal proceedings, regulate labour relations and monitor the work of young people, women and persons.

The Office of the Equal Opportunities Ombudsperson and the State Labour Inspectorate have signed an agreement to collaborate in matters of equality between women and men.

1.3 Job classification

There is a job classification system to determine pay in the public sector, and Annex 1 of the Act on Civil Service provides for 37 levels and categories of civil servants in the Parliament, the offices of the President and the Prime Minister, Ministries, County

Governors' Offices, and municipal administrations. The level of pay is established for each position, subject to the minimum living standard and in accordance with a fixed index.

The minimum wage in the private sector is regulated by a contract between the two parties in accordance with the Civil Code and labour legislation; there is no room for state intervention in this area.

1.4 Available legal procedures in cases involving the violation of the principle of equal pay for work of equal value

According to the Code of Administrative Offences, a violation of the equal rights of men and women is punishable by a fine. The Ombudsperson can impose a fine ranging from 100 to 4,000 Litas (approximately €28–1,130) in case of a violation of the prohibition of discrimination on grounds of sex, and a fine of between 500 and 2,000 Litas (approximately €141–565) in case of a failure to implement the requirements of the Equal Opportunities Ombudsperson. Section 247(6) of the Code of Administrative Offences establishes the personal responsibility of the Ombudsperson in imposing administrative sanctions and investigating cases.

Article 9 of the Act on Equal Opportunities grants victims of discrimination the right to appeal to the Equal Opportunities Ombudsperson and, in accordance with generally established procedures, to appeal to the court of general jurisdiction. There are certain additional possibilities when appealing to the *Seimas* Ombudsperson, whose jurisdiction extends to civil servants.

In addition to the legal instruments available to employees in this field, legal consultations for socially unprotected groups are provided free of charge in the municipalities, as well as the Citizens Advice Bureaus throughout Lithuania, which are financed by the state.

1.5 Means of informing employees of their right to equal pay for work of equal value

Intern users can obtain the current version of any legal act in the database of the *Seimas* free of charge, and the labour laws are available in national labour exchange offices. The Labour Inspectorate is also empowered to consult and provide information to employers and their organisations, job safety services, employees, trade unions on such matters as labour, job safety, and concluding and carrying out collective agreements.

However, in practice, without being a member of a trade union, members of working collectives do not usually receive detailed information about their rights, in particular social rights. The Office of the Equal Opportunities Ombudsperson uses awareness raising campaigns to disseminate information on gender equality rather well, and this is clearly reflected in the amount of work it receives: the rather newly established institution[6] is approached by no fewer people than its Scandinavian counterparts, which were instituted decades ago.

1.6 Role of trade unions

Although trade unions can protect individuals' rights in Lithuania, including in cases involving equal pay, and trade unions can demand that an employer annul such decisions that violate the labour, economic, and social rights of their members provided for by law, it is evident that since the collapse of the Soviet counterparts, trade unions have not yet realised their true value and have failed to exploit their possibilities and to defend employees' interests. There are fields of activity with up to 17 trade unions in one working collective (for example, in healthcare). On the other hand, only a very small number of employees are members of a trade union and very few working collectives are fortunate enough to have acting trade unions today.

Collective work agreements must respect the principle of equal pay for women and men, and several laws establish this obligation for trade unions. Article 6 of the Act on Collective Agreements provides that payment conditions must be agreed upon by trade unions and an employer. The law further provides that disputes between employees and employers shall be settled in judicial proceedings.

At the end of March 2001, a new amendment of the above law was passed, making the dissolution of a labour contract more liberal. As a result, no trade union mediation is now necessary to end a labour contract. The provision evoked disappointment and reactions from employees and trade unions.

---

[6] The Office of the Equal Opportunities Ombudsperson was set up on 25 May 1999.

1.7 Women's factual situation regarding the principle of equal pay for work of equal value

Data on women's and men's pay can be found in special monthly, quarterly and annual publications of the Department of Statistics,[7] and also occasionally in the daily *Respublika*.

The average wages of men and women do differ in Lithuania, and confirm women's disadvantaged position in the labour market. In the first quarter of the year 2000, women received 81.3 percent of men's wages;[8] the ratio for the first quarter of the year 2001 was 88 percent.[9] Women are only exceptionally employed in leading positions, which are paid more generously than lower positions.

In the private sector, and especially in organisations where the relations regulated by contract deal only with two parties and no collective agreements are signed, some violations of the principle may occur.

---

[7] The publications *Wages and Salaries* and *Women and Men in Lithuania*, both of which are issued by the Department of Statistics under the Government of the Republic of Lithuania.
[8] Lithuanian Department of Statistics (2000: 106).
[9] Data was provided by the Department of Statistics.

2. Equal treatment for women and men as regards access to employment, vocational training and promotion, and working conditions

Council Directive 76/207/EEC of 9 February 1976 *on the implementation of the principle of equal treatment for women and men as regards access to employment, vocational training and promotion, and working conditions*

2.1 National legal framework concerning the principle of equal treatment for women and men: General provisions

The equal rights of women and men are guaranteed in the basic legislative acts in Lithuania. In addition, Article 29 of the Constitution states that "all persons shall be equal before the law, the courts, and other State institutions and officers and no person may have his/her rights restricted in any way or be granted any privileges on the basis of his or her sex [...]."

The definition of equal opportunities in the Act on Equal Opportunities is not concrete, but the legal text allows the use of a wide range of provisions from international human rights documents.

2.2 The concept of discrimination on grounds of sex: Definition and legal sanctions

According to the Act on Equal Opportunities, "the violation of the equal rights of women and men [discrimination] shall mean passive or active conduct expressing humiliation and contempt, and the restriction of rights or granting of privileges by virtue of a person's sex [...]," except in certain legally defined cases.

The Constitutional Court has held[10] that positive discrimination should not be treated as granting privileges. The Act on Equal Opportunities defines positive discrimination,[11] suggesting that organisations and institutions, particularly public ones, willing to take

---

[10] Opinion of the Constitutional Court of the Republic of Lithuania on the compliance of the Articles of the Fourth Protocol of *The European Convention on Protection of Human Rights and Fundamental Freedoms* with the Constitution of the Republic of Lithuania of 24 January 1995.

[11] The newest amendment to the Act on 18 June 2002.

action to improve the position of women or men would no longer encounter legal barriers.

In the year 2000, the Office of the Equal Opportunities Ombudsperson asked six public agencies and 90 private companies to explain discriminatory announcements. Following thorough investigations, three persons have been subject so far to administrative fines for violating the provisions of Article 8 of the Act on Equal Opportunities.[12] One administrative penalty was incurred by the director of a joint-stock company for publishing an advertisement in which only women were invited to attend special courses for secretaries. Another two also related to advertising vacancies in the newspapers.

The Act on Equal Opportunities defines cases in which the granting of privileges shall not be considered discrimination, and exceptions include the special protection of women's health – taking into account their particular physiological nature, such as pregnancy, childbirth and breastfeeding.

The Act on Equal Opportunities defines direct and indirect discrimination, but Lithuanian society is able to perceive direct discrimination better than it perceives indirect discrimination.

2.3 National legal framework concerning the principle of equal treatment as regards access to employment, vocational training and promotion, and working conditions

The Act on Employment Contracts prohibits employers from refusing employment on grounds of sex or any other factors that do not affect the person's professional qualifications.[13]

The Act on Equal Opportunities provides that institutions of education and science must ensure equal conditions for women and men regarding: 1) admission to vocational educational institutions colleges, institutions of higher education, and qualification improvement courses; 2) award of grants and student loans; and 3) the selection of curricula and knowledge assessment.[14]

---

[12] "It is prohibited to specify requirements in job or educational advertisements that give priority to either sex (with the exception of the case referred to in Article 2[2][5]) and to request information from job seekers about their civil status, private life or family plans."

[13] Article 19 of the Act on Employment Contracts.

[14] Article 4(1) of the Act on Equal Opportunities.

Despite the legal acts and institutions guaranteeing equal opportunities, in practice women and men are not in the same situation in the labour market. The results of a survey of women job seekers revealed that the majority of women have experienced a diverse range of offences and humiliation at work. Every second respondent (47 percent) noted that she was (is) treated as an inferior employee compared to her male colleagues.[15] Almost half of the married women with childcare responsibilities (42 percent) indicated that motherhood was the cause of many difficulties at work. The results of the survey showed that middle-aged women suffer discrimination in the workplace more often due to staff cuts and redundancies. It is also much more difficult for them to secure future employment, as the major success factor in seeking work is young age. It is common for younger women to be told that they will not be employed because they might get married or become pregnant. According to the respondents, women's position in the private sector was much worse than in the public sector, where gender inequality was not so evident and issues of discrimination against women were related to traditional stereotypes, attitudes and values, whereas the position of women in private enterprises depends upon the economic interests of employers and competitiveness, and the laws are often completely ignored in this sphere.

At the beginning of 1998, the share of the private sector in terms of the national employment structure was almost 68.3 percent, compared with 34.5 percent in 1991. More than half (around 58 percent) of the employees from the state sector were women, while men were more active in private sector activities (making up 57 percent).[16] There has been a slower feminisation of the private sector because the so-called 'feminine' branches of the economy (education, healthcare and social work) are actually maintained as part of the state sector. In contrast, the 'masculine' spheres of activity (construction and some branches of the processing industry) are almost completely privatised. As indicated by special surveys, women get involved in private businesses much less readily than men, although the number of women starting their own business in the private sector is slowly increasing. 33 percent of founders/managers in the small and medium business of newly created enterprises in 1999 were women (compared with 27.4 percent in 1990–1995).[17]

Irrespective of the recent data showing that it is difficult for women to find employment, the average unemployment rate for men as of 2000 was 12.3 percent, compared with 10.8 percent for women. This phenomenon is the result of the economic recession in the country, which exerted a negative influence on the industrial sector, small and medium-size businesses, where mostly men are employed.

---

[15] Kanopienė (2001).

[16] Ibid.

[17] Lithuanian Department of Statistics (2000).

In 2000, 58.2 percent of job seekers directed to training were women, and women comprised 57.8 percent of the total number of individuals improving their qualifications. It is impressive that among the people who improved their qualifications in high schools and higher education, the number of women was much higher.[18]

With reference to vocational training, as in many countries and due to persisting stereotypes, men, as a rule, choose the so-called 'masculine' professions and women choose the so-called 'female' professions although the law allows both men and women to choose any profession or work they like without restriction. As a result, a strong segregation on grounds of sex is observed among persons who study and work.

2.4 Protective measures with regard to women's participation in the labour market

The Ministry of Health and the Ministry of Social Security and Labour approved the list of processes not recommended for women wanting to retain the function of maternity and the list of agents that are harmful and hazardous to women in the working environment. After the Act on Labour Protection was adopted, there were discussions as to whether the listed agents were only dangerous for women wanting to retain the 'function of maternity'.

In an attempt to facilitate opportunities for women with small children to find employment after childcare leave or a period of unemployment, the Act on Support for the Unemployed provides for employment programmes and additional guarantees. There are discriminatory provisions concerning fathers with children under the age of 14, who are only eligible for the respective guarantees if they are raising the child alone.

In the year 2000, the Labour Exchange registered fewer women than men (43.1 percent and 56.9 percent respectively). 655 new work places were established in 2000 and financed by the employment fund; 343 of those places were occupied by women.

2.5 Women's and men's jobs

No legislative acts prohibit the division of work into masculine and feminine spheres. However, employers do sometimes specify gender when advertising vacancies, and certain suffixes in the Lithuanian language indicate whether a woman or man is required for the position advertised without stating this directly. Due to deep-rooted traditions and stereotypes, there are professions or positions that are identified as only feminine (for

---

[18] Data provided by the Lithuanian Labour Exchange.

example, home help and nursemaids). To escape common misunderstandings arising from this, the Commission on National Lithuanian Language has established that professions and positions are only to be written in the masculine gender.

Legal acts establish several cases in which certain work can only be done by women or men (for example, psychological consultations for women abused by men). However, the exceptions made with regard to women's physiological characteristics do raise concerns and have the potential to put women in a disadvantaged position, thereby limiting their right to choose certain jobs.

2.6 Legal status of sexual harassment

The Act on Equal Opportunities prohibits sexual harassment, which is defined in Article 2(3) as "conduct of a sexual nature, verbal or physical, towards a person with whom there are work, business or other relations of subordination." Sexual harassment may take the form of humiliating words or photos, postcards, or drawings that are visible to the victim; letters received by the victim by post or e-mail and any other communications; or any kind of physical contact of a sexual nature. According the Act on Equal Opportunities, the employer must take appropriate measures to prevent and avoid sexual harassment.[19]

---

[19] Article 5(5).

3. Protection of pregnant women from the inherent risk of certain activities and related employment rights

Council Directive 92/85/EEC of 19 October 1992 *on the introduction of measures to encourage improvements in the safety and health at work of pregnant workers and workers who have recently given birth or are breastfeeding*

3.1 Legal and conceptual framework

Article 2 of the Act on Labour Protection defines the terms 'pregnant woman', 'woman who has recently given birth' and 'worker who is breastfeeding',[20] and such workers are included in the group of individuals whose functional capacity is limited because of their health. The law fixes the limited functional capacity until the child reaches the age of one.

Article 38 of the Constitution states that the family is a fundamental unit of society and the State. In accordance with Article 39, the State shall protect families raising children at home and support them in accordance with legally established procedures. The law provides that working mothers shall be granted paid leave prior to and following childbirth, and provided with favourable working conditions and other privileges.

3.2 Assessing the risk to the safety or health of a pregnant worker and employers' obligations

In accordance with Article 62 of the Act on Labour Protection, a pregnant or breastfeeding woman or woman who has recently given birth must be provided with safe and healthy working conditions. General provisions on the safety and health at

---

[20] "A 'Pregnant worker' shall mean a worker who submits a certificate issued by a health care institution to her employer; a 'worker who has recently given birth' shall mean a worker who submits [to her employer] a certificate issued by a health care institution and who cares for her child until the age of one; a 'worker who is breastfeeding' shall mean a worker who submits a certificate [to her employer] issued by a health care institution confirming that she cares for her child and breastfeeds until the age of one." Articles 2(28)–(30) of the Act on Labour Protection of 7 October 1993 (New version: the Act on Safety and Health at Work of 17 October 2000).

work for pregnant women, women who recently gave birth or are breastfeeding are established in Article 63 of the same law.

According to Section 41 of the Code of Administrative Offences, employers whose act or omission constitutes a violation of health and safety regulations shall be held liable under the law. The State Labour Inspectorate shall impose sanctions provided for under the laws of the Republic of Lithuania on employers and workers who violate legal acts on safety and health at work.

Disputes related to the application or violation of these legal acts shall be settled in accordance with the procedures established by law. Collective labour disputes related to safety and health at work shall be settled in accordance with the procedure established in the Act on Settlement of Collective Disputes.

3.3 Night work

In Lithuania, night work (i.e. work performed between 10 p.m. and 6 a.m., the duration of which shall not exceed eight hours a day) is prohibited for pregnant women and, unless the employee consents, it is prohibited for women who recently gave birth and are breastfeeding.[21] The provision for pregnant women is imperative, and they cannot work at night under any circumstances. There is no established procedure in Lithuanian legislation for women who engaged in night work prior to pregnancy to be transferred to daytime work during the period of pregnancy.

In accordance with Article 63 of the Act on Labour Protection, where the elimination of dangerous factors is impossible, the employer shall implement measures to adjust the working conditions so that risk exposure to a pregnant woman, a woman who has recently given birth or a breastfeeding woman is avoided.[22] In addition, the employer must provide for shorter working days or workweek at the request of a pregnant or breastfeeding woman or a woman who has recently given birth.[23]

---

[21] Article 45 of the Act on Labour Protection.

[22] "[…] 4. Having been moved to another job, pregnant women, women who have recently given birth or breastfeeding women shall be paid not less than the average pay they received before being moved to another job. 5. If moving a pregnant woman to another job that does not affect her or her future child's health is not technically feasible, the worker concerned shall be granted, upon her consent, unpaid leave until she goes on maternity leave. The period of the unpaid leave shall not be counted in the insured period and shall be excluded when calculating the average pay that is liable to indemnity." Article 63(3–6) of the Act on Labour Protection of 7 October 1993 (New version: the Act on Safety and Health at Work of 17 October 2000).

[23] Ibid, Article 46(2).

In addition, *overtime work* is prohibited for pregnant women, women who recently gave birth and breastfeeding women. Individuals raising one or more children up to three years of age may work overtime, on days off or holidays only with their consent. In addition to general breaks to rest and eat, breastfeeding women shall be provided with no less than half hour breaks every three hours to breastfeed a child. At the woman's request, breastfeeding breaks may be combined or added to the break to rest and eat or transferred to the end of the working day. Women are to be paid the average salary during such breaks.

3.4 Maternity leave

In Lithuania, in accordance with the provisions of Article 18 of the Act on Holidays, women shall be granted maternity leave for a period of 70 calendar days prior to the birth of the child and 56 calendar days following the birth (or 70 days in the event of a complicated childbirth or multiple births). Maternity leave shall be calculated and granted to the woman in full, regardless of the number of days actually used prior to childbirth. Lithuanian legislation also provides for so-called childcare leave (which is referred to in the EU Directive as 'parental leave').[24] Requirements regarding maternity leave, as a rule, are not included in an employment contract, and the Act on Employment Contract does not require this.

Benefits established by the Law on Sickness and Maternity Social Insurance shall be paid for the period of the maternity leave. The Act on Sickness and Maternity Social Insurance provides for the right to maternity benefits and stipulates explicitly in which cases such benefits should be provided.

In addition, in accordance with Article 8 of the Act on Holidays, annual leave is granted to women, upon their request, prior to maternity leave or immediately after it without requiring six months of uninterrupted work at that enterprise. Pregnant women and women with a child under the age of 14 or a child who is disabled shall be granted holidays at the requested time.

---

[24] Ibid, Article 19: "Upon her request, a mother shall be granted childcare leave until the child reaches the age of three. Upon the family's decision, leave shall be granted to the father, grandparents, or other relative who is raising the child. Leave may be taken either in full or in part, and persons entitled to this leave may alternate turns. Benefits established by the State shall be paid for the period of leave, and the working place shall be kept for the person, except in the event that the enterprise is completely liquidated."

Antenatal examinations

Pregnant and breastfeeding women, as well as women who have recently given birth, must be released from work to attend a medical examination without loss of pay if such examinations must take place during working hours.

3.5 Prohibition of dismissal and employment rights

Article 35 of the Act on Employment Contracts prohibits the termination of an employment contract with pregnant women and women with a child under three years of age. Under the Criminal Code, criminal responsibility is foreseen for the dismissal or refusal to employ a pregnant or breastfeeding woman.[25] According to Article 42, pregnant or breastfeeding women, and women who recently gave birth, must be reinstated if the court establishes a case of unlawful dismissal. In practice there are no known cases involving a violation of the social protection and health requirements set forth to protect pregnant and breastfeeding women, and women who recently gave birth.

---

[25] Section 140 of the Criminal Code.

4. THE BURDEN OF PROOF IN CASES OF DISCRIMINATION BASED ON SEX

Council Directive 97/80/EC of 15 December 1997 *on the burden of proof in cases of discrimination based on sex*

4.1 Legal and conceptual framework concerning indirect discrimination and specific legal means to implement the principle of equal treatment for women and men

In accordance with Lithuanian legislation, persons may defend their rights in judicial and non-judicial institutions if an employer violated the principle of equal treatment regarding employment, vocational training and promotion, and working conditions. Upon the establishment of the Office of Equal Opportunities Ombudsperson, this office has become the only non-judicial institution to which both men and women apply in cases involving a violation of this principle as it is the only public institution in Lithuania that specialises in this field. It has been observed that the Equal Opportunities Ombudsperson's call to an employer for an explanation and the relevant documents is an effective measure in preventing future violations and facilitates bringing an end to current violations.

Individuals may also appeal to the court in such cases, but this practice is not popular for several reasons, including the fact that the principles of equal treatment were only formalised in 1998, and because if an employer violated the principle of equal treatment for women and men regarding employment, vocational training and promotion and working conditions, the victim, under Lithuanian legislation, is not entitled to any material compensation. Lithuanian legislation fails to provide for a specific procedure applicable to individuals appealing to court in order to ensure application of the principle of equal treatment for men and women.

Each individual who has been discriminated on grounds of sex in the field of labour relations, education, science or studies, shall have the right to lodge a complaint with the Office of the Equal Opportunities Ombudsperson. Article 19(2) of the Act on Equal Opportunities provides that "attached to the complaint may be: [...] 2) the available evidence and its description; 3) a list of persons recommended for examination, with their addresses and the circumstances each of them can corroborate." Article 19(3) provides that the "failure to adhere to the form of the complaint specified in paragraph 1 of this Article or the failure to provide the necessary information may not justify a refusal to consider the complaint." Thus, the law provides the possibility, rather than the obligation, for a complainant to file the evidence he/she wants.

During an investigation of complaints on sex-based discrimination, the Equal Opportunities Ombudsperson is the main subject on whom the burden of proof lies (i.e. who must collect evidence, etc.). Such an investigation procedure for complaints involving the application of the principle of equal treatment regarding access to employment, vocational training, promotion and working conditions, significantly facilitates the position of complainants. It also creates more favourable conditions insofar as a complainant is not obliged to obtain documents or any other evidence from the person who committed the violation, as such a process is, as a rule, a difficult task. The Equal Opportunity Ombudsperson, after investigating the complaint and assessing the collected evidence, shall make a decision in accordance with the Act on Equal Opportunities.

Individuals who were discriminated against on grounds of sex may also appeal to the Commission on Labour Disputes, whose activities are regulated by the Act on Labour Disputes. In accordance with Article 5(1) of the Act on Labour Disputes, "an employer, upon receipt of the employee's request to restore the violated rights, shall, within 10 working days from the date he/she received the employee's request, begin direct negotiations with the employee and inform him/her of his/her decision. 2.) An employer, upon acknowledging the violation of rights, shall restore those rights within the term fixed in paragraph 1 of the current Article." Any party who is dissatisfied with the Commission's decision may appeal to court. It can be concluded that an employee appealing to the Commission to ensure the application of the principle of equal treatment for women and men regarding access to employment, vocational training, promotion and working conditions, is not obliged but has the right to submit evidence corroborating his/her requirements.

Another non-judicial institution to which individuals may have recourse in order to ensure the application of the principle of equal treatment for women and men regarding access to employment, vocational training, promotion and working conditions is the trade union, which to a certain extent plays the role of a mediator and conciliator.

4.2 The burden of proof procedure in litigation concerning the violation of the principle of equal treatment for women and men and rules of evidence

Lithuanian legislation has established rules and principles that are generally applied to all civil and administrative cases.

In Lithuanian, a plaintiff must prove the legality and corroboration of his/her requirements, while the defendant must prove the grounds for not recognising the action. Plaintiffs shall, in their action, specify the evidence they intend to use to prove their case. As a rule, defendants shall produce evidence after they receive a copy of the legal action.[26] A similar procedure is provided for in the Act on Administrative Proceedings. Incidentally, the court may require the parties involved to produce relevant evidence that has not been specified by them. According to the law, the burden of proof does not lie with the court; however, it is within the court's jurisdiction to gather evidence in two ways (firstly to demand evidence itself, i.e. to forward the demand directly to an organisation or individual to produce the necessary or to issue a certificate on the right to obtain such evidence for its submission to the court).

Article 57(4) of the Act on Administrative Proceedings also stipulates that "evidence shall be produced by all parties to the proceedings and any other participants. If necessary, the court may offer the above-mentioned individuals the possibility to produce additional evidence or, at the request of such individuals or on its own initiative, to demand the necessary documents [...]."

4.3 Case law on the violation of the principle of equal treatment for women and men

There have not yet been any civil cases in Lithuania concerning the violation of the principle of equal treatment for women and men regarding access to employment, vocational training and promotion and working conditions.

The Office of the Equal Opportunities Ombudsperson regularly publishes flyers on equal rights for women and men as regards access to working conditions, promotion, payment conditions and vocational training. Non-governmental organisations have also made similar publications. Flyers are disseminated in conferences, seminars, health

---

[26] Section 164(3) of the Code of Civil Procedure.

institutions, schools, and at meetings with public officials; they are also disseminated by various public organisations.

In general, one may say that in defending rights concerning the violation of the principle of equal treatment for women and men in non-judicial institutions, a positive feature is that the burden of proof lies with the institution investigating a complaint and the alleged perpetrator. In Lithuanian civil court practice related to the application of labour laws, the burden of proof in such disputes falls on the defendant. This may be applied by analogy to the investigation of cases concerning sex-based discrimination.

5. Non-discrimination against part-time workers

Council Directive 97/81/EC *concerning the framework agreement on part-time work concluded by UNICE, CEEP and the ETUC*

5.1 National legal framework and employment conditions concerning part-time workers

The terms 'part-time worker' and 'comparable full-time worker' are not defined in Lithuania in accordance with the Directive. Nevertheless, in practice, 'part-time workers' are deemed to be persons who work fewer than normal working hours and are paid in proportion to the time worked. In defining the term 'comparable full-time worker' it is necessary to follow the normal working time for a full-time employee, established by law or collective agreements. In accordance with Article 40 of the Act on Labour Protection, the standard duration of work may not exceed 40 hours per week, while the average duration of working time cannot exceed 48 hours.

A shortened working day or week may be provided for the worker at his/her request and with the agreement of the employer. Employers are obliged to provide a shorter working day or week schedule to pregnant or breastfeeding women, women who recently gave birth, as well as female workers raising a child under 14 years of age or a handicapped child under 16 years of age. Fathers also have the right to shorter working hours if they are raising a child under 14 years of age or a disabled child under the age of 16 years alone.

The Government Decision on Establishing a Part-Time Working Day or Week provides for several options of part-time work and the possibility to divide part-time work hours. It is permitted to reduce the number of work hours per day and the number of working days per week, as well as to combine both alternatives.

Article 22 of the Act on Employment Contracts grants employers the right to change an employee's working or other conditions, including the work regime, only when this change is related to changes in production or technology, or when the organisation of labour is being changed. This provision applies to both full-time and part-time workers, as well as in cases of compulsory transfer from full-time working regime to part-time or *vice versa*. All employees must be given written notice of the planned changes in working conditions no later than one month prior to the introduction of such changes. If the changes are related to production technology, the employer must provide conditions for the employees to improve their qualifications or change their specialisation so that they will be able to work after the changes in production or production technology are introduced. The collective agreement may require a longer notice period, as well as additional obligations for the provision of conditions that would enable the employee to prepare for work after the introduction of changes in production or production technology.

If an employee refuses to work under changed working conditions, he/she may be dismissed from work in accordance with the provisions of the Act on Labour Contracts, which is applied equally to both full-time and part-time employees. "If changes are introduced and, as a consequence, an employee's salary is reduced [i.e. in a transfer from full-time work to part-time work] for reasons beyond his/her control, the employee shall be compensated for the disparity in wages for at least three months after the introduction of the changes in working conditions."

From the above, it is clear that the terms applied to part-time and full-time workers are more or less the same. Part-time work does not lead to restricted social benefits, reduced job security and fewer career opportunities than full-time work. The hourly rate of pay is not lower for part-time employees than for full-time employees.

According to the Act on Holidays, the duration of the annual leave is not limited for part-time workers, and during annual leave the employees shall be paid an average pay regardless of whether they are employed full-time or part-time. The proportion of the pay to the time of work or result is further consolidated in Article 10 of the Act on Wages.

The comparatively less favourable treatment of part-time workers is deemed to be a violation, and an employee who feels wronged because of this has the right to complain in accordance with the general procedures set forth in the Act on Labour Contract and the Code of Civil Procedure. Career servants in the public sector have the right to complain about certain violations under the Act of Civil Service and the Code of Administrative Offences.

There is currently no provision in force that prohibits the persecution of an employee who lodged a complaint on grounds of discrimination (except for the Act on Equal Opportunities), although the new draft Labour Code provides for an obligation to define measures to be taken in order to avoid the persecution of an employee who lodged a complaint based on the failure to apply labour law regulations.

The Act on Labour Protection provides that only those fathers raising a child alone can demand that their employers provide them with an opportunity to work part-time. This provision was considered discriminatory by the Office of the Equal Opportunities Ombudsperson and upon the recommendations submitted to the Ministry of Labour and Social Security amendments to the draft Labour Code were made, providing both mothers and fathers with an equal opportunity to work part-time.

Legal provisions in Lithuania do not differentiate between the employment and treatment of full-time and part-time workers in public and private sectors.

If the working time is shortened or prolonged, the employee's salary will be proportional to the time of work or result. However, a change in working time or conditions does not limit or expand employees' rights when establishing the duration of annual leave, periods of work or implementing any other labour rights. No laws or administrative procedures stipulate concrete measures to be taken to facilitate access to part-time work. Accordingly, practice shows that part-time work in general is not popular at all levels of the enterprise. However, the statistics agencies do not provide statistical data on the division of part-time work regarding to the levels of enterprise or skilled and less skilled positions.

No concrete measures to facilitate part-time workers' access to vocational training to enhance career opportunities are stipulated by law or administrative procedures. Nevertheless, action has already been taken to include certain provisions in the new Labour Code on the prohibition of discrimination when promoting or improving qualifications.

Related research

In Lithuania, men are still considered to be the family's main breadwinner, while women's income is merely supplementary. Despite this stereotype and the fact that the level of unemployment is increasing, it is not yet popular for either women or men to work part-time in Lithuania: only 11.6 percent of employees held part-time positions in 1998 (and only 6.9 percent in 1999).[27] In 1998, more women (55.2 percent) than men had a shortened workday. In 1999, by contrast, men comprised 50.4 percent of part-time workers.[28] The fact that women with a shorter workday made up 12.3 percent of all working women and 10.3 percent of married women shows that a shortened workday correlates more to the lack of available work, rather than a devotion to the family or responsibilities at home.[29] According to data from the Labour Exchange, a total of 8.4 percent of persons were unemployed in 1999 (8.2 percent of women and 8.5 percent of men), with an ever-growing tendency towards unemployment.[30] The unemployment rate reached a total of 14.1 percent in 1999 according to the labour force survey; 12.6 percent among women and 15.6 percent among men.[31]

There is still a lack of information in this sphere in terms of available statistics and conducted research. For instance, it is difficult to evaluate the segregation of part-time workers at various levels of enterprises, and segregation in terms of age differences,

---

[27] Lithuanian Department of Statistics (2000: 95).
[28] Ibid, p. 95.
[29] Purvaneckienė (1999: 118).
[30] Lithuanian Department of Statistics (2000: 84).
[31] Lithuanian Department of Statistics (2000: 88).

which would actually be important when trying to assess whether the differences between men and women in terms of income and terms of employment constitute gender-based discrimination.

One of the major steps in the sphere of collecting data on part-time employment was made in 1995, when the Department of Statistics began converting the wages of part-time employees into full-time wages when counting the average salary received by employees. The situation in Lithuania appeared to be similar to that in other EU countries: the wages paid to full-time employees are higher than those paid to part-time employees converted to full-time equivalents, and this applies both to women and men. The statistical research conducted does not concentrate on part-time surveys, and part-time questions are only included briefly in the research. Still, through the accession process more attempts have already been made to develop research in this field.

6. THE PRINCIPLE OF EQUAL TREATMENT TO SELF-EMPLOYED WORKERS AND THEIR ASSISTING SPOUSES

Directive 86/613/EEC of 11 December 1986 *on the application of the principle of equal treatment between women and men engaged in an activity, including agriculture, in a self-employed capacity, and on the protection of self-employed women during pregnancy and motherhood*

6.1 National legal framework on self-employment: General provisions

Definition of self-employed workers

There is no direct definition of a self-employed person in Lithuania, although there are provisions concerning such persons' rights to develop a business, and their social insurance. The terms 'self-employed' and 'contributing spouse' are defined in the Act on Farmers.

Owners of private enterprises, individuals working under a licence issued in accordance with the procedures established by the Government of Lithuania, lawyers, assistant attorneys and notaries are all ascribed to the category of self-employed.

Laws and the regulations related to the directive

The legal acts regulating self-employed activities consolidate provisions on the equal opportunities for women and men, married and unmarried, to establish and develop a business, to register a farm, and to borrow and receive state aid for business development. For example, in order to register a farm the area of agricultural land must be at least one hectare, and this requirement applies to all individuals, irrespective of their sex or family status.

The social insurance for self-employed persons and contributing family workers are regulated in great detail by legal acts and in general comply with the provisions of the Directive. Lithuania has both compulsory and voluntary social insurance schemes. Four branches of the state social insurance are provided for by law and include pension insurance, sickness and maternity insurance, insurance against unemployment, and insurance against occupational accidents.

6.2 Social rights of spouses

Formation of companies by unmarried persons

Both married and unmarried persons have the right to establish a company or a farm. Spouses of self-employed workers often assist in the business, particularly in agriculture, where deep-rooted patriarchal traditions are especially prevalent. Women in rural areas have much fewer opportunities to choose another field of activity and find employment than women in urban areas, and therefore frequently help their husbands in farming activities or farm alone.

Stereotyped gender roles remain strong in Lithuania and prevent men from treating women as equal or even better business partners without any derogatory or ironic attitude. For their part, many women lack resolution and self-confidence, and consider men to be more successful in business.

Nevertheless, Lithuania has started to break with tradition and women are gradually coming to realise their potential and develop and manage businesses. In 1997, women made up 28.8 percent of all business managers, compared with 33.9 percent in 1999.[32]

6.3 Contributory social security schemes for self-employed workers and spouses

The Act on State Social Insurance stipulates obligatory basic pensions insurance for the following self-employed persons: owners of private companies, farmers and contributing family members, licensed individuals, lawyers, assistant attorneys and notaries. A parent raising a child under the age of three, irrespective of whether she/he is on child care leave or not, must be given compulsory state social insurance, which is paid from public funds.

Contributing family members of self-employed workers who are not protected under a compulsory pension social insurance scheme may join a voluntary state pension social insurance scheme and this provision fully complies with the requirements of the Directive under review. The Act on State Social Insurance allows individuals who are insured (self-employed persons and contributing spouses) to be eligible for a social insurance pension if they meet the statutory requirements and reach the statutory pension age, or are certified as disabled. Upon the death of such individuals, this eligibility is transferable to other family members.

---

[32] Lithuanian Department of Statistics (2001: 107).

National legislation provides that self-employed workers and contributing spouses may be insured under voluntary insurance schemes for sickness and maternity benefits, irrespective of their sex, but there is no obligatory insurance for such workers in this area. Voluntary social insurance for sickness and maternity benefits guarantees self-employed workers and their spouses benefits during a period of sickness, pregnancy and childbirth and thus fully complies with Articles 6 and 8 of the Directive. Individuals insured for sickness and maternity benefits on a voluntary basis are eligible for sickness benefits or benefits in case of occupational accidents. In the event of the death of the insured person, any unpaid benefit shall be paid to the individual who covered the insured person's funeral expenses.

In addition to social insurance benefits for sickness and maternity, families, including self-employed workers, raising children shall be paid benefits from public funds; for example, the childbirth benefit and state benefits for families raising three or more children.

6.4 Related research and statistics

Statistics show that in 1991, less than 30 percent of the working population was employed in the private sector. By 1999, this percentage had increased considerably, rising to 70 percent of the working population.

Social perceptions of self-employed women, including women in agriculture

Statistics show that in Lithuanian rural areas in 1998, the number of female self-employed workers was slightly higher than the number of male self-employed workers, and recent trends show the number of female self-employed workers to be declining compared with men. Women more often contribute as assisting spouses to the farming activities of their husbands. In general, small agricultural farms prevail among the self-employed in rural areas. The productivity of small agricultural workers is extremely low, although in most cases they manage to provide themselves and their families with basic food products from a plot of land no larger than three hectares.

Although women make up 53 percent of total population in rural areas, female employment in rural areas is only 45 percent.[33] "This is because […] many women raise small children at home, they are housewives, and they retire earlier […] Therefore, the number of inactive women is twice as high as the number of inactive men."[34] The author of the survey noted that the number of employed women in rural

---

[33] Motiekaitienė (1999: 12).
[34] Motiekaitienė (1999: 12–13).

areas was less than the number of men, except in the age group of 45–54. The higher employment among women of this age is due to the fact that they have already raised their children and are free to devote more time to work.

The majority of rural women (52 percent) are engaged in agriculture, hunting, forestry and fishery, while 12 percent of women are employed in the field of education, 11 percent in industry, eight percent in commerce, hotel and restaurant business, seven percent in the field of health and social services, four percent in transport, warehousing and communications, two percent in public and social services, and four percent in the field of public administration, compulsory social insurance, brokerage and in the real estate business. The data shows the rate of female employment in rural areas is currently stable.

Percentage of self-employed women and men

The table below reveals more specific statistics on the gender breakdown of self-employment in rural and urban areas, submitted by the Department of Statistics as of May 2001 (the figures are in thousands):[35]

Table 1. Self-Employment in 2001

	Total	*Men*	*Women*	*Urban*	*Rural*
Farmer	23.2	19.1	4.1	1.8	21.4
Agricultural worker	121.4	73.6	47.7	3.2	118.1
Individual working with a business licence	37.0	16.7	20.2	31.8	5.2
Other self-employed worker without employees	18.0	11.8	6.2	14.6	3.4
Self-employed worker with employees	35.7	25.0	10.7	30.1	5.6
Contributing family member (in an enterprise or farm)	49.7	23.0	26.6	6.9	42.7
Farmer with employees	1.1	0.8	0.3	0.8	0.3

The table shows that a major share of self-employed workers and contributing family members are engaged in farming.

---

[35] Lithuanian Department of Statistics (2001b).

Past and recent trends on self-employment

In Lithuania, the smallest share of the population is employed in small size businesses. Official figures from the Department of Statistics for 2001 show only 13.6 percent of the employed population in this category.[36] Farmers (contributing family members, employed workers and agricultural workers) made up 16.9 percent of the employed population.[37]

It must be noted that general statistics on the segregation of self-employed workers in rural and urban areas by sex, as well as statistics on business development trends, etc., are very scarce or unavailable. Upon the adoption of the Act on Equal Opportunities, the collection of gender desegregated data has been encouraged. However, such statistics fail to cover all economic activities.

Research on the status/rights of self-employed women

Private enterprises make up an increasingly large share of the companies under liquidation. According to the 1999 survey carried out by the Small and Medium Business Development Agency, private enterprises accounted for 82.6 percent of all small-size businesses and 67.3 percent of all registered companies under liquidation.[38] In 2000, this tendency became even stronger: private enterprises made up 90.6 percent of all liquidated small businesses and 58.3 percent of all registered companies facing liquidation. The large number of private enterprises under liquidation is the result of a complicated economic situation in Lithuania, the strong influence of local market demand and significantly reduced volume of exports, fierce competition, and the temporary enforcement (between 1 January 2000 and 3 July 2000) of the Act on Amending of the Social Insurance Act, which led to a considerable increase in social insurance contributions.[39]

It should be noted that both women and men are involved in traditional agricultural activity as self-employed workers and that this trend in agricultural business prevails.

According to the 2001 survey "The Situation and Needs of Business Women in Lithuania," commissioned by the Finish Ministry of Foreign Affairs, although theoretically women could develop businesses in the same fields as men, in reality women's business activities are concentrated in traditionally female-dominated sectors, such as dressmaking, grocery stores, souvenir shops, hairdressers, beauty salons, private dentists and doctors, bakeries, small restaurants and cafes and health clubs.

---

[36] Lithuanian Department of Statistics (2001c: 96).
[37] Lithuanian Department of Statistics (2001c: 96).
[38] <http://www.svv.lt>.
[39] Ibid.

In general, the survey results suggest that, in practice, businesswomen and businessmen both face the same obstacles hindering business development, and that national legislation does not restrict women or men or give any advantages to men in this field.

In 2001, the Social Innovations Fund, an NGO working in collaboration with the Coalition of Non-Governmental Organisations, carried out a survey entitled the "Factual Situation of Women's Rights and Opportunities in Lithuania." Representatives of 159 women's NGOs were asked questions concerning the awareness of national and international legislation (the Directive in question was not mentioned) governing equal rights for women and men. The survey results showed that 30–50 percent of the women questioned were aware of international legislation, but less than 10 percent could refer to the instruments in practice.[40] Only 15 percent of the respondents believed that the national legal framework for implementing equal rights for men and women was adequate.[41]

This survey and other research confirm that in general most Lithuanians know little about the *acquis*, although since job applicants for some public institutions are required to have a good knowledge of EU legislation, public employees are probably the best aware of the legislation in question.

6.5 Legal means of redress

Self-employed workers who consider themselves wronged by a violation of the principle of equal treatment have the right to appeal to court in accordance with the general procedures; however, not a single case has been recorded so far.

Section 72 of the Criminal Code provides for criminal liability for discrimination on grounds of sex in any economic activity. Accordingly, self-employed workers who are discriminated against in this way shall have the right to recourse to law enforcement agencies and be able to defend their rights under the procedure established by law.

---

[40] <http://www.moterukoalicija.webinfo.lt>.
[41] Ibid.

7. THE FRAMEWORK ON PARENTAL LEAVE

Council Directive 96/34/EC of 3 June 1996 *on the framework agreement on parental leave concluded by UNICE, CEEP, and ETUC*

7.1 National legal framework on parental leave: General provisions

Conditions of access and detailed rules for applying for parental leave

The term 'parental leave' does not exist as such in Lithuania, but the Act on Holidays includes references to 'childcare leave', which is defined as leave to care for a child below the age of three. Childcare leave can be granted to the mother, or, at her or the family's decision, to the father, grandparents or other relatives raising the child. Leave may be taken either in full or in part, and persons entitled to this leave may share the entitlement.

In the case of adoption, foster parents have the same rights as natural parents without any restrictions. Persons who adopt a newborn child or assume guardianship are to be granted a period of leave from the time of the adoption or guardianship until the child is 70 days old.

Parental leave is not subject to an employer's will, and although an employer may indicate specific dates (i.e. the beginning and end of the leave), the leave shall be granted at the family's decision and may be taken either in full or in part. The employment contracts for temporary workers must contain a provision stating that the newly-employed person shall work until the permanent employee returns from childcare leave, rather than indicating a specific end-date.

According the Act on Holidays, unpaid holidays due to domestic circumstances and other important reasons shall be granted according to the procedure established in collective agreements or by agreement of the parties, upon the written application of the employee.

At the request of mothers raising a child under the age of 14, annual unpaid leave of up to 14 calendar days shall be granted at a time coordinated by the parties. Mothers raising a disabled child under the age of 16 shall be granted annual unpaid leave for up to 30 calendar days at a time coordinated by the parties. It should be noted that, regrettably, such leave is not granted to fathers.

During maternity leave and leave to care for a child below the age of three, the father, at his request, shall be granted unpaid leave, the overall duration of which may not exceed three months.

7.2 Social security during parental leave

A parental benefit is payable during childcare leave to either parent (or foster parent or guardian), who shall then be insured by the sickness and maternity social insurance; be granted childcare leave until the child reaches the age of one, in accordance with legally established procedures; and have no less than a seven-month sickness and maternity social insurance qualification period in the 24 months immediately preceding the first day of the childcare leave.

If a woman is granted maternity leave and is eligible for a maternity benefit during this leave, she shall either receive the maternity or childcare/parental benefit, whichever is greater, or the one of her choice.

A payment period for maternity (or parental) benefits shall be calculated from the end of the maternity leave until the child reaches one year of age. A monthly maternity (parental) benefit to care for a child below the age of one shall be calculated on the basis of the average number of working days per month in the reference year (based on a five-day week). The rate of the maternity (parental) benefit is 60 percent of the recipient's compensated income. The rate of the benefit during a month shall be no less than one third of the average monthly insured income valid on the month the leave to care for a child under one year old has been granted.

Upon the birth of the child, the family, whether eligible for a maternity (parental) benefit under the Act on Sickness and Maternity Social Insurance or not, shall be paid a monthly benefit in the amount of 75 percent of the so-called Minimum Standard of Living (MSL) for each child from the ages of one to three.[42]

Legal protection against dismissal

The Act on Employment Contracts strictly regulates the basis for a person's dismissal from work and no interpretations or contradicting provisions are permitted in an employment contract or collective agreement. The conditions under which employment may be terminated are specified in great detail in the Act on Employment Contracts and include *inter alia* the liquidation of an enterprise, an employee's refusal to work following changes in the working conditions, upon the agreement of the

---

[42] Article 4 of the Act on State Benefits for Families Raising Children.

employee and employer, etc. If any of these conditions are violated, persons have the right to legal recourse.

Legal entitlement to return to the same, equivalent or similar job

Employees who are granted childcare leave have the right to return to the same position following the leave, except in the event of the liquidation of the enterprise.

7.3 Parental leave and equal opportunities policy

Men are not currently encouraged to take childcare leave in Lithuania, which is traditionally taken by women.

Initiatives to encourage the introduction of new flexible ways of organising work

The right to work part-time is guaranteed irrespective of the sex of a worker. Persons raising a child under 14 years of age or a disabled child under 16 can only be assigned to work overtime or sent on business trips with their consent. Persons raising children under 14 years of age shall, if possible, have priority in choosing shifts.

7.4 Research on the reconciliation of family and professional responsibilities and on sharing responsibilities between men and women

Since 1996, the Department of Statistics has been conducting a household budget survey in accordance with the new programme, abiding by the major requirements of EUROSTAT. The survey reveals the family income share earned by men and women, but fails to show the distribution of roles in family life and work. Employment trends between women and men are monitored, but the distribution of domestic duties between couples is not covered. Surveys of Domestic Living Standards were also conducted in 1998 and 1999, financed by the UNDP.

No statistics were available on the gender segregation of parental benefits prior to 2000. In 2000 though, parental benefits were received by 36,533 women (98.8 percent) and 420 men (1.2 percent).

8. THE PRINCIPLE OF EQUAL TREATMENT OF MEN AND WOMEN IN OCCUPATIONAL SOCIAL SECURITY SCHEMES

Council Directive 96/97/EC of 20 December 1996 *amending Directive 86/378/EEC on the implementation of the principle of equal treatment for men and women in occupational social security schemes*

8.1 National legal framework on social security schemes: General provisions

Social security after regaining independence

Social security reforms in Lithuania began after the restoration of independence, and the legal and institutional reform of the social security system was introduced in 1990-1991. In 1990, the Supreme Council of Lithuania passed a decision "On the reformation of the social insurance system of Lithuania," transferring social security matters from trade unions to the State.

At that time the main goals for social security policy and action guidelines were laid down in legal acts foreseeing social security to include both mandatory social insurance and social assistance, which did not operate prior to independence. A component of special social benefits was also foreseen, and this led to the establishment and operation of the most important elements of this system: (1) the state social insurance fund (SODRA); (2) the labour exchange; and (3) local government assistance institutions.

Between 1991 and 1995 specific action programmes were elaborated on certain social security and labour issues, such as *inter alia* the Employment Programme and the Programme on the Integration of the Disabled.

Pension reform in 1994–1995

The Act on State Social Insurance Pensions came into force in 1995, replacing the Soviet Law on Pensions, which had been in force since 1956.

After the introduction of the laws establishing pension reform in 1995 (the Act on State Social Security, the Act on State Social Security Pensions, the Government's Decision on the Establishment of Regulations on the Appointment and Payment of State Social Insurance Pensions, etc.), three pension systems were created:

1. the state social insurance pensions, based on insurance and dependent on the number of years served and income of the insured person;

2. the system of state pensions, paid to persons with awards from the Republic of Lithuania, victims of the previous regime, officials and military personnel, as well as scientists; and

3. the system of social support pensions, paid to persons with certain disabilities.

The pensions foreseen in the first category are provided for from the state budget for social insurance pensions, others are funded from the state budget.

From 1995 onwards, the retirement age in Lithuania has been raised, and will continue to be raised, annually by two months for men and four months for women, until it reaches 60 years for women and 62.5 years for men.

Act on Pension Funds passed in 1999

The Act on Pension Funds passed in mid-1999 established the possibility for the operation of pension funds providing both state and private sectors with the preconditions to take on responsibility for pension insurance. There are still no pension funds in Lithuania providing the possibility for supplementary old-age income. The reasons for this include a fairly difficult economic situation and low trust in private financial institutions.

Other legal changes included an increase in the social insurance contribution rate from 31 percent to 34 percent of wages at the end of 1999, which had a direct influence on the financial capacity of the State Social Security Fund. This change was accompanied by a change in the redistribution of rates among the various types of social security: 25 percent went to insurance pensions, 3.5 percent to sickness and maternity benefits, 3 percent to health insurance, 1.5 percent to unemployment insurance, and one percent to occupational accidents and loss of health.[43]

In October 2000, the Ministry of Labour and Social Affairs prepared and presented a White Paper on Pension Reforms following the approval of a concept on pension reform passed by the Government in April 2000. The concept for pension reforms foresees the introduction of a three-pillar system:

1. pay-as-you-go (social) pensions based on current contributions;

2. mandatory funded social insurance pensions;

3. voluntary funded pensions.

The system of protecting women in maternity has been revised, laying down more modest provisions in the field than had been in operation in the Soviet times, but the system has retained its general features.

---

[43] Poškutė (2000: 60).

A new type of social insurance was established in 2000 relating to insurance for occupational accidents and professional diseases.

Compliance of the legislation with the directives

Everyone has the right to social security in Lithuania, irrespective of sex and social security provisions generally implement the principle of equal treatment of women and men in social security schemes set forth in the Directives.

Social support to families as well as diverse benefits to mothers are outlined in Article 39 of the Constitution, which also provides that the law shall provide for paid maternity leave before and after childbirth, as well as for favourable working conditions and other privileges.

State social insurance constitutes the largest and the most important part of the social security system in Lithuania; and it does not anticipate to grant any special privileges or rights to certain social groups or professions.[44]

Article 5 of the Act on the Principles of the Social Security System provides that all persons in Lithuania are to be granted social security benefits in case of complete or partial loss of their work-related income if they are working or have employment insurance for the service years or in other cases outlined by law. This basic rule is applied to both women and men without distinction.

In particular, the law provides for social security benefits in the following situations:

- for persons of or below retirement age if they cannot continue to work in accordance with their vocation due to their age;
- for disabled persons with a temporary incapacity to work;
- for families upon the death of their breadwinner;
- for persons in need of medical treatment, preventive treatment and rehabilitation;
- for families raising children;
- for persons suffering a temporary loss of work;
- for persons in need of state support.

Retired and disabled persons

In the system of state social insurance, old-age, disability, and survivor's pensions are provided for under Article 4 of the Act on State Social Insurance Pensions. The right to

---

[44] Ministry of Social Protection and Labour (2000: 67).

receive the old-age pension is guaranteed to all persons of retirement age, and the amount of social insurance paid is dependent on the amount of years served and certain other requirements. The disability pension is calculated and paid in the same way as the old-age pension.

Persons who are not entitled to these benefits may voluntarily choose this kind of insurance in accordance with the Government's Decision on the Establishment of Rules for the Voluntary Insurance of State Social Pensions.

Maternity

The right to sickness and maternity social insurance benefits, conditions of access and their calculation are set forth in the Act on Sickness and Maternity Social Insurance, which was passed in December 2000. The procedure for granting sickness and maternity social insurance benefits is foreseen in the Government's Decision on Regulations of Sickness and Maternity Social Insurance Benefits.

Sickness and maternity insurance is compulsory for permanent residents in Lithuania who work and receive remuneration for their work. Self-employed and other persons may voluntarily choose this kind of insurance if they are not entitled to it in accordance with the Government's Decision on Establishment of the Rules for State Voluntary Social Sickness and Maternity Benefits Insurance.

The maternity benefits are granted to eligible women during pregnancy and childbirth leave. Either parent (or step-parent or foster parents) caring for the child has the right to receive the maternity benefit if he/she is insured by the sickness and maternity social insurance.

Accidents and involuntary unemployment

According to the Act on Social Insurance of Occupational Accidents and Diseases, this sort of insurance is granted to employer persons and others stipulated by law if they receive wages for their work.

The rules for the payment of benefits in case of occupational accidents or diseases are set forth in the Regulations on Occupational Accidents and Diseases Social Insurance Benefits.

Seeking employment

According to Article 15 of the Act on Support for Unemployed Persons, unemployed individuals with at least a 24-month state social insurance record within the three years immediately preceding their registration with the labour exchange, and other persons who do not have the full required state social insurance record for valid reasons set forth in the Article 16, shall be entitled to an unemployment benefit – provided that the labour exchange did not offer them employment that would suit their particular skills and state of health, or any opportunity for vocational training.

The amount of unemployment benefit shall depend on the unemployed individual's state social insurance record and reasons for loss of work.

Self-employed persons

Social insurance for self-employed persons does differ from that of other employees. The rules for the payment of state social insurance contributions by self-employed persons are established in Article 34 of the Act on State Social Security and the Rules on the Formation and Execution of the State Social Insurance Budget.

According to Article 34 of the Act on State Social Insurance, self-employed persons are obliged to contribute to the social insurance fund in order to receive the basic pension benefit in accordance with the established provisions.

The employer's contributions are calculated as a percentage of the wages paid to the employee. The contribution rate paid to the fund was set forth by the Government in 1991 and constituted 31 percent of the employee's wages until 1999. As of the beginning of 2000 the contribution rate is established by the *Seimas* and constitutes 34 percent of the wage paid to the employee.[45]

Provisions contrary to the principle of equal treatment with regard to social security schemes

During a review of social security legislation in 1999 carried out by the Ministry of Social Security and Labour, some provisions in the Act on State Social Security Pensions, the Act on Employment of the Population and the Act on State Social Benefits to Families were regarded as potentially provoking indirect gender discrimination. Those provisions regulated benefits relating to illness; caring for a family member; the pension age; and self-employed workers. However, since that time the provisions have either been amended or are now considered permissible exceptions according to the Directives.

Discriminatory provisions can no longer be found in the Act on Support to Unemployed Persons, although additional guarantees were previously granted to women with a child under the age of 14 and fathers raising a child under the age of 14 alone. In addition, Article 16(1) had previously foreseen the granting of unemployment benefits to persons dismissed from work or persons without the full required state social insurance record for valid reasons, including women raising a child

---

[45] The Act on the Establishment of Rates of the Budget of the State Social Security Fund for the Year 2000.

up to the age of eight, and men if raising such a child alone. Those provisions have been replaced in the law currently in force,[46] which now foresees the same guarantees and conditions for both mothers and fathers.

No violations of the principle of equal treatment for women and men were found in Lithuanian legislation in terms of (a) determining the persons who may participate in an occupational scheme; (b) fixing the compulsory or optional nature of participation in an occupational scheme; (c) laying down different rules for the reimbursement of contributions where a worker leaves a scheme without having fulfilled the conditions guaranteeing him a deferred right to long-term benefits; (d) setting different conditions for the granting of benefits or restricting such benefits to workers of either sex; (e) suspending the retention or acquisition of rights during the period of maternity leave or leave for family reasons which are guaranteed by law or agreement and are paid by the employer; or (f) setting different levels of benefit or worker contributions as laid down in the Directive on occupational social security schemes.

The Act on Collective Agreements and Contracts does not allow the provisions of collective agreements to violate the principle of gender equality.

Discriminatory provisions with regard to different rules of entry into the scheme, minimum period of employment and memberships have been removed, and as of 1 January 1995 the obligatory insurance period is to be increased annually by one year until the periods are equalised for women and men at 30 years.[47]

Different retirement ages (60 years for women and 62.5 for men) are set forth in Article 18 of the Act on State Social Insurance Pensions, but there is no legal provision obliging either women or men to retire from work after reaching the retirement age.

As regards occupational social security schemes, there are no known cases where the employer granted a pension supplement to persons who did not reach the statutory pension age but are already in a position to receive a pension by virtue of an occupational scheme in order to equalise their situation with persons of the opposite sex who have already reached the statutory retirement age.

Occupational social security schemes are established by collective agreement or contract.

Article 3 of the Act on Collective Agreements and Contracts provides that the following issues are to be addressed in collective agreements:

1. the terms of payment for work and its regulation;

---

[46] Entered into force on 21 December 2001.
[47] Article 55 of the Act on State Social Security Pensions.

2. admissibility to work and working conditions;

3. health and safety at work;

4. the terms of work organisation, as well as the terms of work and rest regimes;

5. the training and re-qualification of employees;

6. social guarantees for employees and their family members;

the terms for terminating work contracts and the size of redundancy benefits and compensation;

1. other work, social and economic questions.

Consideration of the principle of equal treatment

The policy of equal opportunities in Lithuania includes the implementation of the principle of equal treatment in matters of social security. As established by the Constitution and social security legislation, all persons in Lithuania, irrespective of their gender, have a right to social security.

Article 3(1) of the Act on Equal Opportunities provides that "within the limits of their competence, state government and administration institutions must ensure that equal rights for women and men be guaranteed in all the legal acts drafted and enacted by them." This accordingly obliges all institutions to take into account the principle of equal treatment when dealing with social security schemes. The Equal Opportunities Ombudsman and the Department of Labour and Equal Opportunities at the Ministry of Social Affairs and Labour monitor the social security laws in order to prevent gender discriminatory provisions.

The Equal Opportunities Programme, which is now under preparation, aims to include a chapter on social security, setting forth the obligation and means to implement the principle of equal treatment in social security matters.

There is a possibility that maternity benefits provided only to women could worsen their situation in the labour market in terms of admissibility to work. For example, employers could avoid employing women in order to avoid the provisions on maternity benefits. Unfortunately, there is no statistical or other reliable data in this field, and it is therefore difficult to prove that this occurs in practice. Some provisions of the Act on Equal Opportunities aim to overcome this potential obstacle: In particular, Article 8 prohibits employers from requesting information from job seekers about their civil status, private life or family plans.

Working mothers are also protected under the Act on Employment Contracts, according to which the employer cannot terminate a contract at his/her own initiative with pregnant women or mothers raising a child under the age of three.

Legal mechanisms to declare null and void any discriminatory provisions

Collective agreements cannot alter provisions of a mandatory nature established by law, and the Act on Collective Agreements and Contracts provides that those "terms, regulations, and obligations of a collective agreement [contract] that provide employees with conditions that are less favourable than those established by the laws of the Republic of Lithuania shall be invalid."[48] This also applies to the principle of equal treatment in social security legislation.

Disagreements between employees and employers on the non-compliance with the collective contract or its improper implementation are to be resolved in court.[49]

Article 18 of the Act on Equal Opportunities grants everyone the right to file a complaint with the Equal Opportunities Ombudsperson in case of the violation of his/her right to equal treatment. This includes the obligation to implement the principle of equal opportunities for women and men in the field of social security. According to Article 24, upon the completion of the investigation, the Ombudsperson may decide to address an appropriate person or institution with a recommendation to discontinue the actions violating equal opportunities or to repeal a legal act relating thereto.

8.2 Legal means of redress

Protection against dismissal

Employees can only be dismissed at the employer's initiative on the grounds foreseen in Article 29 of the Act on Employment Contracts. Employers may not dismiss an employee in response to a complaint aimed at enforcing compliance with the principle of equal treatment.[50]

---

[48] Articles 3 and 12.

[49] Articles 3 and 12.

[50] According to Article 6 of the Act on Equal Opportunities, the acts of an employer shall be deemed discriminatory if, because of the person's sex, he/she applies less (or more) favourable terms of employment or payment for work; in organising work, creates worse (or better) working conditions for an employee; imposes a disciplinary penalty on an employee, changes working conditions, transfers him/her to another work or terminates the employment contract; or persecutes an employee who filed a complaint of discrimination.

According to Article 42 of the Act on Employment Contracts "if the employee disagrees with his or her discharge, removal from work, or transfer to another job, he or she shall have the right to appeal to court […]. If the employee is discharged, removed from work, or transferred to another job without legal grounds, or in violation of the procedures established by law, he or she shall be reinstated in his last employment by the court. […] When an unlawfully discharged employee declares that unfavourable conditions would be created for him if he were to be reinstated, the court […] may, at the employee's request, award him compensation."

8.3 Research on the impact of social security systems on women

Historical developments in the field of social security are best depicted in the Human Development Reports issued each year by the UNDP in Lithuania, which not only describe the trends, but also foresee the future challenges as well as problematic areas. The Social Reports issued by the Ministry of Social Affairs and Labour also provide information in this area.

Nevertheless, there is a substantial lack of research evaluating the impact of social developments and trends on women, and the reports referred to above in general fail to provide gender-segregated data, making it difficult to assess the impact of the social security system on women.

In fact, the economic recession and resulting difficult financial situation of the last years suggest the low level of social security in general. Districts in which economic reforms have been more successful have a higher standard of living and therefore more sufficient level of social security. Other districts, however, particularly many small towns, continue to suffer a deep recession. As a result of the failure to restructure and renovate their manufacturing base, the unemployment rate is higher there with fewer opportunities for social protection. Many persons of working age do not contribute to social security for a variety of reasons (low income, etc.), thus making it difficult for the social security schemes to be applied to them. Persons with no insurance record are not able to benefit from the basic old-age, disability and other benefits, except for six-month social assistance payments. There is little doubt that women comprise a large part of persons not eligible for pensions; but unfortunately there is no precise data on this issue.

REFERENCES

Bibliography

Anciuvienė, Marija (1999) "The Harmonisation of the Lithuanian Legal System with that of the European Union: Gains and Challenges." *Lithuanian Human Development Report 1999.* Vilnius: United Nations Development Programme, pp.129–141.

Lithuanian Labour Exchange (2001) *Annual Report of Lithuanian Labour Exchange, 2000.* Vilnius.

Burows, Noreen and Jane Mair (1996) *European Social Law.* Chichester: John Wiley and Sons, pp.151–175.

Dilba, Rimvydas (2000) "Employment." *Lithuanian Human Development Report 2000.* Vilnius: United Nations Development Programme, pp.37-47.

Kanopienė, Vida (2001) "Women and the Labour Market in Lithuania." In *Women in Lithuania.* Women's Issues Information Centre. Vilnius: Via Recta.

Lithuanian Department of Statistics (2001) *Labour force, employment and unemployment*, May 2000, No. C321.

Motiekaitienė, Vitalija (1999) *Women employment in rural areas in 1998.* Vilnius.

Nielsen, Ruth and Erika Szyszczak (1997) *The Social Dimension of the European Union.* Third edition. Copenhagen: Handelshojskolens Forlag, pp.363–366.

Poškutė, Virginija (2000) "Social Security." *Lithuanian Human Development Report 2000.* Vilnius: United Nations Development Programme, pp.59–69.

Purvaneckienė, Giedrė (1999) "Women in Lithuanian Society." *Lithuanian Human Development Report 1999.* Vilnius: United Nations Development Programme, pp.115–129.

European Commission (2000) *Regular Report from the Commission on Lithuania's Progress Towards Accession*, 8 November 2000, pp.60–62.

European Commission (2001) *Regular Report. Lithuania's Progress Towards Accession.* <http://europa.eu.int/comm/enlargement/report2001/lt_en.pdf>, accessed on October 12, 2002.

Ministry of Social Protection and Labour (2000) *Social Report.* Vilnius: Ministry of Social Protection and Labour.

Lithuanian Department of Statistics (2001b) Labour force, employment and unemployment, No.C321, May 2000.

Lithuanian Department of Statistics (2001c) *Statistical Yearbook of Lithuania, 2001.* Vilnius: Lithuanian Department of Statistics.

Lithuanian Department of Statistics (2000) *Women and Men in Lithuania, 1999.* Vilnius: Lithuanian Department of Statistics.

Lithuanian Department of Statistics (2001) *Women and Men in Lithuania, 2000.* Vilnius: Lithuanian Department of Statistics.

Women's Issues Information Centre (1999) Women in Lithuania. Vilnius.

List of Legislation Screened

Acts

Criminal Code of the Republic of Lithuania of 26 July 1961, entered into force on 1 September 1961.

Civil Code of the Republic of the Republic of Lithuania of 7 July 1964, entered into force on 1 January 1965.

Code of Administrative Offences of the Republic of Lithuania of 13 December 1984, entered into force on 1 April 1985.

Constitution of the Republic of Lithuania, entered into force on 25 October 1992.

Civil Code of 18 July 2000, entered into force on 1 July 2001.

Act of 27 September 1990 on Individual Income Security, entered into force on 27 September 1990.

Act of 23 October 1990 on the Principles of the Social Security System, entered into force on 23 October 1990.

Act of 13 December 1990 on the Employment of the Population, entered into force on 13 December 1990.

Act of 9 January 1991 on Wages, entered into force on 9 January 1991.

Act of 4 April 1991 on Collective Agreements, entered into force on 30 April 1991.

Act of 21 May 1991 on State Social Security, entered into force on 20 June 1991.

Act of 21 November 1991 on Trade Unions, entered into force on 10 December 1991.

Act of 28 November 1991 on Employment Contracts, entered into force on 31 December 1991.

Act of 13 December 1991 on Support the Unemployed, entered into force on 13 December 1991.

Act of 17 December 1991 on Holidays, entered into force on 17 December 1991.

Act of 7 October 1993 on Labour Protection, entered into force on 22 October 1993 (New version: the Act on Safety and Health at Work of 17 October 2000).

Act of 18 July 1994 on State Social Security Pensions, entered into force on 3 August 1994.

Act of 25 October 1994 on the State Labour Inspectorate, entered into force on 31 December 1994.

Act of 3 November 1994 on State Benefits for Families Raising Children, enforced on 1 January 1995.

Act of 15 January 1998 on Support for the Unemployed, entered into force on 15 January 1998.

Act of 1 December 1998 on Equal Opportunities, VIII-947, entered into force on 1 March 1999.

Act of 14 January 1999 on Administrative Proceedings, entered into force on 1 May 1999.

Act of 4 May 1999 on Farmers, entered into force on 19 May 1999.

Act of 3 June 1999 on Pension Funds, entered into force on 1 January 2000.

Act of 8 July 1999 on Civil Service, entered into force on 30 July 1999.

Act of 23 December 1999 on the Establishment of Rates of the Budget of the State Social Security Fund for the Year 2000, entered into force on 29 December 1999.

Act of 23 December 1999 on Social Insurance of Occupational Accidents and Occupational Diseases, entered into force on 1 January 2000.

Act of 20 June 2000 on Labour Disputes, entered into force on 12 July 2000.

Act of 31 August 2000 on Amendments of Article 72 of Criminal Code and the supplement of Article 72.

Act of 21 December 2000 on Sickness and Maternity Social Insurance, entered into force on 1 January 2001.

Government Decisions

Government's Decision of 18 November 1994 on the Establishment of Regulations on the Appointment and Payment of State Social Insurance Pensions, entered into force on 1 January 1995.

Government's Decision of 9 January 1995 on Approval Procedure of the Establishing of Part-time Working Day or Part-time Working Week, entered into force on 14 January 1995.

Government's Decision of 11 May 1998 on Increasing the Minimum Wage, entered into force on 16 May 1998.

Government's Decision No. 1191 of 19 November 1999 on Approval of the Rules of Voluntary Social Insurance for Sickness and Maternity Benefits, entered into force on 19 November 1999.

Government's Decision of 8 May 2000 on the Regulations of Occupational Accidents and Occupational Diseases Social Insurance Benefits, entered into force on 11 May 2000.

Government's Decision of 19 July 2000 on the Description and Evaluation of the Positions of Civil Servants, entered into force on 24 July 2000.

Government's Decision No. 1094 of 13 September 2000 on Issuance Procedure of Mandatory Licences to Natural Persons, entered into force on 1 January 2000.

Other legal sources

Opinion of Constitutional Court of the Republic of Lithuania of 24 January 1995 on Compliance of Articles 4,5,9,14 and Article 2 of the Fourth Protocol of The European Convention on Protection of Human Rights and Fundamental Freedoms with the Constitution of the Republic of Lithuania, entered into force on 27 January 1995.

Order No. 18/12 of 13 January 1998 of the Ministry of Health and Ministry of Social Security and Labour of the Republic of Lithuania on Processes Prohibited for Pregnant, after Childbirth and Breastfeeding Women, also on Processes Not Recommended for Women Willing to Retain the Function of Maternity, and List of Harmful and Hazardous Agents for Women in the Working Environment and the Order of Application, entered into force on 14 February 1998.

Equal Opportunities for Women and Men in Poland

Table of contents

Executive summary 359

Country report: Introduction 367

1. The Principle of equal pay for work of equal value 370
   1.1 National legal framework: General provisions 370
   1.2 Legal foundations and institutional structures 371
   1.3 Job classification 372
   1.4 Available legal procedures 372
   1.5 Means of informing employees of their rights 373
   1.6 Out of court alternatives 373
   1.7 Role of trade unions 374
   1.8 Women's factual situation 374

2. Equal treatment for women and men as regards access to employment, vocational training and promotion, and working conditions 376
   2.1 National legal framework: General provisions 376
   2.2 The concept of discrimination on grounds of sex: Definition and legal sanctions 376
   2.3 Access to employment, vocational training and promotion 377
   2.4 Protective measures for women in the labour market 378
   2.5 Prohibition of dismissal 379
   2.6 Women's and men's jobs 380
   2.7 Legal status of sexual harassment 380

3. Protection of pregnant women from the inherent risk of certain activities and related employment rights 381
   3.1 Legal and conceptual framework 381
   3.2 Risk assessment and employers' obligations 381
   3.3 Case law 382

3.4	Night work		382
3.5	Maternity leave		383
3.6	Prohibition of dismissal and employment rights		384

4. The burden of proof in cases of discrimination based on sex 385

4.1	Legal and conceptual framework concerning indirect discrimination	385
4.2	The burden of proof and rules of evidence	385
4.3	Case law	386

5. Non-discrimination against part-time workers 387

5.1	National legal framework and employment conditions concerning part-time workers	387

6. The principle of equal treatment for self-employed workers and their assisting spouses 389

6.1	National legal framework: General provisions	389
6.2	Social rights of spouses	390
6.3	Contributory social security system for self employed workers	393
6.4	Related research and statistics	393
6.5	Legal means of redress	396

7. The framework on parental leave 397

7.1	National legal framework: General provisions	397
7.2	Social security during parental leave	400
7.3	Parental leave and equal opportunities policy	401
7.4	Research on sharing family and professional responsibilities	402

8. The principle of equal treatment in occupational social security schemes 404

8.1	National legal framework: General provisions	404
8.2	Legal means of redress	409
8.3	Implementation of the principle of equal treatment	410

Executive summary for Poland

INTRODUCTION

In its 2000 Regular Report, the Commission noted that, with regard to equal opportunities, "against the objective criterion of adoption of the *acquis,* Poland has made no progress in this area over the reporting period," and, furthermore, that "the issue of equal treatment of women and men still requires urgent attention."[1] In 2001, however, the European Commission[2] recognised that "Considerable efforts to align with the EC *acquis* have been undertaken and should continue to receive high priority [...]. While the amendments to the Labour Code constitute good progress, the necessary institutional framework for implementing and enforcing the *acquis* in this area should still be established. Furthermore, actions should be undertaken to raise awareness of equal treatment for women and men, to improve the position of women in the labour market and to increase their representation in decision making."

Regrettably, gender equality has not featured high in hierarchy of issues in the policy implemented by the Ministry of Labour and Social Affairs, and, therefore, in the policy of the Government of the Republic of Poland as a whole. In 1999, the Parliament rejected the draft Act on Equal Status, which provided, *inter alia,* for special means of protection against discrimination in employment and easily accessible means to pursue claims in case of a violation of the principle of equality of women and men.

It is clear that major efforts are still needed to bring national legislation wholly into line with the *acquis communautaire,* and to ensure the provisions of effective monitoring and implementation mechanisms. At the same time, since existing stereotypes and prejudices, such as those related to women being the primary caretakers, continue to run deep, there must be an unequivocal government commitment to educating society as a whole on the value of gender equality, together with viable opportunities for it to be achieved.

---

[1] European Commission (2000).

[2] European Commission (2001).

Summary of key points

Defining principles

The principle of equal pay for women and men is contained in the Polish legal system, both directly and indirectly in the Constitution, as well as in the Labour Code. However, Polish law does not provide a definition of the term 'work of equal value'. Polish law does not define discrimination on grounds of sex or indirect discrimination, although the latter term is not unknown within the Polish legal system and it has featured in particular in the interventions undertaken by the Ombudsperson. The Labour Code does not provide for any discriminatory legal provisions for women and men that are contrary to the principle of equal pay, although such provisions appear in other domains of the law; for example, social security, the law on employment and unemployment. There is no legal definition of sexual harassment.

Protective measures

Polish law provides for wider protection of pregnant and breastfeeding women than is set forth in the European Union. The Labour Code stipulates that pregnant woman may not be employed at night or in overtime work, and pregnant women may not be delegated to work outside their usual work place without their consent. The right to maternity leave is the personal right of an employee, and employers are legally obliged to grant pregnant women free time to undergo antenatal examinations and medical tests ordered by a physician if those tests cannot be performed outside working hours. The Labour Code stipulates that the employer may not give notice of termination or terminate the contract of employment (when notice has been previously given) during the pregnancy or maternity leave of an employee. There are, however, legally prescribed exceptions to this rule.

Burden of proof

Until the 2001 Amending Act entered into force, the principle set forth in the Polish Civil Code applied, whereby the burden fell on the person making the legal claim. The Amending Act introduced a legal shift in the burden of proof to the Labour Code, but the formulation and scope of application are limited and do not cover situations provided for in the relevant Directives. Pursuant to a newly introduced article to the Labour Code, it shall be a violation of the principle of equal treatment of men and women for an employer to differentiate between workers on grounds of sex with regard *inter alia* to a refusal to conclude or continue an employment relationship, or provide less favourable remuneration "unless the employer proves that he/she was guided by other reasons."

Part-time workers

Until the amendments to the Labour Code were prepared in 2000, there were no particular provisions that referred to the employment conditions of part-time workers, which are established exclusively by contract. It should also be noted that, so far, part-time employees have not constituted a major subject of interest for the legislator, the courts or for academics, nor has Polish labour law contained any anti-discriminatory clause that refers *expressis verbis* to part-time workers. The amendment of the Labour Code, adopted by the *Sejm* in February 2001, however, harmonises Polish law with the relevant Directive.

According to the data of the Main Statistical Office of 1999, the percentage of women working part-time in the main workplaces (employing more than nine persons) amounted to 66 percent of part-time employees (and has slightly diminished in comparison to 1995).

Self-employed workers

In the second half of 2000, the number of self-employed women amounted to 1.2 million, which was equal to 18 percent of all women employed and to 37 percent of all self-employed persons in Poland.[3] The principles of equal treatment enshrined in the Constitution have a general character and therefore apply also to self-employed men and women, although there is no specific reference to them. In the new system of social security in force since 1 January 1999, all insured persons are treated equally. This is a common system, providing for the same mechanisms for all social and professional groups, including self-employed workers, except for individual farmers.

Parental leave

Despite clear social expectations that both parents should be equally responsible for a child's education, the main burden of childcare and education is borne by women. Although men were granted access to maternity and childcare leave in the late 1970s (and on an equal basis with women, in the 1990s), men rarely exercise these rights. The lack of precise statistical data makes it impossible to present this phenomenon in

---

[3] Compare GUS (2000: 13).

figures. In 2001, as the result of amendments to the Labour Code, women and men were given the right to take a part of the childcare leave simultaneously, for a minimum period determined in the Directive.

Social security schemes

The system of social security in Poland has undergone many significant changes in the last 20 years. An example of a violation of the principle of equal opportunities for women and men is the provision limiting early retirement (after 20 years of work) options for the father of a child requiring constant care if the mother is unable to provide the care. In 1999, the Constitutional Tribunal held this provision unconstitutional given the differentiation of rights of women and men and the limitation of their discretion in deciding which parent may retire earlier in such cases. Subsequent changes to the system of social security were not inspired by the principle of equal treatment in matters of social security, but were rather a result of the inefficiency of the previous system.

RECOMMENDATIONS RELATED TO EACH SPECIFIC DIRECTIVE

Council Directive 75/117/EEC of 10 February 1975 *on the approximation of laws of the Member States relating to the implementation of the principle of equal pay for women and men*

- The term 'equal pay for equal work' should be introduced into Article 33 of the Constitution,[4] and the principle of 'equal pay for work of equal value' and its definition should be introduced into the Labour Code.

- There should be a system of work evaluation that allows for the comparison of different types of work.

Council Directive 76/207/EEC of 9 February 1976 *on the implementation of the principle of equal treatment for men and women as regards access to employment, vocational training and promotion, and working conditions*

- The term 'indirect discrimination' should be compatible with Article 2 of Directive 97/80/EC.

---

[4] Matey-Tyrowicz (2000: 93).

- A provision should be adopted to set forth the conditions in which preferential treatment in employing a person belonging to an underrepresented sex[5] is admissible in order to achieve real equality.

- References to the sex and age of potential employees in job announcements should be prohibited, as should questions regarding family or marital status, plans for children and the establishment of pregnancy.

- Provisions should be adopted to guarantee equal treatment with regard to professional training.

- There should be an explicit legal provision defining and prohibiting sexual harassment.

- The law should stipulate *expressis verbis* that disputes relating to discrimination constitute cases involving the employment relationship, and effective judicial remedies for discriminatory practice should be made available to victims.

- Protection against the termination of the employment relationship in reaction to a complaint of discrimination should be legally guaranteed.

- The existence of independent authorities should be encouraged, and NGOs should be encouraged to provide expertise on cases of discrimination cases, including through legal aid and representation.

- Specialised training should be provided for judges and lawyers on how to identify and handle cases of discrimination.

- A broad public information campaign should be carried out to educate society in general on these issues.

Council Directive 92/85/EEC of 19 October 1992 *on the introduction of measures to encourage improvements in the safety and health at work of pregnant workers and workers who have recently given birth or are breastfeeding*

- The obligation to transfer pregnant women to other work and the related guarantees outlined in the report should be extended to breastfeeding women.

- There should be a clear obligation to notify a pregnant woman employee of the hazards to her health and security due to working conditions.

- It should be made possible for the father to benefit from part of the maternity leave (after the time necessary for the woman to fully recover from the birth). In

---

[5] Kaczyński (1997: 8).

the case of adoption or for raising a child, the father should be allowed to totally or partially use the leave 'treated as maternity leave', which has so far been granted exclusively to women.

Council Directive 97/80/EC of 15 December 1997 *on the burden of proof in cases of discrimination based on sex*

- There should be a presumption of indirect discrimination where non-favourable action is directed towards a high number of representatives of one sex.

- Employees should be made aware of the reversal of the burden of proof and offered the necessary support mechanisms to bring legal action in cases of discrimination.

Council Directive 97/81/EC of 15 December 1997 *concerning the framework agreement on part-time work concluded by UNICE, CEEP and the ETUC*

- Continuous research should be carried out to determine how many women engage in part-time work, and the reasons for doing so.

- Part-time work and the flexible organisation of working hours should be encouraged not only for women, but also for men, in order to ensure a more just distribution of responsibilities in the home.

Council Directive 86/613/EEC of 11 December 1986 *on the application of the principle of equal treatment between men and women engaged in an activity, including agriculture, in a self-employed capacity, and on the protection of self-employed women during pregnancy and motherhood*

- The Act on the System of Social Security should be amended to include a provision regulating the compensation available to a worker who suffered detriment as a result of the violation of the principle of equal treatment.

- The principle of equal treatment should be included in the Act on the Social Security of Farmers.

- Self-employed workers engaged in agricultural and non-agricultural work should have the same rights and benefits.

- The provision according to which a spouse who participates in running the business is only entitled to insurance if both persons share the same household should be reconsidered.

Council Directive 96/34/EC of 3 June 1996 *on the framework agreement on parental leave concluded by UNICE, CEEP, and the ETUC*

- Provisions should be adopted to provide for childcare/parental leave to be taken until the child reaches the age of eight.

- Workers should be granted the right to return to the same job or, if this is not possible, to an equivalent or similar job with the same salary.

- Exceptions to the ban on employers terminating an employment contract should be limited (at least during the minimum period of time set forth in the framework agreement).

- More flexible working arrangements should be supported, together with the possibility for each spouse to take childcare leave, so that both partners may reconcile their professional and family responsibilities on equal terms.

Council Directive 96/97/EC of 20 December 1996 *amending Directive 86/378/EEC on the implementation of the principle of equal treatment for men and women in occupational social security schemes*

- Polish law related to the third pillar (old-age insurance schemes) should be harmonised with the provisions of the Directive.

- Equal ages of retirement for women and men should be adopted.

- All risk(s) associated with an employee's inability to work should be transferred to the social security agency, rather than the employer (which currently leads to discrimination against women, who more often take paid days off to care for children, etc.).

- Provisions related to compulsory insurance in open retirement funds, as well as optional insurance in workers' retirement programmes, should be introduced to direct all resulting disputes to social security courts, as opposed to common civil courts.

Country reports: Poland

INTRODUCTION

Women were among the groups that painfully felt the negative consequences of economic changes. Under changed conditions, their old, socialist 'privileges', for example the relatively long maternity leave, right to childcare leave, and the possibility of early retirement, became an obstacle in finding and keeping employment. Moreover, because of childcare obligations and greater number of days off, women were the first to become unemployed due to group lay-offs. The need to reconcile family responsibilities with professional life, due to an unfair division of these responsibilities in married couples in Poland, is an important limitation of women's opportunities in employment. Different ages of retirement, the granting of childcare benefits, and increasing unemployment are among other issues affecting women in Poland.

In its 2000 Regular Report the European Commission emphasised that, regarding the equal treatment of women and men, "against the objective criterion of adoption of the *acquis*, Poland has made no progress in this area over the reporting period," and, furthermore, that the issue of equal treatment of women and men still requires urgent attention.[6]

In this context, it was not surprising that according to the European Commission, Poland was the most reluctant candidate country to adopt EU law on the equal treatment of men and women in 2000, out of the twelve countries seeking membership. It should be emphasised that this statement was accompanied by a warning that if the situation does not change, negotiations will not be concluded with Poland in the area of social policy.[7] This warning did influence the position of the Government in power from 1997–2001, and contributed to the acceleration of the work on amendments to pro-gender equal opportunities legislation just before the September 2001 parliamentary elections. As a result, the preliminary closing of negotiations in the area of social policy and employment took place on 1 June 2001.[8]

---

[6] European Commission (2000). 1.2. Human rights and the protection of minorities. Economic and cultural rights.

[7] *Rzeczpospolita*, 11 April 2001.

[8] See Report on the realisation in 2001 of the *National Program of Preparations for Accession to European Union;* <http://www.sejm.gov.pl/ue/ue/html>.

The 2001 Regular Report of the European Commission[9] stated that "Considerable efforts to align with the EC *acquis* have been undertaken and should continue to receive high priority [...]. While the amendments to the Labour Code constitute good progress, the necessary institutional framework for implementing and enforcing the *acquis* in this area should still be established. Furthermore, actions should be undertaken to raise awareness of equal treatment for women and men, to improve the position of women in the labour market and to increase their representation in decision making."

This considerable change in the European Commission's assessment was mainly due to the adoption in 2001[10] of wide, detailed amendments to the Labour Code, defining more specifically – among other things – the principle of equal treatment, and therefore harmonising the Polish legislation with the provisions set forth in the Directive 76/207/EEC.

Gender equality did not feature high in the hierarchy of policy issues implemented by the Ministry of Labour and Social Affairs from 1997–2001 and, therefore, in the policy of the Government as a whole. The lack of political will to conduct a pro-equality policy in the integration of international standards has been visible in a few decisions taken since 1997 by the Government and the Parliament in power until autumn 2001. Some of its decisions only referred to employment indirectly, but they did demonstrate the level of resistance to gender equality. In 1997, for example, the national gender equality machinery was transformed into the Plenipotentiary of the Government for the Family. As a result, gender equality issues were dropped from the scope of interest of this office, and it began to perceive women only in the context of the family. The National Programme for Women, adopted by the former Government in 1997 in implementing of the 1995 Beijing Platform For Action, has not been implemented or it has been implemented only selectively.[11]

In 1999, the Parliament rejected a draft Act on Equal Status,[12] which provided *inter alia* for special means of protection against discrimination in employment and easily accessible means to pursue claims in case of a violation of the principle of equality of women and men. In 2000, a draft on the creation of the Commission of Equal Status in the Parliament, whose tasks were to include analysing draft statutory acts with regard to their consequences for both sexes, was not adopted.

---

[9] European Commission (2001). Chapter 13. "Employment and Social Policy."

[10] The Act of 24 August 2001 on Amending the Act – the Labour Code and Some Other Acts, (published in Dziennik Ustaw, the Official Journal of the Republic of Poland, hereinafter referred to as the Dz. U., No.128 of 2001, item 1405).

[11] Women's Association for Gender Equality (2000).

[12] Fuszara and Zielińska (1995: 53.); Fuszara and Zielińska (2000: 12).

There have been some serious reservations with regard to the information policy of the Polish Government on the equality of men and women. The provisions of EU law on this issue have been presented only partially to the public, and, moreover, separately from their wider legal context, determining the fundamental Community aims, principles and rules. Moreover, the Government has not made efforts to inform the public of the fact that the promotion of equality of men and women, as well as the elimination of discrimination on grounds of sex, have been *expressis verbis* considered as the fundamental task of the EU through Articles 2, 3 and 13 of the Amsterdam Treaty. The lack of objective information, and even certain misinformation, has related, in particular, to the possibility of applying specific advantages in order to facilitate vocational training activities for the under-represented sex or to prevent or compensate for professional disadvantages. Some of the information material on the EU equality policy published by governmental agencies contains many half-truths and biased statements.[13] As a result, the level of women's awareness of the positive changes they may expect after Poland's accession to the European Union is low.

All of the above, combined with the unfavourable atmosphere in which discussions on the most important issues for women are held, underline fears that there is a lack of political will in Poland to promote women's real equality. Nevertheless, there is a strong feeling among women activists that Poland's accession to the EU, and in particular the harmonisation of Polish law with the *acquis communautaire* in the field of equal opportunities for women and men, will contribute substantially to the elimination of many of the side effects of political and economic transformation.

---

[13] Bochwic (1999).

1. THE PRINCIPLE OF EQUAL PAY FOR WORK OF EQUAL VALUE

Council Directive 75/117/EEC of 10 February 1975 *on the approximation of the laws of the Member States relating to the application of the principle of equal pay for men and women*

1.1 National legal framework concerning the principle of equal pay for work of equal value: General provisions

The principle of equal pay for women and men is contained directly and indirectly in the Constitution, as well as in the Labour Code. However, Polish law does not define 'work of equal value'.

The Constitution

Article 33 of the 1997 Constitution stipulates in Paragraph 1 that men and women shall have equal rights *inter alia* in social and economic life. Paragraph 2 specifies that this principle also applies to employment, and in particular guarantees the equal right of men and women to equal pay for work of similar value.

Article 32 provides for the principle of equality before the law and the principle of non-discrimination for any reason whatsoever. These principles refer to all branches of law, including labour law, and all grounds of discrimination, including discrimination on grounds of sex.

The Labour Code

The principle of equal pay for men and women is provided for in Section 11(2) of the Labour Code.

Following the 2001 Amending Act, Section 11(3) of the Labour Code prohibits any discrimination, both direct and indirect, in employment, in particular on grounds of sex, disability, race, nationality, opinions, especially political or religious, or syndicate membership, is prohibited. The new Section 18(3)(a)(2) provides that "Equal treatment of women and men shall mean non-discrimination in any manner, direct or indirect, on grounds of sex." The 2001 Amending Act provides that indirect discrimination occurs when there is a disproportion with regard to the conditions of employment to the detriment of all or of a significant number of workers of one sex and which may not be explained by reasons other than sex.

The newly introduced Section 18(3)(c) stipulates *expressis verbis* that workers have the right to equal remuneration for equal or for work of the same value, irrespective of their sex.

Section 78 of the Labour Code, pursuant to which remuneration should be fixed in a manner corresponding, in particular, to the qualifications and the quantity and the quality of work performed, remains unchanged. The Labour Code also provides obliges employers to apply objective and just criteria in the evaluation of employees and the results of their work.

1.2 Implementation of the principle of equal pay for work of equal value: Legal foundations and institutional structures

The principle of equal pay for women and men is provided for in both the public and private sectors. The Polish legal system does not, unfortunately, establish any particular institutions to investigate the enforcement of gender equality in employment. Nevertheless, some controlling authorities of an administrative character with more general competencies may investigate the implementation of this principle. An example of such an authority is the State Employment Inspection, which is authorised to control and supervise the observance of the labour law in all workplaces. The competencies of the Inspection also include, *inter alia*, controlling the observance of the provisions referring to the employment relationship, including remuneration for work. However, in case of a violation of the principle of equal pay for equal work, the competent authorities of the State Employment Inspection are only entitled to address a motion to the manager of the workplace or to the entity superior to the workplace concerned.[14] The State Employment Inspection is not entitled to request that sanctions be applied in case the employer determined an amount of remuneration in the employment contract in a discriminatory manner on the basis of sex.

---

[14] It should be noted that on 10 April 2001 the *Sejm* adopted the amendments to the Act on State Employment Inspection, which would seriously expand the powers of the employment inspectors by authorising them to issue orders for an employer to pay remuneration for work or other performance granted to the employee. These orders are to be administratively enforced. However, the intention was not to give the inspectors a possibility to order the employer to pay the employee a sum that would compensate the contractual pay, as a result of the violation of the principle of equal pay.

1.3 Job classification

There is no general job classification system for determining pay in Poland, and Polish labour law does not provide for any precise and comprehensive criteria allowing the comparison of different types of work.

The form and amount of the remuneration for work depends on the parties in the employment relationship, except when determining the minimum remuneration, which is set by the Minister of Labour and Social Policy. The Labour Code provides for a principle whereby the conditions of remuneration for work and work-related performance should be fixed in collective agreements. Remuneration regulations were introduced in Polish law in 1996, according to which an employer engaging more than five persons (not covered by the collective labour agreement) shall set the conditions of remuneration for work.

If justified by the type of work, the Labour Code admits the application of the labour norms to measure the expenditure of work, its efficiency and quality, referring in particular to the piecework system. Since a specified rate of unitary remuneration is attributed to every norm, it is likely that these norms indirectly influence the determination of the amount of the remuneration for work, constituting the basis of its calculation. Unfortunately, there is no information or research verifying whether the norms on the piecework system performed mostly by women have been correctly formulated in comparison to that performed mostly by men.

1.4 Available legal procedures in cases involving the violation of the principle of equal pay for work of equal value

Until 2001, Polish legislation did not clearly stipulate whether an employee who considers himself/herself to be a victim of discrimination due to a violation of the principle of equal pay had a direct possibility to pursue a claim in court, but the Supreme Court[15] has tended towards the opinion that the principle of equality and non-discrimination in employment may constitute an autonomous basis of an employee's claims.

However, the newly introduced Section 18(3)(d) of the Labour Code explicitly stipulates that a victim of the violation of the principle of equal treatment has the right

---

[15] In the decision of 13 February 1997, the Supreme Court stated that the employer, however free to appoint physicians to be on duty, may not persecute or discriminate against any of them. OSNAPiUS 1997, No.20, item 398.

to compensation amounting to no less than the lowest remuneration for work and no higher than six times that amount. Employees in such cases certainly had and still have the possibility of indirect recourse to the courts in some situations.

Labour disputes are considered on the basis of the Code of Civil Procedure and proceedings related the employment relationship are exempt from court fees. In exceptional cases, however, (for example, if the employee's claim was totally unfounded), the court may charge procedural expenses to the employee.

1.5 Means of informing employees of their right to equal pay for work of equal value

Regrettably, until the year 2001, no special measures were undertaken in Poland to bring legal measures regarding the principle of equal pay or available complaint mechanisms to the attention of employees. Following the 2001 Amending Act, the new Section 94(4) of the Labour Code obliges employers to make the text of the provisions on equal treatment accessible to workers, in the form of written information disseminated in the workplace or to ensure access to these provisions in another way.

1.6 Out of court alternatives

There are no specific proceedings available in the Polish legal system for settling disputes related to the violation of the principle of equal pay out of court; however, more general conciliation procedures may be applied in these cases. Although the provisions in force do not provide for compulsory conciliation proceedings, before a case is directed to the court an employee may request the initiation of conciliation proceedings before the Conciliation Committee, pursuant to Section 242(2) of the Labour Code.

Section 244 of the Labour Code stipulates that such committees may be appointed jointly by the employer and the establishment's trade union organisation in order to settle disputes concerning the claims of employees connected with the employment relationship. If the proceedings before the Conciliation Committee do not result in a settlement, the committee shall, at the request of the employee, transfer the case to a labour court without delay.

Despite these provisions though, this way of settling labour disputes, including in cases of gender discrimination, is not applied in practice.[16]

---

[16] Women's Rights Centre (2000: 58).

1.7 Role of trade unions

Pursuant to the legal regulations in force, trade unions can play a significant role in proceedings related to the violation of the principle of equal pay in Poland, both outside and within the judicial system.

The role of trade unions is important already at the stage of setting the conditions of remuneration for work, and they can have some influence on the composition of the Conciliation Committees.

According to Section 462 of the Code of Civil Procedure, trade unions may initiate labour proceedings on behalf of employees, and pursuant to Section 465, a trade union representative may take part in judicial proceedings as a representative of the employee (although the cassation appeal may only be lodged by a barrister or legal counsellor of the trade union).

Section 9(2) of the Labour Code stipulates that the provisions of collective labour agreements and arrangements may not be less favourable to employees than the provisions of the Labour Code or other acts and executive acts. If the collective labour agreement or regulations of remuneration binding a particular employer contain provisions contrary to the principle discussed above, the court or other authority competent to consider the individual case of an employee shall recognise such provisions as invalid and issue a decision accordingly.[17]

According to the newly adopted Section 18(3) of the Labour Code, provisions of employment contracts and other acts on which the employment contract is based that violate the principle of equal treatment in employment shall be invalid.

Collective work agreements do not usually include the principle of equal pay for women and men, apparently due to the conviction that the provisions of the Labour Code are sufficient in this matter. It may also be connected to the fact that great importance is not attached to the practical meaning of this principle.

1.8 Women's factual situation with regard to the principle of equal pay for work of equal value

Research shows that women earn between 60 and 70 percent of men's pay, although they are often better educated.[18] Such a difference was confirmed by the Government's

---

[17] Zieliński (2000: 162).
[18] Compare to G. Domański (1992).

Report prepared in 1996,[19] and the need to eliminate such disproportional differences was emphasised in the Recommendations of the Committee for Human Rights in July 1999, as well as in the Recommendations of the Committee on Economic, Social and Cultural Rights in 1998.

Data collected by the Main Statistical Office in 1999[20] indicates that women's national salary was equal to 79 percent of men's average salary (compared with 82 percent in 1998). The gender pay gap was greatest in the occupational group of crafts and related trades, where women earned 63 percent of men's average salary, but also visible among members of the Parliament, where women (who comprise 13 percent of deputies and senators) earn 79 percent of men's salaries on average. Differences are apparent in feminised occupational groups such as teaching professionals too, where women earn approximately 80 percent of men's average salary. Women make up 75 percent of persons earning less than the average salary and only 20 percent of persons earning the highest salaries.[21]

Further data presented in a report of the State Employment Inspection on employers' observance of provisions protecting women's work and the prohibition of discrimination on grounds of sex from 1997–1999 showed that discrimination with regard to pay took place in 29 percent of establishments.[22]

---

[19] Government of the Republic of Poland, Report on the fulfilment in legislation and practice of obligations under the provision of Articles Nos.6–15 of the International Covenant on Economic, Social and Cultural Rights for the period from 1 January 1992 to 31 December 1994, Warsaw, January 1996. p. 33–35.

[20] Main Statistical Office (2000a: 164).

[21] Women's Rights Centre (2000a: 63).

[22] State Employment Inspection (2000: 28–31).

2. Equal treatment for women and men as regards access to employment, vocational training and promotion, and working conditions

Council Directive 76/207/EEC of 9 February *1976 on the implementation of the principle of equal treatment for men and women as regards access to employment, vocational training and promotion, and working conditions*

2.1 National legal framework concerning the principle of equal treatment for women and men: General provisions

Polish law guarantees the principle of equality when searching for employment. The Act on Employment and Counteracting Unemployment obliges district employment offices to provide assistance in finding employment to all persons searching for work, regardless of the person's sex. This principle is assisted by the principle of transparency, according to which every free post notified to the employment office shall be made public to everyone.

Although Polish law does not list marital or family status among the possible grounds for discrimination in Section 11(3) of the Labour Code, etc. such circumstances could be taken into account given the open character of the provisions.

2.2 The concept of discrimination on grounds of sex: Definition and legal sanctions

Polish law does not define discrimination on grounds of sex. However, Poland has ratified ILO Convention No.111 and the UN Convention on the Elimination of All Forms of Discrimination against Women, which are a part of the domestic legal order.

In a 1997 judgement, the Supreme Court stated that the illegal deprivation or limitation of rights resulting from an employment relationship or unequal treatment of employees on grounds of *inter alia* sex, age, and disability constitutes discrimination within the meaning of Section 11(3) of the Labour Code, as does the granting of some employees fewer rights than other employees in the same factual and legal position, for one of the reasons enumerated."[23] The Supreme Court has also held that persecution of

---

[23] Judgement of the Supreme Court, in I PKN 246/97, OSNAP 1998, No.12, item 360.

any kind or discrimination against an employee *inter alia* on grounds of sex is inadmissible.[24]

Section 11(3) of the Labour Code does not provide for any specific sanctions against an employer who applies discriminatory practices. As a result, protection from discrimination on grounds of sex is weaker than, for example, protection from discrimination on grounds of union membership, where such sanctions are clearly provided for by law.

2.3 National legal framework concerning the principle of equal treatment as regards access to employment, vocational training and promotion, and working conditions

In terms of discriminatory treatment in access to employment, employers often refused to employ women, fearing they would exercise their rights in relation to motherhood. In such a case, the refusal to employ did not justify a claim concerning the conclusion of the employment contract, and the law in force did not directly provide for a possibility to pursue such claims before the court. An injured person might, however, pursue a claim for damages in tort on the basis of Section 415 of the Civil Code.[25]

The situation in this regard improved after the 2001 Amending Act entered into force, and the newly introduced Section 18(3)(b) of the Labour Code explicitly provides that any differentiation by the employer between workers of the same sex, resulting in, for example, a refusal to conclude or continue the employment relationship, ignoring the worker in promotion or granting other benefits relating to the work, shall be considered a violation of the principle of equal treatment.

The obligation to treat employees equally is among the fundamental obligations of the employer, and according the Labour Code, a serious violation of this obligation may justify a termination of the employment contract without notice from the employee. However, it is not clear how a 'serious violation of this obligation' should be understood, leaving it to be interpreted by the employee and the court.

In practice, women are very often asked additional questions about their family situation and plans for children during job interviews. Women are even sometimes obliged to sign a statement waiving the right to free days to which they are entitled in

---

[24] The case refers to remuneration due to the employee for the time of non-performance of work for reasons due to the employer.
[25] K. Rączka, in Salwa (ed.) (2000: 37).

case of a child's sickness in order to be employed. Moreover, employers sometimes demand medical certificates from young women seeking a job stating that they are not pregnant.

It should be noted that the Ombudsperson has signalled that group lay-offs, applied more frequently to women than to men, constitute discrimination on grounds of sex.

2.4 Protective measures with regard to women's participation in the labour market

Although Section 10 of the Labour Code stipulates everyone's right to freely choose employment, women may not be employed in work that is particularly onerous or harmful to health and this prohibition is absolute. A female employee who is ordered to perform such work may refuse to do so, and an employer who employs women in such work violates these provisions and shall be subject to a fine. The specification of occupations that are onerous or harmful to health is set forth by the Council of Ministers in the Annex to the Ordinance on the Specification of Occupations Prohibited to Women.[26]

The provisions in force do not directly enumerate occupations prohibited to women (the specification previously in force covered 90 occupations prohibited to women in 18 branches of professional activity). However, they do set forth the highest admissible norms for lifting, transporting and carrying burdens by women. Generally speaking, the occupations prohibited to women are those related to a particular physical effort and transporting of burdens, a forced body position, work in noise and vibrations, and underground work (except for specified posts). Women's circles in particular have raised concerns that these norms exclude women's right to freely choose employment, and limit in advance their professional possibilities, regardless of their individual predispositions and preferences. It has been emphasised that the protection of women's work is justified in relation to pregnant women,[27] but that in relation to other women there should be an obligation to estimate the eventual risks in each particular post.

In 1999 the number of women employed in prohibited work decreased three times in relation to 1998, the proportion of employers being comparable.[28]

---

[26] Dz. U. of 1996, No.114, item 545.
[27] Nowakowska (2000: 13).
[28] State Employment Inspection (2000: 29).

The Polish Government does undertake a few effective positive measures or programmes to increase women's participation and access in the labour market.[29] Such measures are connected, *inter alia,* with the pro-family policy. It should be noted that generally both working and unemployed women perceive the changes that have taken place in the employment market in Poland in the 1990s very negatively.[30] This is very strongly related to the fact that the rate of unemployment has been constantly increasing, and faster in relation to women (while in 1998 the rate was 9.3 percent for men and 12.2 percent for women, in 1999 it rose to 14.4 percent and 18.4 percent respectively). According to the data from the Main Statistical Office, the unemployment rates for women have been higher than men's by 23.8–37.6 percent.

The attempts to cope with unemployment do not refer to women especially,[31] although particular district employment offices sometimes have special offers addressed to women, for example with regard to training aimed at professional re-orientation. However, according to the information published by the Polish public TV in April 2001, in one of the regions of Poland only 28 out of 300,000 unemployed persons (10 percent of the total national number of unemployed persons) have completed training aimed at their professional activation.

Women's NGOs are active in dealing with women's unemployment, but due to limited financial means, which come mainly from foreign sources, only a small number of women can benefit from their activities.

2.5 Prohibition of dismissal

Following the 2001 Amending Act, Section 18(3)(e) of Labour Code provides that an employer may not terminate an employment contract with or without notice because an employee exercises his/her rights in case of a violation of the principle of equal treatment.

---

[29] Such actions have been foreseen in the National Programme of Action for Women, the tool for the realisation of the Beijing Action Platform. Compare to P. Kołodziejczyk (2000: 110).

[30] Żylicz (2000: 33).

[31] Ordinance of the Minister of Labour and Social Politics of 9 February 2000 on Detailed Rules of Running the Labour Intermediation, Professional Counselling, Organisation of Training for Unemployed Persons, Creation of Methodical Background for Professional Information and Professional Counselling and Organisation and Financing of the Labour Clubs, Dz. U. 2000, No.12, item 146.

2.6 Women's and men's jobs

Jobs are prevented from being classified as specifically for women or men in Article 2(2) of an Ordinance of the Minister of Labour and Social Policy from 9 February 2000, which provides that the employer's notification of the available position (at the district employment office) may not contain requirements that discriminate between candidates on grounds of sex, age, nationality, religion and other circumstances.

2.7 Legal status of sexual harassment

Sexual harassment is not defined in Polish law or referred to in the Labour Code. In 1996, a new Section 11(1) was introduced in the Labour Code obliging employers to respect the dignity and other personal rights of employees.[32] Nevertheless, this general provision is imprecise and it is not clear whether it protects the employee exclusively against harassment in the form of sexual blackmail performed directly by the employer or if this protection also covers situations in which the employer allows the employee to be exposed to sexual harassment by other employees or, for example, by clients.

The provisions concerning discrimination on grounds of sex may also serve as the basis of a claim by an employee who has been sexually harassed, but in Poland the qualification of harassment as behaviour that violates the dignity of the employee ensures better protection for the employee than the anti-discriminatory clause.

In some cases sexual harassment may also qualify as an administrative offence or an offence under the Penal Code.

---

[32] Employees also have the right to dignity and other personal rights on the basis of Section 23 and 24 of the Civil Code.

3. Protection of Pregnant Women from the Inherent Risk of Certain Activities and Related Employment Rights

Council Directive 92/85/EEC of 19 October 1992 *on the introduction of measures to encourage improvements in the safety and health at work of pregnant workers and workers who have recently given birth or are breastfeeding*

3.1 Legal and conceptual framework

Polish legislation does not define the concept of 'pregnant worker', and while the Labour Code does not contain an obligation to notify the employer about the pregnancy, there is an obligation to confirm the pregnancy with a medical certificate.

The term 'breastfeeding worker' is referred to in Section 187 of the Labour Code, which guarantees such women employees breaks to breastfeed a child during working hours and without loss of pay. At the request of the employer the breastfeeding worker should present a relevant medical certificate.[33]

The term 'worker who has recently given birth' does not exist explicitly in Polish law.

3.2 Assessing the risk to the safety or health of a pregnant worker and employer's obligations

In accordance with the Council of Ministers Ordinance of 10 September 1996 every employer is obliged to establish the specification of works prohibited to pregnant and breastfeeding women in a given workplace.

Pursuant to Section 227(1)(2) of the Labour Code and Article 39 of the 1997 Ordinance of the Minister of Labour and Social Policy on General Provisions on Safety and Hygiene at Work, the employer is obliged, at his own expense, to determine factors harmful to health involved in particular work, as well as register the results of such research and make it available to employees.

The Labour Code obliges employers to inform all employees of occupational risks connected with the performed work and of the rules for protection against hazards, according to the procedure provided for in the regulations in the Labour Code. Such

---

[33] Hintz, in T. Zieliński (ed.) (2000: 821).

information should be given to the employee once the work begins, and whenever there is a new professional risk or hazards.

Employers' obligations

Following the 2001 Amending Act, employers are obliged to transfer pregnant or breastfeeding workers whose employment involves a risk of contact with dangerous or harmful factors to other work, or, if necessary, relieve them from work without affecting the right to remuneration. There is a further obligation to adjust the working conditions of female workers employed in work prohibited to pregnant or breastfeeding women and of workers possessing a medical certificate stating health contraindications to the requirements set forth in the legal provisions, or to shorten their working time.

3.3 Cases in which exposure is prohibited for pregnant and breastfeeding workers

Polish law grants wider protection to pregnant and breastfeeding women than is set forth in EU law. According to the appendix of the 1998 Ordinance of the Council of Ministers on work prohibited to women, twenty additional or modified positions are included in the activities prohibited only for pregnant and breastfeeding women, including *inter alia* work involving manual lifting, forced positions, sudden changes in air temperature, decreased pressure, viruses, carcinogenic factors, etc.

3.4 Night work

The Labour Code stipulates that pregnant woman may not be employed at night or in overtime work, and pregnant women may not be delegated to work outside their usual work place without their consent. It is also forbidden to employ pregnant women for a time exceeding eight hours per day, even if in a given workplace this is compensated with rest days. These prohibitions do not apply to breastfeeding women.

If the transfer of a pregnant employee to day work leads to a reduction in pay, she is entitled to a compensatory allowance, even if the type of work does not change.[34]

The Supreme Court has upheld the view that pregnancy and the protection of pregnant women cannot serve as a reason for depriving an employee of some of her income.

---

[34] Judgement of the Supreme Court of 15 March 1979, ref. V PZP 13/78, OSNCP 1979, p. 6, item 110.

3.5 Maternity leave

The right to maternity leave is related to the birth of the child within the duration of the employment relationship. It is a personal right of an employee, which may be used in kind. The employer has an absolute obligation to grant the employee the maternity leave either on the basis of a medical certificate on the anticipated date of birth, or, in the case of birth in hospital, on the basis of a certificate of the date on which the birth took place (Section 180[1] of the Labour Code). Adoptive and foster parents are entitled to leave treated as maternity leave, but in a smaller amount determined according to the age of the child.

The provisions on maternity leave have been amended several times in recent years. The 2001 Amending Act changed the title of the chapter in this area to "Workers' right relating to parenthood." As a result, it is possible for the father to take a part of this leave or for both parents to benefit from it at the same time. The length of maternity leave was shortened again in 2002,[35] and female workers are currently entitled to 16 weeks maternity leave for the first child, 18 weeks for a second child, and 26 weeks for subsequent children or in the case of multiple births. Two weeks may be taken before the birth of the child, and 14 weeks of the leave are obligatory. Female employees may submit a motion to the employer to shorten the remaining two weeks of the leave, and employers are obliged to accept this. In such cases, the father caring for the child may seek to take the remaining part of the leave, and to obtain the benefit accordingly.

The right to maternity leave is usually not stipulated in the employment contract because of the existing legal provisions and labour law regulations.

Pursuant to Section 184 of the Labour Code, employees are entitled to a maternity allowance in accordance with the principles and conditions defined by separate provisions.[36] The monthly maternity allowance is equal to 100 percent of the remuneration based on the average monthly salary for the six months immediately prior. If the mother dies or abandons the child, the maternity allowance shall be granted to the father or other closest family member who is insured if they interrupt employment or other profit-making activity in order to personally care for the child.

In addition, the insured mother or other person is entitled to a single birth allowance amounting to 20 percent of the average monthly remuneration.[37]

---

[35] Act of 21 December 2001, Amending the Labour Code, Dz. U. of 2001, No.154, item 1805. The Act came into force as of 13 January 2002.

[36] Articles 29–31 of the Act on Pecuniary Allowances from the Social Security Fund in Case of Sickness and Maternity.

[37] Articles 27–28 of the Act of 25 June 1999 on the Pecuniary Allowances from the Social Security System.

Antenatal examinations

Section 185(2) of the Labour Code obliges employers to grant pregnant women time off from work without loss of pay to undergo antenatal examinations and medical tests ordered by a physician if those tests cannot be performed outside working hours.

3.6 Prohibition of dismissal and employment rights

Section 177 of the Labour Code stipulates that an employer may not give notice to terminate or terminate an employment contract during the pregnancy or maternity leave of an employee unless the woman is at fault and the workplace trade union organisation representing the employee consented to the termination of the contract, or in the event of bankruptcy or liquidation of the workplace.[38] Following the 2001 Amending Act, this protection also extends to fathers on maternity leave, but the prohibition of dismissal does not apply to employees during a trial period of less than one month.

Section 42(1) of the Labour Code, which governs notice of the termination of, or changes to, working conditions and remuneration, also applies during pregnancy and maternity leave.

If an employment contract is unlawfully terminated while a woman is on pregnancy, maternity or childcare leave, the employee has the right to pursue a claim on the basis of general provisions contained in the Labour Code (Section 45 and 57), and can seek to be reinstated or compensated for the unlawful action of the employer. If the employee is reinstated and resumes employment, the Labour Code guarantees her compensation for the material detriment she suffered during the period of unemployment.

According to the State Employment Inspection, among the complaints submitted in 1998 most referred to the termination of employment contracts with pregnant women and about 15 percent of the complaints referred to the non-transfer of pregnant women to other jobs, despite the submission of a medical certificate confirming contraindications. Approximately 80 percent of the complaints were found to be totally or partially justified.

---

[38] If it is impossible to give the employee other work, she is entitled to an allowance amounting to the motherhood allowance up to the birth of the child.

4. The burden of proof in cases of discrimination based on sex

Council Directive 97/80/EC of 15 December 1997 *on the burden of proof in cases of discrimination based on sex*

4.1 Legal framework concerning indirect discrimination and specific legal means to implement the principle of equal treatment for women and men

Until 2001, indirect discrimination was not explicitly defined in the Polish legal framework, although the term was not unknown within the Polish legal system and it has featured in particular in the interventions undertaken by the Ombudsman. Specifically, through the Ombudsman's motions, the following provisions and practice, among others, have been changed: provisions that are indirectly discriminatory towards women, and provisions referring to the possibility of joint taxation of revenues of single parents (single mothers comprise around 13 percent of families, whereas single fathers only comprise two percent).

The 2001 Amending Act defines indirect discrimination and provides for special legal means to implement the principle of equal treatment for women and men, but the EU definition of indirect discrimination is more developed than the one adopted in Poland and there is no presumption in Poland that action which is unfavourable to a significantly higher number of representatives of one sex constitutes indirect discrimination.

4.2 The burden of proof procedure in litigation concerning a violation of the principle of equal treatment for women and men and rules of evidence

Prior to 2001, the principle set forth in Section 6 of the Civil Code provided that the burden of proof rested with the plaintiff. It had been proposed to amend the Labour Code to include a presumption that, in the event of any doubt, an employment contract would be presumed, thereby putting the burden of proving the employment relationship on the employer. However, such a provision was not adopted due to resistance from trade unions.

Fundamental changes in this area were set forth in the 2001 Amending Act and the newly introduced Section 18(3)(b) of the Labour Code stipulates that it shall be considered a violation of the principle of equal treatment of women and men for an employer to differentiate between workers' situation on grounds of sex, resulting in particular in the refusal to conclude or to continue an employment relationship, unfavourable remuneration, etc., "unless the employer proves that he was guided by other reasons."

Some women's NGOs provide brochures that publicise the legal regulations for bringing a case involving the violation of the principle of equal treatment to court, and with the support of the Parliamentary Women's Group and some political parties these circles organise seminars and conferences to spread knowledge about European standards on equal treatment. However, there are practically no activities on behalf of the Government or social partners in this field.

4.3 Case law on the violation of the principle of equal treatment for women and men

The Ombudsman has intervened in some cases of discrimination and, for example, initiated changes to the rules referring to two-days of paid leave in order to care for a child under 14 years of age and the childcare allowance, which was previously granted only to women employees, unless the man could prove he was the "sole carer." The Ombudsman has indicated to the Minister of Labour and Remuneration that the unequal treatment of women and men in access to employment is visible, *inter alia,* in "attempts to dismiss women first in so-called group lay-offs, and women that take leave from work relatively more often due to their care duties."[39] The Ombudsperson has also proposed that the preferences for women in employment should be facultative, because otherwise, in the present conditions, they act against women.[40]

A few cases, in particular referring to the retirement ages for men and women, have been recognised by the Supreme Court and the Constitutional Tribunal. The dysfunction of the Polish system in terms of protection against discrimination on grounds of sex was illustrated by the case of Mrs. Paruszewska,[41] who was employed in one of the central governmental offices and forced to retire at the age of 60 against her will. Despite using all accessible legal means to pursue her claim (ranging from administrative courts to the European Commission on Human Rights in Strasbourg), she has not managed to have the detrimental decision changed or to receive compensation.

---

[39] *Biuletyn RPO* (Ombudsman's Bulletin), RPO /135587/93/III of 25 October1993.
[40] Zieliński (1995: 28).
[41] Paruszewska (2000: 39).

5. NON-DISCRIMINATION AGAINST PART-TIME WORKERS

Council Directive 97/81/EC of 15 December 1997 *concerning the framework agreement on part-time work concluded by UNICE, CEEP and the ETUC*

5.1 National legal framework and employment conditions concerning part-time workers

The concept of part-time worker

According to the data of the Main Statistical Office part-time employees are persons who work part-time on the basis of an employment contract for an undetermined period of time. This term is not defined in any statutory acts.

Legal provisions

Until the amendments to the Labour Code were prepared in 2000, there were no particular provisions referring to the employment conditions of part-time workers, which are established exclusively by contract. It should also be noted that, so far, part-time employees have not constituted a subject of interest for the legislature, the courts or academics, nor has Polish labour law contained any anti-discriminatory clause that refers *expressis verbis* to part-time workers. The amendments to the Labour Code provide for some important provisions concerning the status of such employees, and the proposed amendments in this area have been positively evaluated in the opinion of the European Integration Committee as compatible with the above Directive in the positive approach to part-time work.[42]

The amendments include *inter alia* the inclusion of part-time employment among the possible grounds for discrimination in the anti-discriminatory clause in Section 11(3) of the Labour Code. In addition, a new Paragraph 6 was added to Section 29 of the Labour Code, stipulating that the conclusion of a part-time employment contract with may not establish less favourable conditions of work and remuneration than for full-time employees, while considering the proportionality of remuneration and work-related performance.

Despite these amendments though, the obstacles that may limit the opportunities for part-time workers are not of a legal or administrative nature (or only to a limited extent); they result rather from the psychological barriers towards such employees, who are treated as 'not fully valuable' and the dominant work ethic which places flexibility

---

[42] Opinion of 13 June 2000, ref. JSW/420/2000/DHP.

(understood as the readiness to work in violation of the provisions of the Labour Code referring to working time) high on the list of employers' expectations.

There have been no special provisions so far on the transfer of employees from full-time to part-time work and vice versa, although the Act amending the Labour Code proposed the introduction of such a possibility. In addition, there are no legal or administrative procedures that require concrete measures to facilitate access to part-time work at all levels of the enterprise, including skilled and managerial positions. Measures to facilitate part-time workers' access to vocational training and enhance career opportunities have only recently become an area of concern for the Polish legislator and the Government.

Related research

The lack of relevant research makes it impossible to determine whether there are any important legal or practical differences regarding the treatment of part-time workers in the public and private sectors. According to the data of the Main Statistical Office of 1999, women comprised 66 percent of part-time employees in the main workplaces (employing more than nine people). The percentage of female part-time workers among all female employees in the main workplaces was five percent.[43]

---

[43] Main Statistical Office (1999: 138).

6. THE PRINCIPLE OF EQUAL TREATMENT TO SELF-EMPLOYED WORKERS AND THEIR ASSISTING SPOUSES

Directive 86/613/EEC of 11 December 1986 *on the application of the principle of equal treatment between women and men engaged in an activity, including agriculture, in a self-employed capacity, and on the protection of self-employed women during pregnancy and motherhood*

6.1 National legal framework on self-employment: General provisions

The principle of equal treatment contained in Articles 32 and 33 of the Constitution has a general character and therefore applies also to self-employed women and men, although there is no specific reference to them.

The principle of equal treatment set forth in Article 2(a) of the Act on Social Security Systems does not provide such specification, and the principle of equal treatment in the Act on Economic Activity is formulated in general terms.

Definition of self-employed workers

Polish law does not define the term 'self-employed workers', but Article 2(2) of the Act on Economic Activity defines the term 'entrepreneur'. The Act on Social Security Systems defines the term with regard to self-employed persons working outside the agriculture domain, and the Act on Social Security for Farmers defines a farmer as "any natural person conducting agricultural activity for this person's own account as the possessor (with owner or dependent status) of an agricultural farm situated within the borders of the Republic of Poland."

Acceptance of the directive

The general level of public awareness of the principle of equal opportunities is very low in Poland and while it may be better known in the context of employment relationships, it certainly does not refer to self-employed persons, especially in agriculture.

There are no known initiatives undertaken in Poland to examine the conditions under which recognition of the work of spouses referred to in Article 2(b) of the Directive may be encouraged, nor do any appropriate steps appear to have been considered or taken, especially by the Government, to encourage such recognition.

6.2 Social rights of spouses of self-employed workers

All persons are treated equally in the new system of social security in force since 1 January 1999; it is a common system, providing for the same mechanisms for all social and professional groups, including self-employed workers, except for individual farmers. The Act on the Social Security Systems clearly stipulates that the insurance provided therein covers not only persons performing non-agricultural activity and persons performing contract work, but also persons cooperating with them.

In the context of this Act, 'cooperating persons' include a spouse, children, the spouse's children, adopted children, parents, step-parents and adoptive parents. In order to be covered by the insurance, these persons must share a common household with the person performing non-agricultural activity and cooperate with them in running this activity or performing work on a contractual basis. This provision does not refer to persons with whom an employment contract for vocational training was concluded. Total retirement and disability insurance contributions for cooperating persons are paid by the person performing the economic activity.

According to Act on Social Security Systems, social insurance includes old-age and disability pensions; sickness and maternity insurance; and insurance against accidents at work and occupational diseases. Both persons running the activity and cooperating persons are subject to obligatory retirement and disability insurance.

The social insurance of farmers with Polish citizenship covers farmers themselves and members of their household working with them. The provisions also apply to the farmer's spouse, unless the spouse does not work in the farmer's agricultural farm or in the household directly associated with it. In a given case a disability pension may be granted to a farmer's spouse despite that person's total inability to work, as the work in an agricultural farm may consist, for example, only in managing it. Legally, it does not matter whether the farm constitutes the joint property of spouses or not.

The social insurance for farmers includes insurance against accidents, sickness, maternity, as well old-age and disability pensions. Other farmers or members of their households for whom agricultural activity constitutes a permanent source of income are also insured against accidents, sickness and in case of maternity only upon a motion.

Formation of companies by unmarried persons

The Act on Economic Activity regulates the running of non-agricultural businesses and does not contain any provisions that violate the principle of equal opportunities. It does not seem that it is legally more difficult for spouses to form a company. Chapter 6 deals with small and medium enterprises and provides that the State must create favourable conditions for them to function, respecting the principles of equality and fair competition.

Many discriminatory provisions were in force until recently. For example, in 1991, the Commissioner for Civil Rights made a successful intervention in a case of discrimination against married persons in which the right to a tax exemption was not applied because the taxpayers were married.[44] In 1993, the Commissioner filed a motion with the Constitutional Tribunal, pointing out that provisions depriving female spouses of farmers of the right to single compensation for agricultural accidents at work were inconsistent with the constitutional principle of equality. The Act on the Social Security of Farmers did not list farmers' wives as close persons entitled to a single financial compensation[45] and as a result of the intervention, the Constitutional Tribunal ruled that Article 10(2) of the Act was unconstitutional, and the provision was amended.

Recognition of the work of spouses

The introduction of equal rights for the spouses of self-employed business persons took place relatively recently. Before its reform in 1998, the social security system generally excluded not only spouses employed in a business run by the other spouse, but also a wide range of relatives employed or cooperating with the self-employed business person and sharing the same household with this person. On the basis of a special act, these persons were vested with a smaller range of benefits, connected with a lower social security contribution than usual.[46] However, a spouse who is not cooperating in the business is not, in principle, insured.

Discriminatory provisions related to the social security system

The 1991 Act on Personal Income Tax introduced, among other things, the possibility of joint taxation of spouses. In effect, this meant that the majority of single mothers had to pay higher taxes than married couples. It is also significant that the Commissioner referred different aspects of this provision to the Constitutional

---

[44] Complaint of the Commissioner for Civil Rights, *Biuletyn RPO* 82737/91/VI. Report of the Commissioner for Civil Rights for 1991 to the Diet, on the observance of citizens' rights and freedoms. Parliamentary Paper No.32, 10 December 1991, p. 25.

[45] *Biuletyn RPO* 92655/93/III. In the judgement of 23 February 1993, the Constitutional Tribunal sustained the arguments of the Commissioner (K10/92). Compare Arcimowicz (2002: 114).

[46] Such a principle was applied under the provisions previously in force. Compare a judgement of the Supreme Court of 20 March 1996, II URN 51/95, OSNAPiUS 1996/18, item 278, cited after Gudowska (1998: 51).

Tribunal three times, emphasising the inequality to the detriment of single parents, and especially the most economically vulnerable (i.e. single mothers).

Another example of legislation favouring employees over self-employed persons and that affects women more than men concerns early retirement. According to the legislation previously in force, employees (but not self-employed persons) had the right to take early retirement. Under the new unified system, this is temporarily still the case, although the rule excluding self-employed workers is scheduled for repeal.

Also under the provisions previously in force, a person who was entitled to retirement or reached the regular retirement age had no possibility to benefit from the means left by a spouse who predeceased them and was a member of an open retirement fund. In amending this provision, it was emphasised that these means should be available during the retirement period as a single payment in cash because only small amounts of money may be kept in open retirement fund accounts in the next few years.

The rights of self-employed workers whose operational activity is interrupted owing to pregnancy or motherhood

There are no provisions in Poland entitling either female self-employed workers or the wives of self-employed workers to maternity coverage or benefits during interruptions in their occupational activity owing to pregnancy or motherhood. Unlike employees, for whom insurance coverage is obligatory, female self-employed workers and cooperating spouses are subject to optional contributory insurance in case of sickness or maternity. Moreover, self-employed workers and their cooperating spouses working in agriculture are subject to a different period of entitlement to benefits than persons performing non-agricultural work.

Self-employed non-agricultural workers enjoy the right to maternity benefits, but not maternity leave, if childbirth (or other circumstances such as adoption or fostering of a child) occurs within the insured period. For self-employed non-agricultural workers and employees the maternity benefit is, in principle, granted for a period of 16 weeks (18 weeks in the case of a second child, and 26 weeks in the case of a subsequent child or multiple births).

The Act on the Social Security of Farmers grants insured persons the right to a maternity benefit in an amount equal to the sickness benefit for eight weeks. This benefit is paid together with the childbirth benefit or the benefit for adopting a child below the age of one, if during this period a claim for adoption has been registered.

6.3 Contributory social security system for self-employed workers

Because social insurance is compulsory for all working persons, including the self-employed, optional contributory insurance has limited importance. In the present retirement system, all workers (including self-employed persons) have the right to insure themselves additionally in the so-called third insurance pillar, i.e. workers' retirement programmes, which do not fall within the public social security system. These programmes function on the basis of voluntary participation, are a part of private law and are not secured with state guarantees.

According to the Act on Social Security Systems, the right to voluntary contributory retirement and disability insurance (as with obligatory insurance) is granted, in principle, exclusively to workers or cooperating persons.[47] Although certain groups of persons not covered by obligatory insurance may enter the system of social security, non-working wives, including the spouses of self-employed workers, are not mentioned in this regard.[48] Nevertheless, in certain circumstances, such spouses are entitled to benefit from this form of insurance if they meet the requirements for a carer's benefit; they are not eligible for compulsory retirement or disability insurance while completing university or doctoral studies.

Significantly, farmers may not benefit from the optional insurance within the so-called third pillar since they do not fall within the common system of social security. Accordingly, a farmer's spouse may not benefit from these provisions either.

6.4 Related research and statistics

It should be emphasised that in Poland the percentage of the population employed in agriculture is relatively high and amounts to 18.7 percent, which is 30 percent more than in other countries such as the Czech Republic or Hungary.[49] Individual agricultural farms, which are traditionally family-run businesses in Poland, have not changed structurally. Nevertheless, the widespread impoverishment of family-run farms, and the families themselves, occurred during the period of transformation. The

---

[47] It should be noted that contributory social insurance of this type was created already in 1991. Recently, a respective provision was implemented into the Act on the System of Social Security.

[48] Only the spouse of a person sent to work in consular and diplomatic agencies and missions in international organisations.

[49] Compare *OECD Quarterly Labour Force Statistics 2000*, No.4.

majority of women polled in a survey rated the failure of the farm to generate a profit first among the problems in rural life.[50]

Social perceptions of self-employed women, including women in agriculture

Although it is widely believed that women are mostly involved in commercial enterprises, a survey of city-based women entrepreneurs showed only one third are running commercial companies, and most companies are both production and service oriented, or production, commerce and service oriented.[51] Among female-run companies, agricultural and similar businesses predominate (61.7 percent), followed by companies connected with commerce and repair services (20.3 percent), which prevail in the cities. Clear professional segregation based on sex, which is seen among men and women employees, is not found among women and men entrepreneurs.[52]

The same survey revealed that unemployment, not only actual but also imminent, was the main reason that women establish their own businesses. The three major factors motivating women to work for themselves included: a desire for independence, an innate sense of enterprise, and the desire for a higher income. Although the same three factors apply to male entrepreneurs too, a further motive – the wish to prove one's value to a life-partner – was much more frequently quoted by women than by men.[53]

Percentage of self-employed men and women

The percentage of self-employed women (including women working in agriculture) was 39 percent in 1992 and 1993, 38 percent from 1995–1997, and 37 percent in 1998. The drop was mainly due to the continuous decrease of the percentage of women working in agriculture. As of the end of December 1998, women comprised 59.3 percent of all assisting family members (a slight increase from 1995, when women comprised 57.3 percent of this category). In cities, self-employed persons, regardless of gender, constitute a decidedly smaller group than in the countryside.

Past and recent trends on self-employment

The transition from the so-called planned economy to a free market economy in Poland provided the impetus for the expansion of private businesses. This is evident in

---

[50] See Maria Daszyńska.

[51] Women managers exist in the most diverse fields, from production of dental instruments, repairs of machines and appliances, to accounting services for firms, event organization. Compare Ewa Lisowska (2001: 56–57).

[52] Lisowska (2001: 56–57), and Tryfan (1998).

[53] Acording to a poll of 142 women company-owners in Poland. See: Lisowska (1997: 4ff). Similar results were also obtained by a telephone poll of 150 entrepreneurs (including 40 women), see Zapalska (1997: 76–82).

the three-fold increase of self-employed businesspersons between 1985 and 1993. During the same period the number of self-employed women increased five-fold. After 1993, the rate of increase of the number of self-employed women slowed, attaining its highest level in 1998, and then starting to fall in 1999 and 2000. The reason for the rise of women entrepreneurs between 1989 and 1998 was a move from the public sector following the collapse of state light industry plants. The decrease of the overall number of self-employed persons observed after 1998 should be linked with the implementation of the new system of social security.

Official figures show that in Poland most company owners are men, but also that the percentage of businesswomen is constantly increasing. Before 1989, the number of female entrepreneurs among all women employed outside agriculture amounted to 3.7 percent, increasing up to 7.3 percent in 1990 and to almost 10 percent in 2000.[54] Women employers make up 31 percent of all self-employed women in cities and six percent in the countryside (compared with 34 percent in cities and almost nine percent in rural areas for men).[55]

Research on self-employment in Poland showed that, for women, founding a business is easier than getting a senior management post in another company, since self-employment means more autonomy and less dependence on formal education or qualification requirements as well as professional experience confirmed by the merits in the professional circle.[56]

The rise of women in business in the last ten years is a result of their exclusion from traditional employment, and not because of state policy supporting this development. No special credit opportunities or relaxation of formal credit requirements are offered to women in Poland. There are no centres of information, training or advice for women in business. Within the governmental programme launched in Poland to support small and medium-size companies, a separate programme for women and a drive to promote women in particular enterprises should be undertaken, since this has not taken place so far.[57]

---

[54] Lisowska (2001: 53–54).

[55] Łagodziński (1995: 38).

[56] Lisowska (2001: 29).

[57] In the first half of 2000, an offer to refund training costs for owners or co-owners of small enterprises was made by the Ministry of Economy, according to which women would get a higher refund than men, but this was valid only to the end of 2000. See: Lisowska (2001: 101–102).

6.5 Legal means of redress

In accordance with the provisions of the Act on Social Security Systems, an appeal may be filed regarding any decision of the social security authorities with the labour and social security court. Theoretically speaking, the claim may also refer to a violation of the principle of equal treatment. The procedure takes place pursuant to the provisions of the Code of Civil Procedure on separate proceedings. In these proceedings, the insured person is exempt from court costs.

Pursuant to the Act on the Social Security of Farmers, a decision of the President of the Farmer's Social Insurance Agency may be subject to a court appeal in accordance with the rules set forth in the Code of Civil Procedure.

Bringing measures adopted pursuant to the directive to the attention of representative bodies

Polish law does not require that the measures adopted pursuant to this Directive are brought to the attention of bodies representing self-employed workers and vocational training centres. Nonetheless, such an obligation may be deduced from the Act on Economic Chambers.

7. THE FRAMEWORK ON PARENTAL LEAVE

Council Directive 96/34/EC of 3 June 1996 *on the framework agreement on parental leave concluded by UNICE, CEEP, and ETUC*

7.1 National legal framework on parental leave: General provisions

Polish provisions referring to the Directive comply in principle with the requirements of the framework agreement. In 1996, upon a motion of the Commissioner for Civil Rights (the Polish Ombudsman), a provision that had granted the childcare benefit only to the mother, and to the father only if the mother was away from home, was amended.

Conditions of access and detailed rules relating to parental leave

As a result of the amendment of Section 189(1) of the Labour Code in 2001, women and men were granted the right to take a part of the childcare leave simultaneously, for a minimum period determined in the Directive.

The childcare leave rights provided in the Polish legal system correspond with the parental leave rights set forth in the framework agreement under review. This leave is provided for in Section 186 of the Labour Code. The benefits are currently provided for in Chapter 2(a) of the Act on Family, Care and Childcare Benefits.

As of January 2002, both parents or carers may simultaneously take the childcare leave for a period of up to three months, although the benefit will only be paid to one of them. The relevant amendment to the 1996 Ordinance, providing the detailed procedure for applying for childcare leave in such situations, had not been adopted at the time of writing.

Employees on a trial period, a temporary contract, or working on commission are also entitled to childcare leave, but persons performing cottage industry work are not.[58] Despite this restriction, the scope (relating to entitlement) of childcare leave corresponds to the rules set forth in the Directive.

---

[58] The legislator did not explain why but it can be assumed that this solution derives from the conviction that work performed at home may be combined with childcare, on the basis of the Ordinance of the Council of Ministers, dated 31 December 1975 on Workers' Rights for Persons Working in Cottage Industry. Published in *Dz. U.* 1976, No.3, item 19 with subsequent amendments.

The 1996 Council of Ministers Ordinance cites two categories of persons able to take childcare leave, parents and carers, but does not specify who carers are. Leave can also be granted to non-adoptive parents caring for a child.[59]

The framework agreement provides for granting parental leave for a minimum three-month period. The Polish provisions (according to which, upon an application of a female or male worker, childcare leave may be granted for a period up to three years as mentioned above, clearly go beyond the required minimum standard.

According to Article 1 of the 1996 Ordinance, the female/male worker may take childcare leave until the child reaches four years of age. Polish legislation does not meet the requirement to grant childcare leave until the child is eight years old, despite the provision according to which if, for reasons of health, particularly chronic disease, mental or physical handicap, the child requires personal care, the female/male worker may take childcare leave for up to three years until the child is 18 years old. This right may be granted to a female/male worker irrespective of whether they were previously granted childcare leave before the child reached the age of four. In this case the total duration of the childcare leave may not exceed six years. The birth of another child or fostering/adoption of a child qualifies the parents to receive further childcare leave to the full amount.

The employee must give notice to the employer of the intention to take childcare leave and inform the employer of plans to return from leave earlier than originally agreed. The employee may terminate the childcare leave at any moment with the consent of the employer, after notifying the employer at least 30 days before the planned return to work.

Polish provisions do not clearly determine the nature of the employment relationship as required by the Directive. It can, however, be established on the basis of the normative model in force. During leave, the employment contract between the worker and the employer is not terminated but rather suspended.[60] Therefore, during this time the employee may not be granted vacation leave or benefits, the payment of which depends on the work performed. This relationship is stable nevertheless because it may be terminated only in specifically determined cases. Childcare leave may be split into no more than four portions; the provisions do not, however, stipulate how long these portions should be.

A female/male worker who stopped caring for a child is obliged to notify the employer no later than 20 days after the termination of the care period, whereupon the employer is obliged to allow their return to work within 20 days after notification. If an

---

[59] Sanetra (2000: 282).
[60] See Rączka in Salwa (ed.) (2000: 535).

employer is informed that a worker stopped caring for a child, he or she shall notify the worker of the obligation to return to work on the indicated date.

Legal protection against dismissal on the grounds of an application for, or the taking of, parental leave

Polish provisions afford employees on childcare leave strong protection from dismissal. The employer may not give notice or terminate the employment contract from the date of submission of a claim for childcare leave by the worker until the end of this leave. Dismissal in such cases is permitted only for economic, organisational, or technological reasons connected with production, declaration of bankruptcy, or liquidation of the company.

The Commissioner for Civil Rights has signalled, however, that some employers have dismissed women on childcare leave in order to reduce costs.[61] Termination under these circumstances may take place before the three-month termination notice period and without an indemnity payment because the female/male worker does not obtain remuneration during this period.[62] Many specific provisions also allow the termination of employment during childcare leave,[63] severely weakening the principle of protecting the stability of employment relationships.

Legal entitlement to return to the same, equivalent or similar job

The employer is obliged to allow the worker to return to a post equal or corresponding to that held before leave was taken, with remuneration not lower than that provided for in the contract previously held. According to case law, an employer violates the legal provisions when offering a woman returning from childcare leave less remuneration than she received prior to the leave.[64]

The legal guarantees for workers returning from childcare leave are weaker than in the framework agreement: Polish provisions do not oblige the employer to offer the worker the same post as held before leave was taken, even if this is possible. The new job may correspond with the worker's professional qualifications, but may still be very different from the previous job. At the end of childcare leave, an unemployed women may be

---

[61] See Complaint RPO/122523/93/III. See also Zieliński (1995: 24).

[62] Patulski (2000: 784).

[63] For example, Article 13 section 1 of the Act of 18 September 1982 on Employees of Public Administration Institutions, published in Dz. U. of 1982, No.31, item 214, Article 10(1)(2) of the Act of 22 March 1990 on Territorial Governments' Workers, published in Dz. U. of 1990, No.21, item 123.

[64] Resolution of the Supreme Court of 30 December 1985, III PZP 50/85, published in OSNCP 1986 Nos.7–8, item 118 and OSPIKA 1986 No.6, item 120.

granted benefits for each calendar day following registration in a district labour office, aslong as registration took place six months prior to the end of the childcare leave.[65]

7.2 Social security during parental leave, especially related to healthcare

In accordance with the 1996 Council of Ministers Ordinance, women employees retain the right to health benefits for herself and her family during childcare leave, as well as the right to occupy the home or other premises occupied before the childcare leave if occupancy is dependent on the employer.

The duration of the childcare leave is included in the period of employment, but it is not included in the employment period required to perform work of a given type or work in a given post according to specific provisions. A worker has the same rights connected with disability if it began during the childcare leave.[66]

Pursuant to Article 15(a) of the 1994 Act on Family, Care and Childcare Benefits, a person entitled to childcare leave is also entitled to the childcare benefit if the average monthly income per capita in the entitled person's family does not exceed 25 percent of the current average monthly retirement pension. As of 1 January 1999, childcare benefits are funded from the State Budget. Between 1 June 2002 and 31 May 2003, all social benefits, including childcare benefits, may only be granted to the poorest families, whose per capita income does not exceed the social minimum (548 PLN, approximately €136). A single parent is entitled to 491 PLN (approximately €122),[67] regardless of the number of children in the family.

The right to the childcare benefit may be granted until the end of the childcare leave, but no longer than 24 months (or longer if there is more than one child, a single parent, or a child with special needs). This benefit may not be granted if the childcare leave lasted less than three months, if the per capita family income is too high, if the parents or carers ceased to personally care for the child, if employed or working on another basis, undertaking paid activity, receiving an old-age pension or disability pension, or when the joint income exceeds the set limit.

---

[65] Judgement of the High Administrative Court dated 4 January 1991, II S.A. 878/90, published in OSDP 1992, No.3, item 62.

[66] The judgement of the Supreme Court of 15 January 1987, published in II URN 290/86, PIZS 1987, No.7, p. 17.

[67] There has been criticism that an unfair practice towards childcare recipients has been established.

The notion of the time off from work on grounds of *force majeure* corresponds in Polish law with leave from work for reasons of urgent necessity to care for the child or a sick family member, as well as other cases of justified absence at work for family reasons (not necessarily on grounds of *force majeure*). According to Section 188 of the Labour Code, a female/male employee raising at least one child under 14 years of age shall be entitled to two paid days off in the year.[68] If both parents or carers are employed, this right may be granted to only one of them. The right to receive benefits during this leave is regulated by the Act, on Pecuniary Benefits Paid by Social Security in Case of Illness and Maternity.

The benefit is granted in order to personally care for a healthy child under eight years of age in case of unexpected closing of the nursery, kindergarten or school, or an illness of the person normally caring for the child; to care for an ill child under 14 years of age; in the event of the illness of a family member (up to 14 days). The monthly care benefit is equal to 80 percent of the basic level, calculated on the basis of the average remuneration paid to the worker over the previous six months. Polish provisions are compatible with the requirements set forth in the framework agreement.

7.3 Parental leave and equal opportunities policy

The policies implemented by the Government from 1997 to 2001 consistently supported the preservation of the traditional family model and the equality provisions of the Directive were not complied with. A prolongation of obligatory maternity leave from 16 to 26 weeks, aimed at focusing care responsibilities on women and removing women from the labour market, was prevented by the opposition, so that ultimately 16 weeks further leave was optional, and men as well as women could take the leave and associated benefits. The former government also tried to extend family benefits, and grant them to families with many children, irrespective of their financial situation.

To save public funds, the present coalition Government has so far only reinstated the 16-week maternity leave, with the reservation that only the mother may take the first 14 weeks, and the remaining two weeks may be taken also by the father. It has not restored benefits for pregnant women, but has abolished the universal childbirth benefit, limiting the entitlement to childcare, family and care benefits, and reducing the amount of these benefits.

---

[68] It is emphasised that this right is granted to a working father (carer) even if the mother is not employed on the basis of an employment contract, because it is also related to the minor child's rights to have personal contact with both parents. See Patulski (2000: 794).

Initiatives to encourage the introduction of new flexible ways of organising work

The Government has not undertaken any public education campaigns explaining the change of the family model or the reorganisation of worktime to allow workers to reconcile professional and domestic responsibilities. No such actions seem to be planned for the near future. It should be emphasised that the establishment of 'parental' rights is, in principle, the only action so far undertaken to facilitate the reconciling of professional and family responsibilities. The possibility of more flexible working arrangements was included in a draft of amendment to the Labour Code, but it was not adopted.

7.4 Research on the reconciliation of family and work responsibilities and on sharing responsibilities between men and women

Public opinion polls in Poland have showed a slight difference in favour of the traditional marriage model over the partner-based model.[69] A 1996 survey of Polish women indicated that despite these preferences, the traditional division of labour in the home predominates in Polish families.[70] Irrespective of the family model, women perform the majority of everyday, time-consuming domestic tasks. The vast majority of women (83 percent) take care of handicapped and permanently ill persons. Husbands take responsibility for only a few activities (such as heating the house and ordering outside services). The division of house responsibilities is influenced mostly by the financial situation of the family, and the level of the woman's education. It is evident that women with the highest social and financial status are most burdened when it comes to domestic duties, since less educated women in a poor financial situation often have the help of children.

Research also shows that working women spend only slightly less time than non-working women on housework. Men rarely take over the sole responsibility for any domestic duties,[71] and working mothers spend three times more time than their

---

[69] Report from research prepared by Centre for Public Opinion Polls (hereinafter referred to as "CBOS"), BS/53/2000: *The situation of Polish families – estimations and propositions,* Warsaw, March 2000. Research on "Current problems and events" (117), made between 3 and 8 February 2000, on a representative sample of the Polish adult population (1,100 persons).

[70] CBOS Report No.1716, *Women on the division of domestic responsibilities in the family,* January 1997. Research between 9 and 13 November 1996, on a representative sample of the Polish adult female population, chosen by drawing (1,101 persons).

[71] Duch (2002: 132).

husbands on housework.[72] In Poland, even unemployed husbands fail to relieve the burden of housework from their wives, where the household relies on her income alone.[73]

Demographic, social or cultural considerations affecting the reconciliation of professional and family responsibilities

Despite clear social expectations that both parents should be equally responsible for a child's education, the main burden of childcare and education is borne by women. Although fathers become more involved as the children get older, the burden of education is borne by women in 45 percent of families with children in elementary school and in almost one-third of the families with older children (32 percent).[74]

Although men in Poland were granted access to maternity and childcare leave in the late 1970s (and on an equal basis with women in the 1990s), men rarely exercise these rights, although lack of precise statistical data makes it impossible to present this phenomenon in figures. Restricted access to nursery and kindergartens (the number of state-run institutions has been severely cut back and only high earners can afford private nurseries) forces women to use other forms of childcare; for example, older relatives, etc. Nevertheless, it remains extremely rare for the father to share childcare responsibilities on an equal basis.[75]

The cultural norms dictating that women are responsible for the home and men are responsible for financially supporting the family are among the reasons for the persisting inequalities in the division of household labour. These norms are deeply internalised by both sexes and even if a woman works, her salary only supplements the family budget. Social stereotypes referring to marital roles strengthen this imbalance. Educational materials reinforce the traditional family model, as well as the male and female roles. The media also perpetuates stereotypes portraying professional women as ordinary wives who maintain their traditional work at home, while minimising the value of their work in the public sphere. Neither the State nor employers do anything to counteract these stereotypes.

---

[72] Main Statistical Office (1987).

[73] Anna Dukaczewska-Nałęcz (2000) *Women's activity in the private sphere as a substitute of male domination in the public sphere* (facsimile of a dissertation). Institute of Philosophy and Sociology of the Polish Academy of Sciences. Warsaw, 1997, cited after Duch (2002: 128).

[74] Report on research by CBOS No. BS 168/168/98 "Raisingand caring for children in the family." Warsaw, December 1998. Research carried out by CBOS poll "Actual problems and events" (101), between 15 and 20 October 1998 on a representative sample of Polish adult population (1,094 persons).

[75] Nowakowska (2000: 14).

8. THE PRINCIPLE OF EQUAL TREATMENT OF MEN AND WOMEN IN OCCUPATIONAL SOCIAL SECURITY SCHEMES

Council Directive 96/97/EC of 20 December 1996 *amending Directive 86/378/EEC on the implementation of the principle of equal treatment for men and women in occupational social security schemes.*

8.1 National legal framework on social security schemes: General provisions

The system of social security in Poland has undergone many significant changes in the last 20 years. New types of social security benefits have been introduced (including some particularly important ones from the point of view of women), the substantive scope of already existing benefits has been increased, and the circle of persons entitled to these benefits has been extended (gradually covering more members of working persons' families).

When reforming the system of social security, the legislator gave it a common and unified character. The fundamental basis of the reform that entered into force on 1 January 1999 was that it obliged workers to pay a part of the contribution and its diversification due to different risks.

The first pillar is based, similarly to the old system, on the so-called 'intra-generation agreement', i.e. the repartition system, in which money paid by persons presently working is transferred to retired persons through the reformed Social Security Agency (ZUS). However, in contrast to the previous system, the amount of the old-age pension paid out from this pillar depends on the sum of paid contributions, saved in an individual account, and re-evaluated every year. In this system, the contribution to social security is paid in one sum, without relation to particular risks.

In the second pillar, part of the contributions paid by the insured person is invested within an open private retirement fund, administrated by the Universal Retirement Society. In the new system, the contribution is divided among four funds: old-age, disability, sickness and accidents. The legislature introduced an enumerative catalogue of persons, who must or may voluntarily be covered by particular types of insurance.

The third pillar encompasses all forms of voluntary insurance programmes, including Workers' Retirement Programmes.[76] According to the Act on Workers' Retirement Programmes, participation is not related to the coverage by the new retirement system. Therefore, workers who are subject to the old retirement rules due to their age may also join this programme. A worker may join or leave the programme any time. The contribution is proportional to remuneration and constitutes the worker's revenue, who must pay tax from the contribution paid on his/her behalf. Additional contributions, the amount of which is set as a given sum or as a percentage, are financed by the worker, but this is not obligatory.

The new system is obligatory for persons born after 31 December 1968, which means that the contribution paid from their income is shared between the first and second pillar. Persons born before 1 January 1949 and working exclusively in agriculture remain in the old system.[77] Persons with fewer than 15 years to retirement when the reform was introduced were excluded from the new system, because the new rules could significantly decrease their benefits.

The new retirement system complies with the requirements of the Directives insofar as it provides for the principle of equality, and theoretically speaking, the possibility to pursue a claim arising from the violation of this principle in court. Until recently there were no professional systems of social security within the meaning of the Directive 86/378/EEC and Directive 96/97/EC. The Act on Pension Schemes, which entered into force on 1 April 1999, does not fully comply with the requirements of the Directive with regard to different retirement age of women and men.

The actual situation after reform indicates even greater differences in pension amounts, to the detriment of women, because the new retirement system retained the different retirement age for men and women, while introducing a link between the amount of the old-age pension and the length of employment for which contributions were paid, as well as with the average life expectancy of persons of retirement age (both women and men). It is predicted that in the new system, the old-age pensions received upon retirement will be at least 50 percent lower for women than for men.[78] This problem

---

[76] The possibility to accumulate means of support in old-age took several forms. When the reform of the retirement system was introduced, it created another possibility in the form of Workers' Retirement Programmes, that seem favourable to both employers and workers. These programmes were regulated by the Act on the Workers' Retirement Programmes, dated 22 August 1997, Dz. U. of 1997, No.139, item 932 with subsequent amendments.

[77] As well as certain other categories of persons specified by law.

[78] Compare Wiktorow (2000: 51). The issue was also signalled by the Federation for Women and Family Planning in its independent report on the Observance of International Civil and Political Rights in Poland, submitted to the Committee for Human Rights of the United Nations. July 1999, p. 12.

may be worsened by persisting differences in women's and men's salaries. At the same time, the new retirement system has extended the average working time by around ten years, by gradually phasing out early retirement (by the year 2006).[79]

A draft legal act is currently being discussed that would essentially limit the employment possibilities for retirees. It was not mentioned during the debate that there are indirect disadvantages for women as a result of the lower retirement age. For instance, a 60-year-old woman loses the status of 'unemployed person' five years before a man does. This means the loss of the right to unemployment benefits, as well as pre-retirement benefits.[80]

An 'elastic retirement age' is being prepared according to which any working person, irrespective of sex, may retire between the ages of 62 and 65 years. This system would extend workers' protection against dismissal, since a worker may not be dismissed two years prior to retirement.

The length of the absence from work due to pregnancy and childbirth is regulated by the Labour Code, and the legal acts on social security enumerate the conditions for granting maternity benefits during maternity leave. These two rights usually go together, but not always. For instance, women in cottage industries have the right to maternity leave but not the right to maternity benefits.

Compliance of the legislation with the directives

It is difficult to determine whether the reform process regarding social security took account of the requirements set forth in the three Directives, or criticisms relating to the violation of the principle of equal treatment of men and women.

A provision of the 1991 Act on Employment and Unemployment, abolished as a result of a claim by the Commissioner for Civil Rights, deprived unemployed persons sharing a household with a spouse whose remuneration twice exceeded an average salary of the right to unemployment benefits. Although the provision was formulated in a fairly neutral way in terms of sex, in practice it discriminated against women primarily.

The Commissioner for Civil Rights has also handled cases where discrimination affected both men and women. For instance, on the basis of provisions of the Act on

---

[79] Wiktorow (2000: 50).

[80] See Matey-Tyrowicz (2000) However, as from 1 January 2002, due to the amendments to the Act on Employment and Counteracting Unemployment, pre-retirement benefit will be paid on the basis of more severe criteria and in a lower amount (80 percent of the old-age pension, but no less than 120 percent and no more than 200 percent of the unemployment benefit, currently equal to 476 PLN). Moreover, the unemployment benefit received will not be included into the required period of employment.

System of Social Security, health service institutions imposed an additional obligation upon female workers to prove that the disability of an unemployed husband prevented him from working. In contrast, male workers could receive the health benefit for an unemployed wife without having to prove her inability to work.[81]

Several claims of the Commissioner and judgments of the Constitutional Tribunal have referred directly to the different retirement ages for men and women. In the first case of this kind, the Tribunal recognised as unconstitutional provisions providing for the termination of the employment relationship of certain categories of academic teachers after they reached retirement age. Since these provisions referred to the general regulations on the retirement age, they meant in practice that the employment contract concluded with a woman had to end five years before the employment contract concluded with a man,[82] although work performed by academic teachers was recognised as work that is not affected by the specific biological or social situation of women. A similar opinion was delivered by the Constitutional Tribunal in 1994.[83] However, for procedural reasons it was impossible to give a judgement on the provisions of the Act on Employees of State Institutions, which provided for the possibility of earlier termination of female workers' employment contracts.

Generally speaking, the Tribunal has considered that the privileged treatment of women was admissible in certain situations, but it was forbidden to transform these 'equalising rights' into a form of differentiation of obligations, which in practice limited women's professional opportunities. However, the introduction of a legal provision allowing for earlier and forced termination of the employment contract for women should be recognised as a limitation of professional chances, contrary to the Constitution. Despite the determined and consistent position of the Constitutional Tribunal on this issue and pressure from women's groups, the process of eliminating provisions contrary to these principles may be gradual. By the end of 2000, four legal

---

[81] *Biuletyn RPO* 24859/97/III. A similar example of discrimination outside the sphere of social security was set forth in the Ordinance of the Council of Ministers from 1987, granting railway workers a 50 percent reduction for spouses' rail travel – this was always granted in case of a male worker, and in case of a female worker only when her husband was unable to work or she maintained him (RPO/60496/90/III). Compare Arcimowicz (2002: 113ff).

[82] Judgement dated 24 September 1991, KW 5/91, published in *OTK* 1991, item 96.

[83] Decision of the Constitutional Tribunal dated 15 November 1994, KW 9/94, published in *OTK* 1994, vol. II, p. 81.

acts still contained provisions inconsistent with the principle of equality, which were abolished only later.[84]

Article 40(1) of the Act on Pharmaceutics, Medical Materials, Pharmacies, Wholesale Houses and Pharmaceutical Inspection required that pharmacy managers be below the retirement age. This was recognised by the Constitutional Tribunal as contrary to Article 33(2) and Article 65(1) of the Constitution, and Article 11 of the UN Convention on Elimination of All Forms of Discrimination Against Women. The judgement confirmed that there was no difference in the ability of men or women to fulfil the duties required of a pharmacy manager, based on age.

Direct and indirect discrimination on the basis of sex in social security schemes

The Act on Workers' Retirement Systems (pension schemes) does not contain any provisions that directly discriminate against workers of one sex. In particular, it does not contain provisions contrary to the principle of equal treatment in terms of determining the persons who may participate in an occupational scheme.

Provisions contrary to the principle of equal treatment with regard to social security schemes

The Act on Workers' Retirement Systems explicitly stipulates that the pension scheme agreement may not set forth any other conditions for participation except those specified in the Act, but it would be advisable to add gender perspective to this provision.

A lack of data makes it impossible to assess how workers' pension schemes function in practice in terms of calculating the contributions. However, the provisions of the Act itself, which make the amount of the basic contribution paid by the employer dependant on the amount of the participant's salary, raise the fear that the system may turn out to be discriminatory against women, because in practice the principle of equal pay is not observed.

The payment of funds accumulated within the workers' retirement programme takes place upon a motion of the worker or *ex officio*. Payment upon a motion takes place after the worker reaches 60 years of age or upon early retirement or if a competent authority grants the rights to retirement benefit because of work. Payment *ex officio* takes place after the programme participant reaches 70 years of age. Although both age limits set in this provision are the same for women and men, since the reformed retirement system retains the retirement age difference for women, the age difference occurs also in case of

---

[84] For example, the Teachers' Charter was amended by an Act of 23 August 2001 (Dz. U. 2001 No.111, item 1194). The respective provisions of other acts became invalid with the publication of the last decision of Constitutional Tribunal on this issue from 5 December 2000 (Dz. U. of 2000 No.109, item 1165).

applying for early retirement. As a result, in the case of early retirement women are entitled to submit a motion for a payment of funds accumulated within the workers' retirement programme at the age of 55, while men may only do so at the age of 60. Regarding the provisions above, and the fact that the employer will pay the contribution for a male worker for a longer period of time, the provisions of the Act on the Workers' Retirement Programme are not consistent with the Directive under review.

Legal mechanisms to declare null and void any discrimination

The legal character of the retirement agreement within pensions schemes gives rise to much controversy and it is therefore difficult to state definitively whether it is possible for persons who consider themselves wronged by the failure to apply the principle of equal treatment to pursue a remedy in court. However, disputes between the parties may be recognised by the common courts, pursuant to the general provisions of the Code of Civil Procedure, although recourse through the courts is an expensive and time-consuming process. This could be partly resolved it the legislator were to provide for this agreement as a type of collective agreement, because the courts would have to apply the provisions on separate proceedings in social security matters free of charge, and apply the principles of the Labour Code, according to which provisions of a collective agreement that violate the principle of equal treatment in employment are not binding.

8.2 Legal means of redress

Protection against dismissal in the case of complaint of non-compliance with the principle of equal treatment

Although this matter is not explicitly regulated, it should be considered whether the provisions in the Labour Code on occupational schemes should be applied, pursuant to which an employer may not terminate an employment contract because an employee exercises his/her rights in case of a violation of the principle of equal treatment.

Monitoring mechanisms

There is no special monitoring mechanism to evaluate the legislation itself and its implementation from the perspective of the principle of equal treatment of women and men in social security. The Governmental Plenipotentiary for Equal Status of Women and Men may perform such a function to a certain extent. Traditionally, the function of monitoring the observance of the principle of equality, also in this field, was performed by the Commissioner for Civil Rights, and sex-based discriminatory provisions were abolished under the influence of the case law of the Constitutional Tribunal.

8.3 Implementation of the principle of equal treatment in matters of social security and equal opportunities strategies

It is difficult to speak of any effective strategy on equal opportunities in Poland, and subsequent changes to the social security system were not inspired by the principle of equal treatment, but were rather the result of the inefficiency of the previous system. This is clear from reading governmental substantiations to subsequent drafts of legal acts and the opinions of the Office of the Committee for European Integration, which do not refer to the Directives under review. The opinions of the Committee are similar in all cases – "the subject of the planned amendment to the act is not covered by the scope of the law of the European Union."

Perceived protection of women concerning maternity and social security

The protection of women in maternity is considered a factor in the *de facto* discrimination of women, however rather in employment than in social security. The social security benefits relating to maternity in Poland are comprehensive (for instance, until January 2002, Poland had the second longest compulsory maternity leave in Europe – 26 weeks, during which women obtained a benefit equal to 100 percent of their salaries). Reports of the Public Labour Inspection (the administrative authority charged with controlling employers' observance of employees' rights) show that at the time of recession, the dismissal of women returning to work after maternity leave became a common phenomenon.[85] However, the fact that the benefit period is included in the contributory period for retirement pension entitlements constitutes a positive feature of maternity leave regulations.

The amendment of the Act on Social Security Systems, planned by the current Government and aimed at budgetary savings, will also affect women's situation. Among other things, the age of a child whose parent may receive a guaranteed periodical benefit designated for single and unemployed parents raising a child was lowered from 16 to seven years. This benefit aims to help such persons adjust to a new situation and find new work.

---

[85] Kowalczyk (2002).

References

Bibliography

Proposition of harmonisation of the Polish law to the Communities' legislation as regard the equal treatment of men and women, in: Equality of the rights of men and women. Legislation of the European Union and the Council of Europe, Case-Law of the European Court of Justice and the European Court on Human Rights. Texts and Commentaries. Women's Rights Centre, Warsaw, 2000.

Arcimowicz, Jolanta (2002) The issue of discrimination of women in the activity of the Commission for Civil Rights. In Małgorzata Fuszara (ed.) *Women in Poland at the turn of the XXI century. New contract of the sexes?* Warsaw: Public Affairs Institute.

Baran, E. and K. W. Baran (1997) "Contraventions against the rights of the employee after the amendments of Art. 281 and 282 of the LC," *Prawo i Prokuratura* 1997, No.10.

Barzycka-Banaszczyk Małgorzata (2001) *Labour law.* 5th ed. Warsaw: C. H. Beck.

Bińczycka, T. (1998) "The protection of pregnant women and women during the motherhood period in the Community law and in the Polish labour law." *Praca i Zabezpieczenie Społeczne,* No.5.

Bochwic, T. (1999) *European Union – Women.* Warsaw: Information Centre of the Committee for the European Integration.

Boruta, Irena (1996) *The equality of men and women at work in the light of the European Community law.* Łódź: The University of Łódź.

Boruta, Irena (1998) "Protection of personal goods of the employee." *Praca i Zabezpieczenie Społeczne,* No.2.

Daszyńska, Maria Social and professional situation of women in the light of the poll of the Main Statistical Office. Analysis of the social and professional situation of women conducted on the basis of the research on women between 18–59 years of age in the year 1983, 1987, 1991. In *Women in the research of the Main Statistical Office.* Chancellery of the Diet. Bureau for Research and Expertise. Materials and Documents No.140. M-140.

Domański, G. (1992) *Satisifed slave? Studium o nierównościach między mężczyznami a kobietami w Polsce.* Warszawa: Instytut Filozofii i Socjologii PAN.

Duch, Danuta (2002) *On the power in the family.* In: Fuszara, Małgorzata, (ed.) *Women in Poland at the turn of the XXI century. New contract of the sexes?* Warsaw: Public Affairs Institute.

Dukaczewska-Nałęcz, Anna (2000) *Women's activity in the private sphere as a substitute of male domination in the public sphere* (facsimile of a dissertation). Institute of Philosophy and Sociology of the Polish Academy of Sciences. Warsaw, 1997.

Ereciński, T., J. Gudowski and M. Jędrzejewska (1997) "Commentary to the Civil Procedure Code." In T. Ereciński (ed.) *Civil Procedure Code, Part I, vol. 1.* Warsaw: Wydawnictwo Prawnicze.

Florek, Ludwik (1997) "The prohibition of discrimination in employment relationships." *Praca i Zabezpieczenie Społeczne,* Nos.1–2.

Florek, Ludwik (1998) "Expertise: Equal treatment of men and women as regard the labour law." In *Bureau of the Committee for European Integration. Labour law. Part I. Analysis*, Warsaw, 1998.

Florek, Ludwik (2000) "Equal treatment of men and women." In *Equality of the rights of men and women. Legislation of the European Union and the Council of Europe, Case-Law of the European Court of Justice and the European Court on Human Rights. Texts and Commentaries.* Warsaw: Women's Rights Centre.

Florek, Ludwik, Tadeusz Zieliński (2000) *Labour law*. 3rd ed. Warsaw: C. H. Beck.

Fuszara, Małgorzata (ed.) (2002) *Women in Poland at the turn of the XXI century. New contract of the sexes?* Warsaw: Public Affairs Institute.

Fuszara, Małgorzata, Eleonora Zielińska (1995) "Obstacles and Barriers to an Equal Status Act in Poland." In *Women: the Past and the New Role, Bulletin of the Centre for Europe,* No.1. Warsaw: Warsaw University.

Fuszara, Małgorzata, Eleonora Zielińska (2000) "Short but complicated history of the draft of the act on the equal status," *Prawo i Płeć*, No.1.

Fuszara, Małgorzta, Eleonora Zielińska (1998) "Faces of discrimination." In *Rzeczpospolita* 21 December 1998.

Garlicki, Leszek (2000) "Constitutional complaint as a mean of protection against discrimination." In *Equality of women and men in European retirement systems. Bulletin of the Centre for Information and Documentation of the Council of Europe.* No.2 2000. Warsaw: The Warsaw University European Centre.

Gersdorf, Małgorzata, Krzysztof Rączka, and Skoczyński Jacek (1999) "Commentaries." In Zbigniew Salwa (ed.) *Labour Code. Commentary,* Warsaw: Wydawnictwo Prawnicze.

Gersdorf, Małgorzata, Małgorzata Iżycka-Rączka, Jacek Jagielski, and Krzysztof Rączka (2000) *Allowances. Commentary to the act on pecuniary allowances from the social security system in case of illness or motherhood.* Warsaw: Przegląd Ubezpieczeń.

Gudowska, Beata (1998) *The social security law. Provisions, case-law, doctrine.* Kraków: Zakamycze.

Gutkowska, Krystyna *Peasant women on their families and conflicts therein.* Facsimile.

Iwulski, Jan, Walerian Sanetra (1996) *Labour Code. Unified text. Commentary,* Warsaw: Wydawnictwo Prawnicze.

Jackowiak, Urszula (1994) *Occupational situation of women.* Gdansk: Wydawnictwo Prawnicze Lex.

Jedrasik-Jankowska, Inetta (2001) *Old-age insurances. Three pillars.* Warsaw:b Wydawnictwo Prawnicze PWN.

Jedrasik-Jankowska, Inetta (2002) *Insurance against accidents and diseases.* Warsaw: Wydawnictwo Prawnicze Lexis-Nexis.

Kaczyński, L. (1997) "The principle of freedom of contracts in the labour law after the amendments of the Labour Code," *Państwo i Prawo* No.3.

Kłos, B. *Assistance to lonely mothers. Comments on the draft of the act on amending the act on unemployment and counteracting the unemployment.* Parliamentary facsimile No.2314, Bureau of Expertise of the Diet, Economic and Social Analysis Department, Information No.773.

Knothe, Maria Anna, Ewa Lisowska (1999) *Women in the labour market; negative changes and enterprise as consequences of economical transformation.* Warsaw: Foundation Centre for Promotion of Women.

Kołodziejczyk, Piotr (2000) "The harmonisation of the law in the area of social policy – basic directions of amendments of the Polish law." *Bulletin of the Centre for Information and Documentation of the Council of Europe.* No.2 2000. Warsaw: The Warsaw University European Centre.

Kowalczyk, Aleksandra (2002) "Work and Career." *Profit,* No.4/2002.

Kurzynowski, Adam (ed.) (2001) *Social-professional situation of unemployed women. Barriers and stimulators of their activation.* Warsaw: Szkoła Główna Handlowa. Instytut Gospodarstwa Społecznego.

Łagodziński, Wiesław (1995) "Women in the labour market in the light of the Survey on Economical Activity of the Population (BAEL)." In *Participation of women in public life.* Bulletin of the Centre for Information and Documentation of the Council of Europe, 1995, No.5. Warsaw: The Warsaw University European Centre.

Łętowska, Ewa (1992) *How Did the Commissioner for Civil Rights Begin?* Łódź: Wydawnictwo Master.

Lisowska, Ewa (1997) "Women entrepreneurs in Poland, Lithuania and Ukraine – comparative analysis." In *Kobieta i Biznes,* No.1–2/1997.

Lisowska, Ewa (2001) *Enterprises of women in Poland in comparison to countries of Central and Eastern Europe.* Warsaw: Szkoła Główna Handlowa.

Liszcz, T. (1998) *Introduction to the Labour Code.* Kraków: Zakamycze.

Main Statistical Office (GUS) (1987) *The Analysis of the Time Budget of the Polish Population in 1976 and 1984.* Warsaw: GUS.

Main Statistical Office (GUS) (1999) *Statistical Yearbook of Labour.* Warsaw: GUS.

Main Statistical Office (GUS) (2000a) *Statistical Yearbook of the Republic of Poland 2000,* Year LXI. Warsaw: GUS.

Main Statistical Office (GUS) (2000b) *Economic activity of the population of Poland,* Second half of the year 2000. Information and Statistics series. Warsaw: GUS.

Matey-Tyrowicz, Maria (2000) "The principle of equal treatment of men and women in the light of the Constitution of the Republic of Poland and European law." *Bulletin of the Centre for Information and Documentation of the Council of Europe.* No.2 2000. Warsaw: The Warsaw University European Centre.

Muszalski, Wojciech (ed.) (2000) *Labour Code. Commentary.* Warsaw: C. H. Beck.

Nałęcz, A. (ed.) (1999) *The Labour Code with Commentary.* Gdańsk.

Nowakowska, Urszula (2000) "Study of the legal situation." In Barbara Żylicz (ed.) *The impact of the process of privatisation on the situation of women. Polish women and the economy of the transformation period. Report of the research of 1999,* No.2. Warsaw: Women's Rights Centre.

Oniszczyk, Jerzy (1998) "The unconstitutionality of regulations discriminating women in employment due to attaining the retirement age." In *Prawa i Zabezpieczenie Społeczne*, No.4/1998.

Paruszewska, Wanda (2000) "The new retirement system – a financial trap for women." In *Prawo i Płeć*, No.2/2000.

Patulski, Wladyslaw (2000) "Comments on Article 186 of the Labour Code." In Wojciech Muszalski (ed.), *Labour Code. Commentary*, Warsaw, C. H. Beck.

Pawłowska, Jadwiga, Krzysztof Walczak (eds.) (2001) *Social security: contribution payer's service.* Warsaw: Beck Info Biznes.

Romer, Maria (2000) "Rules of granting old-age pensions to women in the Polish legal system and courts practice." In *Equality of women and men in European retirement systems. Bulletin of the Centre for Information and Documentation of the Council of Europe.* No.2 2000. Warsaw: The Warsaw University European Centre.

Romer, Maria (2000) *Labour law. Commentary.* Warsaw: Wydawnictwo Prawnicze.

Salwa, Zbigniew (ed.) (2000) *Labour Code. Commentary.* 2nd ed. Warsaw: Wydawnictwo Prawnicze.

Sanetra, Walerian (2000) "Expertise on Directive 96/34/EC on parental leave." In Maria Matey-Tyrowicz (ed.) *Harmonisation of the Polish law with European Communities' law.* Vol. 9 *Labour law.* Part I. *Analysis.* Warsaw: Office for the European Integration Committee.

Sikorska, Jadwiga (ed.) (1996) *Women and their husbands.* Warsaw: Institute of Philosophy and Sociology of the Polish Academy of Sciences.

Skoczyński, Jacek *The lowest remuneration, Encyclopaedia of the labour law and the social security.*

Skoczyński, Jacek (1999) "The principle of equal treatment of employees." In *Praca i Zabezpieczenie Społeczne*, Nos.7–8.

Skoczyński, Jacek (2000) "Amendments in the Act on Workers' Retirement Programmes." In *Praca i Zabezpieczenie Społeczne*, Nos.7–8.

Sobczyk, Adam (1999) "The principle of equality of employees in the employment relationships." In *KPP*, No.1/1999.

Social policy towards families of single mothers in Poland. Documents for conference, Warsaw, 15 January 2001, Public Affairs Institute, facsimile.

State Employment Inspection (2000) "Report on the Observance of Provisions Protecting Women's Work and the Prohibition of Discrimination on Grounds of Sex." *Prawo u Płeć*, 2000 No.2, 28–31.

Teutsch, Agata (2000) "Women's Organisations facing the new retirement system." In *Equality of women and men in European retirement systems. Bulletin of the Centre for Information and Documentation of the Council of Europe.* No.2 2000. Warsaw: The Warsaw University European Centre.

Tomaszewska, Ewa (2000) *"Retirement age of women and men."* In *Equality of women and men in European retirement systems.* Bulletin of the Centre for Information and Documentation of the Council of Europe. No.2 2000. Warsaw: The Warsaw University European Centre.

Tryfan, Barbara (1998) *Enterprise of Peasant Women in Poland in Comparison with Selected Countries*. SCRIPT. Warsaw.

Warylewski, J. (1999) *Sexual harassment in the workplace*. Sopot: Wydawnictwo Prawnicze Lex.

Wichrowska-Janikowska, Ewa (1996) "Women's rights in the activities of the Commissioner for Civic Rights." In *Bulletin of the Commissioner for Civic Rights*, No.30.

Wiktorow, Aleksandra (2000) "Differentiated retirement age – encouraging discrimination against women." In *Equality of women and men in European retirement systems*. Bulletin of the Centre for Information and Documentation of the Council of Europe. No.2 2000. Warsaw: The Warsaw University European Centre.

Women's Rights Centre (2000b) "Proposition of harmonisation of the Polish law with the Community legislation as regard the equal treatment of men and women." In *Equality of the rights of men and women. Legislation of the European Union and the Council of Europe, Case-Law of the European Court of Justice and the European Court on Human Rights*. Texts and Commentaries. Warsaw: Women's Rights Centre.

Wratny, J., D. Kotowska, B. Skulimowska, and J. Szczot (1999) *New Labour Code with the commentary*. Warsaw: Wydawnictwo Prawnicze.

Zapalska, Anna (1997) "A Profile of Women Entrepreneurs in Poland." In *Journal of Small Business Management*, 35(4): 76–82.

Zielińska, E. (2000) "Burden of proof in case of discrimination on grounds of sex." In *Equality of the rights of men and women: Legislation of the European Union and the Council of Europe, Case-Law of the European Court of Justice and the European Court on Human Rights. Texts and Commentaries*, Warsaw: Women's Rights Centre.

Zielińska, E. (2000) "Sexual harassment in the legislation of the European Union." In *Equality of the rights of men and women: Legislation of the European Union and the Council of Europe, Case-Law of the European Court of Justice and the European Court on Human Rights. Texts and Commentaries*, Warsaw: Women's Rights Centre.

Zieliński, Tadeusz (1995) "The position of woman in the family and political life." In *Participation of women in public life. Bulletin of the Centre for Information and Documentation of the Council of Europe*. No.5, 1995. Warsaw: The Warsaw University European Centre.

Zieliński, Tadeusz (1997) "Report on the discrimination in employment." In *Documents for the 15th World Congress of the International Society for Labour Law and Social Security*.

Zieliński, Tadeusz (ed.) (2000) *The Labour Code with Commentary*. Warsaw: Dom Wydawniczy, ABC.

Żylicz, Barbara (ed.) (2000) "The influence of the privatisation process on the situation of women." *In Polish women in the economy of transformation period. Research Report*. Warsaw: Women's Rights Centre.

Żylicz, Barbara (2000) "Polish women and the economy of the transformation period. Results of in-depth group interviews, carried out by the Women's Rights Centre in 1999." In *Prawo i Płeć*, No.2/2000.

Reports

Centre for Public Opinion Polls (1993) Report from research on *"Traditional or partner-based family model."* Warsaw, 1993.

Centre for Public Opinion Polls (1993) Report from research on *"Women on their private life."* Warsaw, October 1993.

Centre for Public Opinion Polls (1997) Report from research on *"Women on the division of domestic responsibilities in the family."* Warsaw, January 1997.

Centre for Public Opinion Polls (1998) Report from research on *"Bringing up and caring for children in the family."* Warsaw, December 1998.

Centre for Public Opinion Polls (1999) Report from research on *"Opinions on retirement age of women and men."* Warsaw, November 1999.

Centre for Public Opinion Polls (2000) Report from research on *"The situation of Polish families – estimates and proposals."* Warsaw, March 2000.

Commissioner for Civil Rights (1991) Report for 1991 on the observance of the law and citizens' freedoms. Parliamentary paper No.32, dated 10 December 1991.

Commissioner for Civil Rights (1997) Report for the period between 13 February 1994 and 12 February 1995. Bulletin of the Commissioner for Civil Rights – Materials. 1997, No.33.

Council of Ministers (1997) *National Action Programme for Women*, adopted on 7 May 1997 by the Council of Ministers. Warsaw.

Council of Ministers (1999) *State Pro-Family Policy Programme*, adopted on 3 November 1999 by the Council of Ministers. Warsaw.

European Commission (2000) *Regular Report on Poland's Progress towards Accession*, facsimile.

European Commission (2001) Chapter 13 – "Employment and Social Policy." In *Regular Report on Poland's Progress Towards Accession.*

Government of the Republic of Poland (1996) *Report on the fulfilment in legislation and practice of obligations under the provision of Articles 6–15 of the Internal Covenant on Economic, Social and Cultural Rights for the period from 1 January 1992 to 31 December 1994*, Warsaw, January 1996.

Government of the Republic of Poland (1999) *Report on the realisation of the National Programme of Preparation for Accession to the European Union in 1998*, Employment market and social policy, facsimile.

Ministry of Labour and Social Policy (2000) *Proposition of harmonisation of the Polish law with the Community provisions as regard the equal treatment of men and women, Equality of the rights of men and women: Legislation of the European Union and the Council of Europe, Case-Law of the European Court of Justice and the European Court on Human Rights: Texts and Commentaries*, Women's Rights Centre, Warsaw.

Negotiation position of Poland in the area of social policy and employment, facsimile.

State Employment Inspection (2000) *"Report on the evaluation of the observance of the provisions referring to the protection of women's work and the interdiction of discrimination on grounds of sex."* In *Prawo i Płeć,* No.2.

Women's Rights Centre (2000) *Report – Polish Women in the 1990s.* Warsaw.

Women's Association for Gender Equality (2000) Beijing 1995, Implementation of the Platform for Action by the Polish Government: Alternative report prepared for 44th session of the Commission on the Status of Women, Warsaw, January 2000.

Women's Rights Centre (2000) The impact of the process of privatisation on the situation of women. Polish women and the economy of the transformation period. Research report 1999, ed. B. Żylicz, Warsaw 2000 No.2.

List of legislation screened

Acts

Act of 17 November 1964, the Civil Procedure Code, in Dziennik Ustaw (Official Journal) of 1964, No.43, item 296 with subsequent amendments.

Act of 26 June 1974, the Labour Code, unified text in Dz. U. of 1998, No.21, item 94, with subsequent amendments.

Act of 17 December 1974 on Pecuniary Benefits in Case of Illness and Maternity, unified text in Dz. U. of 1983, No.30, item 143, with subsequent amendments.

Act of 12 June 1975 on the Benefits for Accidents at Work and Occupational Diseases, unified text in Dz. U. of 1983, No.30, item 144, with subsequent amendments.

Act of 19 December 1975 on the Social Insurance of Persons Performing Work on the Basis of Contract of Agency or Contract of Mandate, unified text in Dz. U. of 1995, No.65, item 333, with subsequent amendments.

Act of 18 December 1976 on the Social Security of Persons Performing Economic Activity and Their Families, unified text in Dz. U. of 1989, No.46, item 250, with subsequent amendments.

Act of 6 March 1981 on the State Employment Inspection, unified text in Dz. U. of 1985, No.54, item 276, with amendments.

Act of 26 January 1982, Teachers' Charter, Dz. U. of 1997, No.56, item 357 with subsequent amendments.

Act of 18 September 1982 on Employees of Public Administration Institutions, published in Dz. U. of 1982, No.31, item 214.

Act of 24 June 1983 on the Social Employment Inspection, Dz. U. of 1983, No.35, item 163, with amendments.

Act of 25 July 1985 on Research and Development Units, Dz. U. of 1991, No.44, item 194, with subsequent amendments.

Act of 25 November 1986 on the Organisation and Financing of the System of Social Security, in force until 1 January 1999.

Act of 22 March 1990 on Territorial Governments' Workers, Dz. U. of 1990, No.21, item 123.

Act of 29 November 1990 on Social Assistance, unified text in Dz. U. of 1998, No.64, item 414, with subsequent amendments.

Act of 20 December 1990 on Social Security of Farmers, unified text in Dz. U. of 1998, No.7, item 25, with subsequent amendments.

Act of 23 May 1991 on the Trade Unions, Dz. U. of 1991, No.55, item 234 with amendments.

Act of 10 October 1991 on Pharmaceutics, Medical Materials, Pharmacies, Wholesale Houses and Pharmaceutical Inspection, Dz. U. of 1991, No.105, item 452 with subsequent amendments.

Act of 17 October 1991 on the Revalorisation of Retirement Pays and Pensions, Dz. U. of 1991, No 104, item 450, with amendments.

Act of 16 December 1991, The European Agreement, establishing the association of the Republic of Poland and the European Communities and the Member States, Dz. U. of 1994, No.11, item 38.

Act of 1 December 1994 on Family, Care and Childcare Benefits, unified text in Dz. U. of 1998 No.102, item 651, with subsequent amendments.

Act of 14 December 1994 on Employment and Counteracting the Unemployment, unified text Dz. U. of 1997, No 25, item 128, with amendments.

Act of 14 December 1994 on Employment and Counteracting Unemployment, unified text in Dz. U. of 2001, No.6, item 56, with subsequent amendments.

Act of 2 February 1996 on Amending the Labour Code and Some Other Acts, Dz. U. of 1996, No 24, item 110.

Act of 23 September 1996 on Amending the Act on the Social Security of Farmers, Dz. U. of No.124, item 585.

Act of 2 April 1997, the Constitution of the Republic of Poland, Dz. U. of 1997, No 78, item 48.

Act of 6 June 1997 on the Penal Code, Dz. U. of 1997, No.88, with amendments.

Act of 22 August 1997 on the Workers' Retirement Programmes, Dz. U. of 1997, No.139, item 932, with subsequent amendments.

Act of 13 October 1998 on the Social Security System, Dz. U. 1998, No.137, item 887, with amendments.

Act of 17 December 1998 on Old Age Pensions and Disability Pensions Paid by the Social Security Fund, Dz. U. of 1998 No.162, item 1118, with subsequent amendments.

Act of 25 June 1999 on Pecuniary Benefits Paid by the Social Security in Case of Sickness or Maternity, Dz. U. of 1999 No.66, item 636, with subsequent amendments.

Act of 19 November 1999 on Economic Activity, Dz. U. of 1999 No.101, item 1178, with subsequent amendments.

Act of 24 August 2001 on Amending the Labour Code and Some Other Acts, Dz. U. of 2001, No.128, item 1405.

Decrees and Ordinances

Ordinance of the Council of Ministers of 31 December 1975 on the Workers' Rights for Persons Working in Cottage Industry, Dz. U. of 1976, No.3, item 19 with subsequent amendments.

Ordinance of the Council of Ministers of 28 May 1996 on Childcare Leave and Childcare Benefits, Dz. U. of 1996 No.60, item 277, with subsequent amendments.

Ordinance of the Council of Ministers of 10 September 1996 on the Specification of Occupations Prohibited to Women, Dz. U. of 1996, No.114, item 545.

Ordinance of the Council of Ministers of 20 October 2001 on the Establishment of the Governmental Plenipotentiary for Family and Equal Status, Dz. U. of 2001, No.122, item 1331.

Ordinance of the Council of Ministers of 27 November 2001 on Amending the Ordinance of the Council of Ministers on the Establishment of the Governmental Plenipotentiary for Family and Equal Status, Dz. U. of 2001, No.140, item 1572.

Ordinance of the Minister of Health and Social Security of 11 September 1996 on Carcinogenic Factors in the Work Environment and the Supervision Over the Health of the Employees Exposed to These Factors, Dz. U. of 1996, No.121, item 571.

Ordinance of the Minister of Labour and Social Policy of 29 May 1996 on the Method of Determination of the Remuneration during the Period of Non-Performance of Work and the Remuneration Constituting the Basis for Calculation of the Compensation, Severance Pays, Compensatory Allowances to the Remuneration and Other Fringe Benefits Provided for in the Labour Code, Dz. U. of 1996, No.62, item 289 with amendments.

Ordinance of the Ministry of Health and Social Security of 9 July 1996 on Research and Measurements of Factors Harmful to Health at Work, Dz. U. of 1996, No.86, item 394.

Ordinance of the Minister of Labour and Social Policy of 26 September 1997 on General Provisions on the Safety and Hygiene at Work, Dz. U. of 1997, No.129, item 844.

Ordinance of the Minister of Labour and Social Policy of 29 January 1998 on the Minimum Salary for Work for the Employees, Dz. U. of 1998, No.16, item 74.

Ordinance of the Minister of Labour and Social Policy of 9 February 2000 on Detailed Rules of Running the Labour Intermediation, Professional Counselling, Organisation of Training for Unemployed Persons, Creation of Methodical Background for the Professional Information and Professional Counselling and Organisation and Financing the Labour Clubs, Dz. U. of 2000, No.12, item 146.

Equal Opportunities for Women and Men in Romania

Table of contents

Executive Summary 425

Country report: Introduction 433

1. The principle of equal pay for work of equal value 436
    1.1 National legal framework: General provisions 436
    1.2 Legal foundations and institutional structures 437
    1.3 Job classification 438
    1.4 Available legal procedures 438
    1.5 Means of informing employees of their rights 440
    1.6 Out of court alternatives 440
    1.7 Role of trade unions 441
    1.8 Women's factual situation 441

2. Equal treatment for women and men as regards access to employment, vocational training and promotion, and working conditions 443
    2.1 National legal framework: General provisions 443
    2.2 The concept of discrimination on grounds of sex: Definition and legal sanctions 443
    2.3 Access to employment, vocational training and promotion 444
    2.4 Protective measures for women in the labour market 445
    2.5 Prohibition of dismissal 446
    2.6 Legal status of sexual harassment 446

3. Protection of pregnant women from the inherent risk of certain activities and related employment rights 448
    3.1 Legal and conceptual framework 448
    3.2 Risk assessment and employers' obligations 448
    3.3 Case law 449
    3.4 Night work 450

3.5   Maternity leave 450
3.6   Prohibition of dismissal and employment rights 451

4. The burden of proof in cases
   of discrimination based on sex 453
   4.1   Legal and conceptual framework
         concerning indirect discrimination 453
   4.2   The burden of proof and rules of evidence 453
   4.3   Case law 454

5. Non-discrimination against part-time workers 456
   5.1   National legal framework and employment
         conditions concerning part-time workers 456

6. The principle of equal treatment
   for self-employed workers and their assisting spouses 458
   6.1   National legal framework: General provisions 458
   6.2   Social rights of spouses 459
   6.3   Contributory social security schemes 460
   6.4   Related research and statistics 460
   6.5   Legal means of redress 462

7. The framework on parental leave 463
   7.1   National legal framework: General provisions 463
   7.2   Social security during parental leave 465
   7.3   Parental leave and equal opportunities policy 465
   7.4   Research on sharing family
         and professional responsibilities 466

8. The principle of equal treatment
   in occupational social security schemes 470
   8.1   National legal framework: General provisions 470
   8.2   Legal means of redress 476
   8.3   Implementation of the principle of equal treatment 477

Executive summary for Romania

INTRODUCTION

Since the Revolution of December 1989, Romania has undergone a dramatic period of integration into the international legal order, withdrawing reservations formulated during the communist period for certain international human rights conventions and now boasting a well-articulated and non-discriminatory framework *de jure*.

While the promotion of equal opportunities and treatment did not constitute a priority for any of the governments of the last decade, the necessary preconditions for improving the legislation have been created through *inter alia* the ratification of the Revised European Social Charter, to which Romania acceded with certain reservations, and the adoption of the National Action Plan for Equal Opportunities for Women and Men in 2000.

The establishment in 2000 of the Commission for Equal Opportunities within the Economic and Social Council, aimed at ensuring the permanent exchange between different partners of information, experiences and measures in the field of equal treatment and the elaboration of recommendations for the authorities of the central public administration, was a positive step towards guaranteeing the *de facto* implementation of equal opportunities, but the activities developed by this and other structures for the promotion of equality are not sufficiently coordinated and, as a result, limited in their impact. The absence of a single, comprehensive strategy to prioritise this issue, which is due largely to the lack of political will, is a significant deficiency in the Romanian approach towards ensuring equal opportunities.

SUMMARY OF KEY POINTS

Defining principles

The principle of equal pay for equal work is explicitly enshrined in the Romanian Constitution, the Labour Code and the Act on Remuneration. The recently promulgated Act on Equal Opportunities for Women and Men is the only legal text providing for the principle of equal pay for work of equal value. Furthermore, it explicitly defines and prohibits both direct and indirect discrimination, and sexual harassment, which will also constitute a punishable offence in the Criminal Code.

Protective measures

Romanian legislation does not oblige employers to evaluate the conditions, processes and risk agents that could endanger the health and safety of pregnant or breastfeeding workers, but there is a general legal obligation whereby employers must inform each person prior to his/her employment of the risks s/he will be exposed to at the workplace, including the necessary prevention measures. The Collective Work Agreement extended the prohibition of night work for pregnant women from five months, as stipulated by the Labour Code, to six months. Women are entitled, but not obliged, to take maternity leave of 126 days. The Labour Code prohibits an employer from terminating an employment contract during medical leave, pregnancy, maternity leave, or while breastfeeding or caring for a sick child until the age of three, or while the husband is performing compulsory military service.

Burden of proof

Current legal provisions in Romania, contrary to the EU Directive, stipulate that the burden of proof rests with the plaintiff. As a result, it is very difficult for employees to prove discrimination and they are discouraged from bringing cases to court. Between 1990–2000, no cases were taken to court involving the violation of the principle of equal treatment for women and men in relation to employment, vocational training, remuneration, social protection and promotion, or working conditions. The new Act on Equal Opportunities does not shift the burden of proof from the employee to the employer or the alleged perpetrator. According to the Code of Civil Procedure though, the judge must play 'an active role' in determining the truth and judges have always obliged the defendant (mainly in labour law cases) to provide all the necessary documents. This means that the burden of proof has shifted more or less in practice. The problem with this approach, unlike where the principle is legally provided for in accordance with the Directive, is that if the defendant cannot provide proof of his/her innocence, there is no automatic presumption in favour of the plaintiff.

Part-time workers

There is no legal or contractual definition *in terminis* of the concept of a part-time worker in Romanian legislation, but the Collective Work Agreement does stipulate that part-time programs may be established for certain activities, positions and categories of personnel provided in the collective work agreements for institutions/companies with a duration of working time of six, four or two hours per day. During the period of transition, however, a number of new labour patterns emerged, including part-time work, which are not yet entirely regulated. In the period of 1994–1998, the number of part-time workers did not vary much, ranging from 13 percent to 15 percent of the total number of workers. In 1998, 15 percent of employed Romanians worked part-time, more than half of whom were women.[1] In the year 2000, part-time workers and full-time workers who worked less than 40 hours per week represented 32.2 percent of the total occupied population. Of the persons working part-time, 55.4 percent were women.[2] It is significant that part-time work is seen as an alternative to unemployment and that over 90 percent of part-time workers interviewed stated that they were searching for a full-time job.[3]

Self-employed workers

The term 'self-employed' is not legally defined, but statistically it is defined as "a person who conducts his/her activity at his/her own headquarters or runs an individual business without employing other persons, with the possibility of assistance from unremunerated family members." Because self-employed persons are not conceptually deemed an important component of the labour market, the legislation in force does not include any special provisions regarding this category. Neither the political decision makers nor civil society have been specifically concerned with the status of self-employed persons and even less concerned with promoting equal treatment for men and women engaged in independent activities. Statistics indicate that the number of the self-employed persons in Romania in 2000 was 1,717,000 (29.1 percent of whom were women and 15.2 percent in urban areas),[4] and that self-employed persons and unpaid family members comprised 42.4 percent of the active population, including 91 percent in rural areas. These statistics are misleading, however, since self-employment in rural areas is a means of survival, and not an income-generating enterprise.

Parental leave

According to tradition and religious customs, the role of Romanian women is to raise, care for and educate children in the family. However, following an increase in the rate of unemployment among men, they were forced to take over some of the family obligations of their working partners. One of the few legislative exceptions encouraging

---

[1] UNDP (2000b: 22).
[2] UNDP (2000a: 23).
[3] UNDP (2000b: 22).
[4] UNDP (2000a: 21).

men to engage in childcare activities is Act No.210 of 1999,[5] which stipulates that family doctors shall issue a certificate to fathers who acquire childcare knowledge. The right to parental leave is legally provided for, but there are no specific references regarding the possibility to divide the leave into several fragments or for both parents to benefit alternatively from such leave. The right to parental leave is also not part of a complex program of measures explicitly intended to harmonise professional and family life and there are no measures to guarantee the professional reintegration of employed parents who interrupt their activity to raise young children, with the result that for the most part they are unemployed at the end of the leave.

Social security schemes

Romanian legislation on social security system generally complies with the EU directives, and with the exception of the different retirement ages for women and men, there are no regulations that are discriminatory towards women. However, the social security system has a different impact on men and women, as the level of protection provided by the system is directly proportional to the level of income obtained prior to the occurrence of the insured risk. The effect of this proportionality principle is the preservation of the *de facto* differences between the salaries of men and women and primarily differences in their social security rights.

---

[5] Act No.210 of 1999 on Paternity Leave, published in *Monitorul Oficial,* Part I, No.654 of 31.12.1999.

Recommendations related to each specific directive

Council Directive 75/117/EEC of 10 February 1975 *on the approximation of laws of the Member States relating to the implementation of the principle of equal pay for women and men*

- Specific measures should be adopted to ensure that provisions appearing in collective agreements, wage rating lists or individual work agreements that are contrary to the principle of equal pay shall be, or may be, declared void.

- Statistical or jurisprudential records should be developed to determine the extent of discrimination in the public and private sectors.

- Surveys should be carried out to determine whether the lack of case law in this field is due to difficulties posed by court proceedings or whether it is because the principle is observed in practice.

Council Directive 76/207/EEC of 9 February 1976 *on the implementation of the principle of equal treatment for men and women as regards access to employment, vocational training and promotion, and working conditions*

- Protective provisions, particularly those related to night work, should be revised.

- *De facto* equal access to jobs and promotions should be monitored.

- Vocational training should be made more accessible to girls and women, who should also be encouraged to acquire it, including through nationwide information campaigns.

Council Directive 92/85/EEC of 19 October 1992 *on the introduction of measures to encourage improvements in the safety and health at work of pregnant workers and workers who have recently given birth or are breastfeeding*

- The terms 'pregnant worker', 'worker who has given birth' and 'breastfeeding worker' should be legally defined.

- Employers should be legally obliged to evaluate working conditions and to inform pregnant and breastfeeding workers and workers who recently gave birth of those conditions.

- There should be a legal provision stipulating an exemption from work if it is not possible to transfer the employee to a different working place.

- There should be a legal provision stipulating that a female employee may attend a medical examination during working hours without a decrease in pay.

- There should be a legal provision stipulating a proportional increase (according to the inflation rate) of allowance during maternity leave and during leave to raise children until the age of two.

- There should be a legal provision stipulating measures to be taken in cases where a transfer to other work is technically and/or objectively unfeasible.

- Those agents, processes, and working conditions that physically and/or mentally affect pregnant and breastfeeding employees should be listed.

Council Directive 97/80/EC of 15 December 1997 *on the burden of proof in cases of discrimination based on sex*

- A legal provision regulating the reversal of the burden of proof should be adopted.

- Efficient means by which to inform employees how to bring a case of discrimination to court should be elaborated.

- Lawyers and judges should be given appropriate teaching and practical training on how to handle cases of gender-based discrimination.

Council Directive 97/81/EC of 15 December 1997 *concerning the framework agreement on part-time work concluded by UNICE, CEEP and the ETUC*

- The term 'part-time worker' should be legally defined.

- Flexible work programs, including part-time work, that would allow inter alia women and men to reconcile their professional and family responsibilities, continue studies, or prepare for retirement, should be developed.

Council Directive 86/613/EEC of 11 December 1986 *on the application of the principle of equal treatment between men and women engaged in an activity, including agriculture, in a self-employed capacity, and on the protection of self-employed women during pregnancy and motherhood*

- Special regulations should be adopted in order to clarify the legal status of self-employed persons in accordance with the meaning and intent of the Directive, and – to the greatest possible extent – to establish a clearer demarcation between a freelance profession or trade exercised in order to earn a living for self-employed persons and his/her family, and a commercial activity conducted with a view to obtaining profit.

- The notion of self-employed farmer should be legally defined.

- Once a special regulation referring to self-employed persons has been adopted, it should include provisions on the measures intended for the application of the principle of equal treatment and equal opportunities for men and women also with regard to this category of workers.

- A review of the statistical indicators used in Romania should be carried out in order to harmonise them with those used in the European Union. Comparisons should be made between elements of the same type, and measured with the same units in order to facilitate a comparative analysis.

Council Directive 96/34/EC of 3 June 1996 *on the framework agreement on parental leave concluded by UNICE, CEEP, and the ETUC*

- Research should be carried out to determine the de facto situation regarding the distribution of responsibilities and time budget allocated to household activities by both parents.

- Measures should be adopted to protect employed parents against the risk of dismissal/change in position/loss of rights held prior to or during parental leave.

- Provisions should be adopted to guarantee the professional reintegration of employed parents who interrupt their activity to raise young children.

- Affordable care services for children, elderly and disabled persons should be created.

- Employers should be encouraged to adopt efficient measures to support employees with family responsibilities.

- Trade unions, employers' associations, etc. should make it a priority to support the reconciliation of family and professional responsibilities.

- Social partners should monitor the fulfilment of the obligations regarding the adaptation of community provisions referring to the reconciliation of professional and family responsibilities.

- The matter of equal opportunities for men and women should be included in school curricula in order to teach young people respect for the partnership principle in family life and equal opportunities in employment and public life.

Council Directive 96/97/EC of 20 December 1996 *amending Directive 86/378/EEC on the implementation of the principle of equal treatment for men and women in occupational social security schemes*

- Gender and social security statistics should be systematised to enable comparisons between the situation of men and women, as well as an evaluation of the progress in the application of the principle of equal opportunities and treatment within social security schemes.

- A national organisation, independent from the public authorities, should be set up and authorised to monitor the application of the principle of equal treatment, including in the field of social security.

- A unique procedure for the settlement of litigation related to social security rights should be established.

- There should be a legal obligation to inform the public, free of charge and in an accessible way, of their rights and obligations under the social security systems in which they are included.

Country reports: Romania

INTRODUCTION

After the Revolution of December 1989, Romania passed through a spectacular period of reintegration into the international legal order, becoming a party to numerous international legal instruments and at the same time adopting provisions to bring its internal legislation in line with the requirements of international conventions. Romania also withdrew reservations formulated during the communist period for certain international human rights conventions.

The principle of equality between the sexes is explicitly regulated under Article 4 of the Romanian Constitution and in a number of other national regulations, and Romania can boast a well-articulated and non-discriminatory *de jure* framework. In fact, the European Commission emphasised in the evaluation document Agenda 2000 that in the field of equal opportunities, the national legislation covers the provisions of the Community legislation on non-discrimination on account of gender. At the same time, it was noted that there are no specific provisions that guarantee equal opportunities and treatment for women and men.

The Act No.202 of 2002 on Equal Opportunities aims to incorporate the provisions of the EU Directives on equality into Romanian legislation. The law regulates those measures that would promote equal opportunities for women and men, forbids direct and indirect discrimination based on sex in the fields of work, education, health, culture, information, decision-making, and establishes the means to resolve notifications and complaints of discrimination. It also establishes the public authorities responsible for implementing the law in accordance with international documents to which Romania is a party, as well as with Community provisions in this field.

The Department for the Promotion and Monitoring of Women's Rights Observance was established in 1995 within the Ministry of Labour and Social Protection. In 1999, the department was transformed into the Directorate for the Equal Opportunities – the only structure of the central administration with responsibilities in the field of observing and promoting women's rights and responsible for ensuring equal opportunities and treatment for women and men. One of the important objectives of the Directorate has been to incorporate the provisions of EU Directives on equal opportunities into national legislation and current practice. However, certain normative acts were blocked during the process of adoption, as was the case with the draft law on equal opportunities. Although the difficulty in approving draft laws is due rather to a general overloading of the Parliament, there is a certain indifference or lack of interest on behalf of decision-makers in relation to a series of acute women's problems, including an increase in domestic violence and unemployment and poverty among women, the weak participation of women in decision-making in political or economic fields, and the limited statistical data and studies on women's participation in social, economic and political life.

Still, the necessary basis for improving legislation in this area has been created, especially following the ratification of the Revised European Social Charter and after the adoption of the National Action Plan for Equality of Opportunities between Women and Men.[6]

The national mechanism for promoting equal opportunities was enlarged through the creation, within the Romanian Parliament, of the Sub-Commission for Equal Opportunities within the Joint Parliamentary Commission for European Integration (which functioned until the elections of 2000). The office of the Ombudsman also has a department working on protection of the family, children and women. In 2000, a Commission for Equal Opportunities was founded within the Economic and Social Council, and at the initiative of the Ministry of Labour and Social Solidarity, a Consultative Inter-Ministerial Commission on Equality of Treatment for Men and Women[7] was established to ensure a permanent exchange of information on the experience and measures in this field and the elaboration of recommendations for the authorities of the central public administration.

Despite these advancements, the activities developed by the structures for the promotion of equality are not coordinated and there is no single, comprehensive strategy in this field, mainly due to the lack of political will to prioritise this issue.

Women only represent 45.15 percent of the employed population and work primarily in agriculture, the processing industry, commerce, health, and education. The comprise 71.1 percent of unpaid family workers, 98.8 percent of whom work in agriculture. The number of female managers and high-position public officials in public administration and economic units is about one-fourth of the number of men.

The professional segregation of women leads to income disparities, even though the principle of equal pay for equal work is legally accepted. The segregation of the work force is perpetuated to women's disadvantage both horizontally and vertically, thereby explaining the feminisation of poverty as a characteristic of the transition towards a market economy. Since 1999, the rate of female unemployment has begun to decrease, and at the end of 2000 it had reached a value less than that of male unemployment.[8]

---

[6] Governmental Decision No.1273 of 2000.
[7] Governmental Decision No.967 of 1999.
[8] Ministry of Labour and Social Solidarity (2000), Fourth Quarter, 2000 data.

The first period of the transition (1990–1996) was characterised by the low representation of women in politics and in decision-making structures at an economic level. For example, after the 1992 elections women only comprised 4 percent of all members of Parliament; in 1996, this percentage rose to 6 percent. Certain changes began to occur after 1996 and although the presence of women in the Romanian Parliament far from illustrates the principle of equal opportunities, the evolution has been positive. After the elections in 2000, women make up 10.3 percent of all Members of Parliament (50 women of a total of 485 Members of Parliament).[9]

---

[9] Partners for Change (2000).

1. THE PRINCIPLE OF EQUAL PAY FOR WORK OF EQUAL VALUE

Council Directive 75/117/EEC of 10 February 1975 *on the approximation of the laws of the Member States relating to the application of the principle of equal pay for men and women*

1.1 National legal framework concerning the principle of equal pay for work of equal value: General provisions

In addition to the general provisions on equality in the Constitution, the principle of equal pay for equal work is explicitly enshrined in the Constitution, the Labour Code, the Act on Remuneration and the Act on Equal Opportunities. The relevant texts stipulate the following:

The Constitution

Article 38(4) of the Constitution provides that, for equal work with men, women shall receive equal wages.

The Labour Code

The Labour Code provides that remuneration shall be determined according to the quantity, quality, and social importance of the work, and ensures the principle of equal pay for equal work.

Act No.14 of 1991 on Remuneration

Article 2 prohibits discrimination on the basis of political beliefs, ethnicity or confession, age, sex or material situation.

Act No.202 of 2002 on Equal Opportunities For Women and Men

The recently promulgated Act on Equal Opportunities is the only legal text that explicitly provides for the principle of equal pay for work of equal value, which is defined in Article 4(e) as "paid activity that shows, when compared with another activity using the same indicators and units of measure, that similar or equal knowledge and professional skills were used and that similar amounts of intellectual and/or physical effort were exerted."

Relevant international provisions

The Romanian authorities have assumed an obligation to ensure the right to equal treatment and equal pay for equal work through the ratification of the Convention on the Elimination of All Forms of Discrimination against Women, ILO Convention No.100 of 1951 regarding Equal Remuneration of the male and female workers for work of equal value, the International Covenant on Economic, Social and Cultural Rights and the Revised European Social Charter.

1.2 Implementation of the principle of equal pay for work of equal value: Legal foundations and institutional structures

As a rule, the labour law norms apply to all Romanian wage earners, irrespective of the sector in which they work, and the principle of equal pay accordingly applies to both the public and the private sector. The norms contained in the collective Work Agreement on a national level are valid for all wage earners, irrespective of the type of capital of their respective companies/institutions.

The Work Inspection Authority, a specialised body of the central public administration subordinated to the Ministry of Labour and Social Solidarity, verifies, among other things, the implementation of labour law provisions, and can order that a violation be remedied immediately or within a definite period of time. The refusal of the employer to take the compulsory measures imposed by the Labour Inspector constitutes a violation and is punishable by a fine, and employers or legal entities may be deleted from the Commercial Register if repeated serious violations of the provisions of the labour legislation are discovered.[10]

The Act on the Status of Public Officials instituted a system of remuneration meant to exclude gender discrimination, and the National Agency of Public Officials was created to ensure the observance of this principle. According to Article 98 of the Collective Work Agreement, the implementation of the principle of equal pay for equal work can also be controlled by trade union representatives.

Under the Act on Equal Opportunities, the Ministry of Labour and Social Solidarity is the public authority responsible for monitoring the implementation of this law within its sphere of activity and also eliminating provisions that run counter to the principle of

---

[10] Act No.108 of 1999 on the Creation and Organisation of the Work Inspection Authority; *Monitorul Oficial* No.283 of 21 June 1999, Article 24.

equal opportunities and treatment. The Work Inspection Authority oversees the implementation of this law in both the public and the private sector.

The Ministry of Education and Culture oversees the introduction of measures aimed at observing the principle of equal opportunities and treatment in education plans and curricula, as well as in the current activities of educational establishments.

Gender statistics, which are an important tool in assessing the actual implementation of the law, are to be developed by the National Statistics Institute.

1.3 Job classification

There is no unified system of job classification in Romania, and the hierarchy of wages is conceived in relation to an abstract unit, which differs in accordance with the degree of complexity of the work. It is established for each position either through normative acts or through clauses of the Collective Work Agreement. In the private sector, the coefficients are related to the minimum wages negotiated by each institution/company.

The provisions of the Act on Collective Work Agreements and the clauses in the Collective Work Agreement on a national level do not contain discriminatory elements on the basis of sex.

The system of remuneration established by Act No.188 of 1999 on the Status of Public Officials employs categories, degrees, classes and stages so that competence takes precedence in the professional careers of public officials. In certain fields of activity, the wages of public sector employees are calculated in accordance with special laws that do not contain any discriminatory provisions on account of sex.

1.4 Available legal procedures in cases involving the violation of the principle of equal pay for work of equal value

Under the Constitution, every person is entitled to bring a case before a court to defend his/her legitimate rights, liberties and interests, and it is possible in accordance with the provisions of the Labour Code to seek legal redress in any litigation connected with the conclusion, execution or modification of individual work agreements.

Labour litigation is exempt from court tax, but the lack of concrete regulations on the implementation of the principle of equal pay serves as an obstacle in such cases.

The Law on Equal Opportunities provides that if a complaint against an employer is not resolved through mediation with the help of the trade union or of the employees' representative in that company, the employee can submit a complaint to the competent legal authority. The judicial instance is authorised to order *ex officio* that the individual(s) responsible for the discriminatory situation put an end to it within a given timeframe, and that the person responsible for the discrimination pay damages to the victim of the sex-based discrimination.

The right of non-governmental organisations to defend the rights of a community or group of persons, or individual, that has suffered discrimination before a court was established for the first time in Romanian legislation in 2002.

It is prohibited to dismiss an employee in reaction to a complaint of discrimination, and the provisions of the Labour Code and law on work conflicts offers employees rather strong protection. The cases in which an employer may terminate a contract of employment are explicitly and restrictively provided for in the Labour Code.

Statutory Order No.137 of 2000 provides that individuals who have been discriminated against have the right to sue for compensation proportionate to the damage they incurred, and to demand a reinstatement of the situation prior to the discrimination. As of 1999, the refusal of an employer to implement a final court decision ordering the reinstatement of an employee constitutes an offence and is punishable by six months to one-year imprisonment, or a fine.[11] Employees can only benefit from free legal assistance in exceptional cases where the person involved is unable to pay the lawyers' fees. There is no information available on whether this assistance has ever been granted in cases of labour litigation.

Contractual clauses that run counter to the law are void, and although the nullity of remuneration agreements or individual work agreements that violate the principle of equal pay is not explicitly provided for, on the grounds of this general principle the court may assess the nullity of such a provision at the request of the interested party. The court may also assess the nullity of clauses included in collective work agreements. If the court determines that certain provisions are void, the interested party may demand the re-negotiation of the respective rights.

Collective work agreements do not contain explicit provisions on the principle of equal pay, but they do include provisions on non-discrimination from which the above can be implied.

---

[11] See Act No.168 of 1999 on Collective Work Conflicts, published in *Monitorul Oficial* No.582 of 2 November 1999, Article 84(b).

1.5 Means of informing employees of their right to equal pay for work of equal value

In addition to general provisions in the Collective Work Agreement Act, the Act on Equal Opportunities obliges the employer to inform employees, on a regular basis and including by posting information in visible places, of the legal provisions regarding the implementation of the principle of equal pay and mechanisms for submitting a complaints.

The Work Inspection Authority is charged with coordinating activities to instruct and inform employees in the fields of health, security and work relations, but in practice employees are deprived of useful information regarding their rights and the means by which they can be exercised.

1.6 Out of court alternatives

A person claiming a violation of the principle of equal pay for work of equal value can turn to the relevant trade union or employees' representatives or address the National Council for the Prevention of Discrimination. The Council's role is to implement the principle of equality among citizens and its activities are carried out independently, without any limitations or influence from other institutions or public authorities. The Council proposes, among other things, actions or specific measures for the protection of disfavoured persons or categories when they do not benefit from equal opportunities, and receives complaints and information regarding the infringement of legal provisions related to the principle of equality and non-discrimination submitted by citizens, non-governmental human rights organizations, and public institutions.

Another out of court alternative is the office of the Ombudsperson, whose role is to protect citizens' rights and freedoms, as well as to formulate, in the periodical reports submitted to Parliament, legislative recommendations and concrete measures in this regard.

Collective work agreements do not provide for special procedures for the amicable resolution of individual complaints formulated by employees, although such provisions may be included. Women's associations within trade unions recently elaborated regulations for the amicable resolution of disputes between employers and employees, including those related to the non-application of the principle of equal pay, and these regulations are to be included in the national Collective Work Agreement.

1.7 Role of trade unions

Trade unions play an important role in the protection of rights and in the promotion of the professional, economic and social interests of employees in Romania. According to the Act on Trade Unions, employees have the right to specific means (collective negotiations, mediation, conciliation and arbitration) and legal action in the protection of members' rights. Trade unions can hire lawyers to formulate an action, assist or represent union members in court, or they may employ their own legal counsellors or employees for this purpose. According to their own statutes, trade unions are committed to helping their members by granting them free consultations and legal assistance, and this obligation is observed in practice.

However, because only persons prejudiced in their rights can bring legal action, trade unions may only intervene in cases against their members by way of a special civil procedure allowing someone who is not a party to the lawsuit to intervene in the trial in support of one of the parties or by delegating a legal counsellor.

According to the Act on Equal Opportunities, trade unions and NGOs can represent victims of discrimination in court, and can undertake this free of charge if the claimant does not have the financial means to pay for the service.

1.8 Women's factual situation with regard to the principle of equal pay for work of equal value

Studies[12] show that the legal provisions on non-discrimination in the matter of equal pay for equal work are not always enforced. In particular, one survey[13] revealed the gender pay gap, and the fact that women's average gross salary is systematically lower than men's. Research shows that girls are directed towards professions that are traditionally poorly paid, and maternity is a serious obstacle in professional evolution and promotion. One report[14] also concluded that women have lower wages than men even in 'feminised' areas of employment and that employers behave in an overtly discriminatory fashion by unfairly dismissing women from employment or, alternatively, by employing cheaper female labour.

---

[12] UNDP and The Romanian Academy (2000); Romanian Society for Feminist Analyses (2000); UNDP (1995); Ministry of Labour and Social Solidarity (2001).

[13] National Institute of Research in the Field of Labour and Social Protection, in June 2000, Program RELANSIN – Life Quality, project *The mechanisms for ensuring equal opportunities and women's access to socio-economic life in Romania*, 2000.

[14] PHARE *CONSENSUS* Project (1998).

Statistics show that in Romania there are more women than men in sectors financed by the state budget; for example, education, health, social services, trade, hotels and restaurants, etc. Remuneration in these spheres is generally up to one third lower than the average salary in the economy as a whole. Men prevail in better-paid sectors, such as mining and quarrying, energy, metallurgy, chemistry, transport and communications. Exceptions include the financial, banking and insurance institutions, which have the highest level of salaries (over 2.5 times greater than the national average) and where women predominate.

According to the results of an inquiry into the cost of the work force between 1994–1998, men's average salary was up to 32 percent higher than women's average salary.[15]

---

[15] UNDP and The Romanian Academy (2000).

2. The principle of equal treatment for women and men as regards to access to the job market, vocational training, promotion and general working conditions

Council Directive 76/207/EEC of 9 February 1976 *on the implementation of the principle of equal treatment for men and women as regards access to employment, vocational training and promotion, and working conditions*

2.1 National legal framework concerning the principle of equal treatment for women and men: General provisions

National legislation includes general provisions on the principle of equality and on the implementation of the principle of equal treatment for women and men as regards access to employment, vocational training, promotion and working conditions.

The Labour Code provides for the principle of equality between women and men with regard to access to the workplace, promotion and vocational training, as well as in terms of social protection.

2.2 The concept of discrimination on grounds of sex: Definition and legal sanctions

Statutory Order No. 137 of 2000

The concept of discrimination based on sex is defined generally in Statutory Order No.137 of 2000 as "any difference, exclusion, restriction or preference based on race, nationality, ethnic appurtenance, language, religion, social category, beliefs, sex or sexual orientation, appurtenance to a disadvantaged category or any other criterion aimed at or resulting in the restriction or elimination of the recognition, use or exercise, in conditions of equality, of human rights and fundamental liberties or of rights granted by law in the political, economic, social and cultural fields or in any other domains of public life."

Article 2(2) of the same Order provides that "Any active or passive conduct which, through the consequences it generates, unjustifiably favours or prejudices an individual, group of individuals or community or which subjects such persons to unjust or degrading treatment, in relation to other individuals, groups or communities, shall entail administrative liability […]."

Article 2(5) stipulates that the elimination of all forms of discrimination shall be achieved by means of affirmative action in favour of persons who do not enjoy equal opportunities, as well as through the punishment of discriminatory behaviour.

Chapter II (Article 1) of the Statutory Order provides that discriminatory action is considered an offence punishable by a fine, the amount of which varies according to whom the discrimination was perpetrated against. A court can also order the competent authorities to withdraw the licence of legal entities that significantly prejudice society through discriminatory action or, although they committed a minor prejudice, repeatedly violate the provisions of the Statutory Order.

In all cases of discrimination provided for by the Statutory Order, victims of discrimination are entitled to claim damages proportional to the prejudice, as well a reinstatement of the situation prior to the discrimination or to the termination of the situation created by discrimination, in accordance with the general legal provisions.

The Act on Equal Opportunities clearly defines direct discrimination as "the differential treatment of a person to his/her disadvantage and as a result of his/her sex […]." Indirect discrimination is defined as "the application of provisions, criteria or practices that appear neutral but which in practice affect people of one sex, unless those provisions, criteria or practices can be justified objectively and without any connection to gender." Article 4(d) also defines positive discrimination.

2.3 National legal framework concerning the principle of equal treatment as regards access to employment, vocational training and promotion, and working conditions

Statutory Order No.129 of 2000 provides in Article 2(1) that persons have equal rights to access to vocational training, without discrimination based on age, sex, race, ethnic origin, political or religious affiliation". Further, Statutory Order No.137 of 2000 provides that discrimination against any person, for any reason with regard to work relations and social protection is a punishable offence.

The Act on Equal Opportunities provides in Article 6(1) that equal opportunities and the equal treatment of women and men in work relations entails non-discriminatory access to employment in all vacant positions or posts and at all professional levels; professional information and counselling, and various trainings; promotion at any professional and hierarchical level, as well as the right to freely choose or perform a profession or activity.

Article 8 of the same law prohibits discriminatory practice with regard to "announcing, organising contests or exams and selecting candidates; concluding, suspending, modifying or ending a certain labour relationship; choosing or modifying the job description; establishing payment; [...] protection and social security measures; organizing information and professional counselling services, vocational and other training; evaluating individual professional performance; promoting employees, as well as implementing any other conditions relating to work as provided for in the national legislation."

According to Statutory Order No.137 of 2000, measures taken by the public authorities or legal entities under private law in favour of a person, group of persons or a community to ensure their natural development and the effective achievement of their right to equal opportunities as opposed to other persons, groups of persons or communities, as well as positive measures aimed at protecting disfavoured groups, shall not be regarded as discrimination. This Order also ensures the application of the principle of equal treatment in terms of selection criteria and job advertisements.

The legal provisions related to the implementation of the principle of equal treatment for men and women as regards access to employment, vocational training and promotion and working conditions apply to both the public and the private sectors.

Despite these provisions, the laws are poorly enforced, especially in the private sector, and indirect discrimination against women in terms of employment opportunities, promotion and remuneration persists.

2.4 Protective measures with regard to women's participation in the labour market

Women are entitled to certain protective measures other than those related to maternity, and the Labour Code adopts the provisions of ILO Convention No.89 of 1948 on Night Work in Article 153, forbidding night work for women in industrial enterprises, with some exceptions.

The ILO Convention No.127 of 1967 on Maximum Weight stipulates that assigning women to the manual transportation of heavy weights must be limited, and when such an assignment is still given, the maximum weight of the load must definitely be lower than the maximum weight for men.

2.5 Prohibition of dismissal

The Labour Code stipulates those cases in which an employer can terminate an employment relationship, and work agreements cannot be annulled at the employer's initiative for any reasons other than those stipulated by law. However, in practice, an employer may well terminate an employment agreement if he/she is involved in litigation with the employee.

The Act on Equal Opportunities prohibits an employer from unilaterally modifying work relations or conditions, including dismissing an employee who submitted a notification or complaint to the company or to a court.

There are no legal provisions that prevent jobs from being classified as specifically for women or men. In the classified lists of occupations, trades and specializations for which training is ensured in pre-college education, out of 660 occupations and trades only one has a female designation (a female housekeeper, although men are allowed to work as housekeepers also); all others are in masculine terms.

There are no discriminatory legal provisions based on sex with regard to choosing one's workplace or professional route, but according to available information, a series of restrictions are applied when hiring women for certain workplaces, such as the Ministry of the Interior, the Ministry of National Defence[16] and the Church.

2.6 Legal status of sexual harassment

The Criminal Code will contain a new article on sexual harassment, which provides that "The harassment of a person using threats or pressure in order to acquire favours of a sexual nature by a person abusing his/her authority or influence conferred by the position in the workplace shall be punished by imprisonment from three months to two years or by a fine."

The Act on Equal Opportunities also defines sexual harassment in Article 4(c) as "any form of sexual behaviour known to affect a person's dignity if the behaviour is unwanted and constitutes an underlying factor in any decision affecting that person." Article 10(2) stipulates that sexual harassment shall be considered discrimination based on sex if it aims to "create an atmosphere of intimidation, hostility or discouragement in the workplace for the person who is affected by it" or to "adversely influence the situation of the employee with regard to professional promotion, payment or income

---

[16] Recently, by Order of the Minister of Defence, women are allowed to take part in admission exams for officers, but certain age restrictions apply, and it is prohibited to study while pregnant.

of any nature, or access to vocational and professional training, if the employee rejected the unwanted sexual behaviour."

According to the law, the employer must provide for internal disciplinary legal measures, inform all employees that sexual harassment is forbidden in the workplace, and implement the disciplinary measures immediately upon learning of the harassment.

3. PROTECTION OF PREGNANT WOMEN FROM THE INHERENT RISK OF CERTAIN ACTIVITIES AND RELATED EMPLOYMENT RIGHTS

Council Directive 92/85/EEC of 19 October 1992 on the introduction of measures to encourage improvements in the safety and health at work of pregnant workers and workers who have recently given birth or are breastfeeding

3.1 Legal and conceptual framework

The terms 'pregnant worker', 'worker who recently gave birth' and 'breastfeeding worker' are not defined in Romanian legislation, but in practice the employer must consider the following:

- An official document must be issued by a medical doctor in order to prove a pregnancy;
- A medical certificate must be issued in order to prove the birth of a child;
- There is a legal presumption in the Labour Code that mothers breastfeed their babies until the age of nine months, thus once the birth is proven there is no need to produce further evidence of breastfeeding until the child reaches that age. An extension of the breastfeeding period is allowed on the basis of a medical certificate and only in the case of premature or dystrophic babies, or babies in need of special care, following medical recommendations.

3.2 Assessing the risk to the safety or health of a pregnant worker and employer's obligations

Romanian legislation does not oblige employers to evaluate the conditions, processes and risk agents that could endanger the health and safety of pregnant or breastfeeding workers, but there is a series of legal and contractual provisions that partly ensure the protection of such employees. There is a general legal obligation under Act No.90 of 1996 on Protection in the Workplace, whereby the employer must inform each person prior to his/her employment of the risks s/he will be exposed to at the workplace, including the necessary prevention measures. The violation of this obligation is punishable by a fine.

At the same time, Article 27(2) and (3) of the Collective Work Agreement on a national level stipulates that, both upon hiring and changing one's workplace or working conditions, the workers must not only be informed of the risks and briefed on the applicable work protection norms, but they must also be tested to measure to what extent they know these norms. The Labour Code stipulates a compulsory medical examination for potential employees, as well as for persons who will be transferred to a workplace that can only be accepted if certain health requirements are met, in order to assess whether their health status allows them to perform their work. The Collective Work Agreement and Norms on Health in the Workplace also contain provisions on medical examinations for employees.

The General Work Protection Norms provide that the employer is obliged to organise a general introductory training for employees, as well as a training at the workplace, at least once every six months to inform employees of their working conditions, risks and work protection measures; there are no special provisions for pregnant or breastfeeding workers.

Because there is no legal obligation to hold information activities as provided for by the relevant Directive, no specific punishment is provided for either. The Work Inspection Authority must verify and control the observance of specific norms regarding the working conditions of young people and women, but there is no legal obligation to inform pregnant or breastfeeding workers of the results of the workplace evaluation.

According to the Labour Code, pregnant and breastfeeding women cannot be employed in workplaces with harmful, hard or dangerous conditions, or in conditions that are medically forbidden, and they should be transferred to another workplace without any decrease in their pay. There is no express obligation for the employer to improve the working conditions or working hours for pregnant and breastfeeding women.

3.3 Cases in which exposure is prohibited for pregnant workers and workers who are breastfeeding

There are no imperative prohibitions provided for by the national legislation that address the exposure of pregnant and breastfeeding women to risk factors. Article 127 of the General Work Protection Norms only stipulates that "on assigning women to a workplace, consideration shall be given to the morphological, functional and specific physiological states (menstruation, pregnancy, birth, the period following birth, menopause), and, as a rule, assignment to places with exposure to trepidations, certain chemical substances (lead, mercury, carbon sulphur, benzene, etc.), ionising radiations, lifting and carrying weights, and prolonged orthostatic positions must be avoided."

3.4 Night work

Article 154 of the Labour Code prohibits night work for pregnant and breastfeeding women starting from the sixth month of pregnancy. The provisions of Article 33(3) of the Collective Work Agreement extended the prohibition of night work for pregnant women starting from the fifth month of pregnancy. Women are prohibited from performing night work in industrial units, according to Article 153 of the Labour Code (in accordance with ILO Convention No.89 of 1948 on Night Work), with some exceptions (for example, women in managerial positions or working in jobs of a technical character, in sanitary and social assistance services, etc.).

Because Romanian legislation prohibits night work for pregnant and breastfeeding women and women who have given birth, there has been no need for special provisions obliging employers to transfer women to daytime work. For the same reason, the legislation does not provide the possibility of leave other than maternity leave.

3.5 Maternity leave

Following the entry into force of Act No.19 of 2000 in 2000, maternity leave lasts for 126 calendar days (18 weeks total), i.e., 63 days prior to the birth and 63 days following the birth of the child, with some flexibility given to the employee to choose when to take the leave. Disabled women are to take maternity leave from the sixth month of pregnancy. After the expiry of maternity leave, either parent can be granted paid leave to raise the child until the age of two. The law also provides for the right to paid medical leave for the care of a sick child until the age of seven (or the age of 18 if the child is disabled) for a maximum of 14 days per year. According to Article 61 of the Collective Work Agreement, mothers can be granted unpaid leave to care for a child or children aged two to three.

Women are entitled, but not obliged, to take maternity leave, and Article 119(2) of Act No.19 of 2000 provides for the possibility to compensate maternity leave in accordance with the recommendations of a medical doctor and the woman's choice. Maternity leave is regulated by the provisions of the state social security system and is a right deriving from law, thus there is no need for it to be mentioned in the work agreement.

During maternity leave, women are entitled to 85 percent of the individual average monthly income they received in the last six months before the leave. This amount may not exceed three times the national gross monthly income, provided that a legal share/quota was paid for at least six months during the last 12 months prior to the leave. Employers are obliged, according to Article 66 of the Collective Work Agreement, to pay female workers an allowance equal to the difference between their wage and the legal payment they now receive for at least six weeks of the maternity leave. This period can be extended through work agreements within each institution.

If the mother relinquishes her right to take the leave intended for raising the child/children until the age of two, and chooses, upon returning to work, to reduce her normal hours from eight to six, she will receive the wage she would be entitled to if she worked eight hours, according to the provisions of Article 17 of the Collective Work Agreement. This lasts until the child reaches the age of nine months or, if there is a medical recommendation to extend breastfeeding beyond the nine months, a further three months at the most. On the basis of Article 50(c) of the Collective Work Agreement, employers are obliged to pay the mother an allowance equal to a regular wage upon the birth of the child. If the mother does not work, this allowance will be paid to the father.

Antenatal Examinations

There are no legal or contractual provisions that allow an employee to undergo antenatal examinations during working hours without her salary being diminished.

3.6 Prohibition of dismissal and employment rights

Article 146 of the Labour Code provides that the work agreement cannot be cancelled at the employer's initiative during medical leave, pregnancy, maternity leave, or while breastfeeding or caring for a sick child until the age of three, or while the husband is performing his compulsory military service. However, Article 130 does stipulate the following exceptions to that rule: if the institution moves to another town and can hire locally; if the institution moves to another town and the employee refuses to relocate; if the employee retires due to invalidity of the first or second degree; if the employee is sentenced for a work-related crime, and it is inappropriate for her to continue work; or if the employee was temporarily or permanently prohibited by a court decision to work in that specific profession.

Case law has established that the protection provided for in Article 146 of the Labour Code could not apply in cases where the position of the protected employee is cancelled due to reorganization and a similar position no longer exists in that institution. The Collective Work Agreement on a national level provides that an employer cannot cancel the work agreement of an employee on unpaid leave to raise a child/children from two to three years of age and the employer can only hire a replacement for a predetermined period of time. If an institution is reorganized and this inevitably entails a cut back in personnel, Article 79(2) of the Collective Work Agreement stipulates that dismissals should affect women raising children as a last resort.

Because of the legal and contractual prohibitions to dismiss women who are pregnant, on maternity leave or breastfeeding, such women, if they are nevertheless dismissed during any of these periods, may go to court to obtain a decision that annuls the dismissal and reinstates them in their previous position; they can also claim damages. An employer's refusal to implement a final court decision stipulating the reinstatement is a crime punishable by imprisonment from six months to one year, or by a fine.

4. THE BURDEN OF PROOF IN CASES OF DISCRIMINATION BASED ON SEX

Council Directive 97/80/EC of 15 December 1997 *on the burden of proof in cases of discrimination based on sex*

4.1 Legal framework concerning indirect discrimination and specific legal means to implement the principle of equal treatment for women and men

As described in Section 2, indirect discrimination is defined in the Act on Equal Opportunities. It is not explicitly defined in Statutory Order No.137 of 2000, but Article 2(2) provides that "any active or passive behaviour that in effect unjustifiably favours or prejudices a person, group of persons, or community, or which subjects them to unjust or degrading treatment compared with other persons, shall be subject to administrative liability, unless the behaviour falls under the ambit of criminal law." The general nature of this text allows for varied interpretations, and given that the normative act in which it is included is too recent to have generated judicial practice or doctrine, it is difficult to assess how the text will be interpreted in the future.

The punishment in cases of discrimination were described in Section 2, and are included in the Act on Equal Opportunities, which devotes an entire chapter to resolving notifications and complaints regarding cases of discrimination based on sex.

Procedures involving mediation or conciliation that would ensure the implementation of the principle of equal treatment for women and men have been included in the Act on Equal Opportunities.

4.2 The burden of proof procedure in litigation concerning the violation of the principle of equal treatment for women and men and rules of evidence

The regulations in cases of litigation concerning the violation of the principle of equal treatment for women and men in relation to access to employment, vocational training and promotion, and working conditions, run counter to the EU Directive, which recommends the reversal of the burden of proof in cases of discrimination based on sex.

The provisions of the Act in Equal Opportunities do not shift the burden of proof from the employee to the employer or person perpetrating the discrimination. Articles

33–38 outline judicial procedures similar to those in civil law, whereby the plaintiff must prove the discrimination. There is no legal presumption of discrimination in the national legislation that the plaintiff might invoke to support his/her case. In Romania, the judge must play an active role in accordance with the provisions of Article 129(5) of the Civil Procedure Code. According to the consulted judicial practice, as well as from the recent issue of the magazine *Dreptul* (The Law),[17] however, it does not appear that discrimination or equal opportunities and treatment are topics of interest for legal theorists or practitioners, so it is difficult to establish to what extent judges would manifest their active role provided by the law.

The consequence of the current provisions whereby the burden of proof rests with the plaintiff is that it is very difficult to prove the existence of discrimination, and employees who find themselves in this situation no longer go to court. As a result, there is a serious lack of case law in this field.

There are no special means to make public the regulations on access to justice in cases involving the violation of the principle of equal opportunities and treatment. Legally, publicity is ensured for all normative acts through their publication in *Monitorul Oficial*, the Official Gazette of Romania, which may be purchased by anyone. However, this is not a system to which citizens would turn on a daily basis for information, given that they must have an active interest in order to find out their legal rights, as well as the material means to purchase the publication.

As a rule, the main source of information is the media, which does not provide much information in the matter of equal opportunities and treatment. On the whole, the mass media has not succeeded in conveying the general issue of women's rights in the transition period. The message of the mass media oscillates between helpless recordings of individual cases of women as victims and the image of women as a sexual object. Furthermore, the media is not sufficiently trained to articulate, at the level of collective consciousness, the general problems faced by women in contemporary Romanian society, much less the formulation of an agenda of socio-political and cultural action in this field.[18]

4.3 Case law on the violation of the principle of equal treatment for women and men

Out of 300 decisions handed down by the Constitutional Court between 1995 and 1996, only one referred to the violation of the principle of equal treatment (in the matter of social security). The woman in the case claimed that legally imposing a lower

---

[17] *Dreptul* is published by the Union of Lawyers of Romania.
[18] UNDP and The Romanian Academy (2000).

retirement age for women violates the principle of equality enshrined in Articles 16, 38 and 43 of the Constitution. In its judgment, the Constitutional Court maintained that the difference of age limits imposed on account of sex is not founded on the 'difference of sex,' but on the social status that results from this difference, citing the practice in western European countries (Germany and Austria), where legislative authorities have considered that, given current socio-professional realities, the maintenance of different ages of retirement is justified.

Between 1990 and 2000, there are no cases involving the violation of the principle of equal treatment for women and men in relation to employment, vocational training, remuneration, social protection and promotion, or working conditions.

5. NON-DISCRIMINATION AGAINST PART-TIME WORKERS

Council Directive 97/81/EC of 15 December 1997 *concerning the framework agreement on part-time work concluded by UNICE, CEEP and the ETUC*

5.1 National legal framework and employment conditions concerning part-time workers

There is no legal or contractual definition *in terminis* of 'part-time worker' in Romanian legislation, but the Collective Work Agreement for 2000–2001 on a national level provides that "for certain activities, positions and categories of personnel provided for in the collective work agreement, part-time programs may be established corresponding to fractions of the norm, with a working time of six, four or two hours per day." The full-time norm is 170 hours per month, and the fractions regulated by the Collective Work Agreement are strictly related to this norm only.

There are certain categories of workers (persons whose working conditions are hard or detrimental to health) determined through collective negotiations in conformity with the law, according to which the full-time norm is less than the general norm and their daily working program may not exceed 6 hours.

Part-time employment is not subject to different legal or contractual stipulations than full-time employment, and part-time workers have the same rights as full-time workers, although they are granted proportionally to the time worked. The social security allowances for part-time workers are also based on the principle of proportionality.

Although there are no specific legal provisions on non-discrimination against part-time workers, no cases have been reported in which they were subjected to discriminatory treatment for this reason. Since no differential treatment has been reported in this regard, the possibility of introducing a special procedure in litigation has not been raised.

No legal or administrative obstacles that limit the opportunities of part-time work have been identified. In practice though, this form of work is taken up primarily by women.

The law does not stipulate differences in the treatment of workers in the public and private sectors. In practice, although such differences have not been reported (either as a widespread phenomenon or as an isolated situation), no research has been conducted to confirm or deny their existence.

According to the Collective Work Agreement, at their request, "part-time workers can be employed in a full-time norm if there are vacant positions and if they meet the criteria for occupying such a position." The regulation of part-time work, including the right of the employee to demand a transfer to full-time work, has remained unchanged in the national Collective Work Agreement since 1992.

Section 158 of the Labour Code provides that women caring for children up to the age of six may work part-time if they do not have the benefit of a childcare facility or kindergarten, and this period is to be considered as a full-time norm. The Collective Work Agreement also provides for this right.

There are no legal or administrative measures to facilitate or restrict access to part-time work in any type of organisation and at all professional levels. The Ministry of Labour and Social Solidarity is currently drafting a law on the occupation of the work force, which will extend the possibility of implementing flexible work programs, including part-time work. There are no legal or administrative procedures that require concrete measures to facilitate access by part-time workers to vocational training to enhance their career opportunities.

Romanian law stipulates a 40-hour working week, but during the period of transition a number of new occupational patterns emerged, including part-time work, which is not yet entirely regulated. From 1994–1998, the number of part-time workers did not vary much, ranging from 13 to 15 percent of all workers. In 1998, 15 percent of employed Romanians worked part-time, more than half of whom were women.[19] In 2000, women comprised 55.4 percent of part-time workers.[20] Significantly, part-time work is seen as an alternative to unemployment; thus, over 90 percent of part-time workers interviewed stated that they were searching for a full time job.[21]

---

[19] UNDP (2000b: 22).
[20] UNDP (2000a: 23).
[21] UNDP (2000b: 22).

6. THE PRINCIPLE OF EQUAL TREATMENT TO SELF-EMPLOYED WORKERS AND THEIR ASSISTING SPOUSES

Directive 86/613/EEC of 11 December 1986 on the application of the principle of equal treatment between men and women engaged in an activity, including agriculture, in a self-employed capacity, and on the protection of self-employed women during pregnancy and motherhood

6.1 National legal framework on self-employment: General provisions

Definition of self-employed workers

There is no legal definition of the term 'self-employed' in Romania, but statistically it is defined as "a person who conducts his/her activity at his/her own headquarters or runs an individual business without employing other persons, with the possibility of assistance from unpaid family members." This category includes self-employed entrepreneurs, day labourers, persons employed part-time by state or private companies based on retainer agreements, holders of management lease or concession agreements, or farmers who work individually or in farming associations.[22]

Laws and regulations related to the directive

Because self-employed persons are not conceptually deemed an important component in the labour market, the legislation does not include any special provisions in this regard, although legal regulations do refer to independent activities and Act No.54 of 1991 does stipulate the right of this category to become associated or affiliated to trade union organizations.

The status of self-employed persons is somehow assimilated to the category of entrepreneurs and persons who conduct an activity to obtain profit, and not persons who conduct their activity in order to earn a living. Under these circumstances, it is difficult to address any concern for the application of the principle of equal opportunities for self-employed men and women, including those working in agriculture.

However, although there are no specific programs intended for the organised application of the principle of equal opportunities for self-employed men and women

---

[22] UNDP (2000a: 13).

in the spirit of Directive 86/613/EEC, national legislation is, to a large degree, in harmony with the requirements of the Directive.

With regard to freelance activities, the national legislation does not contain different provisions for men and for women; the license to conduct such an activity is granted only on the basis of documents attesting the necessary skills and qualification.

The principle of equal treatment and self-employed workers

Political decision makers and civil society have not been specifically concerned with the status of self-employed persons and even less concerned with promoting equal treatment for men and women engaged in independent activities. At the same time, self-employed persons have not asserted their status as an important social category themselves, having no trade unions to promote their interests and defend their rights, although, theoretically, the legal regulations in force allow the organisation of such trade unions.

6.2 Social rights of spouses

Formation of companies by unmarried persons

The legal regulations in this field make no reference to the marital status of persons starting a company. According to Section 35 of the Family Code, the spouse who alone exercises the right to manage and use the communal goods is deemed to have the consent of the other spouse, and that by including certain movable assets in the contribution to the registered capital, such goods remain the common property of the two spouses, by their share equivalent.

There is no statistical data available on the occurrence of married couples who start a business together, but such situations do exist in practice.

Recognition of the work of spouses

Several years ago, a female deputy tried to initiate a bill intended to grant recognition of the social usefulness of women's unpaid work in the home, but the bill did not consider the particular status of the wives of self-employed men, and the initiative was abandoned due to a lack of support.

6.3 Contributory social security schemes for self-employed workers and spouses

There are no differences between the social security rights of self-employed persons and persons hired on an employment agreement basis. Self-employed women and the wives of self-employed men benefit from the same maternity protection as women employed on an employment agreement basis if they are insured within the public social security system.

6.4 Related Research and Statistics

Research on women in agriculture

Research shows that this category of persons, comprised of both men and women, is practically ignored, not only statistically, but also by society in general. There is very little statistical data available in this respect, and there are no available surveys or research expressly dedicated to this social category.

This may be because the activity of freelance entrepreneurs was discouraged during communism in Romania by the legal provisions in force at the time: the majority of persons who were not state employees were forced to become members of the cooperation system, in agriculture or in the handicraft field. This category was practically eliminated eventually, since their existence was not justified by the low number of independent workers. Although the situation started to change after the Revolution, not enough attention is paid to the contribution of this active category to the economic and social development of the country, despite the fact that their number is currently rather high.

Percentage of self-employed men and women

Statistics indicate that there were 1,717,000 self-employed persons in Romania in 2000 (29.1 percent of whom were women, and 15.2 percent in urban areas);[23] self-employed persons and unpaid family members represented 42.4 percent of the active population, and 91 percent of them worked in rural areas. The share of the active population who were members of farming companies or employers increased compared with the preceding year, but substantially diminished compared with 1996. The number of unpaid family members and self-employed workers has continued to increase over the last few years.[24] The number of private entrepreneurs registered with the Chamber of

---

[23] National Institute for Statistics (2001b: 21).

[24] National Institute for Statistics (2001b: 25).

Commerce and Industry in 2000 amounted to 394,868, including 133,610 family associations and 261,258 natural persons.[25]

It is difficult to state the real number of self-employed persons and freelance farming workers, as official statistics do not indicate separate data for each category, and the existing data does not allow an indirect assessment of their number. As indicated by the global data available, women represent the highest share in farming, i.e., 51.5 percent of the total,[26] a percentage that has remained almost unchanged since 1997. It is also difficult to state the main types of freelance activities women are engaged in or the trends and evolutions in this field, as there are no statistical data or relevant surveys available.

Further research

Privatisation and the decentralization of the economy have significantly influenced the evolution of the labour market, leading to massive dismissals and unemployment. The deterioration of the economic situation restricted employment possibilities; the occupancy rate of the population diminished, and unemployment became a growing phenomenon (according to the Ministry of Labour and Social Solidarity, the rate of unemployment was 10.5 percent in 2000). As a result, the rate of poverty increased 2.2 times during the last four years, rising from 19.9 percent in 1996 to 44 percent in 2000.[27] The percentage of women in the structure of labour resources is close to that of men: according to the National Institute for Statistics and Economic Study, they represented 48.0 percent of the civil active population in January 2000.

In the early 90's women represented the highest share of unemployed persons, but their number has diminished in recent years as the collective dismissals which began in 1997 mainly affected the spheres of mining, construction and metallurgy – fields of activity where men represent the majority. The occupancy rate of the population aged over 15 was 59.1 percent in 1999. Women's occupancy rate was lower than men's (52.9 percent and 65.7 percent respectively) and lower in urban areas than in rural areas (50.8 percent and 69.2 percent respectively).[28]

The changes in the structure of the occupied population by professional status indicate an increase in the categories of employers, self-employed persons and unpaid family members.

---

[25] National Institute for Statistics (2001a: 22).
[26] National Institute for Statistics (2001b: 27).
[27] White Book of Government Take-Over, December 2000.
[28] UNDP (2000a).

6.5 Legal means of redress

Persons who consider themselves wronged by the application of the principle of equal treatment in freelance activities have several possibilities to exercise their rights in court as described in earlier sections and many commercial cases have already been settled or are pending in court where women have appeared either as defendants or plaintiffs. However, no cases are known in which the failure to apply the principle of equal treatment to women and men was expressly invoked.[29]

---

[29] Jurisprudence Bulletin, 1998, Supreme Court of Justice, Commercial Department, Argessis, 1999: Decision No.3736 of 22 October 1998, p. 314–315; Decision No.2167 of May 26, 1998, p. 315–317. See also Bucharest Court, Commercial Department: Decision No.888 of 9 September 1999, p. 54–57; Decision No.160 of 15 March 1994, p. 58–59; Decision No.406 of 7 April 1993, p. 59–64; Sentence No.1705 of 21 April 1997, p. 64–65.

7. THE FRAMEWORK ON PARENTAL LEAVE

Council Directive 96/34/EC of 3 June 1996 *on the framework agreement on parental leave concluded by UNICE, CEEP, and ETUC*

7.1 National legal framework on parental leave: General provisions

The provisions of Directive 96/34/EC are partially adopted in Romanian legislation and are included in the following legal acts:

Act No. 19 of 2000 on the Public System of Pensions and Other Social Security Rights

Social security rights are guaranteed by the State and are assured by the public system of pensions and other social security systems. Insured persons are entitled to benefits to care for children up to the age of two or, in the case of disabled children, up to the age of three.

Either parent shall be granted a child allowance on demand provided that they fulfil the legal requirements regarding payment of the social security contribution; insured persons who are adoptive parents, guardians or foster parents shall benefit from the same rights.

Act No. 210 of 31 December 1999 on Paternity Leave

Fathers are entitled to paid leave of up to five working days in order to help care for a newborn child. Paternity leave shall be granted to fathers who are employed and insured within the state social security system. Fathers shall benefit from paternity leave only once, on demand, during the first eight weeks following the birth of the child. The allowance is paid from the company's salary fund and shall be equivalent to the salary due for the duration of the leave.

In the event that the mother dies in childbirth or during maternity leave, the father shall benefit from the remaining duration of the maternity leave and receive an allowance equivalent to the maternity and post-natal benefit due to the mother for such a period, or, alternatively, an allowance calculated on the basis of his base salary and seniority, granted from the salary fund of the company that employs him. If the father obtained an infant care graduation certificate, the parental leave is extended by a further ten working days (15 days in total).

Act No. 416 of 18 July 2001 on the Minimum Guaranteed Income

This law regulates the granting of social support benefits and child allowances to the wives of men who performed military service.

Through a series of well coordinated and sustained activities of women's organisations affiliated to the Trade Union Confederation, following negotiations with the Government and employers' associations, provisions in favour of employees with family responsibilities were included in the Sole Collective Employment Agreement at the National Level concluded for 2002. The provisions include *inter alia* the possibility of diminished working time by two hours a day for employees caring for children up to the age of two, part-time work for women caring for children up to the age of six, the possibility to change the working schedule; days off for special family events, and protection against dismissal.

Conditions of access and detailed rules for applying for parental leave

The Family Code stipulates that the family is established by marriage, which is based on the free consent of the spouses and that women and men have equal rights with regard to family relations and to the exercise of the rights related to the children. These legal provisions make no reference to the distribution of tasks and responsibilities related to raising and caring for the children.

The Labour Code

The Labour Code stipulates support measures for pregnant women and women who are breast deeding or caring for an infant child, but does not include measures for fathers with family obligations.

It does stipulate the principle of equal rights for men and women and guarantees women's right to fill any position in any work place, but it only refers to employed women in relation to ensuring the necessary conditions for raising and educating children. Thus, it is assumed that employed men have no 'domestic' responsibilities and that only women are involved in raising, caring for and educating children.

It is prohibited to terminate the employment of pregnant women, women on maternity leave, in the period following birth or while caring for sick children up to three years of age. All of these responsibilities and protective measures are addressed only in relation to employed women.

Act No. 19 of 2000 on the Public System of Pensions

This normative act stipulates the conditions under which paid parental leave is granted, in accordance with the new provisions brought about by the reform of the public system of social security rights (pensions and other social security rights).

7.2 Social security during parental leave, especially healthcare

Prior to the adoption of Act 19 of 2000 in 2001, women who were not employed on an employment agreement basis were granted no social security rights during pregnancy or while raising young children, except for social support benefits, provided that they met the legal requirements.

The Act 19 of 2000 with subsequent modifications and additions changed the duration of maternity leave to 126 days, and companies are obliged to allow women to take breaks in order to breastfeed and care for their young children. The right of both parents insured by the social security system to benefit from paid leave in order to attend to children up to the age of two was inserted for the first time into the national legislation; this provision was also amended by Act 19 of 2000 and it refers to all categories of insured persons.

Social security benefits are granted to the sick in conformity with the provisions of Act No.19 of 2000; medical certificates are issued in accordance with the provisions of Order No.343/199 of 2001, the Annex of which contains instructions regarding the granting of medical leave for *inter alia* temporary disability, maternity, attending to sick children up to the age of seven. There are no surveys or statistical data available on the taking of medical leave according to gender.

7.3 Parental leave and equal opportunities policy

Initiatives to encourage the introduction of new flexible ways of organizing work

The national Collective Work Agreement for 2001–2002 further provides that, whenever possible, employers and trade unions should establish flexible work schedules and the possibilities to apply them. Moreover, employees who waive their right to maternity leave may benefit from reduced working hours by two hours a day, without affecting their base salary or seniority. Work schedules may be changed at an employee's request, provided that the activity is not disturbed.

The Act on Equal Opportunities aims *inter alia* to ensure better management and more flexible working schedules, and contains measures for the implementation of strategies and policies intended to protect employees from unemployment, ensure a high occupancy level and adapt to the requirements of the labour market. The law also stipulates measures intended to stimulate employment, both by increasing employment opportunities for unemployed persons and by creating new jobs.

The National Action Plan on Equal Opportunities for Men and Women[30] provides for the development of flexible occupancy and part-time programs, intended equally for men and women, and its third operational goal is to reconcile professional and family life by encouraging men to participate more in family tasks.

The National Action Plan for Occupancy will be adopted in 2002 and aims to consolidate the principle of equal opportunities in all four pillars by addressing the discrepancies between the two genders and by supporting the reconciliation of professional and family life. The means envisaged to accomplish this include the equitable distribution of family responsibilities regarding childcare and household tasks; the development of flexible and part-time work programs; the development of childcare and other services; and professional reintegration after childcare leave. The institutions charged with the application of these measures are the Ministry of Labour and Social Solidarity, the Ministry of Health and Family, the National Agency for Labour Occupancy, and social partners.

Institutional measures

Institutional bodies with distinct responsibilities in implementing the regulations on labour relations and workforce occupation are not concerned in their regular activities with integrating a gender dimension into the occupancy policies and strategies, or with the observance of the principle of equal treatment and opportunities for men and women in the labour market. Such objectives were not included in institutional practices because it has long been considered that Romanian legislation is non-discriminatory. Nevertheless, in recent years, in an effort to harmonise national legislation in this field with EU standards, awareness regarding the importance of the equal treatment of men and women has increased and greater efforts are being made.

7.4 Research on the reconciliation of family and professional responsibilities and on sharing responsibilities between men and women

The United Nations Program for Development Romania, in cooperation with specialists in various fields of activity, annually draft a 'National Report on Human Development,' which contains statistical data regarding women's participation in economic life and examples of inequality in this field.

The National Institute for Statistics quarterly and annually drafts reports on household labour, providing information regarding types of households, activities and sources of

---

[30] Approved by Government Resolution 1273 of 2000.

income. In recent years, the Institute has included a gender evaluation in its research in order to identify economic and social problems facing men and women in society. Based on the information collected for the survey on Time Management (in 2000), an attempt was made to define domestic work and to evaluate the participation of the partners in a couple. The data reflects the different degree of contributions of men and women make in domestic activities. For example, women allocate 2.1 hours per day for 'food management,' while men only allocate 0.3 hours per day; women allocate 0.8 percent hours per day for 'household maintenance,' while men only allocate 0.4 percent hours per day; women spend 0.3 percent hours per day on childcare, while men only dedicate 0.1 hours per day to the same activity.

Traditionally, women handle domestic matters in Romania, while men provide the family income. During communism, women were encouraged to work under the same conditions as men, but they were also in charge of domestic activities, leading to a double workload both inside and outside the household. The major difference compared with the period after 1989 was the high access to childcare services and the low costs of health care and education.

The percentage of women working outside the household increased during the transition period. Thus, the percentage of women working as technicians, forewomen and other similar occupations has increased since 1994 from 59.9 percent to 60.9 percent. The percentage of women specialized in intellectual professions increased from 46.1 percent in 1994 to 49.9 percent in 1998.[31]

Statistics and research on the number of women who return to work after giving birth and men who take parental leave

There is currently little gender disaggregated data in this field, and it is not possible to assess the number of women who resume their activity after giving birth or the number of men who benefit from childcare leave.

A survey entitled *Women and Men in Romania* indicates that after 1990 there was a demographic aging of the population, especially of the rural female population. The level of education and the increasing implication of women in the labour market were important in estimating the number of planned children. Housewives continue to give birth to a higher number of children, compared with women who are self-employed, work in associations or are employers, who gave birth in 1998 to 3.85 percent of all children born alive.[32]

---

[31] National Institute for Statistics (2001b).
[32] UNDP (2000b: 8–9).

Demographic, social or cultural considerations affecting the reconciliation of work and family responsibilities

The increase of women's participation in economic activities

Out of the more than nine million adult and elderly women registered at the 1992 population census, more than one half were active in employment, although their share of the total active population was much lower than men's. The employment rates of married women were higher than that of unmarried women only in the age groups below 20 and over 50.

In contrast to the period before 1989, in recent years, despite the social protection granted to mothers of children up to the age of three, they do resume their activity soon after giving birth for fear of losing their jobs and becoming unemployed. This fact will gradually change the traditional roles played by mothers in child raising.[33]

Within the context of the socio-economic difficulties of transition, the number of working women increased due to the imperative need for a second salary in the family. At the same time, and also due to the deterioration of life standards, women can no longer afford help with domestic activities and are forced to assume responsibility for all household work. The direct consequences of this situation are a decline in the birth rate, and later average ages for getting married and having a first child.

Some of the obstacles to reconciling family and professional life are of an economic and financial nature, others are related to people's mentality or the public institutions' limited understanding of the complexity of the matter. In addition, the current legislation provides no concrete measures, administrative or financial, to guarantee working men and women the possibility to reconcile family and professional responsibilities. Working mothers are encouraged, by the maternity and child protection policies, to raise their children at home and not to resort to private or public services.

While during communism the state provided a sufficient number of kindergartens and nurseries, many of which were for free or very inexpensive, during transition the state reduced its capacity to subsidize social services, and the number of childcare institutions diminished substantially. Childcare services that remained in operation are sometimes too expensive for parents to afford. Private childcare institutions were created, but can only be afforded by a limited category of high income parents, and do not go far in solving the problem at a national level.

Other obstacles include the perpetuation of traditional mentalities regarding women's 'duty' to take care of domestic matters even if she has a job and works as much as the man of the family; the fact that employers are not encouraged to adopt measures intended to support employees with family obligations; the low number of institutions

---

[33] UNDP (2000b).

to care for children, elderly and disabled persons, and the difficult access to such institutions; and the fact that domestic help services (most of which are private) are not affordable to most of the population.

One of the few legislative exceptions encouraging men to engage in childcare activities is Act No.210 of 1999, which stipulates that family doctors will issue a certificate to fathers who acquire childcare knowledge.

The influence of religion and patriarchal traditions continues to be felt at a community level. There are significant differences between the female population in urban and rural areas, especially as regards education, professional training and access to the labour market. Girls who live in rural areas are especially vulnerable to the perpetuation of traditional role patterns and stereotypes (in family and at school) and are prepared for trades or professions considered as typically feminine, but with lower salaries. Statistics indicate that the number of illiterate women in rural areas is three to four times higher than the number of illiterate men.

Statistical data indicates that the men's employment rate is higher than women's in all age groups.

Although men still generally obtain the income necessary for family subsistence, the number of households run by women has increased, especially due to the rise in the number of single-parent families. A survey on life conditions by the National Institute for Statistics in 2000 indicates that households managed by women represent almost 25 percent of the total in Romania. These households are confronted with more difficulties than those managed by men with regard to the capacity to pay bills, the frequent need to borrow and the capacity of the monthly net income to cover everyday needs.

According to data from the National Institute for Scientific Research in the Field of Labour and Social Protection, household-produced goods are an important means of meeting consumption needs, and of survival, and this activity is performed mainly by women, especially in rural areas. Women also succumb to stereotypes whereby they believe that housework is their exclusive territory.

According to the National Institute for Statistics,[34] women in Romania perform three times more housework than men, while their occupancy rate outside the household is very high. The vast majority of women are employed full-time, and housework takes up most of their spare time, often to the detriment of their physical and mental health.[35]

Women have even more responsibilities in poor families, and poverty increases proportionally to the number of children, especially school-age children. Women in families with many retired members are also burdened by a heavy load of housework.

---

[34] National Institute for Statistics (2001b).
[35] National Institute for Statistics (2001b: 40).

8. THE PRINCIPLE OF EQUAL TREATMENT OF MEN AND WOMEN IN OCCUPATIONAL SOCIAL SECURITY SCHEMES

Council Directive 96/97/EC of 20 December 1996 *amending Directive 86/378/EEC on the implementation of the principle of equal treatment for men and women in occupational social security schemes*

8.1 National legal framework on social security schemes: General provisions

The Romanian social security system differs from those in the Western European countries because it includes only two of the three pillars traditional in Europe: the first pillar, referring to collective social security at a national level, and the third pillar, referring to individual social security. The complementary collective social security system (the second pillar) does not exist in the Romania because only the two pillars mentiomed above existed under communism and, after the fall of the regime, social partners were not encouraged to create complementary systems.[36]

With the exception of the difference retirement ages for women and men, the national legislation does not contain any regulations that discriminate against women, regardless of their marital status, concerning access to social security systems, contribution payments obligations or the calculation of benefits, etc. The measures for the protection of maternity do not affect any of the above mentioned elements in any way. However, the social security benefits calculated as a percentage of the individual salary (pensions of all types, benefits for caring for children up to the age of two or for sick children, as well as benefits for temporary disablement) reflect the *de facto* discrimination suffered by women during their professional activity.

The Act No.19 of 2000 stipulates that the right to social security is guaranteed by the state and the public system is organized based on the following principles: unity, equality, social solidarity, obligation, contribution, distribution, and autonomy. These principles apply to men and women who are part of the national social security system. The law makes no distinction between genders with regard to the insured, as participaton to the public social security system is obligatory, under the law, for legally defined categories of persons.

---

[36] A bill was drafted for the regulation of universal pension funds, but it did not reach the final stage of the legislative process, and the Parliament is currently debating a bill that only refers to insurance against occupational accidents and diseases.

The public system of pensions and other social security rights covers the following types of risks: old age, disability, sickness, accident, maternity, and death.

Duration of contribution payment

The right to certain benefits within the system of pensions and other social security rights is granted at different times, in keeping with the benefit type, and the rules regulating them are generally the same for men and women, with some exceptions regarding the age limit for pensions.

Age limit for pensions

In order for both insured men and women to be granted the age limit pension, it is necessary, in addition to reaching the standard retirement age, to have paid a contribution for a minimum period of 15 years. The complete contribution payment period differs for men and women: 30 years for women and 35 years for men.

Early retirement

In order for a person to benefit from early retirement, he/she must have exceeded the complete contribution payment period by at least 10 years, i.e, to have paid a contribution for at least 40 years in the case of women, and 45 years in the case of men.

Although the law theoretically provides the possibility for both men and women to benefit from early retirement five years prior to reaching the standard retirement age, the fact that men must complete obligatory military service does create differences in the enjoyment of this right in practice.

Disability pension due to occupational accidents, occupational diseases or tuberculosis

In the event that the disability is caused by occupational accidents, occupational diseases or tuberculosis, the insured shall benefit from a disability pension, regardless of the period of time for which the contribution was paid.[37] The insured may also be granted benefits in case of temporary disablement caused by regular diseases or accidents not related to work, by occupational diseases and accidents, for preventing diseases and recovery of work ability, for maternity, or caring for a sick child.

All insured persons, without exception, shall be granted benefits for temporary disablement caused by occupational accidents, occupational diseases, surgical emergency cases, tuberculosis and other infectious diseases, as well as death allowances, regardless of the contribution payment period.

---

[37] Act No.19 of 2000, Article 58.

Social security contributions

Contribution quotas are differentiated according to the type of working conditions and are established annually by the State Social Security Budget Act. The contribution quota for normal work conditions established for 2002 is 35 percent.

Special work conditions are deemed to be those that may seriously affect, permanently or temporarily, the insured's work capacity, due to a high degree of risk exposure, and they are stipulated in the collective employment agreement or, in the absence of such an agreement, by the decision of the legally established management body, as provided by law.[38] The rules applicable for such procedures are neutral with regard to the priciple of equal opportunities and treatment of men and women, as they are based on a set of objective and measurable criteria.

Retirement ages

The law stipulates different retirement ages for men and women. The standard pension age limit was 57 for women and 62 for men under the former pension law, and is currently 60 for women and 65 for men. The transition to the standard pension ages established by the current legislation shall be completed within 13 years, in accordance with a legally regulated schedule.[39]

There was no public debate on this issue, but considering the decline in men's life expectancy as indicated by statistics, reservations are occasionally expressed regarding the adequacy of maintaining the different pension ages for men and women.

The health insurance system

The law stipulates the possibility to take out other forms of health insurance policies covering individual risks, under various special circumstances, and participation in such forms of insurance is voluntary.

The following categories of persons shall benefit from health insurance without paying a contribution: children and young people up to the age of 26 if they are pupils, students or apprentices and have no income; disabled persons with no income or who are being cared for by the family; husbands, wives, parents and grandchildren with no income and who are in the care of an insured person; persons whose rights are regulated by special laws, provided that they obtain no other income besides cash benefits granted under the law, or pension benefits.

---

[38] Act No.19 of 2000, Article 19.

[39] Act No.19 of 2000, Article 41(2) and Annex 3.

The following category of persons shall also be deemed insured without paying a contribution for the duration of their situation:[40] persons in the military; persons on medical, maternity or post-natal leave or on medical leave to care for sick children up to the age of six; persons who are imprisoned or in custody; and members of a family who are granted social support benefits in accordance with Act No.67 of 1995.

Health services

The manner in which medical care is offered (frequency, duration, category, and type of medicine) is regulated by law and by legally concluded standard agreements, without any discrimination between men and women.

A characteristic of the Romanian health insurance system is that the insured person does need to pay for the medical services first and be reimbursed later. The settlement is made directly between the health insurance house and the medical service suppliers, without involving the insured in the process. The insured only pays the equivalent value of medical services that are not covered by the public health insurance system.

The unemployment insurance system

The unemployment insurance system has been regulated as of 1991[41] by a law which, without specifically referring to the equal treatment of men and women, does not discriminate on the basis of gender. A new law has recently been adopted,[42] which, contrary to the previous one, specifically includes the principle of non-discrimination.

Periods during which an employer fails to pay contributions to the state social security budget due to reorganization, bankruptcy, cease of operation, dissolution, liquidation or to a force majeure event are taken into consideration upon the calculation of the contribution payment period.

Unemployment benefits

The unemployment benefit is a fixed, non-taxable amount equivalent to 75 percent of the minimum salary at the economy level valid at the time, granted to the unemployed person for variable periods of time in accordance with the contribution payment period.

The principle of unique unemployment benefits adopted by the new law, although it apparently ensures equal treatment for all unemployed persons regardless of gender,

---

[40] Act No.145 of 1997, Article 9.

[41] Act No.1 of 7 January 1991 on social protection and professional redistribution of the unemployed, republished in *Monitorul Oficial*, Part I, No.257 of 14 September 1994.

[42] Act No.76 of 16 January 2002, Act social security of the unemployed and labour occupancy incentives, published in *Monitorul Oficial*, Part I, No.103 of 6 February 2002.

violates a basic principle of any insurance system, i.e., the principle of interdependence between the insured premium and the benefits paid in exchange. No final conclusions can be reached though on the gender impact of this new regulation before it is actually applied and relevant statistical data become available.

With regard to the unemployment benefit, the new law amends a legislative provision that was contrary to the principle of equal opportunities for men and women. Under the old law, only women who intrerrupted their professional activity to care for young children could be granted unemployment benefits. The new law stipulates that both men and women shall be granted unemployment benefits after completing their paid leave to care for children up to the age of two, or the age of three if the child is disabled, if they cannot resume their activity due to the fact that their employer terminated its activity.[43]

Other benefits

As in the case of unemployment benefits, the circumstances and terms under which the insured may profit from other benefits granted within the unemployment insurance system are established equally for men and women.

Possible discrimination may occur in the actual application of the law though, and the absence of statistical data makes this difficult to assess. A section[44] of the new law contains a detailed description of the statistical indicators system set up to monitor the labour market situation and its evolution; however, no reference is made to data collection and processing according to gender.

The minimum guaranteed income

The regulation[45] referring to the minimum guaranteed income sets up a social assistance mechanism intended to assure each family and each single person a minimum amount deemed to be the minimum necessary for survival when incomes obtained by such families or persons, regardless of their source, are lower than such an amount. Social support benefits granted based on this law replace or supplement, as the case may be, insufficient incomes obtained from other sources.

The manner in which the terms 'family', 'single persons' and 'child' are defined such that there is no discrimination. For example, the family is defined as consisting of: a husband and wife; or a husband, wife and their unmarried children; or an unmarried man and woman and their children or the children of either of the two, who share the

---

[43] Act No.76 of 2002, Article 17(1)(h).

[44] Act No.76 of 2002, Section 2 – Statistical Indicators referring to the Labor Market.

[45] Act No.416 of 18 October 2001.

same household. The term 'child' defines children of married couples, children of either spouse, adopted children, foster children entrusted to one or both spouses or for whom guardianship is established under the law.

Compliance with the directive

Insurance against unemployment was only regulated after 1990,[46] since the existence of unemployment was not recognised during communism, and it was even punishable by law.[47]

In an attempt to eliminate certain inequities and to find a steady balance between resources and the needs of beneficiaries, the social security system underwent several adjustments over the last 12 years, and over 30 new modifying acts have been adopted. None of these acts included any structural modifications of the previous social security system. A reform of this system began in 1997 when a new health insurance law was adopted, and continued with the passing of a new law regarding the public system of pensions and other social security rights, and of a law referring to the unemployment insurance system and labour occupancy incentives.

In terms of equal opportunities for men and women, it is not possible to speak of an evolution of the previous social security system. Because equality *de jure* between men and women was and is regulated by the Constitution, *de facto* equality was never questioned during the communist regime. After the fall of communism, the issue of equal opportunities for men and women was included on the politicians' agenda only in 1996, although it has not really constituted a priority thus far. This explains why there are no past or present statistical data in this field enabling a comparison between the status of men and women and offering a scientifically grounded image of the impact of the social security system on women.

Nevertheless, it can be stated that the social security system has a different impact on men and women, as the level of protection provided by the system is directly proportional to the level of income obtained prior to the occurrence of the insured risk. The effect of this proportionality principle is the preservation of the *de facto* differences between the salaries of men and women and mostly of social security rights.

This principle was partially modified as regards pensions, which are still calculated as a percentage of previously obtained incomes, but a maximum pension level was established that cannot be exceeded, regardless of how high the incomes of the pensioned persons were. As this rule was only recently applied, it is difficult to assume

---

[46] Act No.1 of 7 January 1991.

[47] A law adopted in 1974 (abrogated after 1990) obliged all active persons to work; a mechanism intended to assure fulfilment of this obligation, even by force, was also created.

or to anticipate that the new situation may significantly diminish the number of women whose pensions are lower than those of men.

It should be noted that an analysis of the current social security system is extremely difficult, on the one hand, because regulations in this field are included in several regulatory documents, and, on the other hand, because most of them underwent many successive changes and completions.

The imperfections of the new regulations were severely criticized even in their draft stage, especially by trade unions, and some of the subsequent amendments were adopted to eliminate an important number of inequities caused by the legislative solutions.

The process of improving the legislation is still in progress; and the Parliament is debating new changes to be adopted regarding the pension and health insurance system, as multiple negative effects on the insured are found almost daily.

8.2 Legal means of redress

If certain occupational security provisions violated the principle of equal oportunities for men and women, they may be declared null by courts of law.

With regard to rulings concerning the granting, failure to grant, modification, suspension or cessation of payment of benefits intended to assure the minimum guaranteed income, the law stipulates that such rulings may be contested in contencious administrative courts,[48] and the petitions and actions are exempt from court stamp fee.

An action may be brought by the party who considers himself or herself a victim of discrimination, and the manner in which the case is resolved shall depend on the nature of the injury (i.e., litigation in court, a declaration of a provision as unconstitutional, etc.). Furthermore, a special law[49] acknowledges the capacity of human rights NGOs in cases where the discrimination is related to their scope of activity and affects a community or a group of persons.

Monitoring mechanisms

There is currently no institutionalised mechanism to monitor the application of the principle of equal opportunities with regard to social security. The National Agency for

---

[48] Act No.416 of 2001, Article 30.

[49] Statutory Order No.137 of 2000 on the prevention and sanctioning of all forms of discrimination, Article 22.

Equal Opportunities, an independent agency promoting the principle of equal treatment for men and women, intended to monitor the application of the EU Directives.

8.3 Implementation of the principle of equal treatment in matters of social security and equal opportunities strategies

The progresive implementation of the principle of equal opportunities for men and women with regard to social security is not specifically mentioned as an objective in the National Action Plan regarding Equal Opportunities for Men and Women[50] or in the current Government Program. The matter is dealt with in Chapter V of the Government Program, which stipulates that "the Government shall apply, through its Program, measures intended to create a viable and efficient family protection system as part of a complex approach aimed to reform the whole social security system."

The measures referred to in the text are of a very general nature, representing a list of principles and of good intentions, whose primary merit is the expression of the political will "to fully implement the provisions of the European Community Directives."

The fact that the application of the principle of equal oportunities for men and women does not represent a priority in politics also results from the delayed passing of the Act on Equal Oppotunities for Men and Women, which had been due, according to the Governing Program, in December 2001.

Despite the hesitations of political actors, the principle of equal opportunities became a main concern not only for non-governmental organizations expressly dealing with this issue, but also for the social partners active in the labour market. At least three trade union confederations and representatives at a national level[51] adopted such objectives and expressed their support for the activity of their women's commissions, favouring the application of principle of equal opportunities. With a view to reaching some of these objectives, all national trade union and employers' associations were engaged in the negotiation of the unique collective employment agreement for 2002. 90 percent of the amendments proposed in support of the principle of equal opportunities for men and women were adopted, and some of the collective employment agreements

---

[50] Government Resolution No.1273 of 7 December 2000 on approval of the National Action Plan regarding Equal Opportunities for Men and Women.

[51] National Trade Union Confederation *Cartel Alfa*, National Trade Union Block and National Confederation of Romanian Free Trade Unions – *Frăţia*.

concluded at economy branch level[52] included special clauses referring to the protection of maternity or to work conditions for women, even when the negotiation teams consisted only in men. All this indicates that civil society is quite supportive of the principle of equal oportunities and treatment of men and women, and is open to resolving existing problems.

National legislation assures a rather high degree of protection of maternity, and this is accepted as 'normal,' although it can work to the detriment of women. Although no case has reached the court, it is common knowledge that pregnant women have virtually no chance of being employed, which in practical terms means the impossibility of access to the social security system. At the same time, legal practice shows that although pregnant women are protected against dismissal by law, this protection is sometimes ignored by employers.

So far there have been no official initiatives from the public autorities or social partners regarding the elimination of the *de facto* discrimination in this field and, given the precarious general economic situation, it is difficult to expect that the necessary financial resources might be found to apply additional measures for this purpose, considering that at present, social security funds are used to pay allowances to parents who quit their job to attend to children up to two years of age.

Professional social security systems

There are no professional social security systems in Romania and there is only one type of compensation similar to an unemployment benefit recently stipulated in certain collective employment agreements, namely the severance pay, consisting in amounts of money paid by employers to employees affected by mass dismissals.

There are no well-established and consistent rules establishing such payments, but it can be asserted that the variety of rules adopted for such a purpose have never directly implied any discrimination between men and women. However, indirect discrimination can occur related to the base considered for calculating such compensation, as an effect of the discrimination that existed previously.

---

[52] Article 68 of the Sole Collective Employment Agreement in the field of Constructions for 2001, No.53881 of May 29, 2001, published in *Monitorul Oficial*, Part V No.6 of 15 June 2001; Article 123–141 of the Sole Collective Employment Agreement in the field of Machine Building for 2001–2004, No.53875 of 31 May 2001, published in *Monitorul Oficial*, Part V, No.4 of 12 June 2001; Article 103–120 of the Sole Collective Employment Agreement in the field of Electrotechnics, electronics, fine mecanics and defense, for 2001–2002, No.53972 of 28 June 2001, published in *Monitorul Oficial*, Part V, No.6 of 10 July 2001.

REFERENCES

Bibliography

Association for initiative, responsibility, involvement and solidarity (2001) *Contract of employment and equal opportunities.* Bucharest.

Atanasiu, Anca (1994) "Obstacole care impiedica accesul femeilor la functiile de conducere (Barriers Against Women's Access to Decision-Making Positions)." In *Human Rights Review,* 1/1994.

Athanasiu, Alexandru (1996) *Dreptul securitatii sociale* (Social Security Law). Bucharest: Actami.

Beligradeanu, Serban (2000) *Legislatia muncii 1995–2000* (Labour Legislation 1995–2000). Bucharest: Lumina Lex.

Brasov Court of Appeal (1999) *Anthology of Judicial Practice (1994–1998).* Bucharest: Editura All Beck.

Bucharest County Court (1992) Anthology of Civil Judicial Practice (1992). Bucharest: Casa de Editura si Presa Sansa.

Bucharest County Court (2000) Anthology of Judicial Civil Practice (1998). Bucharest: Editura All Beck.

Bucharest County Court (1999) Anthology of Judicial Commercial Practice (1990–1998). Bucharest: Editura All Beck.

Bucharest County Court (1998) Anthology of Judicial Practice (1993–1997). Bucharest: Editura All Beck.

Bureau international du Travail (1999) "Numero special: Femmes, genre et travail (premiere partie)." In *Revue Internationale du Travail,* 138(3). Geneve.

Bureau international du Travail (1999) "Numero special: Femmes, genre et travail (deuxieme partie)." In *Revue Internationale du Travail,* 138(4). Geneve.

Bureau international du Travail (1994) *Conference international du Travail, 81e session 1994 –* Rapport III (partie 4 A), Rapport de la Commision d'experts pour l'implementation des conventions et recomandations (rapport general et observations concernant certains pays), Geneve.

Bureau International du Travail (1995) *Conference International du Travail, 82e session 1995 –* Rapport III (partie 4 A), Rapport de la Commision d'experts pour l'implementation des conventions et recomandations (rapport general et observations concernant certains pays), Geneve.

Bureau international du Travail (1996) *Conference international du Travail, 83e session 1996 –* Rapport III (partie 4 A), Rapport de la Commision d'experts pour l'implementation des conventions et recomandations (rapport general et observations concernant certains pays), Geneve.

Bureau international du Travail (1997) *Conference international du Travail, 85e session 1997 –* Rapport III (partie 4 A), Rapport de la Commision d'experts pour l'implementation des conventions et recomandations (rapport general et observations concernant certains pays), Geneve.

Bureau international du Travail (1998) *Conference international du Travail, 86e session 1998 –* Rapport III (partie 4 A), Rapport de la Commision d'experts pour l'implementation des conventions et recomandations (rapport general et observations concernant certains pays), Geneve.

Bureau International du Travail (1999) *Conference Internationale du Travail, 87e session 1999* – Rapport III (partie 4 A), Rapport de la Commission d'experts pour l'implementation des conventions et recomandations (rapport general et observations concernant certains pays), Geneve.

Bureau International du Travail (2000) *Conference International du Travail, 88e session 2000* – Rapport III (partie 4 A), Rapport de la Commission d'experts pour l'implementation des conventions et recomandations (rapport general et observations concernant certains pays), Geneve.

Ciobanu, Viorel (2000) *Tratat teoretic si practic de procedura civila* (Theoretical and Practical Treaty of Civil Procedure). Bucharest: National.

Constanta Court of Appeal (1994) *Anthology of Judicial Practice (1993–1994)*. Constanta: Dobrogea.

Constitutional Court (1995) *Anthology of Decisions and Resolutions, 1994.* Monitorul Oficial.

Constitutional Court (1996) *Anthology of Decisions and Resolutions, 1995.* Monitorul Oficial.

Crisu, Constantin, Stefan Crisu, Nicorina Crisu Magraon (1995) *Repertoriu de jurisprudenta si doctrina romana (Index of Romanian Doctrine and Case law) (1989–1994)*, vol. I. Bucharest: Argessis.

Crisu, Constantin, Stefan Crisu, Nicorina Crisu Magraon (1995) *Repertoriu de doctrina si jurisprudenta romana (Index of Romanian Doctrine and Case law) (1989–1994)*, vol. II. Bucharest: Argessis.

Crisu, Constantin and Stefan Crisu (1998) *Repertoriu de practica si literatura juridica (Index of Romanian Judicial Practice and Literature) (1994–1997)*, vol. III. Bucharest: Argessis.

European Trade Union Institute (ETUI), Collective Bargaining in Europe (1998–1999), Brussels: ETUI.

Filipescu, Ion, Augustin Fuerea (2000) Drept institutional comunitar european (Institutional Law of the European Community). Bucharest: Actami.

Fischer, Hugh (1997) "Initiative la locul de munca pentru garantarea protectiei familiei (Initiatives at the Workplace Guaranteeing Family Protection)." In *Human Rights Review*, 1/1997.

Galati Court of Appeal (1996) *Synthesis of Judicial Practice.*

Ghimpu, Sanda and Alexandru Ticlea (1997) *Dreptul muncii (Labour Law)*. Bucharest: Casa de Editura si Presa Sansa.

Grunberg, Laura, Mihaela Miroiu (1997) *Gen si societate. Ghid de initiere (Gender and society. Initiation Guide)*. Bucharest: Alternative.

Iasi Court of Appeal (1997) *Anthology of Judicial Practice,* 1997. Iasi.

Legislative Council (1998) *Regulations of Work Relations – European Practice.* Bucharest: Tribuna Economica.

Ministry of Labour and Social Solidarity (2000) *Statistic Bulletin.* Bucharest: MLSS.

Ministry of Labour and Social Solidarity (200a) National Report on the Condition of Women in Romania, 1996–2000. Bucharest: The MLSS Directorate for Equal Opportunities.

Ministry of Labour and Social Solidarity, League for the Defence of Human Rights (2000) *Promotion of Equal Opportunities for Women and Men.* Bucharest: MLSS.

Ministry of Labour and Social Solidarity, Ministry of Health *Practical Guide Concerning the Rights of Women during Maternity.* Bucharest: MLSS.

Ministry of Labour and Social Solidarity, Council of Europe/DG Human Rights (2001) *Good Practices for Gender Equality.* Bucharest: Punct.

Miroiu, Mihaela (1999) *Societatea retro (The Retro Society).* Bucharest: Trei.

Moroianu Zlatescu, Irina (1995) "Drepturile femeii in reglementarile interne si internationale. Realitati si perspective (Woman's Rights in Domestic and International Regulations. Realities and Perspectives)." In *Human Rights Review,* 2/1995.

Moroianu Zlatescu, Irina (1996) *Equal Opportunities, Real Opportunities.* Bucharest: IRDO, Romanian Institute of Human Rights.

National Association of Romanian Jurists, *Revista "Dreptul" ("The Law" Review),* 1990–2001.

National Institute for Statistics (2001a) *Evolution of the Private Sector in the Romanian Economy, 1990–2000.* Bucharest: NIS.

National Institute for Statistics (2001b) *Survey on Household Labor.* (AMIGO), Bucharest: NIS.

National Institute for Scientific Research in the Field of Labour and Social Protection (2001) RELANSIN Program: *Life Quality – Mechanisms to Ensure Equal Opportunities and Access of Women to Socio-Economic Life in Romania.*

National Institute for Statistics and Economic Studies (2000) Demographic Analyses. *The Demographic Situation of Romania in 1999.*

Nicolaescu, Madalina (1996) "Cine suntem noi? Despre identitatea femeilor din România moderna *(Who Are We? About Women's Identity in Modern Romania)."* In *Anima.*

Parliament of Romania, Chamber of Deputies (1997) "Decisions and Resolutions of the Constitutional Court (1996)." *Monitorul Oficial.*

Partners for Change (2000) *Women and Politics.* Bucharest.

Perju, Pavel (1999) Practica judiciara civila, comentata si adnotata (Civil and Judicial Practice – commented and annotated). Bucharest: Continent XXI.

PHARE CONSENSUS Project (1998) *National Social Security Legislation and EU Law on Equal Treatment of Men and Women* (Report by Mita Castle-Kanerova from Birks Sinclair & Associates Ltd., based on the findings by, and in collaboration with two local experts Mircea Dutu Buzura and Codruta Dragoi).

Ploiesti Court of Appeal (1999) *Anthology of Judiciary Practice, 1993–1997.* Bucharest: Lumina Lex.

Ploiesti Court of Appeal (1998) *Anthology of Judiciary Practice 1998, semester I.* Bucharest: Lumina Lex.

Popescu, Andrei (1998) *Dreptul international al muncii (International Labour Law).* Bucharest: Holding Reporter.

Romanian Institute for Human Rights (1999) *The International Labour Organisation's Conventions ratified by Romania.* Bucharest: Romanian Institute for Human Rights.

Romanian Institute for Human Rights (1999) *The European Social Charter.* Bucharest: Romanian Institute for Human Rights.

Romanian Institute for Human Rights (1999) *The Main International Instruments Regarding Human Rights Romania Is a Party To, vol. I – Universal Instruments.* Bucharest: Romanian Institute for Human Rights.

Romanian Institute for Human Rights (1997) *Women's Rights – Equality and Partnership.* Bucharest: Romanian Institute for Human Rights.

Romanian Society for Feminist Analyses (2000) *Women's Non-Governmental Organisations of Romania – Women's Status in Romania.* Shadow report to the CEDAW, 23rd session, 2000. Bucharest.

Stefanescu, Traian (2000) *Dreptul muncii (Labour Law).* Bucharest: Lumina Lex.

Supreme Court of Justice (1993) *Legal Problems from the Decisions of the Supreme Court of Justice (1990–1992).* Bucharest: Orizonturi.

Supreme Court of Justice (1994) *Case Law Bulletin, 1993.* Bucharest: Continent XXI & Universul.

Supreme Court of Justice (1995) *Case Law Bulletin, 1994.* Bucharest: Proema.

Supreme Court of Justice (1996) *Case Law Bulletin, 1995.* Bucharest: Proema.

Supreme Court of Justice (1997) *Case Law Bulletin, 1996.* Bucharest: Proema.

Supreme Court of Justice (1998) *Case Law Bulletin, 1997.* Bucharest: Argessis.

Supreme Court of Justice (1999) *Case Law Bulletin, 1998.* Bucharest: Argessis.

Supreme Court of Justice (2000) *Case Law Bulletin, 1999.* Bucharest: Juris Argessis.

The Center for Reproductive Law and Policy (2000) *Women of the World, Laws and Policies Affecting Their Reproductive Lives.* New York.

Timisoara Court of Appeal (1999) *Anthology of Judiciary Practice, 1998.* Bucharest: Lumina Lex.

United Nations Development Programme (1995) *The Status of Women in Romania, 1990–1994.* Bucharest: UNDP.

United Nations Development Programme (1999) *The Status of Women in Romania, 1997–1998.* Bucharest: UNDP.

United Nations Development Programme, with the Romanian Academy (2000) *National Report on Human Development.* 1999. Bucharest: UNDP.

United Nations Development Programme (2000a) *Survey on Household Labor.* (AMIGO). Bucharest: UNDP.

United Nations Development Programme (2000b) *Women and Men in Romania.* Bucharest: UNDP.

Voicu, Marin, Mihaela Popoaca (2001) *Dreptul muncii – Tratat de jurisprudenta romana si europeana* (Labour Law – Romanian and European Jurisprudence). Bucharest: Lumina Lex.

Zamfir, Catalin (co-ordinator) (1999) *Politici sociale in Romania 1990–1998 (Social Politics in Romania 1990–1998* Bucharest: Expert.

List of Legislation Screened

Acts

Romanian Constitution of 8 December 1991, published in *Monitorul Oficial* (the Official Gazette) No.233 of 2 November 1991.

Civil Procedure Code, promulgated on 11 September 1865 and published in *Monitorul Oficial* No.2000 of 1865, modified and completed by the Emergency Governmental Ordinance No.138 of 2000, published in *Monitorul Oficial* No.479 of 2 October 2000.

Act No.10 of 1972, the Labour Code, published in The Official Bulletin No.140 of 1 December 1972.

Decree-law No.95 of 1990 on the Establishment of a Five-Day Working Week in State Institutions, published in *Monitorul Oficial* No.36 of 19 March 1990.

Act No.14 of 1991 on Remuneration, published in *Monitorul Oficial* No.32 of 9 February 1991.

Act No.50 of 1996 on Other Rights of Personnel Working in the Judiciary, republished in *Monitorul Oficial* No.56 of 18 November 1999, completed by the Governmental Ordinance No.83 of 2000, published in *Monitorul Oficial* No.425 of 1 September 2000.

Act No.54 of 1991 on Trade Unions, published in *Monitorul Oficial* No.164 of 7 August 1991.

Act No.92 of 1992 on the Organisation of the Judiciary, republished in *Monitorul Oficial* No.259 of 30 September 1997, modified and completed by the Emergency Governmental Ordinance No.179 of 1999 on the Modification and Completion of Act No.92 of 1992 for the Organisation of the Judiciary, published in *Monitorul Oficial* No.559 of 17 November 1999.

Act No.90 of 1996 on Protection in the Workplace, republished in *Monitorul Oficial* No.47 of 29 January 2001.

Act No.130 of 1996 on Collective Work Agreement, republished in *Monitorul Oficial* No.184 of 19 May 1998.

Act No.51 of 1995 on Organising and Exercising the Profession of Lawyers, republished in *Monitorul Oficial* No.113 of 6 March 2001.

Act No.90 of 1996 on Protection in the Workplace, republished in *Monitorul Oficial* No.47 of 29 January 2001.

Act No.109 of 1997 on the Organisation and Functioning of the Economic and Social Council, published in *Monitorul Oficial* No.141 of 7 July 1997.

Act No.119 of 1997 on the Supplemental Allowance for Families with Children, published in *Monitorul Oficial* No.149 of 11 July 1997.

Act No.145 of 1998 on the Establishment, Organisation and Functioning of the National Agency for Employment and Vocational Training, published in *Monitorul Oficial* No.261 of 13 July 1998, modified and completed by the Emergency Governmental Ordinance No.7 of 2000, published in *Monitorul Oficial* No.283 of 22 June 2000 and by the Emergency Governmental Ordinance No.294 of 2000, published in *Monitorul Oficial* No.707 of 30 December 2000.

Act No.154 of 1998 on the System of Wage Calculation in the Budgetary System and of the Calculation of Allowances for Persons in Public Office, published in *Monitorul Oficial* No.266 of 16 July 1998 (with further modifications and completion).

Act No.74 of 1999 on the Ratification of the Revised European Charter, adopted in Strasbourg on 3 May 1996, published in *Monitorul Oficial* No.193 of 4 May 1999.

Act No.108 of 1999 on the Establishment and Organisation of the Work Inspection Authority, published in *Monitorul Oficial* No.283 of 21 June 1999.

Act No.168 of 1999 on the Resolution of Work Conflicts, published in *Monitorul Oficial* No.582 of 2 November 1999.

Act No.188 of 1999 on the Status of Public Officials, published in *Monitorul Oficial* No.600 of 8 December 1999, modified and completed by Governmental Ordinance No.82 of 2000 for the modification and completion of Act No.188 of 1999 on the Statute of Public Officials, published in *Monitorul Oficial* No.293 of 28 June 2000.

Act No.19 of 2000 on the Public System of Pensions and Other Social Security Rights, published in *Monitorul Oficial* 140 of 1 April 2000, modified and completed by the Governmental Ordinance No.41 of 2000 for the modification and completion of Act No.19 of 2000, published in *Monitorul Oficial* No.183 of 27 April 2000.

Act No.202 of 2002 on Equal Opportunities between Women and Men, published in *Monitorul Oficial* No.301 of 8 May 2002.

Decrees and Ordinances

Decree No.225 of 1990 on the Withdrawal of Romania's Reservations to Certain Conventions on Humanitarian Law, published in *Monitorul Oficial* No.69 of 14 May 1990.

Governmental Decision No.967 of 1999 on the Establishment and Functioning of the Inter-Ministry Consultative Commission in the Field of Equal Opportunities for Women and Men, published in *Monitorul Oficial* No.583 of 30 November 1999.

Emergency Governmental Ordinance No.24 of 2000 on the System Establishing Regular Wages for People Who Work on the Basis of a Work Agreement in the Budgetary System, published in *Monitorul Oficial* No.138 of 31 March 2000.

Governmental Ordinance No.129 of 2000 on Vocational Training for Adults, published in *Monitorul Oficial* No.430 of 2 September 2000.

Governmental Ordinance (Statutory Order) No.137 of 2000 on Preventing and Punishing All Forms of Discrimination, published in *Monitorul Oficial* No.431 of 2 September 2000.

Emergency Governmental Ordinance No.138 of 2000 on the Modification and Completion of the Civil Procedure Code, published in *Monitorul Oficial* No.479 of 2 October 2000.

Governmental Decision No.458 of 2000, on the Approval of the Classified List of Occupations, trades, and specializations for which training is ensured by pre-college education, as well as of the duration of training, published in *Monitorul Oficial* No.287 of 2000.

Governmental Decision No.1166 of 2000 on the Establishment of the Minimum Gross Salary on a National Level, published in *Monitorul Oficial* No.615 of 29 November 2000, modified by the Governmental Decision No.231/2001, published in *Monitorul Oficial* No.83 of 19 February 2001-03-30.

Governmental Decision No.1273 of 2000 on the Approval of the National Action Plan for Equal Opportunities for Women and Men, published in *Monitorul Oficial* No.659 of 15 December 2000.

Order of State Minister, Minister of Labour and Social Solidarity, No.578 of 1996 on the Approval of the General Work Protection Norms, published in *Monitorul Oficial* No.344 of 16 December 1996.

Order of State Minister, Minister of Labour and Social Solidarity, No.187 of 1998 on the Approval of the Rules of Organising and Functioning of the Committee for safety and health at work, published in *Monitorul Oficial* No.169 of 29 April 1998.

The collective work agreement on a national level for 2000–2001, with the Ministry of Labour and Social Solidarity under No.53518/15 of 10 May 2000, published in *Monitorul Oficial* No.7 of 3 July 2000.

Order No.343/399 of the Ministry of Health and Family and the Ministry of Labour and Social Solidarity of 8 June 2001, on the Approval of the Institutions of Issuing Sick Leave Certificates, on Which the Granting of Social Support Benefits Are Based, published in *Monitorul Oficial* No.732 of 19.11.2001.

International Documents Ratified by Romania

The ILO Convention No.89 of 1948 on the Night Work of Women Who Work in the Industry, ratified by Decree No.213 of 1957.

The ILO Convention No.100 of 1951 on Equal Pay for Male Workforce and Female Workforce for Work of Equal Value, ratified by Decree No.213/1957, published in the Official Bulletin No.4 of 18 January 1958.

The ILO Convention No.127 of 1967 on the Maximum Weight of Loads that Can Be Carried by One Worker, ratified by Decree No.83/1975, published in the Official Bulletin No.86 of 2 August 1975.

The International Covenant on Civil and Political Rights (1966), ratified by Decree No.212 of 1974, published in the Official Bulletin No.146 of 20 November 1974.

The International Covenant on Economic, Social and Cultural Rights, ratified by Decree No.212 of 1974, published in the Official Bulletin No.146 of 20 November 1974.

The Convention on the Elimination of All Forms of Discrimination against Women (CEDAW), ratified by Decree No.342 of 1981, published in *Monitorul Oficial* No.67 of 17 July 1982 with reserves, which were withdrawn through Decree No.225 of 1990, *Monitorul Oficial* No.69 of 14 May 1990.

The European Social Charter revised, adopted in Strasbourg on 3 May 1966, ratified by the Act No.74 of 1999, published in *Monitorul Oficial* No.193 of 4 May 1999.